THE PEOPLES' WAR?

The Peoples' War?

The Second World War in Sociopolitical Perspective

Edited by
ALEXANDER WILSON,
RICHARD HAMMOND,
AND JONATHAN FENNELL

McGill-Queen's University Press
Montreal & Kingston · London · Chicago

© McGill-Queen's University Press 2022

ISBN 978-0-2280-1470-6 (cloth)
ISBN 978-0-2280-1471-3 (paper)
ISBN 978-0-2280-1589-5 (ePDF)
ISBN 978-0-2280-1590-1 (ePUB)

Legal deposit fourth quarter 2022
Bibliothèque nationale du Québec

The production of this volume was assisted generously by a grant from the KCL SSPP Publication Subvention Fund.

Printed in Canada on acid-free paper that is 100% ancient forest free (100% post-consumer recycled), processed chlorine free

We acknowledge the support of the Canada Council for the Arts.

Nous remercions le Conseil des arts du Canada de son soutien.

Library and Archives Canada Cataloguing in Publication

Title: The peoples' war?: the Second World War in sociopolitical perspective / edited by Alexander Wilson, Richard Hammond, and Jonathan Fennell.

Names: Wilson, Alexander, 1989- editor. | Hammond, Richard, 1985- editor. | Fennell, Jonathan, 1979- editor.

Description: Includes bibliographical references and index.

Identifiers: Canadiana (print) 20220272921 | Canadiana (ebook) 20220272999 | ISBN 9780228014706 (cloth) | ISBN 9780228014713 (paper) | ISBN 9780228015895 (ePDF) | ISBN 9780228015901 (ePUB)

Subjects: LCSH: World War, 1939-1945—Social aspects. | LCSH: World War, 1939-1945—Political aspects.

Classification: LCC D744.6 .P46 2022 | DDC 940.53—dc23

This book was typeset by Marquis Interscript in 10.5/13 Sabon.

Contents

Introduction: In Search of a New History of the Second World War 3
Alexander Wilson, Richard Hammond, and Jonathan Fennell

THEME ONE   PROBLEMATIZING "PEOPLE'S WARS"

1 World War, Worldwide Mobilization: How Global History Complicates the "People's War" Narrative 19
Andrew N. Buchanan

THEME TWO   MOBILIZATION AND REMOBILIZATION FOR "PEOPLE'S WARS"

2 Fascist Warfare on the Home Front: War Mobilization and the Fragmentation of Italian Society, 1935–1943 45
Nicolò Da Lio

3 Building an Enemy: Great Britain as Depicted by Italian Fascist Propaganda 71
Jacopo Pili

4 Growing Up in Kaifeng: Young People, Ideology, and Mobilization in Occupied China, 1938–1945 90
Mark Baker

5 "What the Soldier Thinks": Mobilizing the Mind of the American Soldier in the Second World War 113
Edward J.K. Gitre

THEME THREE "PEOPLE'S WARS" AS DRIVERS OF CHANGE

6 Health Care and Disease in Italy's War, 1940–1945 135
  Fabio De Ninno

7 The Second World War and the New Deal for American Science 162
  Richard V. Damms

8 Edward Murrow and the "Little People" of the Blitz: A Study in American Idealism 185
  Sean Dettman

THEME FOUR WARS AMONG THE PEOPLE

9 German Anti-partisan Warfare: The Spectrum of Ruthlessness to Restraint 207
  Ben H. Shepherd

10 Italian Occupation Policies and Counterinsurgency Campaigns in France and in the Balkans, 1940–1943 230
  Emanuele Sica

11 Divided Loyalties: Indian Prisoners of War in Singapore, February 1942 to May 1943 251
  Kevin Noles

12 Spawning Fratricide: Occupation and Resistance in Greece, 1941–1944 276
  Christina J.M. Goulter

13 Gender and Community During War: The Amorous Relationships of Western POWs and German Women in Nazi Germany 300
  Raffael Scheck

THEME FIVE THE HISTORY AND MEMORY OF "PEOPLE'S WARS"

14 Framing Myths of the Second World War through Ministry of Information Propaganda Posters 327
  Katherine Howells

15 Beyond a "People's War": The Polish Past and the Second
   World War in Contemporary Perspective   353
   Jadwiga Biskupska

   Contributors   377

   Index   383

THE PEOPLES' WAR?

INTRODUCTION

In Search of a New History of the Second World War

Alexander Wilson, Richard Hammond, and Jonathan Fennell

In contrast to the military or the political and ideological histories of the Second World War there is no narrative frame for the Second World War as a global economic, social and cultural event.

Michael Geyer and Adam Tooze,
The Cambridge History of the Second World War[1]

The Second World War was a global event of close to unparalleled human significance. Yet, as Michael Geyer and Adam Tooze have argued, a comprehensive and convincing account of the cultural, social, and economic dynamics that influenced its causes, underpinned its conduct, and drove its consequences has yet to be produced. Geyer and Tooze's volume of *The Cambridge History of the Second World War* goes some way to addressing this gap, but it also sounded a clarion call for more research. It invited historians to explore new ways of engaging with the conflict, to rethink "what we ought to know and the way we might wish to tell the history of a war that was fought by peoples against peoples and engulfed the entire world."[2] A key element of the rationale underpinning this volume is a response to that call.[3]

This collection approaches the challenge of a new history of the Second World War in two ways. First, it presents research on aspects of the war that have previously been marginalized in core military and political accounts, as well as in existing social and cultural ones. It includes work on regions and nations that have typically been afforded limited scholarly attention in English-language publications, such as China, Japan, Italy, Poland, Yugoslavia, and Greece.[4] The collection also incorporates under-represented themes and methods of research. It interrogates the wartime experiences of ethnic minorities and colonial subjects, as well as those of women and children. Several contributions focus on the highest levels of civil-military relations and on institutions of wartime governance, while others assess wartime experiences from below, examining the experiences of prisoners of war and the processes of the construction of post-war memory. As we lift our eyes from the battlefield, we see that: enemies fell in love; for the young, the grand ideological narratives meant little; loyalties could wax and wane; and violence always lingered, even if below the surface.

Second, the volume pursues theoretical and methodological insights; it synthesizes and evaluates the new research to fashion fresh understandings. When transcending traditional national boundaries, it interrogates the potential of panoramas that encompass the global nature of the conflict. The volume engages with research on parts of Asia, Africa, Europe, the Pacific, and North America, giving it the capacity to both disrupt prevailing orthodoxies and build bridges between existing accounts that have become siloed in national or campaign-focused histories.[5] The book does not attempt to "go the distance" on producing the comprehensive new account called for by Geyer and Tooze, but instead takes a step toward this important ultimate objective.

THE CONCEPT OF "PEOPLE'S WAR"

The nation is the standard "unit of analysis" employed by scholars writing about the Second World War.[6] These national narratives are constructed even during the war itself, as states mobilize ideas to influence their citizens, sway their allies, or undercut their opponents. This battle of the narrative is waged through political rhetoric, propaganda, and journalism that collectively comprise the first draft of the historical record.[7] In the years immediately after the Second World War, nationally bounded accounts gained credence as new and old nations tried to understand the transformative changes that had just occurred. The war displaced millions in Europe, Africa, and Asia; it created new states

Introduction

Figure 0.1 Women of the Auxiliary Territorial Service run to their posts at an anti-aircraft battery, Britain 1942. © Imperial War Museum, IWM D 8292.

with fresh boundaries; it accelerated processes of imperial decline; and it radically shifted the distribution of global power.[8] All this had to be explained, and in many cases it was done on national terms.

In the United States, for example, the conflict was seen as having been a "Good War"; the war transformed the American economy, created untold wealth for its citizens, and catapulted the United States into a dominant global role.[9] For the Soviet Union (and, later, the Russian state), the blood sacrifice encompassed in the "Great Patriotic War" became a matter of national mourning and pride. This, in line with the wishes of Stalin and his ruling circle, justified their global clout and legitimized their lasting presence in Eastern Europe.[10] The People's Republic of China, meanwhile, emphasized national unity in the face of foreign aggression to smooth over the cracks of a concurrent civil war and pave the way toward a unified Communist state.[11] German popular memory emphasized shared suffering as a means of assuaging the stigma of national shame, but matters were often different for her former allies.[12] In Italy, the fractured nature of the memory of the conflict at least partially mirrors the intensely complex Italian experience of the war itself; this has hindered the creation of any unifying narrative.[13] In Japan, successive administrations eschewed addressing the question of how to remember the war. Instead, commemoration has frequently been left to citizens' movements or special interest groups, each with their own agendas.[14]

The "People's War" narrative in the United Kingdom, from which this collection takes its name, is perhaps the exemplar of a nationally configured account.[15] During the war years, Britons engaged with the conflict on a range of nuanced levels.[16] It was understood, of course, as a national struggle, but it was also interpreted as an imperial, Allied, European, and global endeavour.[17] With the retreat from Empire in the post-war years and the "birth" of the post-imperial British nation, historians increasingly began to treat the war in more national terms. Scholars adopted the term "People's War" to describe the British experience. They held that the war had exposed flaws in the stratified class-based society that had existed in Britain before and during the war. This awakening provided the impetus for national rejuvenation, which, as ordinary Britons shrugged off the power of the patrician classes, invoked the solidarity needed to fight fascism and forge a new national consensus for the future beyond victory.[18] These perspectives reflected the British zeitgeist of the late 1960s through to the mid-1980s and have proven remarkably resilient to challenge.[19] Britain's public service broadcaster (the BBC), for example, has continued to use the phrase "People's War" as the title of its flagship online archive into the twenty-first century.[20]

More recent scholarship, however, has powerfully critiqued the conceptual and empirical underpinnings of the "People's War" paradigm. Historians such as Daniel Todman, David Edgerton, John Darwin, Ashley Jackson, Yasmin Khan, Andrew Stewart, Douglas E. Delaney, and Jonathan Fennell, among others, have re-emphasized the imperial nature of Britain's war, while Sonya Rose and Wendy Webster have highlighted the extensive role played by ethnic minorities and foreign fighters in wartime Britain.[21] Collectively, this new corpus has raised important questions about the limits of nationally configured narratives in a global war.

Beyond the British example, as we shall see, the conceptual limitations of the "People's War" paradigm have also become clear; in many ways, they cast a shadow over fresh approaches of study. "Such ideas," according to David Edgerton, "have powerfully constrained the writing of histories, much more so than they constrained or explained the actions of historical actors." Increasingly, the position is that "we no longer need to think with such clichés, but rather with new principles which help us understand the power they once had."[22] Thus, it does appear to be the right time to revisit nationally configured accounts of the conflict, to search for new principles and seek the rich gains to be had from a more transnational and global approach.

MASTER NARRATIVES AND MULTIPLE NARRATIVES

Many national narratives of the war portray the experience of their populations in exceptional terms. Nevertheless, even a cursory appraisal of the strands that define each national narrative reveals more similarities than differences. When studied in concert, common themes can hold the key to fashioning a global account, one in which the currents that permeated and crossed boundaries are represented in their appropriate historical context. Such an approach certainly does not pave the way toward a single master narrative of the war. It does, however, highlight the potential for "a global history, or rather multiple global histories." As John Horne has argued in relation to the First World War, "if there are to be master narratives, they should at the very least be explicitly multiple."[23]

This collection engages with five of these possible master narratives, or themes. First, it critically interrogates the concept of "People's War" and problematizes nationally configured accounts that treat the nation, and its people, as an unchanging entity and impermeable block. Second, it explores patterns of mobilization and remobilization and challenges narratives that depict these dynamics as virtually unfettered processes; for many, if not all, belligerents, the war was a far cry from an unparalleled moment of national solidarity. Third, it analyzes the war as a driver of change and scrutinizes accounts that emphasize the transformative characteristics of the conflict. Fourth, it delves into the dynamics of a war that was fought not only on far-away battlefields, but also on the doorsteps of people at home; the proximity of the war, and the pressures associated with it, challenged loyalties and left space for the full spectrum of human frailties, loves, and hatreds. Fifth, it engages with the memory of a conflict that still looms as a touchpoint for national shame, pride, and resentment today; it unpacks the ways in which the "People's War" continues and survives as a "living war" into the twenty-first century.

The first theme, "Problematizing 'People's Wars,'" shows what can be achieved by looking beyond the horizon of national history. Andrew Buchanan's survey of the demographic makeup of belligerent forces during the war highlights the complexities and contradictions evident in many histories of the conflict. Buchanan cautions against the notion of national homogeneity, instead emphasizing the ubiquity of diversity and extranational service in the militaries of all major combatant nations. Cossacks, Spaniards, and Danes fought for the *Wehrmacht*; Kyrgyz, Uzbek, and Polish soldiers served the Soviet Union; Imperial Japanese ranks harboured Taiwanese and Korean troops; while Irish and Jamaican pilots flew for the RAF during the Battle of Britain. In many such cases, including that of African Americans, soldiers ostensibly fighting for global freedom were deprived of their own freedoms at home. This suggests that extranational experience was, in fact, characteristic for many soldiers, calling into question the extent to which the nation should continue to form the standard "unit of analysis" in the context of a global war.

The second theme, "Mobilization and Remobilization for 'People's Wars,'" offers a critical appraisal of the processes of national mobilization, and engages with the question of why some states managed to mobilize their societies more effectively than others. Nicolò Da Lio's chapter argues that Italy, the original fascist state, struggled in particular with the challenges of mobilization. When impediments to popular mobilization occurred, the authorities resorted to repressive or punitive measures. Corrupt officials and business elites adeptly evaded these coercive activities, leaving ordinary workers to bear the brunt of the costs of failure. This alienated key strata of Italian society from the regime and hampered Italy's ability to generate military capability. If the Fascist regime encountered challenges with the mechanics of mobilization, it also struggled in the domain of ideas. Jacopo Pili's chapter evaluates the effectiveness of Italian propaganda during the conflict. He looks at patterns of anti-British propaganda and shows that the Fascist regime lost control of its messaging during key moments of the war. If Italy's inability to mobilize effectively has been interpreted typically as a function of deficient expertise and resources,[24] this new research makes the case that the key failings lay in the inability of the Fascist state to generate popular support and arbitrate effectively between sectional interests in society.

There are parallels between Italy's struggle to mobilize its domestic workforce and the Axis experience at the other end of the Eurasian landmass. Using the case study of the city of Kaifeng in occupied China, Mark Baker's chapter argues that Japanese efforts to mobilize Chinese youth behind a new vision for the country failed. Chinese minors, who comprised one-tenth of the global population during the war years, constituted a significant pool of potential person-power. However, Japan struggled to articulate a clear and consistent message to underpin its political agenda in China. In the ensuing ideological vacuum, Chinese youth reacted to the mobilization process with apathy, disengagement, lassitude, and, ultimately, passivity. In fact, sheer lack of interest and detachment ensured that occupation and collaboration passed into irrelevance. Here, again, the post-war narrative championed by the state, the Chinese "War of Resistance," resonates little with some key aspects of the individual lived experience.

The Allied powers faced similar challenges in mobilizing their own societies for war. Edward Gitre's chapter reveals that even in the United States, a country that curates a memory of a "Good War," the wartime authorities grappled hard with the problem of aligning state policy with popular desires. Gitre shows that for military mobilization to work, uniquely intrusive methods were required, including applying social surveys to enable the US Army's command to shape their approach around the sentiments of the millions of ordinary soldiers who were swept into the ranks. These mass surveys provided the Army with the information needed to effectively assimilate citizens into military life. What the contrasting cases of Axis and Allied mobilization show is that the notion of smooth state and societal mobilization cannot be assumed. States with more equitable and efficient processes tended to fare better. Additionally, it was clearly important for states to recognize that national policy had to reflect and coincide with individuals' hopes and experiences. In other words, big ideas and little stories had to align;[25] in this, the Americans proved more astute than many others.

The third theme engages with the Second World War as a "Driver of Change" and challenges the notion of transformation at the core of many national narratives of the struggle. While the contributors to this volume do indeed accept that change occurred, their chapters serve as a call for a more critical approach; the dynamics of change, continuity, and causality remain open for debate. Fabio De Ninno's chapter demonstrates that the Italian state entered the war with a health-care system woefully unprepared for the strains of a high-intensity conflict that would eventually engulf the homeland itself. This led to disaster, with thousands of Italians dying from infectious diseases. These events occupied a central place in Italian wartime experience, and subsequently catalyzed efforts to create a new approach to how the state provided health care in the post-war years. However, the greater effect of this process over time must be explained by looking beyond the wartime and immediate post-war periods, as political frictions delayed the implementation of genuinely sweeping change for decades. Richard V. Damms, in his study of American science, provides insights into how processes of innovation unfolded during the conflict. By scrutinizing the relationships between political elites and American scientists, he demonstrates that while the war created the opportunity for change, bureaucratic politics ultimately determined the shape of this change. This is an underappreciated dynamic within the broader narrative of the American transition to post-war superpower status. Sean Dettman's chapter, meanwhile, addresses the hitherto underexamined role of American reporters, especially Ed Murrow, during the London Blitz, who used their positions of influence to shape ideas. Although they were not actually British citizens, they were key architects of the "People's War" narrative; they positioned a new national solidarity at the centre of their stories and thus habituated global audiences to viewing the war as a dynamic moment of change.

The fourth theme, "Wars among the People," addresses dynamics of occupation, insurgency, civil war, and captivity. It shows, perhaps surprisingly, that love and loyalty can be as central to our understanding of these topics as hatred and violence. Ben H. Shepherd's chapter examines German anti-partisan operations on the Eastern Front, and in the Balkans, Italy, and Greece. He demonstrates that levels of German brutality and restraint fluctuated widely across time and space; structural factors, such as environmental conditions, levels of insurgency, organizational culture, and ideology played their part, as did the outlook and experience of tactical commanders on the ground. These conclusions resonate within Emanuele Sica's assessment of the Italian experience of occupation and counterinsurgency. Whereas the Italian military presence in southeastern France was typically characterized by an absence of violence, Italian anti-partisan activity in the Balkans generally involved high levels of brutality. These variations were influenced by the structural conditions of both occupations, differing levels of reciprocal violence, as well as by Fascist thinking and colonial experience. However, individual responses also played a powerful role in shaping events. Explanations that focus on grand ideological, military, or political determinants of behaviour must always be balanced by an understanding of individual agency and local events.

Questions of loyalty feature in the next two chapters in this theme. Kevin Noles provides fresh perspectives on the birth of the Indian National Army. His chapter engages with the question of why prisoners of war from the British-led colonial Indian Army chose to slip the bonds of their previous life and soldier afresh with a new institution aligned with Japan. Whereas existing accounts have tended to emphasize big reasons, foremost among them the influence of ideology (Indian nationalism) or the fear of coercion, this chapter emphasizes a range of alternatives. Soldiers enlisted or refrained on the basis of friendships, resentment toward rivals, charismatic leadership, and ethno-religious ties. Thus, while loyalties ostensibly switched at the national level, they often did so because of competing obligations and interests at the level of the individual. Christina Goulter, meanwhile, provides new insights into the contest of loyalties encompassed in the Greek Civil War. Her chapter serves as a valuable reminder that civil conflict was a core feature of the experience of global war. Competing visions for the future and the fragmentation of the resistance movement in Greece made the conflict anything but a "People's War."

In contrast to these studies, which to a significant extent place hatred and violence in the fore, Raffael Scheck reminds us of the circumstances in which love could flourish between people caught on opposing sides of the conflict. His chapter on romantic relationships between Allied prisoners of war and German women reveals that the search for intimacy and companionship could not be suppressed, even in the most trying of circumstances. Neither official punishment nor the possible stigma of societal shame could quell love or lust between couples. Moreover, as the judicial records show, the Nazi regime became alarmed over periodic outpourings of sympathy for women on trial, revealing that ideology could not always prevail over human instincts. Collectively, these chapters illuminate the range of human experiences that played out below national flags. Love could coexist alongside hatred; old loyalties could lapse or endure; and new ties could form; while the war could destroy, it could also create.

The fifth theme addresses the "History and Memory of 'People's Wars'" with a view to offering a critical reflection of the processes by which survivors and their descendants have interpreted the conflict. Katherine Howells uses wartime British Ministry of Information posters to evaluate how they function as a touchpoint for memory today. She combines innovative survey methods with visual sources to establish that the posters, and their ongoing circulation, play an important role in perpetuating popularly held myths about the war. Jadwiga Biskupska then rounds off the volume with an analysis of the memory of the war in Poland. Her chapter, which refocuses our attention on the core issue of "People's War," emphasizes what is lost in nationally bounded histories of wartime experience. In contrast to the homogenous national narrative of the war driven by contemporary right-wing Polish politicians, Biskupska argues that the question of a national memory of the Second World War ought to be contested in the case of Poland. While most assessments accept that the story of Poland's war encompasses those who endured Nazi occupation and fought with Allied Armies, many accounts omit the experience of Polish Jews, a large proportion of whom were murdered, and of groups such as ethnic Germans, who were Polish by nationality and residency at the start of the war, but were purged from the nation by its end. Clearly, all of these individuals played a part in the Polish war, but only some loom large in the way it is remembered. Thus, the message from the last theme of this volume is that national narratives and memory tend to curate the past in ways that too rarely reflect the diversity of human experience. Although unpacking memory can prove a challenging task, it can offer powerful insights into why a prevailing consensus exists and why other facets of the war remain far from public consciousness.

MARGINALIZED HISTORIES

In summary, this volume presents novel work addressing hitherto neglected aspects of the cultural, social, and economic history of the Second World War.[26] Within the substance of the chapters themselves, the volume explores five themes that are intended to enrich our understanding of this global conflict. First, it advances a critique of narrowly defined nationally bounded histories and calls for inclusiveness in the writing of national and transnational histories of the war. Second, it shows that the interests of states and their peoples did not always align; the degree of divergence in this respect often made the difference between effective or ineffective popular mobilization. Third, it argues that the study of change needs to be handled with care; the war created possibilities for change, but real change was often determined by complex political and bureaucratic processes that took place in the years following the end of hostilities. Fourth, the volume argues that the dynamics of love and loyalty should be as central to our understanding of the war as the topics of hatred and violence. Finally, it shows that a comprehension of the complex pathways of memory is key to determining what is celebrated, mythologized, and excluded from the public account of the war today.

The book, of course, does not claim to be an exhaustive exploration of these themes and ideas. Instead, it both offers a contribution and acts as a signpost to "point the way." The chapters help us to think about experiences and contributions in regions that are often ignored in the historiography, including parts of Africa, Asia, and the periphery of Europe. However, like so many books on the conflict, the collection adds little to our understanding of the war in the Middle East and Latin America. Its paradigmatic and theoretical insights are necessarily limited by the range of case studies and themes explored; a full understanding of the war's sociopolitical aspects will undoubtedly prove to be an extended pursuit. Rather, it is hoped that the collection will emphasize opportunities and pitfalls for historians engaged with the task of creating new national, regional, transnational, or global accounts. If the study inspires complementary work, which incrementally contributes to overcoming the many gaps in our collective knowledge, then it will have served its purpose.

NOTES

1 Michael Geyer and Adam Tooze, eds., *The Cambridge History of the Second World War*, vol. 3, *Total War: Economy, Society and Culture* (Cambridge: Cambridge University Press, 2015), 1.
2 Ibid., 2.
3 It is also the product of another intellectual agenda, a desire to build a community of practice around the study of the Second World War. With this aim in mind, an international scholarly society, the Second World War Research Group (SWWRG), was set up in 2014. The SWWRG was established to promote innovative research on the conflict and its global aspects and act as a forum for new perspectives and collaboration. It was

also conceived as an organizational hub for conferences, seminars, and other events relating to the conflict. It was at the group's 2018 conference that the chapters comprising this volume were first presented.

4 There remains a dearth of published English-language research into the wartime experiences for each of these nations when held in comparison with those of the major Allied powers, or of Germany as the leading Axis power.

5 Jonathan Fennell, *Fighting the People's War: The British and Commonwealth Armies and the Second World War* (Cambridge: Cambridge University Press, 2019), 5.

6 For a different approach, see for example, Andrew Buchanan, *World War II in Global Perspective, 1931–1953: A Short History* (Chichester: Wiley Blackwell, 2019).

7 For an analysis of how this process develops, see, for example, David Reynolds, *In Command of History: Churchill Fighting and Writing the Second World War* (London: Penguin, 2005).

8 For an over-arching examination of the issue of displaced populations, see Gerard Daniel Cohen, *In War's Wake: Europe's Displaced Persons in the Postwar Order* (Oxford: Oxford University Press, 2012) for a starting point, and Jessica Reinisch and Elizabeth White, eds., *The Disentanglement of Populations Migration, Expulsion and Displacement in postwar Europe, 1944–49* (Basingstoke: Palgrave Macmillan, 2011) for an excellent range of case studies. On the creation of new states, see Oona Hathaway and Scott Shapiro, *The Internationalists: How a Radical Plan to Outlaw War remade the World* (London: Simon & Schuster, 2017); for the comparative British and French "roads" from Empire, see Martin Thomas, *Fight or Flight: Britain, France and their Roads from Empire* (Oxford: Oxford University Press, 2014).

9 For a critique of the "Good War" concept, see Michael C.C. Adams, *The Best War Ever: America and World War II* (Baltimore: John Hopkins University Press, 1994); For a broader assessment of the impact of the war on US society, see James T. Sparrow, *Warfare State: World War II Americans and the Age of Big Government* (Oxford University Press, 2011); On American ascension to superpower status, the latest research by Stephen Wertheim argues that the war offered an opportunity for the United States to assert global dominance that was willingly seized rather than reluctantly accepted, see Wertheim, *Tomorrow the World: The Birth of US Global Supremacy* (Cambridge, MA: Harvard University Press, 2020).

10 For an introduction to the forging and development of Soviet memory of the war, see David R. Marples, "Introduction: Historical Memory and the Great Patriotic War," *Canadian Slavonic Papers* 54, nos. 3–4 (2012), 285–94; on the aims and strategy of the Soviet leadership for superpower

status, see Caroline Kennedy-Pipe, *Stalin's Cold War: Soviet Strategies in Europe, 1943–1956* (Manchester: Manchester University Press, 1995); and Yoram Gorlizki and Oleg Khlevniuk, *Cold Peace: Stalin and the Soviet Ruling Circle, 1945–1953* (Oxford: Oxford University Press, 2004).

11 See Rana Mitter, *China's Good War: How World War II is Shaping a New Nationalism* (Cambridge: Belknap Press, 2020).

12 For an introduction to the German case, see Michael Geyer and Michael Latham "The Place of the Second World War in German Memory and History," *New German Critique* 71 (1997), 5–40; Bill Niven, ed., *Germans as Victims: Remembering the Past in Contemporary Germany* (Houndsmills: Palgrave, 2006); Nicholas Stargardt, *The German War: A Nation Under Arms, 1939–45* (London: Vintage, 2015), introduction.

13 For a starting point on fractured memory and the war, see John Foot, *Italy's Divided Memory* (Basingstoke: Palgrave MacMillan, 2009). See also Robert Ventresca, "Mussolini's Ghost: Italy's Duce in History and Memory" *History and Memory* 18, no. 1 (2006), 86–119; Paolo Pezzino, "The Italian Resistance between History and Memory," *Journal of Modern Italian Studies* 10, no. 4 (2006), 396–412.

14 For an exploration of this, and a starting point on Japanese memory of the war in general, see Franziska Seraphim, *War Memory and Social Politics in Japan, 1945–2005* (Cambridge, MA: Harvard University Press, 2008).

15 The first in-depth scholarly analysis of the concept was the landmark work by Angus Calder, *The People's War: Britain, 1939–45* (London: Jonathan Cape, 1969).

16 For an example of contemporary wartime disagreement over the usage of the term see British Library, IOR: L/P&J/5/163: Fortnightly Reports of Governors, Chief Commissioners and Chief Secretaries: Bombay Fortnightly Report for the second half of June, 3 July 1942.

17 Sonya Rose, *Which People's War? National Identity and Citizenship in Britain, 1939–1945* (Oxford: Oxford University Press, 2003); Andrew Stewart, *A Very British Experience: Coalition, Defence and Strategy in the Second World War* (Brighton: Sussex Academic Press, 2012); Ashley Jackson, Yasmin Khan, and Gajendra Singh, *An Imperial World at War: Aspects of the British Empire's war experience, 1939–1945* (London and New York: Routledge, 2017).

18 Jeremy A. Crang, *The British Army and the People's War* (Manchester and New York: Manchester University Press, 2000); Jeremy A. Crang, "The British Army as a Social Institution, 1939–45" in *The British Army, Manpower and Society: Towards 2000*, ed. Hew Strachan (London: Frank Cass, 2000), 16–35; Paul Addison, *The Road to 1945* (London: Jonathan Cape, 1975); Paul Addison, *Churchill on the Home Front, 1900–1955*

(London: Faber and Faber, 2002); Paul Addison and Angus Calder, eds., *Time to Kill: The Soldier's Experience of War in the West, 1939–45* (London: Pimlico, 1997).

19 For revisions on the part of the authors, see Angus Calder, *The Myth of the Blitz* (London: Jonathan Cape, 1991); Paul Addison and Jeremy A. Crang, eds., *The Spirit of the Blitz: Home Intelligence and British Morale, September 1940 to June 1941* (Oxford: Oxford University Press, 2020); For reflection on the challenge of shifting the public discourse, see David Olusoga, "Lost Empire: It's a Myth that Britain Stood Alone Against Hitler," 2 September 2019, https://www.theguardian.com/theobserver/2019/sep/02/empire-britain-second-world-war-hitler.

20 BBC, "WW2 People's War: An Archive of World War Two memories – written by the public, gathered by the BBC," 15 October 2014, https://www.bbc.co.uk/history/ww2peopleswar/about/archive_information.shtml.

21 Todman, *Britain's War*; Edgerton, *The Rise and Fall of the British Nation*; John Darwin, *The Empire Project: The Rise and Fall of the British World System, 1830–1970* (Cambridge: Cambridge University Press, 2009); Ashley Jackson, *The British Empire and the Second World War* (London: Hambledown Continuum, 2006); Ashley Jackson, *Distant Drums: The Role of Colonies in British Imperial Warfare* (Eastbourne: Sussex Academic Press, 2010); Delaney, *The Imperial Army Project*; Stewart, *A Very British Experience*; Fennell, *Fighting the People's War*; Yasmin Khan, *The Raj at War: A People's History of India's Second World War* (London: Bodley Head, 2015); Wendy Webster, *Mixing it: Diversity in World War Two Britain* (Oxford: Oxford University Press, 2018).

22 David Edgerton, *The Rise and Fall of the British Nation: A Twentieth-Century History* (London: Penguin Books, 2019), xxxv, 72–4.

23 John Horne, "The End of a Paradigm," *Past and Present* 242, no. 1 (February 2019), 185, 192.

24 See, for example, Vera Zmagni, "Italy: how to lose the war and win the peace" in *The Economics of World War II: Six Great Powers in International Comparison*, ed. Mark Harrison (Cambridge University Press, 1998), 213–14.

25 For another example of this concept, see Neil Roos, *Ordinary Springboks: White Servicemen and Social Justice in South Africa, 1939–1961* (Aldershot: Ashgate, 2005), 11, 43.

26 Michael Geyer and Adam Tooze, "Introduction to Volume III," in *The Cambridge History of the Second World War*, vol. 3, *Total War: Economy, Society and Culture*, ed. Michael Geyer and Adam Tooze, 4 (Cambridge: Cambridge University Press, 2015).

THEME ONE

Problematizing "People's Wars"

I

World War, Worldwide Mobilization

How Global History Complicates the "People's War" Narrative

Andrew N. Buchanan

On 8 May 1942, in an effort to meet the demands of its sprawling multi-front war in China, Southeast Asia, and the Pacific, the Japanese cabinet decided to extend conscription to its colony of Korea. Koreans were legally regarded as Japanese nationals, and since Tokyo's invasion of China in 1937 they had been encouraged to join the Imperial Japanese Army (IJA). Nearly 17,000 Korean volunteers were already serving in the Japanese military when the conscription law finally went into effect in 1944, and they were soon joined by over 200,000 draftees.[1] In 1945, Tokyo extended conscription to Japanese-ruled Taiwan, and by the time the war ended in August, around 200,000 Taiwanese had been drafted. Like the Korean conscripts, Taiwanese recruits were not segregated in separate colonial units but were integrated into the regular army. IJA forces were also augmented by troops raised by the nominally independent government of Japanese-occupied Manchuria and by several pro-Japanese regimes in China. Together, these non-Japanese troops made a substantial, perhaps even an indispensable, contribution to Tokyo's war effort.

Tokyo's recruitment of Korean and Taiwanese conscripts highlights the complexity of Japanese colonialism, which combined violent repression with appeals to colonial subjects to view themselves as collaborators working "beneath the emperor's benevolent gaze" to resist European imperialism. These tensions were reflected among

Japanese policymakers, who feared that disloyal Koreans might be "parasites within a lion" while simultaneously recognizing that conscription implied inclusion in a broader "national community" that brought with it at least some limited political rights.[2] Undoubtedly, many Koreans were unenthusiastic conscripts who quickly deserted, but others served their Japanese emperor loyally.[3] In addition to offering insights into Japanese colonialism, the recruitment of nearly 500,000 non-Japanese soldiers pushes us to think about the overall character of Japan's armed forces, challenging pervasive Western images of ethnic homogeneity that are themselves partly rooted in American wartime propaganda that depicted Japanese people as undifferentiated "photographic prints off the same negative."[4]

The participation of these Korean and Taiwanese conscripts, along with millions of other non-nationals in the seemingly homogeneous armies of every major power, is in some ways *the* hidden history of the Second World War. It is not hidden because the basic facts have been lost: on the contrary, the stories of soldiers recruited from the colonies, from prisoner of war camps, from more or less willing allies, and from racial and ethnic minorities within the imperial heartlands are all well-known or easily researched. They are hidden – often in plain sight – because they have been made marginal to historiographies rooted within the nation-state. They are integral to the wartime histories of *all* the major combatants, but their experiences have been reduced to intriguing footnotes to narratives centred on the nation-state and intolerant of complexity. This chapter aims to encapsulate the central message of this volume by situating these stories at the centre of the *world* war and to see them as elements that complicate and globalize the narrative of a "People's War."[5]

NATION-STATES AND IMPERIAL ARMIES

In contrast to Tokyo's conscription of Koreans and Taiwanese, Britain's imperial mobilization has been well studied, and the ubiquitous presence of soldiers from Britain's dominions, colonies, and protectorates suggests that "British" forces should be universally referred to as "British-Imperial."[6] Names matter: imperial troops fought in every major campaign, and to continue to refer to these forces as "British" simply protracts their marginalization. Perhaps most significantly, by 1945 the thirteen infantry divisions of General Slim's Fourteenth Army in Burma were drawn from India (eight), West Africa (two),

East Africa (one), and the UK (two); clearly, it was a "British" army in name only. In addition to providing ground troops, large numbers of personnel from the "White Dominions" and from the West Indies served in the "British" Royal Air Force, while civilian labourers from across the Empire performed critical military tasks, from constructing infrastructure to moving supplies.

The broad mobilization of British-imperial forces also included the recruitment of Indigenous, Aboriginal, and Maori peoples into the armed forces of Canada, Australia, and New Zealand. This was not necessarily a straightforward process: in Canada, for example, both the navy and the air force initially rejected recruits who were not "of pure European descent and of the white race." Barriers fell as the demand for personpower increased, and by the end of the war 5 per cent of the Indigenous population of Australia had been enlisted, along with 3 per cent in Canada and fully 16 per cent in New Zealand. With the exception of the 3,600 men of the 28th Maori Battalion, formed to showcase Indigenous support for the war effort, all served in integrated units.[7]

The Indian Army offers a lens through which to examine some of the broader processes at work. Between 1940 and 1945, the Indian Army was transformed from a 190,000-strong professional army organized to police the borders of empire into a 2-million-person volunteer force tasked primarily with re-establishing British rule in Southeast Asia.[8] The pre-war Indian Army had been organized around a set of organizational practices rooted in the imperial knowledge produced by decades of British colonial rule. In particular, recruitment drew disproportionately upon the Sikh and Muslim "martial races" of northern India. These practices were overwhelmed by wartime demands, and as traditional pools of manpower were drained, recruiters reached into the Hindu populations of central and southern India, encouraging enlistment with promises of good food, regular pay, and technical training.[9] As is often the case, "voluntary" enlistment was prompted more by the pinch of hardship and promise of opportunity than by loyalty to the Raj.

Expansion necessitated far-reaching changes. In 1939, Indians accounted for just 400 of the 5,000-man officer corps, but by 1945 they were providing one-third of the officers.[10] British officials had long regarded Indians as "simple country folk" who were brave and loyal but unequipped to master modern technology; these assumptions were jettisoned to meet the demand for drivers, mechanics, radio operators, and, to a lesser extent, skilled infantrymen, turning the army into a "vast centre of education" that taught literacy and numeracy as well as technical skills.[11] These changes were implemented following the destruction of much of the pre-war Indian Army in Malaya, Burma, and North Africa in 1942, and by 1945 the British had produced a battle-tested new army that was indispensable to the imperial war effort. In the process, this mobilization unsettled the reified rituals and orientalist knowledge upon which the Raj was based, "denaturalizing" colonial rule for "Indians and British alike."[12] Even teaching Indian soldiers to read was a "two-edged sword," enabling them to form new impressions of their place in the world even as it equipped them for service in a modern army.[13] By the end of the war, the Indian Army had become a site of vibrant political discourse and nationalist politics; as army commander Claude Auchinleck noted ruefully, "every Indian officer worth his salt is today a nationalist."[14] The British colonial state made the Indian Army, but that army – or rather the agency of its soldiers – played a major role in unmaking the Raj.

Given the pre-existence of a popular movement for Indian independence, the dialectic between wartime mobilization and anti-colonialism was particularly salient in the Raj, but the same questions were manifest in other British colonies. In much of British-ruled Africa, British officials relied largely on allegedly traditional structures of chiefly authority, carefully buttressed by the colonial state, to coerce military service. But even as they recruited African soldiers, officials worried about the domestic social consequences of military service, and advance planning for *de*mobilization began in 1942.[15] As in India, officials feared that once African soldiers had been exposed to new experiences and a broader world view, they would become hostile to ongoing colonial rule in their homelands. While concern over demobilization may not have been quite a "panic," there was a generalized fear that the war had permanently unsettled colonial rule.[16] These fears were heightened by the fact that as many as 40,000 Indian soldiers captured by the Japanese elected to join the anti-British Indian National Army, an occurrence that Kevin Noles examines in depth within this volume. As Noles argues, these were rarely purely ideological choices, but the scale of the defections did point to underlying issues of loyalty embedded in all colonial military service.[17]

Colonial soldiers contributed to the war efforts of other imperial powers, including the Netherlands, Italy, and France. Much of the defence of the Dutch East Indies fell to locally recruited troops.[18] At the start of its colonial expansion in 1885, Italy began recruiting

World War, Worldwide Mobilization

Figure 1.1 Indian soldiers of the British Empire fraternizing with Italian civilians, n.d. © Imperial War Museum, IWM NA 8533.

Eritrean *askaris*, who played a major part in the disastrous invasion of Abyssinia in 1895, in the 1911–12 conquest of Libya, and in the brutal 1922–31 Libyan counterinsurgency.[19] Paralleling British "martial race" theory, Italian officials developed colonial knowledge with which to understand the military use of Black bodies, imagining that the heroism and resilience they valorized stemmed from an ancestral love of war. At the same time, they argued, the askaris' "impulsive" behaviour required tempering by white male rationality to forge it into an effective instrument of modern war.[20] The benefits of employing Africans went beyond racialized notions of their martial abilities: Italian elites were keenly interested in "empire on the cheap," and the low cost of maintaining the askaris went along with the fact that even heavy casualties produced no adverse domestic political consequences.[21]

Italian authorities added Eritrean cavalry, artillery, and armoured car units for the 1935 invasion of Ethiopia, and they were joined in the *Regio Corpo Truppe Coloniali* (RCTC) by recruits from Libya and Somaliland.[22] The RCTC served as shock troops, and despite the well-publicized aerial and mechanized dimensions of the campaign, their efforts were critical to the Italian victory.[23] Rome expanded the RCTC in the late 1930s, raising two full divisions – including a paratroop regiment known as the "Black Devils" – in Libya and two more in Somaliland. Totalling over 200,000 men, the RCTC made a significant contribution to Italy's offensive campaigns in 1940, with the Libyan *Sibelle* and *Pescatore* divisions providing one-quarter of the infantry in the invasion of British-occupied Egypt, while Eritrean and Somalian askaris facilitated the conquest of British Somaliland.[24] Italian-led advances were quickly followed by British-imperial counteroffensives that outmanoeuvred Italian forces unequipped for modern mobile warfare, effectively destroying the RCTC.[25] The Italian army in North Africa fought on with often-unrecognized determination, but with its former colonies under British occupation it could not rebuild the colonial army.

France's mobilization of colonial person-power is well known but, like Italy's, it is often marginalized. In the First World War, colonial soldiers – including *tirailleurs sénégalais* recruited in French West Africa and units of the *Armée d'Afrique* raised in the Maghreb – served on the Western Front, at Gallipoli, and in the postwar occupation of the Rhineland. The 1928 decision to reduce military service in metropolitan France to one year limited the size of the French Army to around 500,000 troops, producing a force that was "undermanned, ill-trained, and short on modern weaponry."[26] These constraints increased the relative importance of France's colonial troops, 75,000 of whom were serving in France at the time of the German invasion in May 1940. Around 10,000 colonial soldiers were killed, wounded, or captured during the fighting in France, and 1,500 to 3,000 prisoners of war were killed by German troops; arguably, these racially motivated massacres form a "missing link" between German atrocities in Poland and genocidal war in the Soviet Union.[27]

After the fall of France, the French Empire became a site of struggle between the Vichy regime and forces supporting Charles de Gaulle's Free French. De Gaulle made little headway in recruiting French soldiers who had remained in Britain after being evacuated from Dunkirk, and in its early stages the movement relied heavily on colonial troops. Félix Éboué, governor of Chad and the first African to hold high office in the French Empire, rallied his colony to de Gaulle in August 1940. Cameroon and Congo soon followed, giving de Gaulle a territorial base for military operations against Gabon, which was captured in November. In early 1941, a Free French column of Chadian tirailleurs sénégalais and local camel cavalry raided the southern Fezzan region of Italian-ruled Libya, capturing the key oasis at Kufra. The following January, an army largely composed of African troops under Philippe de Hauteclocque – known by his nom de guerre Leclerc – crossed the Libyan desert to join British-Imperial forces in Tripoli for the Allied advance into Tunisia.

Following the Allied victory in Tunisia, Leclerc's command was sent to Britain and re-equipped by the United States as the 2e Division Blindée (2nd Armored Division) for the cross-channel invasion of France. During this process, the division's ethnic composition changed as many Black soldiers were rotated back to North Africa and replaced by white Frenchmen. Nevertheless, in April 1944 the 2e DB was still around 25 per cent North African (3,600/14,490) and its diversity was increased by 350 Republican veterans of the Spanish Civil War.[28] Free French military strength was further reinforced by the Maghreb-based *Armée d'Afrique*, which included Arab and Berber *tirailleurs*, Algerian light infantry *Goumiers, Zouave* regiments of conscripted French settlers, and units of the Foreign Legion. At the January 1943 Casablanca conference, the United States pledged to re-equip 11 divisions of the Armée d'Afrique along US Army lines with the intention of using its 175,000 French and 230,000 African soldiers in an invasion of southern France.[29] American officials also hoped that this force would strengthen General Henri Giraud – Washington's favoured French leader – against de Gaulle.[30]

Rearmament progressed quickly, and in July 1943 a four-division French Expeditionary Corps (CEFI) composed largely of Maghrebis was attached to the US Fifth Army in Italy, where the Moroccan Goumiers distinguished themselves in the battles to break through the German defences south of Rome.[31] The political results of the rearmament were less satisfactory for Washington. During 1943, de Gaulle emerged as the main leader of the French Committee for National Liberation, marginalizing Giraud and ensuring that when the Armée d'Afrique was reformed into Armée B for the invasion of southern France in summer 1944, it was led by loyal Gaullists. The Operation Dragoon landings were quickly followed by Armée B's capture of the ports of Toulon and Marseilles, the ending of the German occupation of southern France, and a rapid advance up the Rhône Valley. More important, Armée B gave de Gaulle's newly established government in Paris its own armed forces with which to buttress its legitimacy and authority in the metropole. The government moved quickly to induct the guerilla forces of the French Resistance, many led by the Communist Party, into the regular army, thereby bringing potential political opponents under military discipline. The flipside of this development was the rapid demobilization of many of the army's Arab, Berber, and West African soldiers in a process referred to as the *blanchiment*, or "whitening." By the time Armé B – now redesignated the First Army – reached the German border, it was possible, as Army Commander Jean de Lattre de Tassigny observed cynically, to "search in vain for a black soldier" in regiments that still bore the title "Senegalese."[32]

The blanchiment helped to create the illusion that the "French" contribution to the ending of the German occupation had been largely the work of white Frenchmen. In fact, the true face of the Free French forces, from the first campaigns in Equatorial Africa, through operations in Libya and Tunisia, to the campaigns of the CEFI and of Armée B, was largely non-white. This dichotomy was heightened by the rapid sharpening of tensions between Paris and its colonial subjects in the Maghreb, where widespread nationalist protests unfolded in 1944–45; as Algerian nationalist Ferhat Abbas noted in his 1943 *Manifesto*, France only "admits equality with Muslim Algeria on one level: sacrifice on the battlefield."[33] Abbas's understanding that, despite promises of sweeping political reforms, French leaders viewed their Maghrebi subjects as disposable (and largely unacknowledged) military assets, fed into deepening popular hostility to French rule. On 8 May 1945, a march in Sétif celebrating the end of the war and calling for the release of imprisoned nationalist leaders led to clashes with French authorities and to massive government repression that left thousands of Algerians dead.[34] Returning home just days after the massacre, the soldiers of the 7th Algerian Tirailleurs were appalled by what they heard and saw; many, including decorated veteran and future National Liberation Front leader Ahmed Ben Bella, concluded that the only solution was to fight for "Algeria for the Algerians."[35] As in British India, the military mobilization of colonial subjects made a key contribution to military victory while simultaneously advancing the disintegration of the empire.

NON-NATIONAL SOLDIERS IN NATIONAL ARMIES

Colonial subjects were not the only non-metropolitan soldiers who changed the face of the armed forces of the major powers. During the Battle of Britain, for example, the Royal Air Force's Fighter Command was a "diverse, international force" in which those who had escaped from occupied Europe flew alongside pilots from Britain and the British Empire.[36] Fliers from Belgium, Czechoslovakia, France, and Poland accounted for around 10 per cent of Fighter Command's front-line strength, and they were joined by men from neutral countries (at least eight from Eire and seven from the United States of America) and one from Palestine.[37] The Poles were particularly effective, with the majority-Polish 303 Squadron shooting down more German aircraft than any other RAF unit in the battle.[38] These pilots were part of a larger Polish military diaspora. After the German invasion of the USSR in June 1941, London encouraged the Polish government-in-exile to sign an agreement with Moscow that freed thousands of Poles from the Soviet prison camps they had been in since the German-Soviet partition of their homeland in 1939. The former POWs were encouraged to join a new Polish Army being formed in the USSR.

Despite the Sikorski-Maisky Agreement, tensions between the government-in-exile and Moscow continued, and in March 1942 the "Anders Army," named after its leader, General Władysław Anders, left the USSR on an arduous odyssey through Iran and the Middle East to British-ruled Palestine. Anders's 110,000 followers included at least 36,000 women and children. Three thousand Polish Jews, including future Israeli leader Menachem Begin, elected to remain in Palestine, but the remainder went on to form the basis of the Polish II Corps attached to British-Imperial forces in Italy.[39] The II Corps also recruited Poles who had been forcibly conscripted into the German military and had subsequently either deserted to the Allies or been captured by them, and by 1945 it numbered over 100,000 men and women.[40] Other Polish soldiers, including an armoured division and a brigade of paratroopers fought in northern Europe, while 300 officers followed an even more tortuous path. After escaping to Britain in 1940, these men were dispatched to British West Africa to provide what Churchill called a "white infusion" needed to train the West African Field Force.[41] British colonial officials soon found the Poles too sympathetic to the African soldiers under their command and too relaxed in their relations with African women, but over 60 of them went on to lead men of the 81st and 82nd West African Divisions in combat in Burma.[42]

Poles also fought in large numbers in the Soviet Red Army, which, by the time of the invasion of Germany in 1945, included two entire Polish armies. The first soldiers recruited into the First Polish Army, or "Berling Army" after its commander, Zygmunt Berling, were former prisoners of war who had remained in the Soviet Union after the departure of the Anders Army, and they were joined by men conscripted into the *Wehrmacht* before being captured by the Soviets.[43] As the Red Army advanced into Poland, the new pro-Soviet Provisional Government introduced conscription, and former combatants of the Armia Krejowa (Home Army [AK]), the guerrilla force loyal to the government-in-exile, were also inducted. There was not much ideological commitment involved: former AK fighters could either join the Red Army or face deportation to Soviet labour camps. Equipped and organized as regular Soviet formations and integrated into the Red Army's command structure, the two Polish armies suffered heavy casualties in the final battles of the war. The Soviets ensured that these forces were led by Soviet officers and trusted Polish communists, but, like their British-Imperial and French counterparts, they always doubted the loyalty of the rank-and-file. Nor was this doubt misplaced: many Polish soldiers in the Red Army hoped that they would be joined in a newly independent Poland by the Anders Army advancing from the west, and while political commissars and secret policemen tried to suppress such sentiments, some of these men did go on to resist the post-war Sovietization of Poland.[44]

Soviet commanders believed they faced similar problems with soldiers recruited from the non-Russian states of the Soviet Union, who by summer 1944 comprised just under 50 per cent of the Red Army's total person-power.[45] Here, again, names matter. Although it has become commonplace to use "Russia" and "Soviet Union" interchangeably, the constant repetition of "Russia" obscures the fact that the USSR was a union, if under Stalin a forced one, of soviet republics, and reinforces a Russian chauvinist vision of the Soviet Union as a homogeneous entity. Moscow's propagandists made strenuous efforts to highlight the participation of non-Russians in the Great Patriotic War, but they did so within the framework of a supranational and pan-Soviet patriotism that was, in fact, as Soviet war correspondent Ilya Ehrenburg explained, simply a "natural continuation of Russian [*rossikkii*] patriotism."[46] "Soviet patriotism" rested on a specifically *Russian* history and genealogy that referenced national heroes from Alexandr Nevskii to Field Marshal Kutuzov.[47] Appeals to a Soviet patriotism that repackaged great Russian chauvinism had little appeal in the non-Russian, non-Slavic, and non-Orthodox republics, particularly since many people were already inclined to view the USSR as an "exploitive, repressive, hegemonic Russian invention."[48] At the same time, an adherence to the 1917 Russian Revolution as a popular and progressive accomplishment continued strongly in Russia despite the repressive character of the Stalinist regime but was much less influential in the non-Russian republics.

As a result of these factors, the non-Russian republics did not experience the great wave of voluntary enlistment that swept Russia following the German invasion, and their rates of draft evasion and desertion were significantly higher.[49] Across much of the *Ostfront*, some non-Russian populations initially viewed the Germans as liberators, and they volunteered to fight with them against the Soviets. The racialized character of the Nazi colonial project rendered Germany entirely incapable of taking advantage of these sentiments. The only partial exception was in relation to the Cossacks, who, in a German version of "martial race" theory, were recognized with "clichéd benevolence" as a warlike people with a long history of opposition to Stalinist centralization.[50] Moreover, despite the difficulty of mobilizing its non-Russian populations, Moscow desperately needed them, and it sought to stimulate recruitment by making concessions that projected confidence in the loyalty of non-Russians.

In fall 1941, Moscow resumed the recruitment of nationally-based units from individual republics, a practice that had been ended in 1938 after Stalin denounced them as potential nuclei of anti-Soviet agitation.[51] The re-establishment of national units seems to have encouraged recruitment, although on occasion looks could be deceiving: only 32 per cent of the newly formed 16th Latvian Rifle Division were ethnic Latvians, with the remainder composed of Russians, Jews, and members of other nationalities living in Latvia and recategorized as Latvians for propaganda purposes.[52] As with its Polish armies, Moscow never entirely trusted the loyalty of its non-Russian forces, but as reserves of military-age Russians were depleted after long years of fighting, it had no choice but to rely on them. As a result, by 1945 the face of the Red Army – particularly in its front-line infantry formations – was strikingly non-Russian and increasingly Siberian,

Mongolian, or Central Asian, a key fact of hybridization obfuscated by constant references to "Russians."

Ironically, the word "German" has a similar effect. The German military in the Second World War has long been imagined in both popular and scholarly history as a force characterized by mechanized modernity and ethnic homogeneity. Scholars like David Stahel have highlighted just how limited the Wehrmacht's mechanization actually was, picturing *two* German armies invading the USSR: one that was small, mechanized, and mobile and one that relied on foot marches and horse-drawn transport and was "large, slow and cumbersome."[53] As losses mounted and supply systems broke down, the Wehrmacht was increasingly *de*modernized; at the same time, it must be noted, it became increasingly de-Germanized.

The precise number of non-Germans serving in the German military's support services and in the allied armies under its command is unknowable, but as Robert Citino concludes, it is clear that by the end of the war the "Wehrmacht wouldn't have been in the field at all were it not for non-German foreigners."[54] Non-Germans served on the Ostfront in three major capacities: first, as volunteer soldiers in special Waffen-SS units enlisted in support of the Nazi crusade against "Bolshevism"; second, as members of national armies – Finnish, Hungarian, Italian, and Romanian – fighting under German command; and third, as former Soviet soldiers recruited from German prisoner of war camps and put to work as *Hilfswillige* (willing helpers) or "Hiwis."[55]

Some Hiwis, particularly those from the Baltic States, Byelorussia, and Ukraine, were opponents of the Stalinist regime who welcomed the opportunity to fight against it, but the great majority were former Red Army soldiers who calculated that their chances of survival were better in the Wehrmacht than in prison camps. At the start of Operation Barbarossa in June 1941, the first two categories of non-Germans contributed well over 700,000 soldiers to a total invasion force of nearly 4 million, and some 1,200 miles (over 1,900 kilometers) out of the 2,000-mile front (over 3,200 kilometers) were held by Finns, Hungarians, and Romanians.[56] As the invasion progressed, German field commanders quickly began to defy official prohibitions on recruiting Slavs and started using captured Soviet soldiers for logistical tasks. By June 1943, at least 800,000 Hiwis were serving in the Wehrmacht in some capacity; given that both Soviet and German authorities had an interest in under-reporting the numbers of Hiwis, the actual figure was probably far higher.[57]

Beginning in 1938, "Germanic" volunteers who were not German nationals were admitted into the Waffen-SS. Recruited from the so-called Germanic lands, these volunteer soldiers initially served primarily to give physical substance to the National Socialist notion of a Greater German Reich and to project political and ideological influence throughout northern Europe.[58] As the Nazis' anti-Bolshevik crusade unfolded following the invasion of the Soviet Union in June 1941, voluntary recruitment to the Waffen-SS swelled to produce a series of "Germanic" formations – from small contingents to entire divisions – composed of Danes, Dutch, Finns, Flemings, Norwegians, and Swedes. Many of these soldiers had participated in fascist organizations in their own countries and were highly motivated and ideologically committed Nazis, and their units, like the 5th SS Panzer Division *Wiking*, were elite formations. As the war went on, however, SS units in occupied territories from the Baltic to the Balkans began forcibly conscripting local men, often for counterinsurgency duties. As many as 500,000 non-Germans served in the Waffen-SS in some capacity, and by 1945 non-Germans outnumbered Germans in the Nazi's signature formation.[59] Faced with an increasingly difficult military situation, racial ideology was set aside in practice; even the last-ditch defence of Berlin fell in part to the Scandinavian volunteers of SS Panzergrenadier Division *Nordland*.[60]

The invasion of the Soviet Union underscored the importance of expanding the armed forces under German command, and a June 1941 meeting involving representatives of the Wehrmacht, the Reich Main Security Office, the Foreign Office, and the Nazi Party determined that some "non-Germanic" soldiers – including French, Croats, and Spaniards – could fight with the Wehrmacht.[61] The largest single group of "non-Germanic" volunteers on Germany's Ostfront were the 45,000 Spaniards who served in the *Division Azul* (Blue Division) between October 1941 and October 1943. The division was raised by an uneasy alliance between army leaders and the fascist Falange, and its ostensibly all-volunteer character was designed to demonstrate Spanish dictator Francisco Franco's support for Germany's anti-Communist crusade while preserving his country's non-belligerent status.

Uniformed, trained, and equipped by Germany, the Division Azul was incorporated into the Wehrmacht as the 250th Infantry Division. Originally slated to support the push toward Moscow, the division was reassigned to the front around Leningrad after German officers expressed doubts about its discipline. The Spaniards finally arrived after a gruelling series of marches that highlight the Wehrmacht's lack of motorized transport. The Division Azul performed well despite its lack of winter equipment, but German commanders thought that the Spanish soldiers were too inclined to fraternize with the local population – including having "orgies with Jewesses" – and they reported a level of technical incompetence that allegedly included using a hammer to assemble MG-34 machine guns. Expressing typical great-power chauvinism, Field Marshal Günther von Kluge asked whether the Spaniards were "soldiers or gypsies?"[62]

The Hungarian, Italian, and Romanian armies fighting on the Ostfront suffered similar German disdain. Although all were signatories of the Tripartite Pact, Berlin viewed its allies as subordinate states whose armies were at Germany's disposal, and there was never any question of integrating them into top-level strategic planning. Hitler respected Romanian leader Ion Antonescu as a loyal anti-communist crusader and an honorary man of "Germanic origin," but lamented that it was his "misfortune to have Romanians under his command."[63] Despite German disdain, Romania committed two armies and over 325,000 soldiers to the war against the USSR, and the other allied nations also made major commitments. By the opening of Operation Blau in summer 1942, Allied troops accounted for around 25 per cent of the "German" force, making it, as General Gerd von Runstedt noted ironically, an "absolute League of Nations army."[64]

German contempt for the armies of the "lower nations" has continued to colour historical memory. Germany's allies largely figure in accounts of the Ostfront as hapless fall guys: the Romanian Third and Fourth Armies, for example, are rarely discussed except in the context of their collapse in the face of the Soviet counteroffensive around Stalingrad in November 1942. The destruction of the Romanian armies allowed the entrapment of the German Sixth Army in Stalingrad, but these poorly equipped and massively overstretched forces could never reasonably have been expected to hold back the Red Army's armoured spearheads; in fact, perhaps reflecting their dismissive attitude toward the Romanians, German commanders refused to take their reports of heavy Soviet attacks seriously until it was too late to mount an effective response.[65] Following the destruction of the Romanian Third and Fourth Armies – some 3,000 survivors were among the 90,000 "German" prisoners captured in Stalingrad – the Italian Eighth Army and the Hungarian Second Army each lost over 80,000 men fighting to defend the line of the River Don, and the survivors were withdrawn from combat and repatriated.[66]

The third and most numerous group of non-Germans on the Ostfront were the Hiwis. From early on in Barbarossa, local commanders began employing increasing numbers of Hiwis, first as non-combatants and then in combat roles. In a triumph of pragmatism over ideology, the Army High Command agreed during the summer of 1942 that up to 10 per cent of the positions in German divisions could be filled by non-combatant Hiwis. Despite this ostensibly temporary concession, racial ideology led senior Nazis to derail army plans for the formation of a "Russian Liberation Army" (ROA) led by former Red Army General Andrey Vlasov.[67] Many of the Hiwis incorporated into German units dug latrines and moved supplies, but some were pulled into combat roles.[68] Many wore German uniforms and were visually indistinguishable from Germans, a fact of integration that has contributed to their historical invisibility. During the Battle of Stalingrad, around 19,000 (10 per cent) of Sixth Army soldiers were Hiwis, and in some divisions they accounted for 50 per cent of combat strength; later, when Army Group Centre prepared for the inevitable Soviet offensive in the summer of 1944, it counted 103,000 Hiwis out of a ration strength of 849,000, and many more no doubt went unrecorded.[69] In the desperate days that followed the collapse of Army Group Centre, Berlin finally approved the creation of the Russian Liberation Army, and Hitler appointed Vlasov "supreme commander of Russian armed forces."[70] It was too little and too late: Vlasov's scattered forces spent the final weeks of the war manoeuvring to surrender to the Americans, but most of the 20,000 ROA soldiers who ended the war in US prisoner-of-war camps were later handed over to the Soviets.

German officials had a more positive attitude to Cossacks than to ethnic Slavs, and in April 1942 Hitler approved them for front-line duty and anti-partisan operations.[71] Eventually, Cossack forces grew to a 25,000-strong cavalry corps, although, perhaps reflecting lingering doubts about their loyalty, they were deployed away from the Ostfront on counterinsurgency operations in Yugoslavia.[72] At the same time, the recapture of Cossack homelands by the Red Army in 1943 ended speculative discussions in Berlin on the establishment of a Cossack puppet state. At the end of the war, some 32,000 Cossacks who had fought under German command were rounded up in Carinthia (southern Austria) by British authorities and turned over to the Soviets.

Hiwis and other forcibly impressed soldiers were concentrated on Germany's Ostfront but, like the Poles who escaped to join II Corps in Italy, they also served in significant numbers elsewhere. In fall 1943, German commanders began assembling *Ost-Bataillonen* or "eastern battalions" for France in preparation for an Allied landing. These units were composed of both Hiwis and non-German volunteers, including Cossacks, Georgians, Turkmens, Volga Tatars, and Azeris, and they made a significant contribution to the Wehrmacht's infantry combat strength; in LXXXIV Corps, for example, they comprised eight out of forty-two battalions.[73]

RACIAL AND ETHNIC MINORITIES IN THE US MILITARY

The numbers make it clear that, despite the obvious ideological difficulties, Germany simply could not have sustained its military effort without the participation of very large numbers of non-Germans.[74] The wartime experience of the United States offers some interesting points of comparison. In the context of fighting a war in which the strategic emphasis on the production of war materiel necessarily limited the availability of Caucasian military manpower, the United States relied heavily on the mobilization of racial and ethnic minorities, colonial troops, and allied armies. US authorities faced an ideological challenge, but whereas German racial ideology had to accommodate mobilizing non-Germans, America fought the war under a banner of democracy and racial equality while actually practising racial segregation. In a manner that paralleled the outlook of other imperial elites, American commanders argued that African Americans were too educationally backward to master modern weapons, but unlike their colonial contemporaries they also argued that Blacks were unsuited for combat. There was no American equivalent of "martial race" theory except, perhaps, in the valorization of a Native American past that had already been effectively extirpated.

During the interwar years, Black soldiers in the remaining four African American regiments had been dispersed into "housekeeping detachments" on bases around the United States.[75] When the wartime expansion of the military began in 1940, the Army agreed to induct African Americans in proportion to the population, but in practice proficiency tests were used to slow their recruitment. Prompted by a public campaign in the Black press, more African Americans were recruited as personnel shortages began to bite, and eventually some 1.25 million served – a number roughly proportional to their weight in the population.[76] Most were assigned to labour or service units, and critical but often unheralded operations like the construction of the Ledo Road in Burma or the Red Ball Express trucking operation in France were carried out largely by African Americans. If technically non-combatant, this work was not without danger: in July 1944, over 250 Black stevedores were killed while loading ammunition at Port Chicago, California.

Manpower shortages prompted the formation of two Black divisions that were deployed in 1944 in Bougainville and in Italy, but poor training and antagonism between white officers and Black soldiers marred their combat performance. By late 1944, however, a lack of trained soldiers in the European Theatre persuaded commanders to assign small African American units – tank and artillery battalions and infantry platoons – to previously all-white formations. The results were impressive.[77] These moves – and parallel developments in the Air Corps and the Navy – were undertaken for pragmatic reasons and stopped short of full integration, but they nevertheless started to break down segregation. Moreover, African American veterans took their experience of fighting racism and segregation in the military home with them, where it helped to fuel the rise of the Civil Rights movement.[78]

Members of other ethnic groups also served in the US military in significant numbers. Precise numbers are impossible to determine, but they include 850,000 Italian Americans, as many as 500,000 Mexican Americans and other "Hispanics," and over 25,000 Japanese Americans.[79] As reported by the Bureau of Native Affairs, around 25,000 Native Americans – around 7 per cent of the Indigenous population – also served, and they were joined by at least another 20,000 "off-reservation" Native Americans.[80] Soldiers from these ethnic minorities did not face the systemic segregation that confronted African Americans, and with the exception of the 53,000 Puerto Ricans who served in the territorially defined Puerto Rican National Guard and the 65th Infantry Regiment, and the Japanese-American members of the 442nd Regimental Combat Team, they did not fight in separate units. Nevertheless, many faced varying degrees of prejudice and discrimination; Italian and Hispanic American men, for example, were held by many US elites to have non-white and feminine characteristics that made them unsuitable for military service.[81] Native

American military service, on the other hand, was often framed by an Americanized version of martial race theory that valorized Indigenous warrior traditions even as it mythologized them. Popular perceptions of martial valour paved the way to acceptance, enabling at least some Native Americans to experience their time in the military as one of "cultural reaffirmation and renewal."[82]

The United States also raised at least 200,000 fighters from its colony in the Philippines where, contrary to popular images of American victimhood, Filipinos accounted for all but 600 of the 7,000 men who died on the 1942 Bataan Death March.[83] In Italy, the American Fifth Army included the 25,000-strong Brazilian Expeditionary Force. Raised in exchange for US economic and military aid, this Brazilian contingent was itself an ethnically diverse force that included a large number of Afro-Brazilians and even some Italian-Brazilians.[84]

CONCLUSION

The work of thinking about the recruitment of colonial conscripts, non-national soldiers, and members of racial and ethnic minorities into the armed forces of *all* the major protagonists in the Second World War adds depth and texture to our understanding of the war on a number of different levels. First, it rescues the stories of millions from what E.P. Thompson called the "enormous condescension of posterity."[85] Second, it illuminates the commonalities of imperial practice, linking the attitudes of the Japanese in Korea, the British in India, and *mutatis mutandis*, of white US officers toward the African Americans under their command. Third, by bringing the subaltern to the centre, these entangled histories challenge the national frameworks that have dominated the historiography of the Second World War, allowing the weight and ubiquity of the worldwide mobilization of military personpower to globalize our understanding of the war itself.

If, as James Belich et al. contend, global history foregrounds "*uneven or differential connectedness*" and is "centrally concerned with the history of *mobility*," then the Second World War can be reimagined as transnational vectors describing the movement of armies, matériel, people, ideas, and – as discussed above – of millions of soldiers recruited outside the imperial metropolises.[86] At the very least, this mobility and connectivity complicates the previously all-pervasive image of the war as a struggle between homogeneous nation-states (and a series of "People's Wars") that careened into each other like billiard balls. What does it mean, for example, when we see that a significant proportion of the "Japanese" Army was in fact Korean, that the Wehrmacht required Soviet Hiwis to sustain its Ostfront, or that the Indian Army fighting for the British Empire in Burma was a mighty incubator for anti-colonial nationalism?

Yet the Second World War, like other modern wars, was waged by nation-states, whether they were fighting to carve out new colonial-autarkic blocs, defend existing empires, secure national borders, or establish a new global hegemony. From this point of view, the global histories of mobility and connectivity discussed here do not *negate* old nation-centric historiographies, but rather unfold in *dynamic tension* with them. So, for example, they help us to see how national military mobilizations had profound consequences that reached far beyond national borders, intertwining the organization of colonial subjects for war with the strengthening of anti-colonial nationalism, complicating Stalinist visions of a new soviet nationality, or re-evaluating the contribution of the "lower nations" bound to Germany by the Tripartite Pact. In this sense, perhaps, global history offers not a new master narrative but an approach that, by simultaneously complicating and connecting nation-centric people's histories, allows a new and genuinely globalized account to emerge.

NOTES

1. T. Fujitani, *Race for Empire: Koreans as Japanese and Japanese as Americans during World War II* (Berkeley: University of California Press, 2011), 44–6.
2. Ibid., 48–52.
3. Ibid., 239–99.
4. Filmmaker Frank Capra, quoted in John W. Dower, *War Without Mercy: Race and Power in the Pacific War* (New York: Pantheon Books, 1986), 19.
5. I have not attempted to extend the analysis to the numerous armies raised in China; this omission stems from time constraints and a lack of suitable English language sources; the war in China could certainly be complicated in similar ways. However, see Mark Baker, "Growing Up in Kaifeng: Young People, Ideology, and Mobilization in Occupied China, 1938–1945" chapter 4 of this book, for an example.

6 See in particular Ashley Jackson, *The British Empire and the Second World War* (London: Hambledon Continuum, 2006).

7 R. Scott Sheffield and Noah Riseman, *Indigenous Peoples and the Second World War: The Politics, Experiences and Legacies in the US, Canada, Australia and New Zealand* (Cambridge: Cambridge University Press, 2019), 63–76.

8 Yasmin Khan, *The Raj at War: A People's History of India's Second World War* (London: Bodley Head, 2015), 22.

9 Tarak Barkawi, *Soldiers of Empire: Indian and British Armies in World War II* (Cambridge: Cambridge University Press, 2017), 8; Khan, *The Raj at War*, 23.

10 Raymond A. Callahan, "Winston Churchill, Two Armies, and Military Transformation," *World War II Quarterly* 5, no. 4 (2008), 41.

11 Barkawi, *Soldiers of Empire*, 233–4.

12 Ibid., 8–9.

13 Ibid., 234.

14 Claude Auchinleck quoted in Callahan, "Winston Churchill, Two Armies, and Military Transformation," 41.

15 See Frank Furedi, "The Demobilized African Soldier," in *Guardians of Empire: The Armed Forces of the Colonial Powers, c. 1700–1964*, ed. David Killingray and David Omissi (Manchester: Manchester University Press, 1999), 183.

16 For "panic," see Furedi, "The Demobilized African Soldier," 179, 182. For a more nuanced view see Ashley Jackson, "Supplying War: The High Commission Territories' Military-Logistical Contribution to the Second World War," *Journal of Military History* 66, no. 3 (July 2002), 756–9.

17 See Kevin Noles, "Divided Loyalties: Indian Prisoners of War in Singapore, February 1942 to May 1943" in this book, chapter 11; Barkawi, *Soldiers of Empire*, 109–17.

18 Around 20 per cent of the Royal Netherlands East Indies Army was composed of Europeans, who provided all the officers and many of the NCOs; 80 per cent of the army was recruited in Indonesia, primarily from Javanese, Ambonese, and Manadonese. See Marc Lohnstein, *Royal Netherlands East Indies Army 1936–1942* (Oxford: Osprey Publishing, 2018), 4–7.

19 Stephen C. Bruner, "'At Least So Long as We're Talking About Marching, the Inferior Is Not the Black, It's the White': Italian Debate over the Use of Indigenous Troops in the Scramble for Africa," *European History Quarterly* 44, no. 1 (2014), 35–6; Nir Arielli, "Colonial Soldiers in Italian Counter-Insurgency Operations in Libya, 1922–1932," *British Journal for*

Military History 1, no. 2 (February 2015), 49–51, 52; 55–7; Alexander De Grand, "Mussolini's Follies: Fascism in Its Imperial and Racist Phase, 1935–1940," *Contemporary European History* 14, no. 2 (May 2005), 130–2, 133.

20 Aldo Giuseppe Scarselli, "'The Eritrean Askari believes to be the best soldier in the world!': How the Eritrean Colonial Soldiers were Represented in Italian Military Memoirs," unpublished MA thesis, Leiden University Institute for History, 2014–15, 24–30.

21 De Grand, "Mussolini's Follies," 132; Arielli, "Colonial Soldiers in Italian Counter-Insurgency Operations," 53–4.

22 Mike Bennighof, "Conquest of Ethiopia: Italy's Eritrean Soldiers," *Avalanche Press Newsletter*, October 2018.

23 Bennighof, "Conquest of Ethiopia"; Giorgio Rochat, "The Italian Airforce in the Ethiopian War, 1935–1936," in *Italian Colonialism*, ed. Ruth Ben-Ghiat and Mia Filler (New York: Palgrave Macmillan, 2005), 43.

24 For numbers, see Giorgio Rochat, *Guerre italiane in Libia e in Ethiopia: Studi militari 1921–1939* (Treviso: Pagus, 1991), 27.

25 Richard Carrier, "Some Reflections on the Fighting Power of the Italian Army in North Africa, 1940–1943," *War in History* 22, no. 4 (2015), 517.

26 Philip Nord, *France 1940: Defending the Republic* (New Haven: Yale University Press, 2015).

27 Raffael Scheck, *Hitler's African Victims: The German Army Massacre of Black French Soldiers in 1940* (Cambridge: Cambridge University Press, 2006), 10–11.

28 Charles-Robert Ageron, "Leclerc, de l'Empire à l'Union Française," in *Du capitaine de Hauteclocque au général Leclerc*, ed. Christine Levisse-Touzé (Paris: Editions Complexe, 2000), 243.

29 Anthony Clayton, *France, Soldiers and Africa* (London: Brassey's Defense Publishers, 1988), 143.

30 Marcel Vigneras, *Rearming the French* (Washington: US Army Center for Military History, 1989), 33–44; Andrew Buchanan, *American Grand Strategy in the Mediterranean during World War II* (Cambridge: Cambridge University Press, 2014), 85–6.

31 Clayton, *France, Soldiers and Africa*, 145.

32 Jean de Lattre de Tassigny, *History of the French First Army* (London: George Allen and Unwin, 1952), 176–7.

33 See Martin Thomas, *Fight or Flight: Britain, France and Their Roads from Empire* (Oxford: Oxford University Press, 2014), 60; Alistair Horne, *A Savage War of Peace: Algeria 1954–1962* (New York: NYRB, 2006 [1977]), 42.

34 See Martin Thomas, "Colonial Violence in Algeria and the Distorted Logic of State Retribution: The Sétif Uprising of 1945," *Journal of Military History* 75 (January 2011), 125–57.
35 Horne, *A Savage War of Peace*, 28.
36 Stephen Bungay, *The Most Dangerous Enemy: A History of the Battle of Britain* (London: Aurum Press, 200), 176.
37 Bungay, *Most Dangerous Enemy*, 175; J. Lee Ready, *Forgotten Allies: The Military Contribution of the Colonies, Exiled Governments, and Lesser Powers to the Allied Victory in World War II* (Jefferson, NC: McFarland, 1985), 1:27–9.
38 Bungay, *Most Dangerous Enemy*, 174.
39 Andrzej Szujecki, "Near and Middle East," in *The Polish Deportees of World War II: Recollections of Removal to the Soviet Union and Dispersal Throughout the World*, ed. Tadeusz Piotrowki (Jefferson, NC: McFarland and Company, 2004), 97; Halik Kochanski, *The Eagle Unbowed: Poland and the Poles in the Second World War* (Cambridge: Harvard University Press, 2012), 198–9, 202, 466–80.
40 British intelligence estimated that 170,000 Poles were conscripted into the *Wehrmacht*. Kochanski, *Eagle Unbowed*, 230, 475.
41 Winston S. Churchill, *The Second World War*, vol. 3 (Boston: Houghton Mifflin, 1950), 686.
42 Czeslaw Jesman, "'The "Polish Experiment' in West Africa during World War II," *Africa: Rivista trimestrale di studi e documentazione dell'Istituto italiano per l'Africa e l'Oriente* 20, no. 4 (December 1965), 421–2.
43 Kochanski, *Eagle Unbowed*, 393.
44 Antony Beevor, *The Fall of Berlin 1945* (London: Penguin, 2002), 64, 199–200. This fractured war experience has led to similarly complex issues when it comes to state-led remembrance of the war in Poland; see Jadwiga Biskupska, "Beyond a 'People's War': The Polish Past and the Second World War in Contemporary Perspective," chapter 15 of this book.
45 Susan L. Curran and Dmitry Ponomareff, "Managing the Ethnic Factor in the Russian and Soviet Armed Forces," (Santa Monica: RAND publications, 1982), 30. In Red Army infantry divisions, Russians accounted for 51.78 per cent of the person-power, followed by Ukrainians (33.93 per cent), Byelorussians (2.04 per cent), Uzbeks (1.25 per cent), Jews (1.14 per cent), and citizens of the various Caucasian and Central Asian republics and autonomous areas.
46 Ilya Ehrenburg, quoted in Roger R. Reese, *Why Stalin's Soldiers Fought: The Red Army's Military Effectiveness in World War II* (Lawrence: University of Kansas Press, 2011), 15.

47 Reese, *Why Stalin's Soldiers Fought*, 18.
48 Ibid., 312.
49 Ibid., 141–6.
50 Rolf-Dieter Müller, *The Unknown Eastern Front: The Wehrmacht and Hitler's Foreign Soldiers* (London: I.B. Tauris, 2014), 216.
51 Juliette Cadiot, "Russian Army, Non-Russians, Non-Slavs, Non-Orthodox: The Risky Construction of a Multiethnic Army," *Journal of Power Institutions in Post-Soviet Societies* 10 (2009), 6.
52 Reese, *Why Stalin's Soldiers Fought*, 147.
53 David Stahel, *Operation Barbarossa and Germany's Defeat in the East* (Cambridge: Cambridge University Press, 2009), 118–19.
54 Robert M. Citino, *The Wehrmacht's Last Stand: The German Campaigns of 1944–1945* (Lawrence: University of Kansas Press, 2018), 436.
55 I use the term *Ostfront* instead of the more usual "Eastern Front" since from Moscow's point of view the front was in the West.
56 Müller, *Unknown Eastern Front*, 255–6.
57 For reasons discussed here, it is hard to give accurate figures. But see Müller, *The Unknown Eastern Front*, 228; Oleg Beyda and Igor Petrov, "The Soviet Union," in *Joining Hitler's Crusade: European Nations and the Invasion of the Soviet Union, 1941*, ed. David Stahel (Cambridge: Cambridge University Press, 2018), 375–6.
58 Sigurd Sørlie, "Norway," in *Joining Hitler's Crusade: European Nations and the Invasion of the Soviet Union, 1941*, ed. David Stahel (Cambridge: Cambridge University Press, 2018), 319–21.
59 George H. Stein, *The Waffen SS: Hitler's Elite Guard at War, 1939–1944* (Ithaca: Cornell University Press, 1984), 137–9.
60 Ibid., 164; Beevor, *The Fall of Berlin*, 257–8.
61 David Stahel, "Introduction," in *Joining Hitler's Crusade: European Nations and the Invasion of the Soviet Union, 1941*, ed. David Stahel (Cambridge: Cambridge University Press, 2018), 5–7.
62 Xavier Moreno Juliá, "Spain," in *Joining Hitler's Crusade: European Nations and the Invasion of the Soviet Union, 1941*, ed. David Stahel (Cambridge: Cambridge University Press, 2018), 207.
63 Stahel, *Joining Hitler's Crusade*, 9.
64 Gerd von Runstedt, quoted in Jonathan Trigg, *Death on the Don: The Destruction of Germany's Allies on the Eastern Front, 1941–1944* (Stroud: The History Press, 2017), 119.
65 Trigg, *Death on the Don*, 162.
66 Müller, *Unknown Eastern Front*, 28, 54, 87.
67 Ibid., 223–8.

68 Beevor, *Stalingrad*, 184–6.
69 Müller, *Unknown Eastern Front*, 225; Citino, *The Wehrmacht's Last Stand*, 171.
70 Müller, *Unknown Eastern Front*, 232–6.
71 Ibid., 217; Beyda and Petrov, "The Soviet Union," 404–11.
72 Müller, *Unknown Eastern Front*, 219–20.
73 Citino, *The Wehrmacht's Last Stand*, 120.
74 See Müller, *The Unknown Eastern Front*, 255–8.
75 Bernard C. Nalty, *Strength for the Fight: A History of Black Americans in the Military* (New York: The Free Press, 1986), 128–9.
76 Fujitani, *Race for Empire*, 209.
77 Nalty, *Strength for the Fight*, 178–9; David P. Colley, *Blood for Dignity: The Story of the First Integrated Combat Unit in the US Army* (New York: St Martin's Press, 2003), esp. 189–94.
78 See Penny M. Von Eschen, *Race Against Empire: Black Americans and Anticolonialism, 1937–1957* (Ithaca: Cornell University Press, 1997), esp. 32–5.
79 Matteo Pretelli and Francesco Fusi, "Fighting Alongside the Allies in Italy: The War of Soldiers of Italian Descent Against the Land of Their Ancestors," in *Italy and the Second World War: Alternative Perspectives*, ed. Emanuele Sica and Richard Carrier (Leiden: Brill, 2018), 302; Fujitani, *Race for Empire*, 207–9.
80 Sheffield and Riseman, *Indigenous Peoples and the Second World War*, 63–4.
81 Andrew Buchanan, "'Good Morning, Pupil': American Representations of Italianness and the Occupation of Italy, 1943–1945," *Journal of Contemporary History* 43, no. 2 (April 2008), esp. 220–1.
82 Sheffield and Riseman, *Indigenous Peoples and the Second World War*, 53.
83 Ronald H. Spector, *Eagle Against the Sun: The American War with Japan* (New York: Vintage Books, 1985), 396–7.
84 Matteo Pretelli and Francesco Fusi, "Fighting Alongside the Allies in Italy: The War of Soldiers of Italian Descent Against the Land of Their Ancestors," in *Italy and the Second World War: Alternative Perspectives*, ed. Emanuele Sica and Richard Carrier (Leiden: Brill, 2018), 312.
85 E.P. Thompson, *The Making of the English Working Class* (London: Penguin, 1980 [1963]), 12.
86 James Belich, John Darwin and Chris Wickham, "Introduction: The Prospect of Global History," in *The Prospect of Global History*, ed. James Belich, John Darwin, Margaret Frenz and Chris Wickham (Oxford: Oxford University Press, 2016), 14–15.

THEME TWO

Mobilization and Remobilization for "People's Wars"

2

Fascist Warfare on the Home Front

War Mobilization and the Fragmentation of Italian Society, 1935–1943

Nicolò Da Lio

This chapter presents the first results of research aimed at understanding the role of military justice on the Italian home front during the decade of fascist wars, 1935 to 1943. It addresses two shortcomings in the historiography on the fascist wars: the first relates to the role of military justice in the Second World War;[1] the second concerns the daily life of mobilized workers between 1935 and 1943.[2] The historiography on Italian mobilization during the Second World War highlights the institutional and political limits of a fascist industrial mobilization based on an antagonistic relationship between entrepreneurs and the state.[3] This historiographical debate revolves around whether the limited Italian mobilization was the consequence of weak institutions, partial totalitarianism, and erratic foreign policy, or the failure of a genuine "people's" project, in which the "fascistization" of Italian society was central to waging total war.

Regardless of the different historiographical positions, Italian war mobilization is considered to have had two distinct phases. The first phase, from 1935 to 1942, departed from the war mobilization experienced in the Great War, as fascist authorities attempted to control and centralize war production. The second started in 1942, when, in an attempt to encourage production efficiency, the Great War model was thoroughly applied by organizing self-governing production groups in which the main industries administered the production process themselves. Both phases were hampered by a lack of well-defined objectives as well as the means to attain them. Because of these limits, the regime failed in its attempts to fully mobilize Italy for a world war.[4]

As authoritative as this understanding of the periodization of mobilization in Italy during the Second World War has become, there is another way to understand the issue. As Massimo Legnani has argued, it is insufficient to study fascist mobilization solely through an institutional lens. Only by analyzing mobilization as an instrument to inspire and discipline Italian people can one understand both the fascist totalitarian aims and the regime's political limits.[5] In this context, the working classes, and their attitude toward the fascist authorities, became central to the success of mobilization. By studying a local case, 506 trials held by the Verona Military Court between 1940 and 1943 – approximately half of the trials held against workers during this period[6] – the chapter shows that workers grew progressively distant from the regime as the war continued.[7] Mobilization became one of the areas used by fascist authorities, ministries, entrepreneurs, and military agencies engaged in a political conflict to control work production and discipline workers. This dynamic played out as early as 1940, well before the 1942 de-centralization of production, and has to be seen as central to our understanding of Italy's Second World War.

MUSTERING AN ARMY OF WORKERS

The lessons of the Great War played a central role in determining the way in which mobilization was organized in the 1920s and 1930s in Italy. General Alfredo Dallolio, who oversaw the mobilization for war between 1915 and 1918, first as head of the *Sottosegretariato* (Undersecretariat) and then the *Ministero per le armi e le munizioni* (Ministry for Arms and Munition), was central to this story. Between 1923 and 1939, Dallolio was directed to prepare Italy for mobilization for a future European conflict.[8] The Italian and fascist doctrine for a future war revolved around the need for a short and decisive conflict, a "fast war," that would require a thorough political, economic, and military mobilization, even in time of peace. The ideological mobilization experienced by Italian society during the Great War would, thus, have to be actively retained, while at the same time, a new social hierarchy based on political and military merit would have to be implemented. Mussolini wanted Italians to think of themselves "as a mobilized army" both in peace and war.[9]

In spite of the creation in 1923 of the *Consiglio Supremo della Difesa* (Supreme Council for Defence) and of the *Comitato Nazionale di Mobilitazione* (National Mobilization Committee), the latter under the presidency of Dallolio, no single organization was tasked with overseeing the "total mobilization" of Italian society during the interwar years. General Dallolio called for a centralized institution, but mobilization was actually implemented by many ministries, provincial, and municipal institutions, as well as the Fascist Party itself.

One of the first important steps was the introduction of new laws. The Great War had increased the grasp that military authorities had on Italian society. In the 1860s, military law had been instrumental in repressing southern "brigands." In the 1890s, it was used to violently quell political protests, and in 1908 it was used to control the civilian population after the disastrous earthquake in Messina and Reggio Calabria.[10] The Great War, to all intents and purposes, represented just another step in the proliferation of special jurisdictions and the use of military justice to control Italian civilians.

In this context, the fascist regime's efforts to use military justice to control Italian society was built on firm foundations. The *Tribunale Speciale per la Difesa dello Stato* (Special Tribunal for the Defence of the State), created in 1926, was manned by military judges tasked with repressing anti-fascists by using wartime military law. Over time, the boundaries separating citizens and military service became blurred and, as the military judge Gaetano Tei summarized, military courts were to "watch over and control" all Italian citizens, who were liable for punishment for "any damaging behaviour."[11] The rule of law was to be subordinated to the regime's objectives.[12]

In 1925, a statute for a National War Organization was passed; this was one of the first laws promulgated by the new fascist government. The framework within which the nation was to be organized for war was not merely technocratic: as the Fascist MP, engineer, university professor, and reserve artillery major Ernesto Galeazzi argued in parliament, organizing the nation for war was the "first step" toward the "new fascist order" and the "militarization of the Nation."[13] This political design was largely supported by the Italian military,[14] who saw an opportunity to cement their place in Italian society. Moreover, the benefits of a mobilization machine that would direct the Italian economy and deal with issues of social justice were hard to ignore.[15]

In this design, fascist corporatism would build an "inclusive union of all social categories"[16] and leave the military authorities to pull the strings and effectively assign "every man [...] to his proper place" in society and in the economy.[17]

The 1925 National War Organization law compelled every citizen without military duties to cooperate in the defence of the nation. Military ministries would retain control of all military aspects of mobilization. To organize the other aspects of mobilization, four central government organs were to be created "when necessary." These organs, and their respective regional delegations, would be tasked with administering commercial operations, war production, food distribution, and propaganda and civil relief. There was little detail, however, on how those in charge of the military and civilian mobilization processes would coordinate their activities. The *Comitato per la Mobilitazione Civile* (Civil Mobilization Committee), which now replaced the National Mobilization Committee, would oversee the civilian mobilization process until, at the beginning of hostilities, the War Ministry took over, and exercise complete authority.[18]

In 1931, a new law on "The Discipline of Citizens in Time of War" was set out. It tasked municipalities with finding workers for war production and with the control and coordination of local war measures through a Civil Resistance Committee – to be formed in the event of mobilization. Henceforth, in a time of war, mobilized workers who went absent would be considered deserters;[19] mobilized workers would consequently have a different judicial status than ordinary workers. In 1935, the newly created *Commissariato Generale per le Fabbricazioni di Guerra* (General Commissariat for War Production [COGEFAG]), was placed under the command of Dallolio and separated from the Civil Mobilization Committee,[20] of which Dallolio retained the presidency. The COGEFAG enforced war discipline on mobilized workers, set working hours, and validated the distribution of raw materials, but did not control the distribution of coal, firewood, fuel, electricity, and tires.

In spite of the legislative effort displayed in ten years of fascist government, it was still unclear who was supposed to control the mobilization of workers. In 1932, the Ministry for Corporations was directed to run a census of workers eligible for mobilization. The ministry completed a card index of 170,000 citizens to meet a demand for 190,000 to 200,000 "civil servants" (a form of universal civic duty) who had been called up for military service. The index was supposed to act as a template for the creation of other indexes to supply industrial and agricultural firms with person-power. However, when this new mobilization machine was tested, in Piedmont and Lazio between July and December 1939, it was shown to be deficient.[21] It was found that the military authorities' indexes only covered men between the ages of eighteen and fifty-five who were eligible for conscription. The ministry, therefore, had to appeal to the Fascist Party for help in filing the new indexes, which were to include senior citizens up to the age of seventy, minors as young as seventeen, and women. As a consequence of the experience gained in Lazio and Piedmont, responsibility for the mobilization of workers was now divided between the Ministry for Corporations, which was responsible for men aged between nineteen and seventy, and the Fascist Party, which focused on teenagers between the ages of fourteen and eighteen and women between the ages of fourteen and seventeen.[22] Efforts to streamline the mobilization process had largely failed.

War broke out in Europe on 1 September 1939. The rapid approach of Italian involvement in the conflict did not, however, lead to the infrastructure for mobilization being organized more efficiently in Italy. Two days after the commencement of hostilities, Dallolio resigned his post at the head of the COGEFAG. At the age of eighty-six, he considered himself too old to lead the mobilization process; he was also a well-known Germanophobe.[23] In May 1940, a new law regulating war mobilization was approved in an attempt to rationalize the situation.[24] Italy declared war on the United Kingdom and France twenty days later. The new law retained most articles from its 1925 predecessor, but because the regulations that should have followed the law did not appear until 1942, the responsibilities remained confused. The judicial status of workers in a time of war remained unclear.

On 23 May 1940, COGEFAG, now led by General Carlo Favagrossa, a Spanish Civil War veteran, was transformed into the Undersecretariat for War Production. Favagrossa retained the power to subject firms to military discipline, by declaring them "auxiliary" industries, but he neglected to ask for more powers for war production.[25] In June 1940, auxiliary industries were militarized,[26] but regulations about their militarization did not follow. The law was therefore repealed in April 1941.[27] At the same time, in addition to auxiliary industries, single firms or workshops were mobilized individually with specific decrees (usually implemented by Mussolini), thus expanding the quantity of workers subject to military law outside COGEFAG's control. A different decree, in November 1940, confirmed that all workers within auxiliary, or mobilized, industries were subject to military law,[28] but up until February 1942 there was no law regulating penalties for workers who had been disciplined.[29]

In the meantime, with the armed forces only partially mobilized in June 1940 and with a short-lived demobilization following the fall of France, workers in auxiliary industries were temporarily exempted from being called up. It was not until July 1941 that matters changed. The armed forces were now remobilized, but a thorough civil mobilization was postponed.[30] Therefore, industries and the public sector were not assigned mobilized personnel to compensate for the loss of workers to military obligations.[31]

It was not until September 1941 that the Fascist Party finally completed its workforce indexes for teenagers and women. The Ministry for Corporations also lagged in finding men without military obligations to meet the needs of industry.[32] Matters were then made more complicated when the Undersecretariat for War Production bent to the needs of industrialists who wanted to retain their skilled labourers and declared that workers could not be substituted with women and minors.[33]

In February 1942, a new law defining a simpler procedure was enacted: the Fascist Party would continue to manage its census, while the Ministry for Corporations would administer the process of drafting and assigning workers.[34] But the executive regulations were not issued before yet another law was enacted in February 1943. This new law represented the first real rationalization of the mobilization process. The Undersecretariat for War Production was now transformed into an independent ministry, and coherent regulations for directing and disciplining the citizen workforce were finally put in place.[35] From now on, mobilized workers would fall into two distinct categories: workers employed in auxiliary industries, which comprised all military-related production, and workers mobilized for the *Servizio Civile* (Civil Service, later called *Servizio del Lavoro*, Work Service).[36] The latter were also divided between workers employed in mobilized institutions (such as workshops, power plants, hospitals, municipal and provincial administrations, civilian transport services, or trash removal services – typically as a consequence of a "Duce's decree"), and people individually mobilized for a mandatory *Servizio Civile*. The *Servizio Civile* was supposed to be a universal civic duty, but it was, paradoxically, also used as an extrajudicial punishment for idle or politically unreliable persons.[37] All of these categories were subject to the jurisdiction of the territorial military courts. Progress had been made, but the years of confusion and competition meant that the legitimacy of Mussolini's mobilization process still lay in doubt.[38]

PRODUCTION AND PRODUCERS

As the Italian "Decade of War" started, national productivity was on the rise. However, by 1940 it had begun to stagnate and then, from 1943, decline.[39] As the system for mobilization was tested and refined, it became clear that, in spite of occasional shortcomings,[40] resources were sufficient given the production capabilities of the Italian war industry. In fact, productivity was hampered more by human factors, such as the complex bureaucracy, a lack of trained engineers and specialists, and the labour-intensive outdated production methods. The prominent Ansaldo and OTO artillery factories are a telling example. The two industries worked at half their potential during the war, not because material resources were insufficient, but because the bureaucracy governing production demands and resource allocation was extremely inefficient, and engineers, technicians, and skilled workers were in short supply.[41]

To make matters worse, the mobilization of workers was neither "total" nor evenly distributed; there were distinct differences in the rates of mobilization by age, gender, social group, and region. Of the total workforce available, only a fraction was actually mobilized before December 1942, when Mussolini issued a decree mobilizing all industrial firms.[42] Before that date, auxiliary firms directly linked to war production had only been able to secure about three-quarters of the 1,320,000 men they needed.[43] This was in spite the fact that in 1942 about 4 million workers were employed in industrial firms in Italy.

Some people looked on the mobilization process positively. Many volunteers hoped to be assigned to a job to avoid military service,[44] and unemployed people could hope to find a job. Even Jews who had recently been expelled from their workplace could try to affirm their right to full citizenship by volunteering,[45] thus highlighting their nationalist or fascist spirit.[46] A total of 794,064 women and 273,217 minors volunteered to work in war industries during the war, out of a total census of almost 4 million women and 1.6 million minors.[47] In 1936, Dallolio had estimated that 300,000 women would need to be conscripted into auxiliary industries in case of war.[48] But the regime was firmly against the idea of mobilizing women for war production, and the available data confirms that the regime mobilized as few women and minors as possible during the war years.[49] By October 1942, 463,049 women had been mobilized for the war effort;[50] the figure subsequently jumped to 1,217,585 in December, when, during the crisis of late 1942, il Duce mobilized all industrial firms to support the war effort.

The number of male workers grew steadily during the war years too, increasing from the 832,838 employed in auxiliary industries in 1940 to around 1 million in 1941 and 1942. By October 1942, the figure for men mobilized for war work reached 2,014,168, jumping again to 3,993,287 in December. At this point, mobilized men and women amounted to 5,210,872, of whom just 1,219,890 were employed in auxiliary industries.[51]

By comparing these numbers with the figures in the 1936 Italian census, which listed the active population as 13,341,000 men and 5,242,000 women, it is possible to deduce that around 29 per cent of active men and 26 per cent of active women were mobilized for war work during the Second World War.[52] The relative proportion of males versus females changed little, however; thus, a considerable opportunity to free up person-power for military service, by substituting female for male labour, was missed. As Mark Baker demonstrates in chapter 4 of this volume, failures to draw on specific pools of person-power could have very negative effects on the ability of belligerents to fight the war effectively.

Other opportunities were missed, too; the most mobilized sectors of the wartime economy were not necessarily the most important, or the most productive, sectors of the Italian economy. Taking the data for October 1942 as an example, it is possible to see that private industries were comparatively more subject to mobilization, accounting for 55.29 per cent of the overall mobilized workforce, than the public sector, which comprised the shipyards, arsenals, arms factories, and workshops of the armed forces, and accounted for 39.48 per cent of the mobilized force. Agriculture was assigned a much smaller proportion of the available workforce, accounting for just 5.24 per cent. In absolute terms, this meant that there were 1,352,199 mobilized workers in private industry, 965,536 in the public sector, and 128,069 in agriculture, for a grand total of 2,445,804 persons.[53]

In addition, the workforce that was mobilized was used inefficiently; many firms experienced difficulties in finding skilled or unskilled labourers. In the hope of freeing up person-power for war production, the textile sector was rationalized in September 1942. Most textile firms worked only twenty hours per week. It was therefore decided to set the minimum work hours at thirty-two per week and close any company that could not keep up the pace. On top of that, any factory that did not have its own power plant was ordered to stop production in winter, when electricity became scarce due to the lack of water for hydroelectric power. In spite of these efforts, most factory owners were able to get dispensations for their firms,[54] therefore freezing manpower in unproductive industries and preventing workers from being allocated to more important sectors.

In April 1943, with the rationalization process proving ineffective, and with local authorities prioritizing their own immediate needs over the perceived national good, men were forbidden to perform jobs that could be done by women.[55] But time was now running out for the fascist authorities. A very last attempt was made, in June 1943, to get more out of Italian industry. The Ministry for Corporations created the *Direzione generale della manodopera* (Workforce General Directorate). This empowered provincial prefects to shut down inefficient textile industries, which could not work forty-eight hours per week, and stop any non-auxiliary business that was not directly involved with food production. The workforce made available in this way was to be relocated by the local provincial employment centres, who could assign individual workers to military works, food production, or auxiliary industries.[56]

It was too little too late. As a result of the shortage in person-power, an inefficient labour market had developed, with negative consequences for the Italian war economy. In some industries, such as the manufacture of clothing, the job market became fossilized as workers tried to retain jobs that required few hours and allowed them to tend to their crops. In others, turnover rates skyrocketed, especially in some of the most important war industries; firms like Fiat, Falck, and Breda struggled to retain their skilled workers. This was partly because their competitors tried to recruit their workforces by offering better wages and other benefits.[57] For example, in Fiat in Turin (vehicles and aircraft) and Ilva in Marghera (steel mills), one-quarter to one-third of the workforce changed yearly, and often many workers were hired and fired within a year.[58] The extractive industries were also particularly affected, as miners sought better pay and less dangerous work.

These high turnover rates, and the large numbers of inexperienced workers that resulted, affected workplace safety. In the second half of 1941, accidents caused 40,410 minor injuries, 9,934 severe injuries, and 93 deaths, affecting, respectively, 3.97 per cent, 0.98 per cent, and almost one worker in every 10,000. In the first half of 1942, workplace safety got a little better, but by the end of the year 5 per cent of the workforce had been injured on the job, 1.4 per cent severely; one in every 7,000 workers had a fatal accident.[59]

It is in this context that the disciplinary measures available to the state mattered. With the fascist government proving incapable of conducting a modern war, with Italian forces losing battles, and day-to-day life on the home front becoming more and more difficult, conditions deteriorated even in industries subject to military law. Even when the hope of winning the war was still high, a little more than one-third of all authorized dismissals in auxiliary industries occurred for disciplinary reasons, while a small but not insignificant fraction occurred for political reasons. It is possible that this high rate was driven by workers who purposely broke disciplinary regulations to find better employment elsewhere.[60] Others clearly left their posts as soon as they learned that their workshop was going to be mobilized.[61] In firms where single departments were mobilized, workers lamented that their non-mobilized colleagues could seek better wages without risks.[62]

In light of these challenges, factory owners encouraged the government to introduce harsher punishments for lack of discipline.[63] In response, they were told to organize dining halls to improve the living conditions of workers, but they were also told to build detention chambers in their factories.[64] All in all, judicial actions against workers became more and more common, especially during the second half of 1942, some months before the crucial defeats at El Alamein and Stalingrad and the intensification of the air bombing campaign over central and northern Italy.

Between 1936 and 1938, military judicial actions against mobilized workers remained at a manageable level. In fact, discipline improved over this period; there were 357 trials in 1936, 208 in 1937, and 125 in 1938.[65] With the start of the war, however, trials became more frequent. The number of workers tried in military courts now increased at a rate higher than the overall increase in the number of mobilized war workers. In the first year of war, between June 1940 and June 1941, there were 590 trials.[66] In the second half of 1941, there were 744.[67] Between January and June 1942, there were 1,077 trials.[68] Between

July and December, the number of trials more than doubled to 2,560.[69] In the first six months of 1943, 2,719 trials took place.[70]

The available data suggests that discipline was particularly difficult to maintain in sectors affected by the war, such as auto and aircraft production and especially in the mines. The lowest rate for disciplinary infringements occurred in 1938, with an average of one mobilized worker in every 5,000 charged by a military court. The rate in the auto and aircraft industries was slightly higher; in the mining sector, however, it was one in every 2,000.[71] By the last six months of 1942, the situation had deteriorated considerably; data for the auxiliary industries, which at this time employed about one-fifth of all mobilized workers, shows that about one worker in every four hundred had to face a military trial.[72] It is safe to assume that the situation was little different for other mobilized workers.

It is clear, therefore, that there were very great differences in the way Italian citizens experienced mobilization on the home front. Italian mobilization, in fact, created conflicting individual and territorial statuses and boundaries. Workers living in the same area and performing similar jobs could be subject to either civil law or military law. Different statuses could also exist within a single firm, as mandatory workers subject to military discipline could be assigned to companies not subject to mobilization law, while non-mobilized industries could fall under military disciplinary scrutiny, sometimes without having been notified.[73] Even individual sectors within a single manufacturing plant could be mobilized.[74]

The complex administrative apparatus did not help matters.[75] Just as Jacopo Pili has identified inconsistencies in Fascist Italy's propaganda messaging (see chapter 3 of this volume), so too there were inconsistencies in its wartime administration. Every institution administered different territories at regional, provincial, and inter-provincial levels. Workers were to be mobilized at the level of the provincial corporative council; the local economy was to be coordinated, therefore, by prefects and by delegates of the different corporations. Draft lists were written by the Fascist Party, while disciplinary matters were handled by the undermanned Delegazione interprovinciale per le fabbricazioni di guerra (DELEFAGS), COGEFAG's regional delegations responsible for different provinces.[76] Meanwhile, coordinating mandatory workers was the domain of the provincial Fascist Party federation.[77] This bureaucratic spiderweb made for anything but a unified experience; there was to be no "People's War" for Italy.

THE VERONA MILITARY COURT

The study of a local court provides some deeper perspectives and allows us to better understand what actually happened in mobilized industries during the war. It also sheds light on how mobilization influenced the daily lives of workers and the strategies that they employed to navigate the challenges of surviving on the Italian home front.

Italian military justice was administered either by permanent territorial military courts, or by special military courts organized by corps, armies or, exceptionally, divisions in combat zones. Military personnel, civilians subject to military law (such as mobilized and mandatory workers), or civilians whose actions affected either military personnel, property, or the war effort were subject to a territorial military court. The "technical hierarchy" within a workshop was considered akin to military hierarchy, and all mobilized or mandatory personnel were subordinated to military men and carabinieri, the army branch tasked with civil policing.

The jurisdiction of the military court in Verona encompassed eastern Lombardy, western Veneto, and Trentino. This area was particularly important for the Italian war economy: many small arms and aircraft armament industries were located in Brescia; most of the Italian aluminium and magnesium production was concentrated in Trentino, and especially in Porto Marghera, Veneto's chemical conglomerate, with its 18,000 workers in peacetime. A large portion of Italian hydroelectric power was also produced in the regions of Trentino and Veneto. Overall, in 1940, 91,593 industrial enterprises of different sizes were operating in Veneto; the region ranked third in industrial production capacity. These industries had a total workforce of 377,848 men and women, but the demographic pressure in the area was high; scores of people emigrated every year and a significant proportion of the population lived in appalling economic and sanitary conditions.

In Veneto, 19,643 enterprises were mobilized in 1940 (21.4 per cent of all local industries), with a workforce of 149,294 men and women (39.4 per cent of the local workforce).[78] These industries added to the auxiliary firms already controlled by the COGEFAG and all fell under Verona's jurisdiction. As of May 1939, more than 8.56 per cent of all primary auxiliary firms in Italy lay in the Verona Military court territory. This proportion remained unchanged when mobilization was extended to secondary auxiliary companies in the event of war.[79]

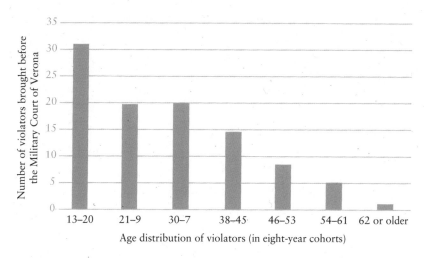

Figure 2.1 The age distribution (in eight-year cohorts) of violators brought before the Military Court of Verona, Second World War. Archivio di Stato di Verona, F. Tribunale Militare, Fascicoli Processuali and Volumi Sentenze.

The first data we can obtain is the violators' age distribution and weighted median age, according to which the typical offender was a thirty-one-year-old unmarried male,[80] without a prior criminal record,[81] and without ties to fascist institutions.[82] The majority of violators were between seventeen and twenty years old.[83] Mobilization laws were broken mostly by people exempted from military service because of their age (individuals between the ages of twenty-one and fifty-five were eligible for call up, but military service fell mostly on those between ages twenty-one and thirty-four). Those outside the window for military service made up the majority of workers and were therefore more represented in the trial data. It is also worth noting that those of military age risked a great deal if they were prosecuted for lack of discipline; if found guilty, they could easily find themselves directed to active military service.[84]

The various juridical statuses can be associated with a range of behaviours. Dissatisfied mandatory workers assigned to agricultural work, for example, were prone to damaging crops in protest against the poor working conditions.[85] But refusing to take service at all was more common. These workers were often forced by local party officials to do mandatory work because they were considered poor or "lazy," or as punishment for voicing protest against their employers.[86] More often, however, absenteeism was caused by the low wages paid by the employers. The Ministry of Finance tried to solve this problem by proposing to raise the wages of mandatory workers to the standard of the private sector, but the Ministry for Corporations opposed the move because it feared that mandatory workers assigned to public offices would then have better wages than the civil servants who had remained at their workplaces.[87]

The dynamics underpinning the behaviour of mobilized workers were even more complex. In 1940 and even in 1941, absenteeism was often caused by a misunderstanding of mobilization laws, by either workers or employers. In the first years of war, some individuals were found not guilty because the employer failed to properly inform the workers of their judicial status.[88] Sometimes, workers did not show up at their workplace because they thought that peacetime bank days or holidays were still in force.[89] A greater problem was encountered when workers tried to leave seasonal low-skilled jobs, even though these jobs were considered militarily important. Employers were also prone to using military law to get rid of workers with health issues or an erratic work attitude.

The greatest number of cases, however, appear to have been caused by workers seeking better wages. Mobilization laws were supposed to freeze wage increases. But to cope with the wage freeze, many workers chose to ignore the law and move jobs. Many were encouraged by auxiliary firms illegally offering better wages. By 1942, enterprises – sometimes encouraged by military authorities[90] – were competing with each other to find skilled and unskilled labourers. In spite of the limitations imposed by mobilization law to job recruitment, employers were eager to "steal" workers from other auxiliary industries to fulfill military contracts. Employers faced few consequences for this behaviour because the only people put on trial for breaching the mobilization laws regulating work mobility were the ordinary workers. Additionally, some workers "deserted" their post in Italian firms and sought better conditions by looking for work in Germany.[91]

In 1942 and 1943, the violations changed both qualitatively and quantitatively. Infringements became more common, and mobilized workers began to skip their jobs because they lacked transportation to the workplace, as public transport lines became more and more erratic and bicycle tires became rare.[92] The work of military courts grew exponentially between Mussolini's dismissal, on 25 July 1943,

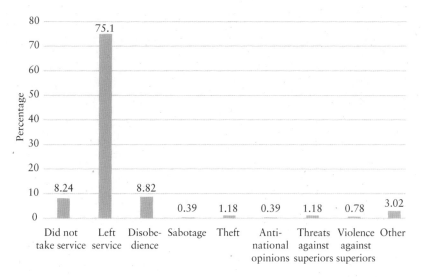

Figure 2.2 Violations by cause, the Military Court of Verona, Second World War. Archivio di Stato di Verona, F. Tribunale Militare, Fascicoli Processuali and Volumi Sentenze.

and the publication of the armistice terms with the Allies, on 8 September 1943. During this period, Badoglio's cabinet facilitated the transition to post-fascism by declaring all Italian territory subject to military law. In a desperate attempt to control the population, tribunals began to condemn the accused without an actual trial (no public hearing was required or defence admitted). In the forty-five days of the Badoglio government, civilians began to serve jail time for having turned on lights at night, for having opened windows on hot summer nights, for having taken a walk after curfew, or for having participated in celebrations or feasts celebrating Mussolini's arrest.

Overall, military justice was quick and severe, but its effectiveness varied. Sentences were usually issued within four months of a violation, with trials typically lasting between twenty minutes and less than an hour. While almost two-thirds of those who stood accused in front of the military court were found guilty, most of the individuals condemned to jail received a suspended sentence (only 6.97 per cent of those found guilty served any time in jail). In fact, it seems that military justice tended to play out before any actual trial, because those indicted were jailed before their trial 66.08 per cent of the time. Thus, individuals were usually jailed regardless of any consideration

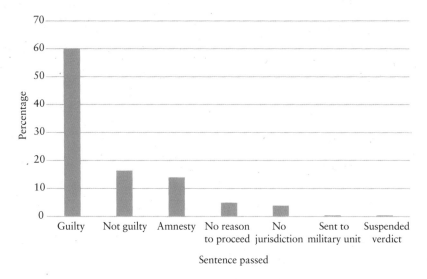

Figure 2.3 Judicial actions of the Military Court of Verona, Second World War. Archivio di Stato di Verona, F. Tribunale Militare, Fascicoli Processuali and Volumi Sentenze.[1]

[1] More than the 0.43 per cent shown were actually sent to military units. Trials were paused for those who served in a mobilized unit. Therefore, when trials resumed after the war all accused were found to be eligible for amnesty.

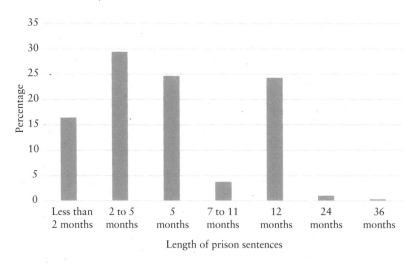

Figure 2.4 Length of prison sentences, Military Court of Verona, Second World War. Archivio di Stato di Verona, F. Tribunale Militare, Fascicoli Processuali and Volumi Sentenze.

of their specific case and were usually freed after the sentence regardless of whether they were found guilty. The typical prison sentence was either 6 months long (24.66 per cent) or 12 months long (24.32 per cent). The median prison sentence length was a little less than 13 months. Many, including Mussolini, the military authorities,[93] and the military general prosecutor, Ovidio Ciancarini, thought that military courts were too lenient,[94] especially when called to punish "civilians perturbing the public order."[95]

Almost all judicial actions were carried out against male workers, in spite of the fact that one-third of mobilized personnel were women. This practice may have encouraged the role of women as public spreaders of a widening social restlessness. Local authorities recognized the need to punish female troublemakers,[96] lest disciplinary violations committed by particularly bold individuals encourage collective protests.[97] By 1942, groups of women, often accompanied by children, were walking the streets and public squares throughout Italy demanding better food allocations and challenging public authorities.[98] Collective anger had become strong enough for individuals and groups to challenge even military courts and, in this respect, the judicial data is extremely interesting. Deteriorating living conditions encouraged collective protests, and the first strikes not limited to local areas took place in May 1942. Less than a year later, the March 1943 strikes affected the industrial cities of Milan and Turin.[99] The military judicial data explored here, however, shows that mobilized workers were clearly dissatisfied with the fascist war even as early as 1940. By 1942, even if political opposition in auxiliary industries was in its infancy,[100] those experiencing the most extreme consequences of the fascist war were clearly voicing their protest in spite of the repressive apparatus available to the state to silence opposition.

CONCLUSION

This research offers new insights into how military justice and mobilization shaped the Italian home front during the fascist wars. The limited success of the Italian mobilization process is already known to historians, but the consequences for the daily lives of the Italian people have been less studied. Military justice acted as a tool to discipline and direct the Italian worker during a period of national crisis. This repressive action underlined the authoritarian nature of fascist society, as only workers bore the brunt of military law, while corrupt officers and industries faced only light disciplinary consequences for their actions.[101] This ultimately fed workers' anger and contributed to the delegitimization of the Fascist Party and the unions.

Italian workers were supposed to be mobilized for a "total war." In the interwar years, fascists and military men alike had hoped to create a single juridical status that encompassed both military men and civilians working on the home front.[102] The reality that emerged, however, was quite different. Italian mobilization relied on a complex and contradictory system of statuses, each of which depended on the conflicting administrative and judicial territories within which individuals lived or worked. The system for mobilization that emerged in Italy did not produce anything close to fair outcomes, or a "classless society." There would be nothing approaching a "people's" mobilization on the home front.[103] In this respect, the military judicial system, through coercion, played an important role in influencing behaviour. From 1940 onwards, the regime's grasp on Italian society was gradually undermined by its failings. Mobilization ultimately highlighted the social stratifications inherent in fascist society.[104] As fascist institutions continued to fail the test of war, they also lost legitimacy, thus undermining their performance and planting the seeds of change for the post-war era.

NOTES

1. Relevant exceptions include: Giorgio Rochat, *Duecento sentenze nel bene e nel male. La giustizia militare nella guerra 1940–1943* (Udine: Gaspari, 2002); Sergio Dini, *La bilancia e il moschetto. I Tribunali militari nella Seconda guerra mondiale* (Milan: Mursia, 2017). On military justice studies, see Nicola Labanca and Pier Paolo Rivello, eds., *Fonti e problemi per la storia della giustizia militare* (Turin: G. Giappichelli, 2004).
2. Work on the daily lives of workers has focused more on the Great War than the Second World War. See, for example, Fabio Degli Espositi, "The Industrial and Agriculural Mobilization of Italy," in *Italy in the Era of the Great War*, ed. Vanda Wilcox (Leiden-Boston: Brill 2018); Santo Peli and Alessandro Camarda, *L'altro esercito. La classe operaia durante la prima guerra mondiale* (Milan: Feltrinelli 1980); Luigi Tomassini, *Lavoro e guerra. La mobilitazione industriale italiana. 1915–1918* (Naples: ESI, 1997); Massimo Mazzetti, *L'industria italiana nella Grande Guerra* (Rome: USSME 1979). Labour conditions in Brescia during the First and

the Second World War have been studied in Santo Peli, "Operai e guerra. Materiali per un'analisi dei comportamenti operai nella prima e nella seconda guerra mondiale," in *Tra fabbrica e società. Mondi operai nell'Italia del Novecento*, ed. Stefano Musso (Milan: Fondazione Giangiacomo Feltrinelli, 1999).

3 Fortunato Minniti, "Aspetti organizzativi del controllo sulla produzione bellica in Italia (1923–1943)," *Clio* 4 (1977), 333–9; Fortunato Minniti, "Aspetti territoriali e politici del controllo sulla produzione bellica in Italia," *Clio* 1 (1979), 118–19.

4 Massimo Legnani, "La guerra totale. Per un'indagine sul progetto e realtà della guerra fascista," *Italia Contemporanea* 213 (1998), 752–9; John Gooch, *Mussolini's War: Fascist Italy from Triumph to Collapse, 1935–1943* (London: Penguin, 2020), 414.

5 Massimo Legnani, "Società in guerra e forme della mobilitazione. Stato degli studi e orientamenti di ricerca sull'Italia," *Italia Contemporanea* 213 (1998), 771–9. A general summary in Ferrazza Paola, "La mobilitazione civile in Italia," *Italia Contemporanea* 214 (March 1999), http://www.italia-liberazione.it/pubblicazioni/1/ic_214_ferrazza.pdf.

6 While the archival records start in 1937, no trials against workers were held until 1940.

7 Luca Baldissara, "Operai e fabbriche nella Seconda Guerra Mondiale," in *Il Novecento. 1896–1945. Il lavoro nell'età industriale*, ed. Stefano Musso (Rome: Castelvecchi 2015), 567–85.

8 On the understanding of "total war" during this period, see Erich Ludendorff, *Der totale Krieg* (München: Ludendorffs Verlag, 1935). Both the German version of the book and its French translation circulated in Italy.

9 Benito Mussolini, Camera dei Deputati, Atti parlamentari, Tornata del 23 maggio 1925, 3788. This can be compared with the American approach to late peacetime mobilization; see Edward J.K. Gitre, "'What the Soldier Thinks': Mobilizing the Mind of the American Soldier in the Second World War," chapter 5 of this book.

10 Carlotta Latini, *Cittadini e nemici. Giustizia militare e giustizia penale in Italia tra Otto e Novecento* (Milan: Le Monnier, 210), 289.

11 Gaetano Tei, *Nuovi lineamenti del diritto penale militare* (Milan: Giuffrè, 1942), 15.

12 Emanuele Landolfi, "Il concetto fascista di giustizia militare," *Esercito e Nazione*, May 1934, 371–3.

13 Ernesto Galeazzi, Camera dei Deputati, Atti parlamentari, Tornata di venerdì 5 giugno 1925, 4214.

14 Archivio dell'Ufficio Storico dello Stato Maggiore dell'Esercito (AUSSME), Fondo (F.) 16, busta (b.) 1, Commissariato Generale per le Fabbricazioni di Guerra, Relazione dei servizi XI-Dima e XII-Dila. 1938.
15 Museo Centrale del Risorgimento di Roma (MCRR), F. Dallolio, b. 1120, Comitato per la Mobilitazione Civile, IX Sessione della CSD, Relazione, February 1932; MCRR, F. Dallolio, b. 1121, Commissariato Generale per le Fabbricazioni di Guerra. Il Commissario Generale, Promemoria per S.E. il Capo del Governo, 27 June 1938; Archivio Centrale dello Stato (ACS), F. Ingravalle, b. 1, Relazione Fabbriguerra dal 1/9/939 al 30/6/941.
16 "La cura del soldato," *Le Forze Armate*, 28 August 1939.
17 G.M. Braga, "Stato totalitario e potenziale bellico," *Le Forze Armate*, 13 December 1938, 3. This principle was confirmed in Article 22 of the Regio Decreto 31 ottobre 1942 n. 1611. See also G. Gaidano, "Di alcuni problemi della difesa nazionale nello Stato corporativo," *Milizia Nuova* 7 (1927), 219–22.
18 Legge 8 giugno 1925 n. 969.
19 Legge 14 dicembre 1931 n. 1699.
20 Regio Decreto Legge 15 October 1925 n. 2281.
21 ACS, Presidenza del Consiglio dei Ministri (PCM), 1940–43, categoria (c.) 1.1.10 fascicolo (f.) 1000.6.3, Ministero delle Coroporazioni, Organo per la mano d'opera, 26 September 1939.
22 ACS, PCM, 1940–43, c. 1.1.10 f. 1000.3.7, Verbali della XVII Sessione della CSD. 8–14 February 1940.
23 Antonio Assenza, *Il generale Alfredo Dallolio. La mobilitazione industriale dal 1915 al 1939* (Rome: Stato Maggiore dell'Esercito. Ufficio Storico, 2010), 657–60.
24 Legge 21 maggio 1940 n. 415.
25 Minniti Fortunato, "Aspetti organizzativi del controllo sulla produzione bellica in Italia (1923–1943)," *Clio* 4 (1977), 329.
26 Regio Decreto 18 giugno 1940 n. 631.
27 Legge 24 agosto 1941 n. 1076.
28 Regio Decreto 1 novembre 1940 n. 1782.
29 ACS, PCM, 1940–43, c. 1.1.10 f. 1000.5.10.3, Lettera del Ministero dell'Interno 8 November 1940; Regio Decreto 16 dicembre 1941 n. 1611, the Royal Decree came into effect after its publication on the *Gazzetta Ufficiale del Regno d'Italia* of 14 February 1942.
30 ACS, PCM, 1940–43, c. 1.1.10 f. 1000.19, Commissione Suprema di Difesa, circolare n. 6940, 2 July 1941. The Air Ministry decided to determine an expiration date applied only to its officers who were temporarily exempted from military service without a defined term *ad quem*, ACS, Ministero della Marina (MM), Gabinetto (Gab.), b. 480, Stato Maggiore

R. Aeronautica, n. 3/15962, Decadimento provvedimenti indisponibilità a tempo determinato nei riguardi Ufficiali R. Aeronautica, 24 August 1942; ACS, MM, Gab., b. 480, Stato Maggiore R. Aeronautica, n. 108200/4, Mobilitazione civile – provvedimenti di carattere eccezionale per il personale delle classi 1910 e più giovani, 30 March 1942.

31 Specific categories were treated differently: specialised workers and technicians working for firms involved in tank production were to be sent back to the industries, or were to be exempted from military service if were still working, ACS, MM, Gab., b. 480, Stato Maggiore R. Esercito. Ufficio Esoneri, n. 2183/2, Provvedimenti di carattere eccezionale, 29 July 1942.

32 ACS, PCM, 1940–43, c.1.1.10 f. 1000.1, Natali a Sorice, 9 September 1941.

33 ACS, PCM, 1940–43, c. 1.1.10 f. 1000.1, Centro Nazionale di M.C., Appunto per il Segretario del P.N.F., 20 January 1942. Six months earlier, the Navy opposed the same reasons, ACS, MM, Gab., b. 480, Ministero della Marina to Partito Nazionale Fascista, 823/MC, Mobilitazione Civile – Richiesta personale minorile, 18 June 1941.

34 Decreto Legge 26 febbraio 1942 n. 82.

35 Regio Decreto 31 ottobre 1942 n. 1611, published in the *Gazzetta Ufficiale del Regno d'Italia* of 18 January 1943.

36 In this chapter, mobilized workers in auxiliary industries or mobilized industries are defined as "mobilized workers," and workers mobilized individually are defined as "mandatory workers."

37 Some Jews were also mobilized for mandatory *Servizio Civile*, spurring a debate about the opportunity to employ them alongside "Aryan" workers. For example, 770 Jews and 1,300 idle citizens were mobilized by the Prefectures in the summer of 1942 (see Ferrazza, "La mobilitazione civile in Italia," 8–9). In July 1943, the Regime ordered the "total mobilization" of the Jewish population born between 1907 and 1925, obtaining between 9,146 and 9,151 workers. Data varies and lacks gender specifications from Zara, Terni, Naples, Frosinone and Apuania, but can be divided between males (4,595 or 4,605) and females (4,474 or 4,484), ACS, Ministero dell'Interno (MI), Direzione Generale Demografia e Razza, Divisione Razza, Affari Diversi, b. 17, f. II 19, Ministero dell'Interno, n. 1321 C.2/1°, Avviamento al lavoro di cittadini di razza ebraica, 14 July 1943; see in ACS, MI, Direzione Generale Demografia e Razza, Divisione Razza, Affarmi Diversi, b. 17, f. II 19, sf. 30.000 R., undated statistical table.

38 ACS, PCM, 1940–43, c. 1.1.10, f. 1000.6.1.5, Luigi Natali ad Amilcare Rossi, 13 March 1943.

39 Zamagni Vera, "Italy: How to Lose the War and Win the Peace," in *The Economics of World War II. Six Great Powers in International Comparison*, ed. Mark Harrison (Cambridge: Cambrdige University Press 1998), 178–89.

40 ACS, Segreteria Particolare del Duce (SPD), Carteggio Riservato (CR), Bollettini e informazioni 1940-43 (BI), b. 164, f. March 1941, Promemoria per il Duce. Situazione del lavoro, 28 March 1941.

41 Fortunato Minniti, *L'industria degli armamenti dal 1940 al 1943: I mercati, le produzioni*, in Zamagni, *Come perdere la guerra e vincere la pace. L'economia italiana tra guerra e dopoguerra* (Bologna: Il Mulino 1997) 97.

42 Decreto del Duce 5 dicembre 1942, GU n. 289 del 7 December 1942. Civilian militarisation in Albania and Puglia was also declared ignoring the previous legislation, Bando del Duce 6 gennaio 1941, n. 19, commented in Sucato Gaetano, *Servizio del lavoro e militarizzazione. Raccolta delle disposizioni vigenti coordinate e annotate* (Rome: Edizioni Stella 1943), 238-43. The decree mobilized all industrial firms represented in a corporation.

43 MCRR, F. Dallolio, b. 1125, Commissione Suprema di Difesa, Verbale della VII Sessione, February-March 1930; MCRR, F. Dallolio, b. 1125, Commissione Suprema di Difesa, Verbale della XIII Sessione, February 1936.

44 ACS, SPD, Carteggio Ordinario (CO), f. 500.005/1, Segnalazione della Segreteria Particolare di S.E. il Capo del Governo, Milano, 9 July 1943.

45 Archivio di Stato di Treviso (ASTV), Prefettura, Gab., b. 301, f. 16/1, Legione cc.rr. di Padova, Istanza del prof. Adolfo Vital, 5 July 1940.

46 Archivio di Stato di Padova (ASPD), Prefettura, Gab., b. 540, f. XVIII/25, Istanza della professoressa Fiorina "Rina" Pisa al Prefetto di Padova, 6 June 1940.

47 Fascist authorities considered 14 million women eligible for mobilization, but were forbidden from recruiting women with children or those who were older than 45. This meant that just 6 million women were actually eligible for recruitment. The census was not yet completed at this point, however. AUSSME, F. 9, b. 71, PNF. Centro Nazionale di Mobilitazione Civile, *Relazione al Ministro Segretario del PNF sulla organizzazione della mobilitazione civile dei minori e delle donne al 31 dicembre 1940–XIX*.

48 MCRR, F. Dallolio, b. 1125, Commissione Suprema di Difesa, Verbale della XIII Sessione, February 1936; AUSSME, L 10, b. 54, f. 3, Comitato per la Mobilitazione Civile, *Raccolta di Elementi per una mobilitazione industriale immediata (prima approssimazione)*, Rome 1928, 33.

49 ACS, Ingravalle, b. 2, Sottosegretario di Stato per le Fabbricazioni di Guerra, Attività svolta dalla 7^ Divisione nel periodo 1° luglio–31 dicembre 1941; Relazione sulla attività svolta dalla 7^ Divisione nel periodo 1° luglio–31 dicembre 1942.

50 The data comprises women working in mobilized firms as well as those conscripted for mandatory work, ACS, SPD, CO, f. 500.005/III, Ministero

delle Corporazioni, Notiziario sul Servizio del Lavoro in Italia e all'estero, 1 October 1942.
51 ACS, Ingravalle, b. 1, Relazione sull'attività del Fabbriguerra nel periodo dal 1°-9–39 al 30-6-1941.; ACS, Ingravalle, b. 2, Sottosegretario di Stato per le Fabbricazioni di Guerra, Attività svolta dalla 7^ Divisione nel periodo 1° luglio–31 dicembre 1941; ACS, Ingravalle, Relazione sulla attività svolta dalla 7^ Divisione nel periodo 1° luglio–31 dicembre 1942; "Economia di guerra," *Autarchia* (febbraio-marzo 1943), 28.
52 *L'Italia in 150 anni. Sommario di statistiche storiche 1861–2019* (Rome: Istat, 2011), 468.
53 ACS, SPD, CO, f. 500.005/III, Ministero delle Corporazioni, Notiziario sul Servizio del Lavoro in Italia e all'estero, 1 October 1942. Soldiers were used as farmers, to transport fertilizers, and for construction works, ACS, PCM, 1940–43, c. 1.2.1, f. 912, Ministero della Guerra, n. 68650, Concessione di mano d'opera militare per la spedizione dei concimi chimici, 6 November 1942; ACS, MA, Gab. 1942, b. 46, f. 3-V-19, Convenzione tra l'amministrazione aeronautica e la ditta Impianti applicazioni telefoniche (I.A.T.) di Venezia, per la cessione di mano d'opera militare per lavori di scavo, 9 September 1942.
54 ACS, SPD, CO, f. 500.005/III, Appunto al Duce da parte del Ministero delle Corporazioni, 14 September 1942; ACS, SPD, CO, f. 500.005/IV, Relazione sulla situazione economica al 10 dicembre 1942 dell'Ispettorato corporativo centrale.
55 Regio Decreto Legge 12 April 1943 n. 271.
56 ACS, Cianetti, b. 8, Appunto al Duce, 15 June 1943.
57 AUSSME, L 10, b. 30, f. 1, Promemoria 26 gennaio 1943 dell'Ufficio esoneri dello Stato Maggiore R. Esercito.
58 Bigazzi Duccio, *Gli operai nell'industria di guerra (1938–1943)*, in *Come perdere la guerra e vincere la pace*, ed. Vera Zamagni, 193–4. Interestingly, while in 1938 public and private data on turnover in industry is coherent, from 1939 onwards private statistics collected by the industry personnel offices are completely different to the numbers collected by the war production officers. This difference may suggest that while 1938 layoffs were authorised by the central administration, as soon as the European war begun and the economy reached full employment, the Government could no longer control the movement of the workforce in spite of its best efforts.
59 ACS, Ingravalle, b. 2, Sottosegretario di Stato per le Fabbricazioni di Guerra, Attività svolta dalla 7^ Divisione nel periodo 1° luglio–31 dicembre 1941; ACS, Ingravalle, b. 2, Relazione sulla attività svolta dalla 7^ Divisione nel periodo 1° gennaio–30 giugno 1942; ACS, Ingravalle, b. 2,

Relazione sulla attività svolta dalla 7^ Divisione nel periodo 1° luglio–31 dicembre 1942.
60 Archivio di Stato di Verona (ASVR), F. Tribunale Militare (TM), Fascicoli Processuali (FP), f. 7280. A similar case in ASVR, TM, FP, f. 9214.
61 ACS, PCM, 1940–43, c. 1.1.10 f. 1000.6.1.6, Ministero delle Corporazioni, Servizio del Lavoro – Istruttoria delle proposte di mobilitazione, 29 April 1943.
62 ACS, SPD, CO, f. 500.023/I, Promemoria per il Duce, Mobilitazione civile dell'industria, 29 November 1942.
63 Bigazzi Duccio, *Gli operai nell'industria di guerra (1938–1943)*, in Zamagni, *Come perdere la guerra e vincere la pace*, 221–5.
64 Ferrazza Paola, "La mobilitazione civile in Italia," *Italia Contemporanea* 214 (March 1999): 9, http://www.italia-liberazione.it/pubblicazioni/1/ic_214_ferrazza.pdf.
65 MCRR. F. Dallolio, b. 1118, f. 3, XVII Sessione della Commissione Suprema di Difesa, XVI Argomento, 12 February 1940.
66 ACS, Ingravalle, b. 1, Relazione sull'attività del Fabbriguerra nel periodo dal 1°-9-39 al 30-6-1941.
67 ACS, Ingravalle, b. 2, Sottosegretario di Stato per le Fabbricazioni di Guerra, Attività svolta dalla 7^ Divisione nel periodo 1° luglio–31 dicembre 1941.
68 ACS, Ingravalle, b. 2, Relazione sulla attività svolta dalla 7^ Divisione nel periodo 1° gennaio–30 giugno 1942.
69 ACS, Ingravalle, b. 2, Relazione sulla attività svolta dalla 7^ Divisione nel periodo 1° luglio–31 dicembre 1942.
70 ACS, Ingravalle, b. 2, Relazione sulla attività svolta dalla 7^ Divisione nel periodo 1° gennaio–30 giugno 1943.
71 AUSSME, F. 16, b. 1, Commissariato Generale per le Fabbricazioni di Guerra, Relazione dei servizi XI-Dima e XII-Dila. 1938.
72 ACS, Ingravalle, b. 2, Relazione sulla attività svolta dalla 7^ Divisione nel periodo 1° luglio–31 dicembre 1942.
73 ACS, PCM, 1940–43, c. 1.1.10, f. 1000.5.8.1.2, Ministero delle Corporazioni, Precettazione di operai del marmo, 12 December 1942.
74 To make matters more complicated, workers serving in auxiliary industries were subject to military law regardless of their age, but, until August 1941, workers of conscription age temporarily assigned to civil jobs were not. The condition and judicial status changed when the Undersecretariat for war production approved a decree modifying the 1940 law on Citizens' Discipline in time of War, ACS, PCM, 1940–43, c. 1.1.10, f. 1000.5.10, Appunto al Duce, 13 August 1941; Regio Decreto Legge 24 August 1941 n. 1035.

75 MCRR. F. Dallolio, b. 1115, f. 1, Verbale della Commissione Suprema di Difesa. Seduta del giorno 31 gennaio 1939.
76 On average, the 16 officers manning the 3rd Delegation controlling Emilia, Veneto, Trentino and Venezia Giulia had to control 108 auxiliary industries and 83 non-mobilized industries, with an average of about 12 firms per officer. Nationwide, 136 officers had to control 880 auxiliary and 83 non-auxiliary industries. In fact, 206 industries were not controlled by officers of the Servizio Disciplina, AUSSME, F. 16, b. 1, Commissariato Generale per le Fabbricazioni di Guerra, Relazione dei servizi XI-Dima e XII-Dila. 1938.
77 Ferrazza, "La mobilitazione civile in Italia," 8–9.
78 Tognato Lorenzo, *Il Veneto e l'economia di guerra fascista. 1935–1946*, (Venice: Marsilio, 2013), 18–35.
79 AUSSME, F. 16, b. 1, Elenco degli Stabilimenti "destinati a divenire ausiliari" in caso di emergenza. January 1940.
80 92.83 per cent.
81 Albeit 20.95 per cent of those for which there is data had one. If we take into account the 28.83 per cent cases for which there is no data, those with prior criminal records are the 14.91 per cent.
82 Of those for which there is data, 64.66 per cent were not enrolled in any fascist organization. Just over half of trial data documenting ties to fascist institutions is missing, but as those ties would have had a positive effect on the accused, we can assume that the authorities would have informed the military court. If that is the case, only 16.47 per cent of the accused were enrolled in the Party or in any of its organizations, including the fascist unions.
83 29.49 per cent. Per year: 17, 5.76 per cent; 18, 6.65 per cent; 19, 10.86 per cent; 20, 6.21 per cent.
84 Ilari Virgilio, *Storia del servizio militare in Italia*, vol. 3 (Rome: Centro Militare di Studi Strategici. Rivista Militare 1990), 312.
85 ACS, SPD, CO, f. 500.005/III, Ministero delle Corporazioni, Relazione sulla situazione dell'autarchia. 10 May 1942.
86 120 rice workers were mobilized and 8 arrested because a group of 300 refused to work in the Vercelli province. Another 107 were later mobilized in different parts of the province, ACS, SPD, CR, BI, b. 166, f. giugno 1941, Promemoria per il Duce, 12 June 1941.
87 ACS, PCM, 1940–43, c. 1.1.10, f. 1000.5.8, Ministero delle Finanze al Ministero delle Corporazioni, 25 April 1942.
88 One of many examples, ASVR, TM, Volumi Sentenze, 4° Trimestre 1941, Sentenza 774.
89 ASVR, TM, FP, f. 3343.

90 ACS, MA, Gab. 1942, b. 46, f. 3-V-18, Ministero dell'Aeronautica. Gabinetto del ministro, Disciplina del collocamento della mano d'opera, 25 August 1942.
91 ASVR, TM, FP, f. 3445.
92 ASVR, TM, FP, f. 8366.
93 AUSSME, L 14, b. 33, f. 5, Procura Generale Militare, n. 4326, Funzionamento dei Tribunali militari, 6 July 1943.
94 AUSSME, M 3, b. 48, f. 3, c. 5213, Procura Generale Militare del Re Imperatore, circolare n. 559, Procedimenti penali per reati commessi da personale civilmente mobilitato, 29 December 1941.
95 AUSSME, L 14, b. 33, f. 5, Stato Maggiore R. Esercito, n. 1168, Tribunali di Guerra, 7 August 1943.
96 ASVR, TM, FP, f. 9200.
97 ASVR, TM, FP, f. 7279, Confederazione fascista dei lavoratori dell'industria, Ufficio Sindacale, 5 January 1943; Archivio di Stato di Milano, TM, Volumi Sentenze, 1943 vol. 3, 458 del 1° maggio 1943.
98 Colarizi Simona, *L'opinione degli italiani sotto il regime. 1929–1943* (Bari: Laterza, 2009), 380–6.
99 Baldissara Luca, "Operai e fabbriche nella Seconda Guerra Mondiale," in *Storia del lavoro in Italia*, vol. 2, ed. Musso Stefano (Rome: Castelvecchi, 2015), 582.
100 ACS, SPD, CR, BI, b. 166, f. giugno 1941, Provincia di Genova. Situazione del mese di maggio 1941; Provincia di Milano. Situazione del mese di maggio 1941.
101 ACS, SPD, CO, f. 500.023/1, Il Sottosegretario di Stato per le fabbricazioni di guerra, Promemoria per il Duce, Raccomandazione per assegnazione di cemento, 26 aprile 1942; *Bollettino Ufficiale. Anno 1941–XIX, 1° Agosto* (Rome: Libreria dello Stato 1941); ASTV, Prefettura, Gabinetto, b. 290, Confederazione Fascista dei Lavoratori dell'Industria, Reclutamento abusivo, 28 March 1940.
102 AUSSME, F. 16, b. 1, Commissariato Generale per le Fabbricazioni di Guerra, Relazione dei servizi XI-Dima e XII-Dila. 1938.
103 As opposed to a "democratising" war mobilization, Angus Calder, *The People's War. Britain 1939–1945* (London: Pimlico 1992), 438.
104 Peli, "Operai e guerra. Materiali per un'analisi dei comportamenti operai nella prima e nella seconda guerra mondiale," in *Tra fabbrica e società. Mondi operai nell'Italia del Novecento*, ed. Stefano Musso (Milan: Fondazione Giangiacomo Feltrinelli, 1999), 214.

3

Building an Enemy

Great Britain as Depicted by Italian Fascist Propaganda

Jacopo Pili

Italian foreign policy under the Fascist regime has been the subject of considerable attention.[1] Similarly, Fascist propaganda efforts abroad during the interwar period have been the focus of significant academic research.[2] But what about the Fascist discourse in Italy? What did the regime tell its people about its enemies? In spite of the importance of the subject, the theme of Italian propaganda during the Second World War has received insufficient attention to date. Luigi Petrella's recent book, *Staging the Fascist War,* analyzes how the Fascist regime dealt with the allied bombings on Italian cities, and how the home front gradually collapsed.[3] Apart from that, the character of propaganda in Italy during the war years has been considered only in a fragmentary way.[4] In particular, a systematic analysis of anti-British propaganda has been missing from the historiography.

In 1990, Renzo De Felice outlined a periodization of fascist propaganda during the conflict that still very much frames our understanding of the subject today. He identified two kinds of fascist discourse regarding Britain: one that he described as permeated by "an extreme verbal violence" and another "more cultured" that developed from an old tradition of Anglophobia. De Felice identified three "eras" of Italian anti-British propaganda: the first spanning the period between June and December 1940; the second lasting until mid-1942; and the third continuing until the end of the regime in 1943. In De Felice's analysis, the first period focused on justifying the war; during this period, a clear narrative emerged, blaming Britain for starting the conflict. During the second phase, propaganda was directed toward an explanation for Italian defeats; it underlined the fundamental weakness of the British Empire: due to a lack of cohesion, it was likely to break up at any moment. The third period, which De Felice described as "far less sophisticated," emphasized the need to hate the enemy and the terrible destiny that awaited Italy should it be defeated.[5]

As authoritative as De Felice's interpretation has become, there is room to reconsider his periodization and to offer a new picture, one that provides a fresh framework for understanding the fascist use of anti-British propaganda during the Second World War. Moreover, by challenging the traditional interpretation of the phases of propaganda in Italy during the war, this chapter sheds new light on Italian perceptions of Great Britain and the extent to which ideology shaped fascist strategy during the Second World War.

DEPICTING AN ENEMY

The most prominent feature of the fascist anti-British discourse was a consistent denigration of British martial abilities. To understand how this discourse developed during the Second World War, it is necessary to go back to the previous decades. The notion that the British armed forces were unfit to defend the empire had been commonplace since the late 1920s. The Fascists thought that the British were simply unwilling to fight because they had been emasculated by wealth and comfort. During the 1930s, the reports of military attachés showed how low the military image of Britain had fallen in the eyes of Italian specialists. For example, in a meeting of the Italian military attachés with Chief of Staff Alberto Pariani, in 1938, the following exchange occurred:

> Pariani: I would want to know what is the effort Britain is capable of, in case of conflict.
> Laderchi: It could provide 170,000 men, which is to say the whole army currently existing, for the defence would be dealt with by the territorial army.
> Pariani: Few [men]. That's why Britain wants peace at any cost.[6]

As early as 1937, Pariani had claimed that, once his new agile army was ready, Italy could crush Egypt and Sudan "whenever and however we want."[7] In June 1938, Pariani had a detailed report on the strategic situation in the Mediterranean drafted by the "Operation office II" (a planning office that reported to the chief of staff). It described the British position as weak; Britain would be forced to avoid any "bellicose attitude" in the area due to the scarcity of its forces and its own strategic doctrine.[8] This attitude helps to explain the increasingly aggressive foreign policy pursued by Mussolini during the 1930s, including his claims to Hitler that he would be able to deal with both Britain and France by himself.[9] While it must be accepted that il Duce was inclined to hyperbole, it is clear that he did not rate the will and fighting ability of Britain very highly during this period.

The Italian press did what it could to communicate these ideas to the Italian people. Articles depicting the strength of the *Regia Marina* and *Regia Aeronautica* were common in the press. Britain, it was claimed, was now the minor force in the Mediterranean.[10] Stereotypes about the undisciplined, unmotivated British soldier abounded.[11] In 1934, *La Stampa* wrote that any foreign observer of "British things" could not but notice that British military might was going through an unprecedented weakening.[12] In 1936, the writer and journalist Guido Piovene wrote in *Il Corriere della Sera* about the dominance of pacifism in Britain; this was especially the case among the common people "who wished to remain at home with their radios, [fishing] line and golf clubs."[13] In March 1937, an article in *Gerarchia* reported how Britain was experiencing "its worst military crisis in 150 years," the causes of which were not only material but also social and moral. The decline of the old "mercenary" model and a fall in recruitment were, it argued, leading to an unavoidable waning of British influence worldwide.[14]

In March 1939, another *Gerarchia* contributor described how the sword (representing violence, the only virtue of the British Empire) had been replaced by gold. Not a single man in the current empire was ready to sacrifice himself for it. The real power, the writer thought, was the Bank of England![15] The writer Giovanni Prezzolini, one of the most important Italian intellectuals of his time and hardly a diehard fascist (he was to become an American citizen in 1940) held similar views. In 1939, he told his friend Pietro Calamandrei that the British and the French were too afraid to fight. Germany, Italy, and the Soviet Union, on the other hand, were ready to fight a proletarian war against the evils of capitalism.[16]

In September 1939, during the period of strained Italo-German relations immediately after the outbreak of war, the press was ordered to take a more considered view of Britain: "[T]o exalt neither the victories of one, nor the heroism of others: it must ... be clear that we take no part [in the unfolding war]." For a short while, the attitude toward Britain was almost balanced.[17] This new "moderate" phase ended even before Italy joined the war. This was in part due to what De Felice has described as "petty vexations on Italian naval traffic" inflicted by the British,[18] but also due to the fascists calculating, from April, that the balance of power was moving in favour of the Germans.

In the period immediately after Italy joined the war, the tone of Italian propaganda turned triumphal. The press indulged in optimistic comments about the hopeless position of the British Empire.[19] Fascist authors now extended British military incompetence to past conflicts. In July, Marco Ramperti mocked the British contribution to the Great War,[20] and Luigi Barzini wrote that while numerically superior, the British forces in Belgium and France had been unable to make any meaningful advance between 1914 and 1918.[21] British military setbacks in Norway and the Low Countries, as well as their idleness while Germany crushed Poland, seemed to confirm the prejudices that had developed over the previous decades. The French defeat was explained in *Gerarchia* as a consequence of the fundamentally weak and cowardly nature of the British people. General Orlando Freri stated that "the English contribution to the Allied cause had been truly insufficient." The British had refused to send a meaningful number of soldiers to France because they cared only about their own interests. More could be expected in Kenya and Egypt, where, Freri felt, the British were more invested. But even here, he thought they would mainly send colonial and Dominion troops.[22]

Giovanni Selvi's thesis, or concept, of "Anti-Heroic War, or English War" is perhaps even more revealing about the Fascist attitude during this period. In June 1940, during the great German offensive in the West, Selvi wrote an article in *Gerarchia* where he laid out the key elements of "anti-heroic warfare": coalition war, the war of bribery and mercenaries; blockade, the war of siege and starvation; and intelligence and propaganda, the war of "spider and woodworm." Such tropes appeared in one form or another in most of the fascist discourse, some of them until the very last days of the war.

Coalition war, Selvi wrote, was the central plank of "Anti-Heroic War" and a long-established British tradition. Using the bogeyman of continental hegemonies as a justification, Britain had "exhausted and dominated" the European continent, become "ruler of the seas," and "stripped" its enemies and friends alike of their wealth and power. For centuries, English influence was behind

> the wars in Europe [...] with the only goal of increasing Imperial power and crushing any new force which threatened its predominance, [...] Anybody who dared to threaten [British] rule was declared an enemy of England and of God. Napoleon's invasion of Egypt, Wilhelm's hopes of a Baghdad-Bahn [railway], Mussolini's desire for work for his people and the conquest of Ethiopia, Hitler's desire for living space [...] they are all the diabolical enemies of England.[23]

Selvi claimed, in a similar vein to Mussolini, that the real victims of British coalitions were the peoples who had unwisely consented to take part in them. A British guarantee was a ticket to misfortune, as the current war had demonstrated.[24]

Others made the same claim. Pietro Caporilli wrote that the British had convinced "other [peoples] to kill each other for centuries, in order to preserve John Bull's five feasts. It is through [their] perfidy and disloyalty that the noble lords of the United Kingdom have perturbed the political life of nations."[25] Roberto Pavese, a professor of psychology at the University of Milan, wrote in July that Britain's usual ploy of fighting and winning with other peoples' blood had been undermined by il Duce. By weakening the hold of freemasonry worldwide and by humiliating the League of Nations, Mussolini had inspired neutrals to resist the pressure of the plutocracies to join in their aggression. German victories, wrote Pavese, had matured from a Mussolinian seed.[26]

The perfidious character of English coalition warfare was underlined by the extent of the suffering of the defeated. France, Orlando Freri wrote, had demonstrated heroism and made a huge "blood sacrifice," yet it had been betrayed by London. Like Poland, Norway, Holland, and Belgium, France had sacrificed itself for England.[27] At the same time, the British practice of hosting governments in exile was widely ridiculed by the press, which mocked the British "alliance with the dead."[28] The theme of perfidious coalition warfare remained popular long after the first phase of the conflict.[29]

THE PERIODIZATION OF ITALIAN ANTI-BRITISH PROPAGANDA

The German victories during the first phase of the Second World War culminated in the expulsion of the British forces from continental Europe. In the first months of the war, Mussolini and many Italians (as well as many others in the rest of the world) did not expect the British to fight on. Decades of discourse about British (and western) softness and feebleness seemed confirmed by the facts on the ground.[30] Accordingly, Italian newspapers did not talk of Britain as a dangerous enemy, but rather as a despised prey that was about to be hunted down and devoured. Less than a month after the declaration of war, the propagandist Mario Appelius proposed the sterilization of millions of Britons so that the European genetic pool could be cleansed, a choice of words that does not fit well into the first more sophisticated and relatively milder phase described by De Felice.[31]

Around the same time, an Italian journalist wrote that "the epilogue of the British farce is too banal to be called drama. It is nothing but a great example of international gangsterism [*gangsterismo*] which has been [...] destroyed and punished."[32] Another journalist wrote that "the greatest Empire in the world," made weak by opulence, had entered its agony, enduring defeat after defeat. It was the end of the "most colossal bluff ever seen."[33] And it was a victory of spirit and soul against material things and gold. The Italian press did little to hide its belief that Britain was almost finished, in what has been described as "the optimistic summer of 1940."[34] While the slow and modest Italian conquests in Somaliland, Kassala, and Sidi Barrani were inflated beyond any measure,[35] newspapers talked of panic overwhelming a Britain under the shadow of German invasion.[36] It was soon claimed that the Italian fleet controlled the Mediterranean. The British fleet and air force were mocked as unwilling to test their strength against their Italian counterparts. So great was the delusion that in July it was reported that the *Regia Aeronautica* had destroyed half of the British fleet in the Mediterranean.[37] The scope of propaganda was clearly not limited to a mild justification of the Italian intervention.

There was a sadistic streak to the discourse as well. The violent German bombing campaign against Britain was celebrated by the fascist press. The word "panic" was used to describe the condition of Londoners, and British people in general, under the bombs.[38] In

September 1940, *La Stampa* laughed at "English contortionism under the avenging bombs," noting how British agitation under the bombs contrasted with the stereotype of the calm Englishman.[39] That same month, another article mocked how Londoners had become "cavemen" to find refuge from the bombings.[40] In October, Luigi Barzini used apocalyptic tones to describe the "rain of fire from the sky" that was annihilating London, recalling the doom of Sodom and Gomorrah. It was, in Barzini's words, a just revenge for all the miseries inflicted by Britain on the world. "If [British] resistance persists" he concluded, "nothing will remain of England but the skeleton."[41] Mussolini was proud to announce to the Italian people that he had obtained from Hitler the chance to join in the Luftwaffe's effort.

The triumphalism of Italian war propaganda did not last into the winter, however. For the Italians, what happened during the grim winter of 1940–41 made it clear that Britain was far from defeated and the war was far from over. Even before the beginning of the military disasters, the prolonged British resistance forced the Fascist press to adopt a different approach. On 21 October 1940, Aldo Valori commented on the admiration of many Italians for the British. He attributed British fortitude to the stubbornness of an ignorant people, a fear among the ruling classes and big business that peace or defeat might dent profits, and most of all to the abiding strength of the British state:

> Britain is not defeated [...] its resources of all kinds, accumulated during centuries of pillaging, are of course not exhausted [...] but let us not attribute to our foe moral virtues that are completely imaginary; let us not credit him with a superiority of character that he has not.[42]

Then defeat struck. The *Regia Marina* suffered a serious blow in November when British aircraft attacked at Taranto. Between December 1940 and February 1941, Marshal Rodolfo Graziani's Italian Tenth Army was routed from Cyrenaica by a small but mobile force commanded by Lieutenant-General Richard O'Connor. Then, the *Africa Orientale Italiana* was overrun, in spite of stubborn resistance in Eritrea. During the winter of 1940–41, as MacGregor Knox has argued, Great Britain broke the independent Italian war effort.[43]

The difficult task of reconciling these defeats with the quite unflattering depiction of the British previously presented forced a change in the prevailing discourse. Victory was still considered certain, but the war was now described as a long business. Britain, it was accepted, was still strong.[44] But, as *La Stampa* commented, this last obstacle on the path to European peace could be conquered if all the forces of the nation were mobilized and focused on the goal.[45] At the same time, the magnitude of British success was downplayed or ignored. In February, Orlando Freri wrote in *Gerarchia* that as England was unable to attack Germany, she had "concentrated all the forces available in her immense Empire against Italy." The Mediterranean and Africa had assumed a central role in the economy of the war.[46] However, the British advance was far from quick or decisive, in spite of the remarkable superiority they enjoyed in men and weapons.[47] The stubborn resistance of "Italian units [who lacked] means of attack and defence" had made all the difference.[48] Britain had used all its strength against what it considered the "minor mass" of the Axis, and that explained the Italian difficulties.[49]

During the following phase of the war in North Africa and in the Mediterranean, the fortunes of the key belligerents fluctuated wildly. The Italian press described the British defeat in Greece as a "new Dunkirk and a new Gallipoli."[50] The recapture of Cyrenaica by Italian and German forces was considered far more impressive than the previous British victory.[51] But the recent defeats had instilled a new caution into the discourse. While violent criticisms of Churchill were extremely common,[52] the new rule was to avoid excessive optimism and predictions about the course of the war.[53] The temptation to interpret victory as a sign of the enemy's weakness or unworthiness was also to be avoided; on 22 April 1941, the press was ordered to "stop underrating the enemy and spreading a sense of euphoria."[54] That spring, the *Ministero della Cultura Popolare* (Ministry of Popular Culture) censored one book because "the experience of the current war in which the Dominions support Great Britain, and India lies more or less quietly under the British heel," had "partially debunked" the argument that the empire was "disintegrating."[55]

A period of violent but indecisive battles in the desert followed. In December 1941, the Italians and the Germans were forced to retreat once again from Cyrenaica. Then, between January and July 1942, the Axis forces in North Africa counterattacked, overwhelming the British and Commonwealth Eighth Army and eventually pushing deep into Egypt. With these remarkable victories, the contemptuous tone of the Italian press resurfaced. In many ways, the attacks on the quality and attitude of the British troops and people mirrored those of the summer of 1940.[56] The fascist authorities considered these stories counter-productive and did their best to limit them. In January, Alessandro Pavolini, the minister for popular culture, insisted that the press not excessively emphasize the difficulties faced on the British home front.[57] As a consequence, morbid descriptions of the suffering of British civilians under German bombs almost disappeared in the early months of 1942. In June, as the Axis forces marched on Egypt, Pavolini ordered the press to adopt a tone of "great sobriety," adding that "we expect victory exclusively through [our] arms, and not from a collapse of the enemy internal front."[58] In July, the orders to the press stated:

> In North Africa, the enemy fought and fights with bravery and stubbornness. To downplay such a truth with vulgar and irresponsible banalities (enemy routs, etc.) would undervalue the heroism and tenacity of our [soldiers]. Also [it is necessary to] refrain from an excessive underrating of the English generals[59] ... The reasons for [our] victories must be exclusively credited to [our] military heroism, strategic genius, and the power of the Italian and German troops" armaments.
> The current order is also valid for the humoristic press and extends to the maritime domain (English ships which do not know but how to sink, etc.)[60]

The press, nevertheless, continued to publish articles that questioned the enemy's will to fight. In September 1942, *Il Corriere della Sera* set out an anthropological explanation of the British martial tradition. The British, it claimed, were happy to flee in a "cowardly" fashion because they waged war like their corsair ancestors, who, in the infinite space of the seas, were used to attacking when superior in forces and withdrawing when the enemy was stronger. In this tradition, there was no room for tactical genius to obviate material inferiority with manoeuvre. This kind of warfare reduced battles to a question of brutal strength, much removed from the spiritual values that were at the core of Italian success. Moreover, it was clear that the British had no problem retreating again and again because they never fought on their home soil. Now, the Tripartite forces, which were attacking Britain from every angle, had ruined this old British game of "space and time." [61]

THE FINAL PHASE

The third period of De Felice's periodization must now be considered. How could the Italians reconcile the need to denounce the brutality of the British bombing campaign in Italy while also praising the Germans, who were wreaking much publicized havoc on their enemies?[62] Initially, as Luigi Petrella has argued, fascist propaganda emphasized continuity in Italian life; it denied "that the war was a destructive break with the deeply rooted rhythms and habits of Italy."[63] This narrative could not last for long. On 13 June 1940, the British bombed Turin; the war had quite clearly come home. A distinction was now made between the British and Axis practices of war; the enemy was willingly targeting people, because their goals were not military but terroristic. The Axis, on the other hand, only attacked military targets. In any case, Britain had started the murderous practice of bombing civilians, and deserved what it got as a consequence.[64] On 21 November 1942, the Ministry of Popular Culture wrote to the press emphasizing that "the enemy increasingly shows that it does not pursue a military goal, but only a criminal one [*camorristico*]. Anyway, the Italians are not and will not allow themselves to be terrorised."[65]

The British, as *La Stampa* put it in July 1941, did not belong to the world of civilized people.[66] In June 1943, a *Gerarchia* article noted that "the Anglo-Saxons" had still not attempted a landing in Europe because they were aware of the heavy price in blood that such a move would entail. They preferred instead to bomb women and children. The Anglo-Saxons were

> in a hurry to eliminate Italy from the conflict, and they would like to do it without a fight. Never were our enemies so concerned with sparing the blood of our fighters. Instead, they shed that of our children, our women, our elders, and our nurses, and destroy our churches and our ancient monuments.[67]

The British goal, it was argued, was clearly to break the spirit of the Italian people. The tools used were characteristic of the British way of warfare; they involved "threats and wheedling, the explosive pencil together with the flattering leaflet, the brutal bombing with the sentimental appeal, the humiliating command with the praise of our soldiers."[68] The writer Dino Brogi wondered how much more worried they would be if they were aware of the real spiritual endurance of the Italian people. "There are many people," he wrote in June, "waiting for the Anglo-Americans in Sicily, Sardinia, Calabria and Grosseto to avenge their killed and maimed children, [their] women bombed on peaceful roads and the old men buried under the ruins."[69] That same month, in *La Stampa*, the prominent fascist journalist Concetto Pettinato underlined that history had proven that the British had "a heart of stone."[70]

This kind of discourse, however, did not resonate with Fascist censors, who were reluctant to depict the Italians as victims. The press was thus ordered to avoid any sentimentality concerning the loss of life and to adopt a more virile and polemic tone that focused on the barbarity[71] and cowardice of the enemy.[72] The Fascist authorities felt that too little space had been given to descriptions of Anglo-Saxon cruelty. In May 1943, orders to the press lamented that "the polemic against the Anglo-American pilots, murderers of children and women, is not "cutting" enough. [It is necessary to] develop the concept of barbarism, *gangsterismo*, cowardice. Avoid any sentimental tone. Do not mention reprisals for now."[73] The appeal did not have a long-lasting effect; later the same month, the Ministry of Popular Culture reminded the press that "after some days, the polemic against the enemy has, again, lost its 'cutting edge': the English and the Americans keep fighting the war like brigands. The reaction of the Italian press is weak."[74] The order added that claims that the Italians were "angels" had to cease too, since it was reminiscent of the "old despicable commonplace of the "good Italian."[75] The Fascist regime had sought to turn the Italian people into a hard race of conquerors; the only acceptable response to the bombings was hatred, not passive martyrdom. An order to the press on 17 May 1943 hammered the point home:

> Today we witness cowardly, atrocious and inhuman acts [...] that have no precedent and remind us of the far gone days of the barbarian invasions. The reaction of the Italian press against these atrocities must be ... expressed in strong terms ...
> GENERAL DIRECTIVE: hatred against the barbarians.[76]

By 1944, the discourse focused on the brutality and arrogance of the invaders. These "new barbarians" were worse than the old ones because they showed no respect for the artistic treasures of Italy.[77] By now, however, the disconnect between Fascist pronouncements and the reality on the ground was so great that propaganda started to lose any meaning. In fact, a sort of grudging respect became more prevalent in the press. For example, an *Il Corriere della Sera* article went so far as to state that if the British had been Italians, Britain would have been defeated in 1940.

> [I]f the British islands had been inhabited by 50 million Italians instead of 50 million Englishmen, Churchill would have been forced to wear a fake beard and run from his home after Dunkirk ... [and] King George would have escaped by night ... But the British islands are inhabited by Englishmen, and forty-three months after Dunkirk the war still continues, King George is still on the throne, Churchill smokes his cigars and Eden still talks about fancy ties.[78]

CONCLUSION

The analysis of the sources presented here suggests a radically different picture of the Fascist regime's anti-British propaganda effort in the Second World War. This chapter has shown that the tone of the Fascist discourse did not progressively degenerate during the war, shifting from a more sophisticated and moderate approach to a more violent and vitriolic one in the last desperate phase of the war. Instead, the chapter has demonstrated that the development of that discourse was far less linear. Verbal violence peaked during the first period of the conflict, the summer of 1940. De Felice rightfully argues that the defeats of the first winter of the Italian war required a shift in emphasis, toward justifying Italian setbacks, but they also forced the Fascist authorities to try to restrain the press and adopt a more balanced approach. Old attitudes, however, kept resurfacing. The last period of the war was indeed characterized by verbal violence and extreme hostility in the press, but this period was no worse than the first. In fact, in some ways it was better, as the contemptuous tones of the first phase were gone by then.

This new periodization of Italian anti-British propaganda in the Second World War offers a fresh perspective on Italian perceptions of Britain during this period and on the character of Fascist propaganda writ large. Ideology clearly played an important role in shaping the image of the enemy in fascist Italy; over the course of the war a significant disconnect emerged between the depiction of Britain in propaganda and the reality on the ground. The Fascist regime's assessment of British military potential, and willingness to fight, was central to Mussolini's decision to join a war he was largely unprepared to fight. Over time, the hard school of war taught the regime about the limits of an ideological approach to military assessment. The press, however, was much slower to take these lessons on board. The regime's repeated, and not always successful, attempts to restrain certain kinds of criticism of the enemy shows that the Fascists experienced very real limits to their control of the war propaganda machine – a topic that deserves to be more thoroughly assessed.

NOTES

1 See for example Nicola Labanca, *Oltremare. Storia dell'espansione coloniale italiana*, Bologna (Bologna: Il Mulino, 2007), 143; MacGregor Knox, *Mussolini Unleashed, 1939–1941: Politics and Strategy in Fascist Italy's Last War* (Cambridge: Cambridge University Press, 1982); MacGregor Knox, *Hitler's Italian Allies: Royal Armed Forces, the Fascist Regime, and the War of 1940–1943*, (Cambridge: Cambridge University Press, 2000); MacGregor Knox, *Common Destiny: Dictatorship, Foreign Policy and War in Fascist Italy and Nazi Germany* (Cambridge: Cambridge University Press, 2000); John Gooch, *Mussolini and his Generals, the Armed Forces and Fascist Foreign Policy 1922–1940* (Cambridge: University Press, 2007); Fortunato Minniti, *Fino alla guerra, Strategie e conflitto nella politica di potenza di Mussolini 1923–1940*, (Napoli: Quaderni di Clio, Edizioni Scientifiche Italiane, 2000); Robert Mallett, *Mussolini and the origins of the Second World War, 1933–1940* (Basingstoke: Palgrave MacMillan, 2003); Enzo Collotti, Nicola Labanca, and Teodoro Sala, *Fascismo e politica di Potenza, Politica estera, 1922–1939* (La Nuova Italia, 2000); Nir Arielli, *Fascist Italy in the Middle East, 1933–40* (Basingstoke: Palgrave MacMillan, 2010); H. James Burgwyn, *Italian Foreign Policy in the Interwar Period, 1918–1940* (Westport, CT, and London: Praeger, 1997).

2 Claudia Baldoli, *Exporting Fascism: Italian Fascism and Britain's Italians in the 1930s* (Oxford: Berg, 2003); Francesca Cavarocchi, *Avanguardie dello spirito: il fascismo e la propaganda culturale all'estero* (Carocci, 2010); Tamara Colacicco, *La propaganda fascista nelle università inglesi: la diplomazia culturale di Mussolini in Gran Bretagna* (Milano: Franco Angeli, 2018), Arielli, *Fascist Italy in the Middle East*; Arturo Marzano,

Onde Fasciste, La propaganda araba di Radio Bari (Rome: Carocci Editore, 2015).
3 Luigi Petrella, *Staging the Fascist War* (Bern: Peter Lang, 2016).
4 Denis Mack Smith, "Anti-British Propaganda in Fascist Italy," in *Inghilterra e Italia nel '900. Atti del convegno di Bagni di Lucca* (La Nuova Italia, 1972); Pietro Cavallo, *Italiani in guerra, sentimenti e immagini dal 1940 al 1943* (Bologna, Il Mulino, 1997).
5 Renzo De Felice, *Mussolini l'alleato*, vol.1 (Turin: Einaudi, 1990), 171.
6 *Resoconto stenografico delle esposizioni fatta dagli addetti militari nei giorni 27 28 e 29 giugno 1938*, L10/8/14, Archivio Ufficio Storico Stato Maggiore Esercito.
7 Minniti, *Fino alla Guerra*, 148.
8 Ibid., 168.
9 Robert Mallett, *Mussolini and the Origins of the Second World War, 1933–1940* (Basingstoke: Palgrave MacMillan, 2003), 14.
10 Ibid., 102. See also Luigi Barzini, *La guerra all'Inghilterra*, 21 July 1939, 19. It has been written that "The airplane [...] was presented as the ideal image of the modernity and military efficiency of the regime, [and was] continuously used by the Fascist propaganda as a symbol of a rising Italian military power's strategic superiority, which could surpass the military potential of Great Britain, which was considered obsolete." See Camillo Zadra and Nicola Labanca, *Costruire un nemico* (Milano: Unicopli, 2012), 178. See also Fabio De Ninno, *I sommergibili del fascismo* (Milano: Unicopli, 2014), 279–82.
11 Unattributed, "Le reclute inglesi brontolano," *Il Corriere della Sera* (afterwards *Il Corriere*), 31 July 1939, 6; and unattributed, "Malcontento e indisciplina fra le reclute inglesi," *Il Corriere*, August 4 1939, 5.
12 R.P., "La nuova tribuna di Mosley," *La Stampa*, 23 January 1934, 1.
13 Guido Piovene, "I ginnetti e i pacifisti," *Il Corriere*, 10 January 1936, 3.
14 Di Saronno, "La situazione militare inglese," *Gerarchia*, March 1937, 176–83.
15 Guido Guida, "L'oro e la spada," *Gerarchia*, March 1939.
16 Duggan, *Fascist Voices*, 335–6.
17 Ministero della Cultura Popolare, Order to the press, 29 September 1943, Busta 70, Varie, Carte Morgagni corrispondenza rivista, Agenzia Stefani, Archivio Centrale dello Stato, afterwards ACS.
18 De Felice, *Mussolini l'alleato*, 1:172.
19 For some examples, see unattributed, "L'Inghilterra cacciata dall'Europa," *Il Corriere*, 27 July 1940, 1; unattributed, "In America, nessuno più crede alla possibilità che la Gran Bretagna si salvi dalla sconfitta," *La Stampa*,

3 July 1940; Giorgio Sanna, "La tenaglia mortale già si stringe intorno ad Albione," *La Stampa*, 26 July 1940, 1. Still in September, Orlando Freri announced on *Gerarchia* that the invasion of the British islands would happen in a short time. See Orlando Freri, "La guerra italo-germanica contro l'Inghilterra," *Gerarchia*, September 1941.

20 Marco Ramperti, "Gli Inglesi nell'altra guerra," *La Stampa*, 9 July 1940, 3. Much later, in more difficult times, Ramperti was to expand the theme of British indignity in the previous conflict by claiming that British discipline was a post-war myth, used to erase a reality of strikes and alcoholism. See Marco Ramperti, "Gli Inglesi nell'altra Guerra, – disciplina e flemma: una leggenda – Birra e whisky e scioperi" *La Stampa*, 11 November 1941, 3.

21 Luigi Barzini, "Il crollo del prestigio britannico," *Il Popolo d'Italia*, 27 June 1940.

22 Orlando Freri, "La guerra," *Gerarchia*, July 1940.

23 Giovanni Selvi, "La guerra anti-eroica, ovvero la guerra inglese," *Gerarchia*, June 1940, 287–95.

24 Il Duce had stated that "the stupid policy of guarantees had [...] shown itself particularly lethal for those who accepted them."

25 Pietro Caporilli, *Come Cartagine* (Roma: Novissima, 1941), 7.

26 Roberto Pavese, "Ieri e oggi," *Gerarchia*, July 1940, 361–3.

27 Orlando Freri, "La guerra," *Gerarchia*, July 1940, 370–84. Regarding Belgium in particular, see also Concetto Pettinato, "Cresce l'elenco delle vittime dell'egoismo britannico," *La Stampa*, 29 May 1940, 6.

28 See unattributed, "Le alleanze coi morti furoreggiano in Inghilterra," *La Stampa*, 26 July 1940, 1.

29 There are many examples of this, in the various phases of the war. In January 1941, when Italy was stuck in Greece and Yugoslavia was progressively assuming a pro-Axis stance that would not last long, the diplomat Giuseppe Solari Bozzi wrote that London's usual attempts to build a coalition in the Balkans had failed. See, Giuseppe Solari-Bozzi, "L'Asse e il nuovo ordine balcanico," *Gerarchia*, January 1941, 14–19. In September 1942, *Il Corriere* remarked that the British, "as long as they will find peoples and armies to tie to their chariot," will only be indirectly hurt by their defeats. See M.C., "Dunkirk-Tobruk," *Il Corriere*, 24 September 1942, 1. In August 1942, the Fascist authorities ordered the press to report the Soviet Ambassador in London's hopes that the other members of the coalition would share with Russia the weight of the conflict. Ministero della Cultura Popolare, Order to the press 8 August 1942, Busta 71, Varie, Carte Morgagni corrispondenza rivista, Agenzia Stefani,

ACS. See also unattributed, "Gli Inglesi non hanno rinunciato a fare la guerra fino all'ultimo francese," *Il Tevere*, 5/6 January 1940; Orlando Freri, "La guerra italo germanica contro l'Inghilterra," *Gerarchia*, November 1941; unattributed, "Il programma di Albione, combattere fino all'ultimo soldato russo," *Il Corriere*, 3 October 1941, 1. Ministero della Cultura Popolare, Order to the press August 8 1942, Busta 71, Varie, Carte Morgagni corrispondenza rivista, Agenzia Stefani, ACS.

30 See Ciano, *Diario*, 30 September 1940, and Aristotle A. Kallis, *Fascist ideology: Territory and Expansionism in Italy and Germany, 1922–1945*, 179.

31 Cavallo, *Italiani in guerra*, 157.

32 Roberto Pavese, "Ieri e oggi," *Gerarchia*, July 1940, 361–3.

33 Felice Bellotti, "Un anno di guerra e di vittorie," *La Stampa*, 1 September 1940, 1.

34 Arielli, *Fascist Italy and the Middle East*, 163.

35 For example, one article talked of "crumbling of [British] African colonies." See unattributed, "Le vittorie italiane," *Il Corriere*, 3 September 1940.

36 Giuseppe Piazza, "Smarrimento a Londra in vista della catastrofe," *La Stampa*, 29 June 1940.

37 Unattributed, "La flotta inglese Battuta," *Il Corriere*, 11 July 1940, 1. See also Mack Smith, "Anti-British propaganda in Fascist Italy," 105–6.

38 See, for example, unattributed, "Giornate di panico in Inghilterra," *La Stampa*, 12 July 1940, 3, unattributed, "Il panico si diffonde in Inghilterra, la legge marziale progettata dal governo di Londra," *La Stampa*, 17 July 1940, 3.

39 Unattributed, "Contorsionismi inglesi sotto le bombe giustiziere," *La Stampa*, 8 September 1940, 2.

40 See Cesco Tomaselli, "Nei sotterranei londinesi, I cavernicoli alla ricerca del più sicuro rifugio," *Il Corriere*, 14 September 1940.

41 Luigi Barzini, "Che cos'è la resistenza inglese," in *Roosevelt e la guerra all'Inghilterra* (Verona: Mondadori, 1942), 207. Other suggestive headlines were Cesco Tommaselli, "A Terrible Punishment Destroys London from the Sky"; Pic., "The Infernal Nights of the British Capital," *Il Corriere*, 11 September 1940, 1.

42 Aldo Valori, *Parole di Fede* (Milan: Mondadori, 1942), 129. One month later, he repeated that British resources were still conspicuous, adding however that it was not due to the merit of modern Englishmen, but of their ancestors, those "magnificent and picturesque delinquents." By any measure, the British were not even that good at using the huge amount of

colonies, resources, and outposts of their Empire. Indeed, he asked his listeners to "think about what we would have done had we had such a powerful Navy ... " See ibid., 141.
43 MacGregor Knox, "Fascist Italy Assesses Its Enemies," in *Knowing One's Enemies*, ed. Ernest R. May (Princeton: Princeton University Press, 1986), 347.
44 Valori, *Parole di fede*, 262, 326.
45 Unattributed, "Lo scopo supremo – la sconfitta totale della Gran Bretagna," *La Stampa*, 19 November 1940, 1.
46 Some authors also commented that Britain had chosen to attack Italy instead of Germany also because they wanted to punish Italian insolence in considering itself on par with the superior British race. See Valori, *Parole di fede*, 242.
47 Orlando Freri, "La guerra italo-Germanica contro l'Inghilterra," *Gerarchia*, February 1941.
48 Mario Montanari, *Le operazioni in Africa Settentrionale*, vol. 1, *Sidi El-Barrani* (USSME, 2000), 379–80.
49 Orlando Freri, "La guerra Italo-germanica contro l'Inghilterra," *Gerarchia*, March 1941.
50 Ministero della Cultura Popolare, order to the press 25 April 1941, Busta 71, Varie, Carte Morgagni corrispondenza rivista, Agenzia Stefani, ACS.
51 The press was ordered to remark that "[the offensive] took Wavell two months. In the way back, the Axis troops regained the ground in 14 days despite the difficult atmospheric conditions." See Paolo Murialdi, *La Stampa del Regime fascista* (Bari: Laterza, 2000), 350.
52 See, for example, Ministero della Cultura Popolare, order to the press 10 June 1941, Busta 71, Varie, Carte Morgagni corrispondenza rivista, Agenzia Stefani, ACS.
53 One example is the following order to the press: "Following the recent air-naval victories do not speak of war virtually won, and in general never indulge in premature and anticipatory optimisms." Ministero della Cultura Popolare, order to the press 25 May 1941, Busta 71, Varie, Carte Morgagni corrispondenza rivista, Agenzia Stefani, ACS.
54 Murialdi, *La Stampa del Regime*, 394.
55 Curzio Villa, *Nemica Inghilterra,* (Brindisi: Editore Oberdan Zucchi, Milano (XIX), 1941).
56 The press was also once again excessively optimistic; in April, an article on the *Corriere della Sera* talked of the "end of British plutocracy," and of a Britain that was already defeated. See Marziano,"Il tramonto della

plutocrazia britannica," *Il Corriere*, 28 April 1942, 1. Another article, in July, stated that the collapse of Britain was by then unavoidable. See C.B., "Di sconfitta in sconfitta, l'Inghilterra va verso il collasso finale," *Il Corriere*, 1 July 1942, 4.

57 Petrella, *Staging the Fascist War*, 171.
58 Ministero della Cultura Popolare, order to the press 26 June 1942, Busta 71, Varie, Carte Morgagni corrispondenza rivista, Agenzia Stefani, ACS.
59 Indeed, the officers were not spared by the Fascist press. One article claimed that the arrogance, ignorance, and intellectual mediocrity of the British ruling classes were the reason of the "pitiful" performance of the British army, as well as of the "humiliating political decadence of England." See unattributed, "Un tipico rappresentante della mediocrità intellettuale inglese," *Il Corriere*, 15 August 1942, 4. Another article mentioned how British officers were despised by the American press. See unattributed, "L'incapacità degli ufficiali britannici additata al pubblico disprezzo dalla stampa americana," *Il Tevere*, 6/7 July 1942.
60 Ministero della Cultura Popolare, order to the press 1 July 1942, Busta 71, Varie, Carte Morgagni corrispondenza rivista, Agenzia Stefani, ACS.
61 M.C., "Dunqueruqe-Tobruk," *Il Corriere*, 24 September 1942, 1.
62 Even that became more difficult once it was clear that the bombing campaign had not defeated Britain. In February 1941, the press was ordered "not to exaggerate in the titles and in the description of the effects of the German air attacks on the English cities." Nicola Tranfaglia, *La Stampa del Regime 1932–1943* (Milan: Bompiani, 2005), 345.
63 Petrella, *Staging the Fascist War*, 15.
64 Aldo Valori, *Parole di fede*, 15. For example, *Il Corriere* claimed that Churchill subverted the truth when he stated that the Germans had attacked civilians first. The article commented that "the bombings of London and of other British towns began after at least three months of British aggressions against the German populations, specifically as a reprisal for these aggressions." Unattributed, "Un nuovo sfogo di odio Churchilliano," *Il Corriere*, 15 July 1941, 6.
65 Ministero della Cultura Popolare, order to the press 21 November 1942, Busta 71, Varie, Carte Morgagni corrispondenza rivista, Agenzia Stefani, ACS.
66 Unattributed, "Come combattono gli Inglesi," *La Stampa*, 18 July 1941, 4.
67 Dino Brogi, "Sintomi," *Gerarchia*, June 1943.
68 The Allies were indeed attempting to undermine the morale of the Italian people through their techniques of psychological warfare. Especially from mid-1942, the intensive dropping of leaflets on Italian cities before and

after the bombings had the effect of both blaming Mussolini and the Germans for the bombings and to underline the desperate situation of Italy in the conflict. See Claudia Baldoli, *I bombardamenti sull'Italia nella seconda guerra mondiale, strategia anglo-americana e propaganda rivolta alla popolazione civile*, DEP, n.13–14, 40–3; Marco Fincardi, "Anglo-American Air Attacks and the Rebirth of the Public Opinion in Fascist Italy," in Bombing, States and Peoples in Western Europe, 1940–1945, ed. Claudia Baldoli, Andrew Knapp, and Richard Overy (London and New York: Continuum, 2011), 244–7.

69 Brogi, "Sintomi," 207–8.
70 Concetto Pettinato, "Cuore di pietra," *La Stampa*, 4 June 1943, 3.
71 The term "barbarous" was one of the most commonly used. See, for example, Alessandro Luzo's criticism of British bombings, in Mack Smith, "Anti-British propaganda in Fascist Italy," 109. See also Petrella, *Staging the Fascist War*, 171.
72 See, for example, Ministero della Cultura Popolare, order to the press 2 May 1943, Busta 71, Varie, Carte Morgagni corrispondenza rivista, Agenzia Stefani, ACS; and Ministero della Cultura Popolare, order to the press 20 July 1943, Busta 71, Varie, Carte Morgagni corrispondenza rivista, Agenzia Stefani, ACS.
73 Ministero della Cultura Popolare, order to the press 3 May 1943, Busta 71, Varie, Carte Morgagni corrispondenza rivista, Agenzia Stefani, ACS.
74 It was ironic that the Regime asked for *more* emphasis on the destruction brought over the country, when its propaganda had refused to admit the severity of the bombings, even after the first, unopposed raids on the Italian cities. See Fincardi, "Anglo-American Air Attacks," 243.
75 Ministero della Cultura Popolare, order to the press 22 May 1943, Busta 71, Varie, Carte Morgagni corrispondenza rivista, Agenzia Stefani, ACS.
76 Tranfaglia, *La Stampa del Regime*, 388.
77 Countless articles mentioned the devastation brought by the enemy on the occupied soil of Italy. See, for example, unattributed, "I barbari vengono dal mare," *Il Corriere*, 18 October 1944, 1; Cesco Tomaselli, "Il ferro e l'oro," *Il Corriere*, 5 May 1944, 1; Massimo Lelj, "Perche gli anglosassoni distruggono l'arte italiana," *Il Corriere*, 23 February 1944, 2. This last article typically stated that "calling them barbarians we honour them [...] they are not worthy of even the delusions of the barbarians, they are simply corrupt."
78 Concetto Pettinato, "Perché la guerra non può essere perduta," *La Stampa*, 25 January 1943, 1.

4

Growing Up in Kaifeng

Young People, Ideology, and Mobilization in Occupied China, 1938–1945

Mark Baker

Kaifeng was once the largest city in the world. As the capital of China's Northern Song Dynasty (960–1127 CE), it had boasted more than one million residents. By the end of the nineteenth century, however, its population had dropped to less than 120,000 people; a series of devastating wars and floods from the nearby Yellow River had left the city a shadow of its former self. Yet Kaifeng was still the capital of populous Henan Province on China's Central Plains (*Zhongyuan*), and the coming of the railroad in 1906 resulted in something of an economic and demographic recovery.[1]

The Japanese invasion brought this revival to a halt. Henan Province played a crucial role during the Sino-Japanese war of 1937–45. In the words of local historian Xie Xiaopeng, it was "the hinterland of China, the gateway to the northwest, the screen for Central China, and the crossroads between northern and southern fronts."[2] What Hans Van de Ven calls a brutal "meat grinder of a war" was perhaps at its worst here. More than 40 per cent of the provincial population fled their homes and millions of civilians lost their lives. In many ways, the plight of the people of Henan matched the demographic catastrophe that played out within the borders of pre-war Poland (see chapter 15 of this volume).[3]

To better understand the occupation-collaboration politics of occupied China during this period, this chapter will focus on the experience of Kaifeng during the War of Resistance. The city was taken by Japanese forces on 5 June 1938, and although always close to the frontline, it remained occupied to the very end of the war. Conservatively inclined inland power centres such as Kaifeng played an important role in Japanese efforts to turn military dominance into political support and ideological hegemony in China. The Central Plains had been a site of such struggles for thousands of years, and for Japanese occupiers and Chinese collaborators alike Kaifeng was the focus of ideological and mobilizing efforts among its civilian population. With its proximity to a hotly contested frontline, the city was described by the official newspaper of the provincial collaborationist regime as the "foremost outpost in establishing the state."[4]

The youth of Kaifeng were absolutely central to this story. The collaborationist authorities in the city saw the young as key to their project of forging a "new people" – organized, moral, and Japanese-speaking. The seven-year occupation was an especially formative period in the lives of these tens of thousands of young people.[5] To better understand their fate, this chapter makes use of a variety of sources, including contemporary newspapers, education journals, and memoirs. It investigates how growing up in this occupied, bombed-out, and shrunken city influenced the attitudes of young people toward the war, mobilization, collaboration, and the future of China. Just as Nicoló Da Lio's chapter demonstrates Italian failures to exploit some potential pools of person-power, this chapter outlines Japanese efforts to mobilize another demographic cohort – the youth of Kaifeng.[6] It argues that the failed efforts by the collaborationist authorities to mobilize Kaifeng's young people expose not only the ideological contradictions of collaboration but also its increasingly empty politics.

By engaging with these issues, the chapter aims to enrich our understanding of the global Second World War in four key ways. First, it aims to expand the study of children and young people in wartime China – which, after all, comprised almost 10 per cent of the world's population in the 1940s – to include areas under Japanese occupation.[7] Second, it intends to shift attention away from the Lower Yangtze toward an area of occupied China that has been overlooked in histories of the war.[8] Third, by focusing on change over time, it sets out to uncover the desperate mobilization of the last months of the Japanese Empire in China, a period often bypassed by historians in favour of the early years of occupation. Finally, this study from the very edges of the Axis-controlled world will aid our comparative understanding

Figure 4.1 Japanese soldiers mount an assault on the town of Kaifeng, China, 1938. © Imperial War Museum, IWM HU 53134.

of fascist and neo-traditional client regimes. By building on the work of historians of Europe, who have used youth to disentangle the ideological strands of mobilization, collaboration, and remobilization, this chapter will add a new dimension to our understanding of the complex dynamics of a "People's War."[9]

"THE GLORIOUS FLAG OF OUR NEW GOVERNMENT": KAIFENG YOUTH AND THE OCCUPATION-COLLABORATION STATE

After an initial period of looting and violence – though not on the scale of the Nanjing Massacre the previous winter – the Japanese military authorities set about building the institutions of the occupation-collaboration state in Kaifeng. As elsewhere in occupied China, the ranks of collaborators included conservative elites, opportunist military strongmen, and officials transplanted from the puppet state of Manchukuo in the Chinese northeast. In theory, civil authority rested with new municipal and provincial governments under the North China collaborationist "Provisional Government" (*Linshi Zhengfu*) in Beijing.[10] In practice, however, multiple institutions were left squabbling for power, including the Japanese garrison and military police (*Kempeitai*), Chinese collaborationist military forces, and informal espionage and smuggling networks.[11] These fragile authorities attempted to establish the foundations of a new urban order based on registering the population, rebuilding war-damaged infrastructure, reviving production, and conducting a concerted propaganda campaign.

Some of this work took place more on paper than in practice, but according to the collaborationist official Xing Hansan, work targeting young people was pursued more seriously than that focused on older Kaifeng residents.[12] For the collaborationist authorities, young people were both a problem and a political opportunity. Kaifeng's municipal authorities were anxious about juvenile delinquency and vagrant young people, as well as the "younger generation of workers" who had missed out on education due to the disruptions of 1937–39.[13]

Alongside these concerns, however, sat the language of hope. The rhetoric of the Japanese authorities stressed the importance of peace and their aspirations for a new start for the young of Kaifeng. As one observer of the occupation in North China put it, the new authorities yearned for a chance to foster a cohort morally superior to those educated under Nationalist rule.[14] Local collaborator Xing Hansan noted that the "Japanese recognized it would be comparatively difficult ideologically to train adults, but young people's thinking is pure" – a view echoed by young people themselves when speaking to the authorities: "[W]e young people are in a time of being simple and unaffected" (*tianzhen lanman*), noted sixth-grader Guo Zhongtian in a mayoral speech contest, "and hence able to have our ideas corrected."[15]

This political focus on young people came in two main strands. The first was elementary education in government schools. Already by the autumn term of 1938, the Kaifeng municipal government had reopened four primary schools in the war-torn city, and by 1941 was spending more than its entire tax income on primary education.[16] With the westward flight of Henan University into unoccupied areas, the highest educational institution in the occupied province was the training college for primary school teachers (*Shifan Xuexiao*). The graduates of this training college, remembered Xing Hansan, were the young people most trusted to spread the political message of the regime.[17] But school education had its limits. Even after two years of occupation, less than a fifth of primary-school-aged children attended government-registered establishments.[18] A 1939–40 push for Japanese language learning also proved limited in its effect: the promise of Japanese teaching in all schools was never followed through, and by 1942 only a third of pupils in Kaifeng were studying even the most rudimentary Japanese.[19]

The limits of school education put extra pressure on the second strand of work focused on young people: extracurricular organization and political training. The key institution in this regard was the youth section of the *Xinminhui* (Renovate the People Association or New People Association), a mass organization centred on occupied North China that paralleled and at times challenged the institutions of the collaborationist government. Beginning in 1939, Kaifeng's Xinminhui youth corps recruited older teenagers into three-month courses to train lower-ranking staff for the regime. By the end of the first year alone, almost 1,000 male adolescents had received such training in Kaifeng, in part because of the promise of a job at the end of the course. Previously unemployed graduates of these programs became neighbourhood heads, low-ranking policemen, and government clerks; those who showed ideological zeal were rewarded with more prestigious roles in the Xinminhui itself.[20] Separate from Xinminhui training, some 3,000 young people – presumably those insufficiently literate for formal courses – were also corralled into a government paramilitary unit (*Bao'an dui*) for urban security work.[21]

As well as this formal training, young people in Kaifeng encountered the propaganda of the regime in a variety of ways. The local radio station included dedicated programs for children and young people, mostly political speeches and songs.[22] Young people were involved in a plethora of annual events, including commemorative parades, official sports events, and speech competitions. Surviving samples of prize-winning speeches by young people give a sense of the political language that they were learning to reproduce: "[O]ppose the CCP who disrupt the world's peace," declared fifth-grader Li Qiuju during 1941

> and the Chiang Kai-shek regime which blindly resists Japan and tricks the people into a deathtrap (*sidi*) ... But fortunately, our allies the Japanese have righteously dispatched troops, and chased the completely evil Communist Party beyond the city. The peace-loving people of Kaifeng have escaped and have new life again, and are now living peacefully under this glorious and magnificent flag (*zhe guangming canlan de qizhi*).[23]

But what did these ideas amount to? Apart from opposition to Communist and Nationalist parties, did the occupation-collaboration state have a positive social vision? Did the new authorities stand for tradition, deference, and the elderly; or progress, modernity, and the young? Were young people to be passively deferential or a mobilized vanguard?

AN "IDEOLOGICAL CLEAVAGE"?
YOUNG PEOPLE AND COLLABORATION POLITICS

The new regime needed an ideological underpinning for long-term state-building and mobilization, but significant tensions emerged about the content of this vision. Lincoln Li described these tensions as an "ideological cleavage" between the traditionalist Confucianism of the North China government and the "progressive and modern image" of the parallel Xinminhui mass organization.[24] Outright traditionalism had been marginal in the struggle for the soul of post-imperial China. Some cultural conservatism, and the ideals of a "national essence," had been incorporated into the Nationalist Party – and were enjoying a wartime revival in unoccupied China – but an unreconstructed traditionalism was revived only under Japanese patronage.[25] Of all China's regional client regimes, the North China government acquired a particular reputation as a traditionalist gerontocracy, dominated by superannuated Confucians who had been prominent in the late Qing and early Republican periods. But, despite Kaifeng's pre-war reputation as a conservative city, it is apparent that these dynamics did not play out fully at the local level – in Henan, for example, over

70 per cent of collaborationist officials, and even a majority of senior provincial ministers, were under the age of 40.[26]

Such conflicts, and contradictions, between traditionalists and modernizers were present across much of the Axis-controlled world, and it is tempting here to see an analogue of defeated France, equating Confucian traditionalism with Pétain's conservative *Révolution Nationale* and the mass mobilization of the Xinminhui with the various modernizing nationalisms and fascisms of Pierre Laval and the Paris collaborationists.[27] Such dichotomies, however, obfuscate rather than clarify the situation in occupied China. Matters were simply more confused. Competing discourses of tradition and modernity were present, of course, and it is possible to chart their changing forms and meanings over time. But, in most cases, these impulses appear simultaneously, jumbled up in the same journals (whether Xinminhui- or government-sponsored), the same speeches, and even the same sentences. Indeed, it is by pursuing the inherent contradictions and confusions of contemporary discourse that the ideological difficulties of the occupation-collaboration state come ever more sharply into focus.

At face value, the discourse on young people in Kaifeng was certainly saturated with the language of traditionalism. This was a rejection of the recent past, of both youthful nationalist movements and the perceived individualism of young people in the 1920s and 1930s. Sun Yat-sen's progressive-sounding Three People's Principles had been taken off the curriculum in 1938 and all books discussing Sun's theories were banned in 1939.[28] The following summer, the education department in Kaifeng issued a profoundly conservative program for the city's young people, enjoining them to "promote China's traditional morality" and "turn to the guidance of Confucianism to eliminate alien Communism and utilitarianism" (*gonglizhuyi*), to "pass on the moral culture of the East."[29]

In a speech to Kaifeng's young people, Zhang Zhengfang, provincial head of the Xinminhui – supposedly the "progressive" force in North China – diagnosed as the root of China's problems "more than one hundred years of young people's deep-rooted bad practice" (*jibi*): "[T]heir twisted hearts have an admiration for western culture from their smattering of knowledge, content with chasing after it in a servile way ... this has caused a disaster for the citizenry, rural bankruptcy, an unsettled society."[30] Kaifeng's education journal was more specific about what had gone wrong: students were disobedient and politicized.

You tell them they should show initiative, and they spontaneously start asking difficult questions of their superiors/teachers; you say that students should pay attention to national affairs, and they start sticking posters everywhere, shouting slogans, and wanting to take part in actual politics (*shiji zhengzhi*) ... Since May Fourth, most students have received the influence of Euro-American "freedom," "equality," "rights" and "struggle," and this is what leads to their superficial clamours and arrogance (*fu xiao qiyan*).[31]

As Jeremy Taylor has shown in his study of propaganda posters in occupied China, young women, in particular, were considered a threat to traditional order.[32] "If a girl receives education, vanity arises out of her arrogant heart," conservative commentator Yang Fuli warned Kaifeng's teachers in 1940, "[S]he envies splendour and wealth, and becomes incapable of coping with bitterness and hard work ... And once arrogance has been born within her, it leads to a wantonness that can't be controlled (*fangdang bushu*)." Influence from Europe and the United States, Yang concluded, had caused "male and female inequality, with women's rights exceeding men's rights" (*nüquan gaoguo nanquan*).[33]

This neo-traditionalism resonated with *Wangdao*, the "Kingly Way" of the Confucian past. The key, according to John Hunter Boyle, was the (re-)creation of a mythologized "passive citizenry," focused on private morality rather than a contested public politics.[34] Similarly, in her study of children's magazines from occupied Beijing, Wang Fanyi notes the focus on harmony, beauty, and the need to grow up as a "good person" in one's private life. Insofar as this was a view of public life, it was a moral "renovation" of politics, restoring a world where ordinary people received top-down protection from honest officials.[35] Young people in Kaifeng were part of this vision. "We must trust and follow the old East Asian Confucian ethical code and morality," declared one student at a speech contest, "be filial sons at home, and act as loyal ministers (*zhongchen*) of the state."[36] School students were fed a diet of obedience, not least in compulsory meetings on "respecting the elderly."[37] As in Pétain's Vichy, this submission was to be reinforced in the hierarchical household. Rather than the school as a site for socializing students *away* from the traditional family, Kaifeng's schools were supposed to ensure the same conservative message by forging stronger links with the home.[38]

While this conservative vision was concerned with fostering private morality, another impulse was to mobilize young people for active political roles. The presence of this alternative discourse is hardly surprising. Joseph Levenson has pointed out, for example, that it was hard to be "authentically" traditional after the fall of imperial China. In equal measure, Prasenjit Duara has noted, in his work on Manchukuo, that even the most pliant and constructed modern state must try actively to involve its subjects in its ideological constructions.[39] For local intellectual and official Xing Hansan, while collaborationist thinking could "take Confucian thought as its root and stem" (*yi ... Rujia sixiang wei gen gan*), the "spirit of the age" needed an ideology "containing a relative active nature" (*hanyou jiaoda de jijixing*) and scope for input from "ordinary people" (*yibanren*).[40] Kaifeng's young people, then, were also cast as participants in an active struggle to build a modern, even progressive, "New China" (***Xin Zhongguo***).

In tension with discourses of harmony and passivity, young people – especially males – were told they had a key role in a world of struggle. A 1941 poem by one Yang Jingwen told its readers:

Young men, do not be timid,
Timidity is the poison of humanity,
It will cause people to belittle and mock you,
And when you receive people's mocking, who will be willing
　　to help you?
The attitude of the world is that everywhere the strong eat,
　　and the weak get eaten (*qiang shi ruo rou*).[41]

Rather than deferential and passive, young people could be described – just as Lily Chang and Laura Pozzi have shown in Nationalist territory – as full and contributing members of society.[42] One speech by Guo Zhongtian of Kaifeng's No. 1 Primary School is strikingly similar to discourses in unoccupied areas: "Although we are young, we are also part of the citizenry. It is very mistaken to think that we do not have responsibility towards the state ... we are the future masters of the Chinese Republic."[43]

While claiming to be restoring old morality, Kaifeng's collaborators sometimes evoked a very different idiom when propagandizing young people. In 1940, activist Li Shiwei urged Kaifeng's young people not to restore the old, but to build the new:

The new order in East Asia is aiming to rescue China from the depths of the water and the heat of the flames ... and we young people, faced with such a new order of grand significance, certainly cannot sit idly by (*xiushou pangguan*) and enjoy its benefits. Instead, our generation of young people (*wo bei qingnian*) should have a grand mission.[44]

The corollary of pro-youth language was a more positive assessment of the May Fourth movement and its social consequences: "For many years," wrote Xie Ziling in a rejection of the old gender order, "our country has emphasized men and diminished women, and there is also a damaging legacy of the idea that women are more virtuous without talents ... [But] since the May Fourth movement, the voice of women's liberation has risen."[45]

As Xing Hansan remembered, this language of mobilization and progress came to the fore in the run-up to the Pacific War, when ideas about protecting the young from sacrifice fell away.[46] In 1941, Japanese advisor Murata Seiji outlined the world situation as

[a] great division between those who would preserve the old order and those who wish to build the new one ... Those who want to build a new order are China, Japan and Manchukuo, as well as Germany and Italy in Europe, who are all relying on a will to the death to advance towards this goal ... our hopes for this in fact rest on our youth.[47]

Shortly before Pearl Harbor, one prize-winning student essay urged that "We young of Kaifeng, of China, of all East Asia, must unite and rise up, rise up! Do not hesitate, see clearly our new era!"[48]

By the closing years of the war, the language of youth power was firmly centre stage. Whereas the legacy of the May Fourth Movement had been rejected by traditionalists, the anniversary of the 1919 youth protests was celebrated by a mass parade of Kaifeng's young people in 1944.[49] Even as he criticized youthful decadence, Xinminhui head Zhang Zhengfang told young people later that summer that they were "the foundation of society, the mainstay (*dizhu*) of the state, the driving force of the era; some have the red blood of passion, some the will of iron, the spirit of steel."[50]

The tension between discourses of old and new is clear, therefore, and young people were caught between these opposing impulses. Yet what were the implications of these differences, and where did the contradiction end? The first and simplest answer is that the struggle between tradition and progress ended with the ascendancy of the new. The imperative of mobilizing young people aided the emergence of pro-youth discourses at the expense of the traditionalism of the early North China collaborators. Although it failed to establish its power in Henan Province, the tone of collaboration also shifted following the establishment of the Wang Jingwei regime in March 1940, with its claims to modernizing nationalism and an inheritance from the pre-war Nationalist Party. Soon after, the Pacific War ratcheted up the language of mobilization and struggle, as well as the claims of fighting against the old European imperial order.

In a second sense, though, the tension between old and new may be read as a false dichotomy. It is striking that whatever the difference in tone, it is hard to chart a programmatic difference between traditionalist and modern discourses on young people in Kaifeng. Both the "Kingly Way" formulation and the slogan of "New China" can be traced back to the foundation of Manchukuo and the work of ideologues such as the Manchuria Youth League's Tachibana Shiraki.[51] Both elements were transplanted to North China after 1937 by Kita Seiichi, who established the Xinminhui as a mass organization.[52] Collaboration ideology was rooted in a call for moral renewal that could be couched in either traditional or modernist terms without changing much of its content. In Kaifeng, one writer of 1940 thought that old and new could be simultaneously achieved: lamenting the peripheralization and decline of the region, he insisted that under the new regime "we will restore the old culture of Henan, and also lay the foundations of a new one."[53]

But if tradition and progress had little to choose between them, did they really mean anything at all? A third reading of this tension is that it ended not in victory for pro-youth ideas, nor in conflation of old and new, but simply in hollow ideology and empty slogans. This was particularly the case by the second half of the Japanese occupation of Kaifeng. A few examples of exhortation to Kaifeng's young people underline this trend toward the vacuous. In his long piece calling on young people to build the new order, Japanese advisor Murata Seiji came to a climax that meant little beyond anti-individualism and loyalty to the authorities: "[W]e must foster our sense of the state, overcome all difficulties, throw aside self-interest, and unite with our comrades, sharing pain and joy together, and achieve the consciousness that we need (*biyao de zijue*)."⁵⁴ A few months later, one Kaifeng pupil gave a similarly meaningless set of prescriptions to his peers:

> We just need to study hard and when we have graduated sacrifice ourselves for the state ... How do we move forward as students now? Have good thoughts, correct concepts, get rid of all that is bad, overthrow evil doctrines, do not receive false propaganda or the temptations of Communism, have a loyal heart, listen to and follow the guidance and plans of the new government of China.⁵⁵

In 1944, this language of obedience was echoed in the empty urgings of a newspaper supplement aimed at Kaifeng's young people: "[O]pen your half-sleepy eyes and change your perspectives, and go toward one's fate of sacrificing one's life for the state, reduce the private and elevate the public and walk on the road to rebirth."⁵⁶ The same supplement also included a poem, presumably intended to stir adolescent readers: "[Y]ou must take an unsurpassably steadfast spirit, earnestly develop your knowledge, cultivate the good and expel the bad, and determinedly train your bodies to walk a thousand *li* on the illuminated road."⁵⁷ It is perhaps no coincidence that a few months later, cadres of the Xinminhui youth corps – the supposed flagship of mobilization – were firmly instructed, "don't talk about theories" (*butan lilun*), but instead focus only on "benefitting the masses" (*hui ji qunzhong*) and "removing their difficulties" (*jiechu yinan*).⁵⁸

One is reminded – albeit here in propaganda rather than administrative mode – of the "flattened prose and numbing dullness" that Ann Stoler describes in Dutch imperial archives.⁵⁹ But as Stoler points out, this tedium can itself show something of the reality of empire – in this case, an ideologically hollow heart of darkness. It is hard to know precisely why political vision became so meaningless as the occupation wore on. Perhaps it underlines the sheer difficulty of real sociopolitical debate so close to the frontline, during the grinding reality of a long war. Without the experience of actual defeat, there is little sign of the intellectual liveliness and sense of hope in youth that marked Vichy France.⁶⁰ Banality may also have been a way of preserving the conscience of reluctant cooperators (not least Kaifeng's educators, many of whom had remained in their posts from before the war) or perhaps it reveals growing disillusionment with the traditionalist project of the North China collaborators.

There may be something in all of these interpretations. More important, though, is the sheer difficulty of a cogent sociopolitics under foreign occupation, of a "real" politics of collaboration in an age of nationalism. As Prasenjit Duara points out, nation-states are constructed along twin strands of sovereignty and authenticity.[61] Without even the barest fiction of sovereignty enjoyed in Vichy, Manchukuo, or even the Wang Jingwei government, North China collaborationists had neither sovereignty nor authenticity to fall back on. Young people could be organized against Communism or Western imperialism, but there was little that was politically meaningful that they could be mobilized *for*.

That did not mean that young people could escape the consequences of occupation. As the Pacific War dragged on, Japanese policy in China turned from longer term state-building and ideological work to a more short-term extraction of resources – as collaborator Xing Hansan later put it, from "raising the chickens and taking the eggs" (*yang ji qu luan*) to "starving the chicken to death."[62] By the last years of the war, Kaifeng's young people were reduced to labour inputs for the doomed Japanese Empire.

"WHAT IS DUTY"? MOBILIZATION AND MILITARIZATION[63]

After the initial effort to co-opt Kaifeng's young people, both in and out of school, the youth work of the occupation-collaboration state entered something of a lull between 1940 and late 1941. Xinminhui youth activity dropped off, and schools began to teach only classroom-based moral education rather than the physical drill training that had been formally mandated.[64] It was the outbreak of the Pacific War that gave new impetus to youth mobilization in Kaifeng. On 11 December 1941, just a few days after Pearl Harbor, Kaifeng's schools joined a mass meeting to celebrate the outbreak of war and to promise to "join together to overthrow American and British imperialism."[65] Student Yi Shuqing of No. 3 Primary School described a role for Kaifeng's youth:

> Although we Chinese people do not have the possibility of going to the frontline to engage in combat with the enemy ourselves, there are a great many roles to play in war, in the war of thought and politics, in the economy and all kinds of struggle, everything

relies on those in the rear... we should certainly take on this burden of rear support, which is sometimes even more important than those at the front.[66]

For the first few months of the Pacific War, though, mobilization was still more rhetorical than real in Kaifeng. A more active role for young people came only with the food crisis of 1942–43. The story of this Henan Famine in Nationalist-held territory is now well known, and although patterns of starvation in occupied and semi-occupied areas are less clear, drought and requisitioning certainly brought widespread death to the countryside.[67] Kaifeng itself seems to have been less hard-hit than its rural hinterland; the city was kept supplied by its railroad link, and a rudimentary rationing system was in place.[68]

Nonetheless, there were certainly serious shortages, and – as elsewhere in the war-torn world of the 1940s – young people were mobilized to raise urban food production. In the critical spring of 1943, the authorities organized young people to farm spaces within the city walls. Fortunately, Kaifeng's long decline had left large open areas within the walls; less propitiously, much of it was poor-quality wasteland or stagnant pools of water. At the beginning of March, Kaifeng's teacher training college organized its students to establish a farm just inside the north gate; soon afterwards, agriculture was built into the regular school curriculum.[69] One *mu* of land (one-sixth of an acre) was parcelled out to every twenty middle-school boys, or to one hundred middle-school girls. Primary-school pupils also got involved in tending these plots, and the education authorities encouraged young people to teach their families to set up vegetable gardens.[70]

It is not known how much extra food was grown by these young producers; what is clear is that 1943 was a turning point in the mobilization of young people in Kaifeng. As the tide of world war began to turn, any pretence of peacetime was dropped from propaganda and, as across the Japanese Empire and in Japan itself, society mobilized for all-out conflict. As had long been the case in unoccupied China, where the struggle for survival had always involved people of all ages, young people entered the war effort in droves. For some young people in Henan, their mobilization for the war effort was a traumatic experience that was life changing – if not life ending: more than 11,000 young men, for example, mostly from rural areas, were sent outside the province for forced labour, many to Manchuria, but many in smaller numbers to Japan itself. Most young people in Kaifeng were more fortunate, however. In and around the provincial capital, labour service was usually more local, and the notorious brutality of the northeastern coal mines could be avoided. As long as they were not caught without papers or seen idling around the railway station, they could hope to see out the war at home.[71]

Escaping the worst did not mean, however, that Kaifeng's young people could avoid giving their labour to the war effort. Under new provincial education minister Sun Jingqing, the Xinminhui youth corps was reorganized in all schools.[72] "The things that students do in school," ran one directive, "from research and moral behaviour, to physical training, skills and entertainment, should as far as possible be performed as part of the youth corps." Half-hearted physical education was transformed into full drilling. Youth corps "labour service training" (*qinlao fuwu xunlian*) put Kaifeng's young people to work, variously digging wells, constructing dikes, mending roads, and building bridges.[73] Still others were corralled into a "voluntary" drive to collect copper and iron, including tearing out metal from schools and public buildings.[74]

The last years of the war also saw the militarization of Kaifeng's young people as auxiliaries for the war effort. Rather than "future masters," adolescents – and not only males – were now cast as "future soldiers." They were to be the "outstanding fighters" who would establish the state and revive Asia.[75] Kaifeng's young people received training in logistics, policing and air-raid protection. Air-raid work began in the summer of 1944, with 130 youth corps members receiving a month's training in fire-fighting, first aid, and radio communications.[76] In addition to these measures, in the summer vacation of 1944, both male and female high school students received two weeks of residential military training. These exercises included (at least for male participants) infantry drilling, field exercises, firearms training, and bayonet fighting.[77] Yet unlike in some parts of the world in 1944–45, where underage youth were pushed into the frontline, those in occupied China were not trusted by the Japanese to serve in any fighting capacity.

By 1945, Kaifeng faced a tension between extreme mobilization and efforts to preserve an air of normality. The civil authorities successfully kept schools open until the summer vacation of that year, but all young men in the city were undergoing intense youth corps training.[78] Eventually, after protests from businesses who had seen teenage apprentices disappear for military training for lengthy periods, youth drill was reduced to a three-hour session three times per week.[79] In July 1945, high school students once again faced compulsory military training, with provincial governor Bao Wenyue overseeing the passing-out parade less than two weeks before Hiroshima. Bao declared that the training would "make young people into cadres who can one day revive the state." What he did not know was that the war would soon be over, even before the end of the summer vacation.[80]

CONCLUSION

This chapter has explored the organization and mobilization of young people in the early and later stages of Kaifeng's long occupation. It has interrogated the discourses surrounding young people in this period and the growing emptiness of collaboration ideologies. What is harder to reconstruct is the reactions of young people to these organizational and discursive attempts at co-option. Contemporary collaborationist sources, of course, usually recount widespread enthusiasm; later Communist sources describe occupation in a heroic resistance mode.

There are signs, however, that the dominant response of Kaifeng's young people was neither enthusiasm nor active resistance, but disengagement from collaborationist structures and language. When it came to the war, the collaborationist newspaper lamented, "most young people think it is of no consequence for them, and wish to continue to live happily on the side-lines." Political celebrations and anniversaries were simply "opportunities for young people to revel in the theatre or the cinema."[81] One official bemoaned the authorities' lack of cultural power, railing at young people for "wearing bourgeois clothing, and dancing the Boston quick-step, into which they degenerate" (*duoluo*).[82] After six years of occupation, the Xinminhui youth corps admitted its own failure: "[T]he results of the young People's movement in Henan have been paltry" (*miaoxiao liaoliao*).[83] Promises of a return to traditional values and visions of a new China had fallen on deaf ears. Whether due to passive resistance or disengagement, Japanese efforts to mobilize the youth of Kaifeng failed.

All the victorious nations in the Second World War have a national epic, a "People's War" story. Historians are rightly suspicious of these narratives and pick away at the inconsistencies and elisions of their construction. In this case, it was not heroic resistance but the sheer detachment of many young people that ensured that the ideological emptiness of occupation and collaboration passed into irrelevance. It is here, in the ideological void and pointless labour of long occupation that we can discover the fissures and forgotten stories lying behind China's national epic, its "People's War."

An autobiographical reflection by Pei Yuanyou, of the Kaifeng Girls' High School, encapsulates this disengagement from the austere strictures of the occupation regime: "What I fear most is the New Year: what new clothes should I wear? New shoes? A new hat? Should a girl wear flowers?" But Pei goes on to hint at a more existential angst, one that perhaps stands as an insightful description of growing up in mid-century China – and a warning to historians tempted to replace national epics with big academic wartime narratives of their own:

> I walk into my room, and at that moment my low spirits reach their worst; if I were an emaciated poet in this situation, he would be able to release a poem of limitless worry, love, suffering, depression; or if I were a calligrapher in this loneliness, in a moment he could produce a beautiful piece to dispel his worries. But at that moment all I can do is just sit there.[84]

NOTES

1. See Zhu Junxian, *Yinge zhi bian: Zhongyuan quyu zhongxin chengshi de jindai bianqian* [Transformations of Inheritance and Renovation: Modern Changes in the Central Cities of the Central Plains Region] (Taiyuan: Shanxi renmin chubanshe, 2013), esp. chapters 4–5.
2. Xie Xiaopeng, "Kangzhan shiqi Henan lunxianqu yanjiu de huigu yu zhanwang" [Research on occupied Henan during the War of Resistance: Review and Prospects], *Henan daxue xuebao* 56, no. 4 (2016), 139–44, 139.
3. Quote from Hans Van de Ven, *China at War: Triumph and Tragedy in the Emergence of New China* (London: Profile Books, 2017), 7. On war in Henan, see Micah Muscolino, *The Ecology of War in China: Henan Province, the Yellow River, and Beyond, 1938–1950* (New York: Cambridge University Press, 2014).
4. *Xin Henan Ribao* [*New Henan Daily*, Kaifeng, 1938–1945], 22 July 1944.
5. Kaifeng had a population of between 180,000 and 200,000 during the occupation (compared with almost 300,000 before the war); of these, at least 40 per cent were under 20. Officials calculated 26,000 residents of

primary school age, but this may be an underestimate. See *Kaifeng Jiaoyu Yuekan* [*Kaifeng Education Monthly*, 1940–42], no. 9 (1940), 3–4. I use "young people" as distinct from "child" to discuss those of upper primary school age and above; i.e., those aged between eleven to twelve and around nineteen (in western counting), described in sources as *shaonian* ("early youth") and *qingnian* ("youth"), and mobilized in Youth Corps (*qingshaonian tuan*). On this and other terminology, see also Aaron Moore, "Growing up in Nationalist China: Self-Representation in the Personal Documents of Children and Youth, 1927–1949," *Modern China* 42, no. 1 (2016), 73–110, 74–5.

6 See Nicolò Da Lio, "Fascist Warfare on the Home Front: War Mobilization and the Fragmentation of Italian Society, 1935–1943," chapter 2 of this book.

7 For Nationalist territory, see Lily Chang, "Contested Childhoods: Law and Social Deviance in Wartime China, 1937–1945" (PhD diss., University of Oxford, 2012), note that Chang's chapter 8 also discusses occupied Shanghai; M. Colette Plum, "Lost Childhoods in a New China: Child-Citizen-Workers at War, 1937–1945," *European Journal of East Asian Studies* 11, no. 2 (2012), 237–58; Laura Pozzi, "'Chinese Children Rise Up!': Representations of Children in the Work of the Cartoon Propaganda Corps during the Second Sino-Japanese War," *Cross-Currents: East Asian History and Culture Review*, no. 13 (2014), 99–133. Historians of Henan have discussed young people under occupation, but usually only in studies of education. See Xie Bingsong, "Kangzhan shiqi Henan lunxianqu de nucai jiaoyu" [Servile education in occupied Henan during the War of Resistance], *Shixue Yuekan*, no. 5 (1999), 84–7; Ruan Yizhao, "Riwei zai Henan lunxianqu de nucai jiaoyu yanjiu" [A study of Japanese-puppet servile education in occupied Henan], (MA diss., Zhengzhou University, 2010).

8 Xie, "Kangzhan shiqi Henan lunxianqu yanjiu," 143. For local studies of occupation, see essays in Christian Henriot and Wen-Shin Yeh, eds., *In the Shadow of the Rising Sun: Shanghai under Japanese Occupation* (Cambridge: Cambridge University Press, 2004); Timothy Brook, *Collaboration: Japanese Agents and Local Elites in Wartime China* (Cambridge, MA: Harvard University Press, 2005); Toby Lincoln, *Urbanizing China in War and Peace: The Case of Wuxi County* (Honolulu: University of Hawai'i Press, 2015), chapters 7–9.

9 Note, for instance, W.D. Halls, *The Youth of Vichy France* (Oxford: Clarendon Press, 1981); Sarah Fishman, *The Battle for Children: World War II, Youth Crime, and Juvenile Justice in Twentieth-Century France*

(Cambridge, MA: Harvard University Press, 2002); Goran Miljan, "'To Be Eternally Young Means to Be an Ustasha': Youth Organizations as Incubators of a New Youth and New Future," in *The Utopia of Terror: Life and Death in Wartime Croatia*, ed. Rory Yeomans (Rochester: University of Rochester Press, 2015).

10 Even after the establishment of the better-known Wang Jingwei government in Nanjing in March 1940, occupied Henan remained under the control of the northern collaborationists (and ultimately, the Japanese North China Area Army), rebranded as the "North China Political Affairs Council" (*Huabei Zzhengwu Weiyuanhui*). For Wang's failed efforts to control Henan, see Xie Xiaopeng and Cao Shulin, "Kangzhan shiqi nan bei weizhengquan dui Henan lunxianqu de zhengduo" [The struggle between northern and southern puppet regimes over occupied Henan during the War of Resistance], *Zhengzhou daxue xuebao* 51, no. 2 (2018), 134–40.

11 On deliberate administrative fragmentation, see Lincoln Li, *The Japanese Army in North China, 1937–1941: Problems of Political and Economic Control* (New York: Oxford University Press, 1975), 64–90.

12 Xing Hansan, "Riwei tongzhi shiqi Henan sheng Xinminzonghui yange ji huodong," *Henan wenshi ziliao* no. 9 (1984), 70–87, 86.

13 *Kaifeng Jiaoyu Yuekan*, no. 9 (1940), 5.

14 George Taylor, *The Struggle for North China* (New York: Institute of Pacific Relations, 1940), 88–95.

15 For Xing's quote, see Xing Hansan, *Riwei tongzhi Henan jianwenlu* [A record of Japanese-puppet rule in Henan based on personal knowledge] (Kaifeng: Henan daxue chubanshe, 1986); for Guo's, see *Kaifeng Jiaoyu Yuekan*, no. 10 (1941), 45.

16 See "Kaifeng shi gongshu sannianlai shizheng jingji gongzuo baogao" [A report on the economic work of city government during the last three years of the Kaifeng municipal office], reproduced in *Xin Henan Ribao*, 3 August 1941. The shortfall was made up by subsidy from the provincial government.

17 Xing, *Riwei tongzhi Henan*, 116.

18 *Kaifeng Jiaoyu Yuekan*, no. 9 (1940), 6. This was primarily due to a lack of schools and teachers, not a wholesale rejection of collaborationist education. More than 3,000 children sat exams for just 588 government school places.

19 Henan sheng zhengfu mishuchu wenshuke, ed., *Henan sheng zhengfu sanshiyinianfen tongji nianjian* [Henan Provincial Government Yearbook for 1942] (Kaifeng: Henan sheng zhengfu mishuchu, 1943), 167; on

the waning of interest in Japanese language, see Xing, *Riwei tongzhi Henan*, 61; for a similar trend elsewhere in Japanese-occupied territory, note Paul Kratoska, *The Japanese Occupation of Malaya and Singapore, 1941–45: A social and economic history*, 2nd ed. (Singapore: NUS Press, 2018), 130–4.

20 Xing, *Riwei tongzhi Henan*, 57–8. On the *Xinminhui* in Henan, see Ma Yiping, "Riwei Henan sheng xinminhui shulüe" [A Brief Account of the Xinminhui in Occupied Henan], *Huabei shuili shuidian xueyuan xuebao* 24, no. 6 (2008), 75–7. The Youth Corps of North China is not to be confused with similar-sounding organizations, including the *Zhonghua Qingniantuan* of the Lower Yangzi Reformed Government and the later Wang Jingwei-backed *Zhongguo Qingniantuan*.

21 Xing, *Riwei tongzhi Henan*, 36. It is unclear if this militia operated only in Kaifeng, or also in other towns in occupied Henan.

22 Radio schedules printed daily in *Xin Henan Ribao*.

23 *Kaifeng Jiaoyu Yuekan*, no. 10 (1941), 45–6.

24 Li, *The Japanese Army in North China*, 114; also quoted in Jeremy Taylor, "Gendered Archetypes of Wartime Occupation: 'New Women' in Occupied North China 1937–1940," *Gender & History* 28, no. 3 (2016), 660–86, 666.

25 On Nationalist Party thought, see Wai-keung Chan, "Contending Memories of the Nation: History Education in Wartime China," in *The Politics of Historical Production in Late Qing and Republican China*, ed. Tze-ki Hon and Robert Culp (Leiden: Brill, 2007), 169–210; Brian Tsui, *China's Conservative Revolution: The Quest for a New Order, 1927–1949* (Cambridge: Cambridge University Press, 2018). For distinctions between conservatisms, see Charlotte Furth, "Culture and Politics in Modern Chinese Conservatism," in *The Limits of Change: Essays on Conservative Alternatives in Republican China*, ed. Charlotte Furth (Cambridge, MA: Harvard University Press, 1976), 22–54.

26 *Henan sheng gongshu zhiyuan lu* [Record of staff of Henan Provincial Government] (Kaifeng: Henan sheng mishuchu, November 1939).

27 See, for instance, Julian Jackson, *France: The Dark Years, 1940–1944* (Oxford: Oxford University Press, 2001), chapters 7 and 9; on a similar view of youth policy, Debbie Lackerstein, *National Regeneration in Vichy France: Ideas and Policies, 1930–1944* (Farnham: Ashgate, 2012), 188–206. Note that this neat division of Vichy policies – going back to Robert Aron's 1954 "Two Vichys" defence of Pétain and denunciation of Laval – has been contested. See Jackson, *France: The Dark Years*, 9–12.

28 *Henan sheng gongbao* [Henan Provincial Bulletin], 1939, no. 9, 74, cited in Ruan, "Riwei zai Henan lunxianqu," 29. On the Three People's Principles, see Chan, "Contending Memories of the Nation," 197.
29 Reproduced in Cheng Ziliang and Li Qingyin, eds., *Kaifeng chengshi shi* [A History of the City of Kaifeng] (Beijing: shehui kexue wenxian chubanshe, 1993), 259–60.
30 *Xin Henan Ribao*, 22 July 1944.
31 *Kaifeng Jiaoyu Yuekan*, no. 3 (1940), 12. "May Fourth" here refers to the nationalist student protests of 1919.
32 Taylor, "Gendered Archetypes."
33 *Kaifeng Jiaoyu Yuekan*, no. 3 (1940), 10.
34 John Hunter Boyle, *China and Japan at War, 1937–1945: The Politics of Collaboration* (Stanford: Stanford University Press, 1972), 92.
35 Wang Fanyi, "Ertong wenyi de niuqu xingtai" [The Distorted Form of Children's Literature and Art], *Dushu yu pinglun*, no. 8 (2007), 126–8. On "Renovation" or "Restoration" (*weixin*), Timothy Brook, "Collaborationist Nationalism in Occupied Wartime China," in *Nation Work: Asian Elites and National Identities*, ed. Timothy Brook and Andre Schmid (Ann Arbor: University of Michigan Press, 2000), 159–90.
36 *Kaifeng Jiaoyu Yuekan*, no. 10 (1941), 45.
37 Note, for instance "Jinglaohui (yaoqinghan)" [Meeting on respecting the elderly (invitation)], Henan Provincial Archive, M10-02-0095.
38 Halls, *The Youth of Vichy France*, esp. 8–9; *Kaifeng Jiaoyu Yuekan*, no. 3 (1940), 14.
39 Noting Joseph Levenson, *Confucian China and its Modern Fate: A Trilogy* (Berkeley: University of California Press, 1968), esp. xxvii–xxxiii; Prasenjit Duara, *Sovereignty and Authenticity: Manchukuo and the East Asian Modern* (Lanham: Rowman & Littlefield, 2003).
40 *Kaifeng Jiaoyu Yuekan*, no. 3 (1940), 1–4.
41 Ibid., no. 16 (1941) 55.
42 Compare Chang, "Contested Childhoods," 88–109; Pozzi, "Chinese Children Rise Up."
43 *Kaifeng Jiaoyu Yuekan*, no. 10 (1941), 45.
44 *Kaifeng Jiaoyu Yuekan*, no. 9 (1940), 65.
45 *Kaifeng Jiaoyu Yuekan*, no. 23 (1942), 1.
46 Xing, *Riwei tongzhi Henan*, 64–5.
47 *Kaifeng Jiaoyu Yuekan*, no. 11 (1941), 16–17.
48 *Kaifeng Jiaoyu Yuekan*, no. 19 (1941), 2.
49 *Xin Henan Ribao*, 5 May 1944.
50 *Xin Henan Ribao*, 22 July 1944.

51 Lincoln Li, *The China Factor in Modern Japanese Thought: The Case of Tachibana Shiraki, 1881–1945* (Albany: SUNY Press, 1996); note also Duara, *Sovereignty and Authenticity*, 61–5.
52 See Boyle, *China and Japan at War*, 86–95.
53 *Kaifeng Jiaoyu Yuekan*, no. 8 (1940), 14.
54 *Kaifeng Jiaoyu Yuekan*, no. 11 (1941), 17.
55 *Kaifeng Jiaoyu Yuekan*, no. 14 (1941), 10.
56 "Qingnian husheng" [Voice of Youth], supplement in *Xin Henan Ribao*, 29 April 1944.
57 Ibid.
58 *Xin Henan Ribao*, 30 July 1944.
59 Ann Laura Stoler, *Along the Archival Grain: Epistemic Anxieties and Colonial Common Sense* (Princeton: Princeton University Press, 2009), 23.
60 Compare Halls, *The Youth of Vichy France*, esp. chapter 1.
61 Compare Duara, *Sovereignty and Authenticity*, 25–33.
62 Xing, *Riwei tongzhi Henan*, 183–4.
63 Quote from *Xin Henan Ribao*, 12 May 1945.
64 "Huabei jiaoyu shi ce yaogang shishi fang'an" [Scheme for implementation of key principles of applying policy in North China education], 19 February 1943, reproduced in Chen and Xu, *Rijun huo Yu* (1986), 366–73, 369.
65 *Kaifeng Jiaoyu Yuekan*, no. 21 (1941), 1.
66 *Kaifeng Jiaoyu Yuekan*, no. 29 (1942), 1. Note that Tokyo refused collaborators' offer to send troops to southeast Asia. See David Barrett, "The Wang Jingwei Regime, 1940–1945: continuities and disjunctures with Nationalist China," in *Chinese Collaboration with Japan, 1932–1945: The Limits of Collaboration*, ed. David Barrett and Larry Shyu (Stanford: Stanford University Press, 2001), 102–15, 111–12.
67 See esp. Muscolino, *Ecology of War*, esp. chapter 3; Kathryn Edgerton-Tarpley, "Saving the Nation, Starving the People? The Henan Famine of 1942–43," in *1943: China at the Crossroads*, ed. Joseph Esherick and Matthew Combs (Ithaca: East Asia Program, Cornell University, 2015).
68 Census data from Kaifeng city shows a much smaller demographic loss (83 per cent of a "normal" cohort) than its surrounding rural area (only 59 per cent of a "normal" cohort). See Anthony Garnaut, "A Quantitative Description of the Henan Famine of 1942," *Modern Asian Studies* 47, no. 6 (2013), 2007–45, 2036–9. On urban provision, see *Xin Henan Ribao*, 28 October 1942; "Kaifeng shi hezuoshe lianhehui," [Kaifeng city co-operative federation] 31 August 1942, Henan Provincial Archive, M10–002–0094.

69 *Xin Henan Ribao*, 26 March 1943; 3 April 1943.
70 *Xin Henan Ribao*, 7 April 1943; 24 April 1943. On vegetable plots, see Ruan, "Riwei zai Henan lunxianqu," 26–7.
71 Xu Youli, "Guanyu kangri zhanzheng shiqi 'qiangpo laodong' wenti de chubu kaocha" [A preliminary investigation into the issue of 'forced labour' during the War of Resistance against Japan], *Shangqiu shifan xueyuan xuebao* 23, no. 2 (2007), 44–8; Huang Zhenglin et al., *Jindai Henan jingjishi (xia)* [An Economic History of Modern Henan (vol. 2)] (Zhengzhou: Henan daxue chubanshe), esp. 408.
72 Xing, *Riwei tongzhi Henan*, 114–20.
73 "Huabei jiaoyu shi ce yaogang shishi fang'an," 369.
74 On metal, see "Kaifeng xie tie tong lei souji shishi fang'an," [Scheme for carrying out collection of scrap iron, copper and the like], Spring 1944 (no date), Henan Provincial Archive, M10–002–0102. Young people collecting metal for the war effort was, of course, happening around the world, witness Halls, *Youth in Vichy France*, 46; Peter Thorsheim, *Waste into Weapons: Recycling in Britain during the Second World War* (Cambridge: Cambridge University Press, 2015), esp. 86–9.
75 *Xin Henan Riabo*, 27 July 1944.
76 *Xin Henan Ribao*, 5 July 1944. This was far from a purely pro forma exercise or a means of controlling young people. There were some twenty-four USAAF raids on Kaifeng between June 1944 and August 1945. For a full list, see Kit Carter, ed., *The Army Air Forces in World War II: Combat Chronology* (Maxwell, AL: Albert F. Simpson Historical Research Center, 1973), http://aircrewremembered.com/USAAFCombatOperations.
77 *Xin Henan Ribao*, 5 July 1944; 7 July 1944; on the nature of youth corps training, 28 July 1944.
78 On municipal efforts to keep primary schools open, see *Xin Henan Ribao*, 6 August 1944.
79 *Xin Henan Ribao*, 10 August 1945.
80 *Xin Henan Ribao*, 31 July 1945.
81 *Xin Henan Ribao*, 29 April 1944.
82 *Xin Henan Ribao*, 12 May 1945.
83 *Xin Henan Ribao*, 23 July 1944. For proposals for improvement, see 30 July 1944.
84 *Kaifeng Jiaoyu Yuekan*, no. 14 (1941), 25–6.

5

"What the Soldier Thinks"

Mobilizing the Mind of the American Soldier in the Second World War

Edward J.K. Gitre

On 8 December 1941, the day after Japan attacked Pearl Harbor, the US Army embarked on a novel social and behavioural experiment.[1] That morning, the first cohort of forty or so men of the 9th Infantry Division stationed at Fort Bragg, North Carolina, were directed to report to a large camp theatre. Neither they, nor the non-commissioned officers who accompanied them, knew the purpose of their orders. When they arrived, a young private informed them, "You are going to be given some questions, and the same questions will be put to hundreds of other soldiers here in this division." The War Department of the United States of America wanted to hear directly from the men themselves "what is going right and what isn't." The private emphasized the novelty of the exercise. "[T]his type of thing," he said, "has never been done in this Army, or in any other Army in the world." To encourage openness and cooperation, the men were promised that their responses would be recorded anonymously.[2]

That day, the same day that the US declared war on Japan, hundreds of soldiers from the 9th were surveyed. In fact, between 8 and 10 December, approximately 1,900 men in total participated in what was referred to as Planning Survey I. Half a million other service personnel and civilian War Department employees would also participate in the months and years to come. Plenty of men doubted whether the army wanted to know truly what the rank-and-file thought. One unconvinced soldier wrote in the open-ended "free-comment" section at the end of the survey that, "I doubt very much if all this stuff shall do much good as it probably is just another army form that they want filled out."[3] The invitation elicited cognitive dissonance for others; one soldier asked, "It isn't verboten, is it, for enlisted men to comment – anonymously – on their 'superiors'"?[4] Doubts were raised and persisted. Yet, by all indications, the vast majority of those surveyed seized the opportunity to speak their mind.[5]

Planning Survey I, and the other surveys that followed, was intended "to increase the Army's efficiency by helping the individual soldier to do a better job."[6] Personnel in this people's army, or army of "citizen soldiers," were promised that command wanted to hear directly from each and every one of them. Some in command were genuinely interested in the thoughts and morale of the ordinary soldier; others, however, were not. From start to finish, morale research in the US Army would remain a controversial topic. Consequently, the civilian scholars who were recruited to run the program were instructed that their contributions to this "practical engineering job" were to receive "no publicity whatever."[7] The ambivalence displayed by the High Command substantially shaped the development of the research program. It also obscured the program's role in influencing the experience, image, and culture of the army in the years after 1941.[8]

This chapter will argue that the research branch played a vital role in helping soldiers "adjust" to military life during the Second World War. It brought the best out of soldiers, both on and behind the frontline. By studying the responses of individual soldiers, and by using data to underpin the decision-making process, the research branch reinforced the connection between the individual and the state. As Frederick Osborn, the man who established the research branch, explained:

> Modern wars are not fought by armies alone, but by peoples sustained by belief in their own way of life. So long as American life is based on freedom and respect for the individual, it is necessary that the Army, so far as possible, base its handling of the soldier on the same principles.[9]

Put simply, "the Army cannot be at odds with the nation on such a basic issue as that of the national character." There could hardly be a purer example of the art and science of the liberal state, instantiated through "statistics," than the part played by the US Army's research branch in eliminating "friction" between citizen soldiers and command during the Second World War.[10]

THE GENESIS OF THE MORALE PROGRAM

Applied social science research was a growth industry well before the outbreak of the Second World War. In the interwar period, corporate America, political parties, governments, periodicals, and various media outlets invested heavily in gathering and analyzing the opinions, beliefs, and habits of US citizens. The assessment of public opinion took on increased significance with the rise of authoritarian regimes abroad.[11] Sustained attention to the views of "the people," as evidenced by George Gallup's American Institute of Public Opinion and other polling outfits, became the lifeblood of American democracy. As President Franklin Roosevelt wrote, in a missive to the National Conference of Jews and Christians, "the whole structure of democracy rests upon public opinion. Indeed, under a government which functions through democratic institutions, we are ruled by public opinion." Now, more than ever, the voice of the American citizen had to be heard, and known. "Only through the full and free expression of public opinion," noted the president, "can the springs of democracy be renewed and its institutions be kept alive and capable of functioning."[12]

Roosevelt's appreciation of the intertwined nature of public opinion and democratic governance may have been widely shared in the political sphere, but it was not the prevailing doctrine of a US military command bracing for war. The sticking point was control, and concerns over losing it. In April 1941, the Army Chief of Staff George C. Marshall brought a proposal to his chiefs. It recommended that Elmo Roper, one of the country's most prominent pollsters, be asked to "obtain reactions" from the army on various aspects of morale, such as post exchanges, the sale of beer, and relations with civilian communities. The chief of staff thought that such a program had "great possibilities."[13]

James Ulio, the head of the Morale Branch of the army, thought it "inadvisable," however. He worried about the "proper supervision and control" of "this vitally important and extremely delicate work" and objected to the prospect of having "civilian "samplers" in the field," no matter how "well qualified and controlled" they were. His branch was in fact working on a program of its own that would ensure control of the undertaking and the personnel to be employed.[14] The Personnel Branch of the army was similarly reluctant, its assistant chief of staff noting that, "to make inquiry through civilians of the state of morale or of matters influencing morale would weaken command and suppress the confidence good leadership places in subordinates." Better to leave the matter to the Morale Branch, who could make use of polling within the "military structure."[15]

A program controlled completely by command was soon ruled out too, however. Giving such freedom to the troops was considered simply too dangerous. As Henry Stimson, the secretary of war, put it in May 1941:

> Our Army must be a cohesive unit, with a definite purpose shared by all. Such an army can be built only by the responsible effort of all of its members, commissioned and enlisted. Anonymous opinion or criticism, good or bad, is destructive in its effect on a military organization where accepted responsibility on the part of every individual is fundamental.[16]

In the face of this opposition stood Frederick Osborn, one of the forgotten architects of America's Second World War. Osborn was a financier and businessman who had turned amateur scholar and fundraiser for the social sciences.[17] In August 1940, he was invited by the statistician Stuart Chase to join the Roosevelt administration to help coordinate research between government departments. A childhood friend of the president, Osborn was soon asked to expend his energies elsewhere. With the country on the cusp of passing its first peacetime draft, a new civilian committee was needed to help write regulations for the controversial measure. The White House asked Osborn to be its chair.

That autumn, while the committee worked day and night to draft six volumes of selective service regulations, Osborn found his attention drifting toward a perhaps greater opportunity. On 23 December, he wrote to Frederick Keppel, the president of the Carnegie Corporation, discussing how "a number of different people have been trying to get permission from the army to make studies of one sort or another on the men drafted." For someone who was deeply interested in the field of population studies and eugenics, "the opportunity to study a cross-section of the entire male population of the United States within the army age groups" was too good to be true.[18]

Osborn's successful stewardship of the selective service committee led to another chairmanship. At Stimson's request, Osborn was appointed to the Joint Army and Navy Committee on Welfare and Recreation (JANC) whose job was to draft civilian resources and expertise to help build a comprehensive armed forces morale program. The committee comprised some of the most prominent figures in the fields of education, business, philanthropy, the arts, and entertainment. The new initiative brought into sharp relief the centrality of ideas and morale as the United States prepared for the possibility of war.

That March, Stimson issued a memorandum authorizing the reorganization of the army's morale services, rechristening Ulio's Morale Division the "Morale Branch." "For the first time in our history," the memo noted:

> [W]e are, in time of peace, mobilizing and training a large Army through the instrumentality of a selective service system ... The success of this civil process will be dependent upon the Army's ability to return these soldiers to civil life in an enthusiastic state of mind toward their period of service. In a larger sense this provides an opportunity to popularize the Army with our people which is essential for an efficient fighting force.

The directive granted the new branch more independence as well as direct access to the chief of staff. Its goal was clear: to ensure that public opinion, or military morale, remained favourable under these preparatory conditions. "High military morale" had to be prioritized if the army was going to be ready to fight when the time came. The "need for mental and spiritual preparation for the struggle which lay ahead" was now considered just as great as the "need for training in the skills of soldiering."[19]

The reorganized Morale Branch and JANC still worked, however, as parallel organizations. Although Stimson had initially banned any opinion polling of troops, his March memo authorized the Morale Branch to "make necessary research on specific morale problems, including the problem of the individual ... and make appropriate recommendations for their improvement."[20] Osborn, unsurprisingly, began to co-opt his networks in the social sciences into his efforts. His relationship with the Roosevelt family, as well as the trust he had earned from Marshall and Stimson, undoubtedly helped in his efforts to involve the Social Science Research Council, the leading academic society of its kind, and the Carnegie Corporation in his morale program.[21]

Events now played a hand. That summer, Ulio fell ill. Stimson and Marshall asked Osborn to take over the Morale Branch. With no little trepidation, he agreed; he was now an "over-night General."[22] Then, on 18 August 1941, LIFE magazine published an unflattering article on the state of morale in the army. The piece was based on an informal survey of 400 privates in an infantry division. The results were devastating. Half said they would desert after their year of service was up; 40 per cent said that they "rue the day they got into the Army." LIFE quoted a private who groused that "the papers are always talking about how good the morale is and how ready the Army is for battle. The hell it is! Why don't they ask us?"[23]

The *New York Times* followed up the LIFE article with its own investigation. Conditions were found to be "so shocking" that the paper decided not to publish the report and instead turned it over to the War Department.[24] With Congress having only just voted to extend military service for the 1,531,000 who had already been called up, it was clear that something drastic had to be done. The timing was auspicious. Two months later, Osborn received approval from Marshall to conduct a "scientific survey" of attitudes in the US Army. The new chief of the Morale Branch was ready to go: he had already started to recruit a research staff and had lined up no less than $100,000 of Carnegie Corporation funds to begin his new morale program.[25]

THE MORALE PROGRAM IN ACTION

Osborn, and the scholars he recruited, would need to continue to "combine science and statesmanship" to overcome the challenges they would face in the years to come.[26] First up, they had to prove that social science methods could make a positive contribution. Samuel Stouffer, the University of Chicago sociologist who Osborn appointed as his director of research, outlined what he took to be the principal purpose of their first survey.

> [T]he central objective now, which, I take it, is to provide an example of the effectiveness of survey techniques which will be convincing evidence to the several branches of the Army of the need for a regular continuous reporting system based

on interviewing samples of soldiers ... Everything in the schedule, every decision as to interviewing procedure or sample selection, every plan for tabulation and analysis should be aimed straight at that purpose.

Surveys, Stouffer maintained, should not be too long and should be clear and convincing. Their results needed to be rapid, specific, meaningful, actionable, and free of any "misleading" implications. Interviewers were to be well adjusted to army life and the scheme for sampling had to be "beyond criticism." "Ten-dollar words" on the survey schedules should be avoided, and any question that might invite enlisted men to make "damaging remarks about officers ... eliminated." Every question, Stouffer continued, had to "be examined with a microscope to make sure it doesn't jeopardize the present main objective." Stouffer and Osborn were so concerned about negative scrutiny that they even called their first study a "planning" rather than "morale" survey.[27]

In spite of these concerns, the team was eager to complete the first survey in time for Christmas 1941, before any international events might influence the "collective state of mind" of American troops. The date for the survey was set for Monday 8 December. But on Sunday afternoon, the 7th of December, just as interviewers and class leaders were receiving their final training and instructions for the following day, a radio flash announced the attack on Pearl Harbor. Certain survey questions became dated "in one split-second," but Osborn's team decided to move forward, and by Wednesday had secured 1,878 responses, sufficient to constitute a cross-section of the entire 13,726-member 9th Division.

Even before the survey was completed, the research team began to analyze the data. Louis Guttman, a statistical mathematician from Cornell University, lent a hand. The university also provided students and laboratory equipment, and a number of specialized coders and clerks were borrowed from various government agencies. The Bureau of Agriculture Economics lent some of its Hollerith electromechanical tabulating machines to transfer the data to punch cards and tabulate the results. For comparative purposes, the team obtained demographic data on the US male population from the Census Bureau. In three brisk weeks, the Census Bureau ran tabulations from 1.25 million punch cards using "literally hundreds of its machines and employees." The Adjutant General's office also ran tabulations on a 20 per cent sample of all enlisted men, adding 300,000 punch cards of data.

The scale of the undertaking was remarkable. Researchers had access to each man's "Form 20," a small card that contained demographic and other background data. Information was collected on the nation's draftees from the Selective Service System, as was information on race and intelligence from the Personnel Procedures Section of the Adjutant General's Office. This mountain of data, once tabulated and analyzed, yielded all sorts of information about America's fighting force, some quite specific and actionable, other data more general but still invaluable to Command.

Three out of every five soldiers surveyed indicated they had spent their own money to have ill-fitting uniforms altered, leading the quartermaster general to establish a fund for uniform alterations. Most of the men wanted more information about the meaning of the war for Americans. It was widely known, and the survey confirmed, that many men had requested a draft deferment. But even knowledgeable officials were surprised by how many had *not* asked for deferment but felt they should have received one. Also, while troops desired more recreational, entertainment, and comfort facilities, as well as certain privileges and personal freedoms, the survey showed these should not be considered a "cure-all" for problems pertaining to morale. The worst cases of maladjustment appeared to result from troop dissatisfaction with classifications and assignments, i.e., those posted to jobs that did not match their skills and qualifications.

Some of what the data showed had already been observed and anticipated by the army. Still, seeing the data visualized could and did have a dramatic effect. It was startling to see graphically, for example, how different the enlisted men of the Second World War were from those of the Great War. Officials suspected that these new recruits were better educated than the old Regular Army. The survey confirmed these suspicions and pointed toward some possible consequences: those least "adjusted" to army life tended to be the most educated, with over half of college-educated enlistees dissatisfied with their assignments. Conscripts were not only better educated than their Regular peers, they were also of higher socioeconomic status. This survey-documented generation gap helped elucidate the friction between the two cohorts, especially among enlisted men who wanted to become officers themselves.[28]

This was a different citizen-soldier force, with different, higher expectations of how a modern American army ought to be run. They expected a more democratic approach to command. Black soldiers, who had been told that they were to defend freedom and democracy, expected to be treated with respect. The uncovering of these radically different expectations justified in no small measure the intensive labour required for the morale research program. As Ernest Burgess, a colleague of Stouffer's at the University of Chicago, put it (in a letter to the executive director of the Social Science Research Council in December 1941):

> In spite of many obstacles which at times seemed insurmountable, [Stouffer] has succeeded in carrying the project to a point where the way will be wide open for the type of studies that Mr. Osborn and he desire to make. The army is beginning to appreciate it is in great need of just this type of material.[29]

Marshall, who had always favoured morale research, ordered an abstract of the report transmitted to all commands and asked that the assistant chief of staff for personnel (G-1) prepare a digest for general circulation. He also issued a directive, which had General Staff approval, instituting continued reporting of research. A copy of the report was also delivered to the president, who, Stouffer highlighted in his notes to Osborn, "directed that a speech be drafted following the lines of our report almost verbatim."[30]

Still, like so many of the new recruits, Osborn's team of researchers experienced their own frustrations. They ran into red tape and bureaucratic walls, challenges that were only heightened as the army further expanded once war broke out. A month after the completion of the Fort Bragg survey, the War Department was reorganized. The Morale Branch was renamed the "Special Services Branch," and the research division's purview was enlarged by placing its services at the disposal of the entire military organization. The branch was now required to help solve administrative and personnel problems across the whole army. But G-1 continued to maintain organizational responsibility for morale and continued to insist that all policy matters be cleared through personnel channels, creating an "inordinate amount of administrative routine."[31]

During another reorganization, which took place only two months later, Osborn took the opportunity to request that he be granted broader approval authority. At the time, even small exploratory studies required prior clearance. It seemed uneconomical and inefficient to Osborn, and his small overtaxed professional staff, to have to prepare and clear constant memoranda, not to mention the time required for G-1 to vet the requests.³² As the organization expanded, so would the need for additional approvals beyond G-1. The reorganizing zeal of the army continued, with some bureaucratic experiments lasting mere weeks.³³

Special Services' survived, yet the branch was vulnerable to the very personnel problems it was tasked to assess. Securing and keeping competent, and just semi-competent, military personnel was a constant battle. Between the time the Morale Branch started testing Planning Survey 1 and June 1942, the turnover rate in Osborn's command was 80 per cent. The problem of finding and retaining competent clerks, let alone field officers to run surveys, frustrated the branch's efforts. In many ways, it was Osborn's and Stouffer's contacts with the outside world that kept the project going. Money from the Carnegie Corporation allowed the team to recruit top and rising talent in the social sciences – such as the Yale psychologists John Dollard and Carl Hovland, the social psychologist Leonard S. Cottrell Jr, and the sociologist Donald Young.

It was not until the end of the summer of 1942 that matters improved considerably. As troop transport ships, filled stern to bow with American soldiers, headed eastward across the Atlantic, Osborn got in contact with Dwight D. Eisenhower. Osborn provided Eisenhower with a copy of Special Services new output, "A Short Guide to Great Britain," a pamphlet designed to help orient troops to British culture. Eisenhower immediately requested 90,000 copies for distribution to arriving US troops.³⁴

Eisenhower, who saw value in Osborn's work, requested that the Special Service Branch assign officers to survey soldiers' attitudes in Britain and propose measures to improve relations between American soldiers and the British Army and British civilians.³⁵ He wrote to the Adjutant General, noting:

> The large problem presented by this subject is the necessary adjustment which must be made by our forces upon entering this densely populated area, mixing with people who have a history and tradition reaching back into past centuries, and to whom that history and tradition are of almost sacred importance ... [T]he most important steps in the orientation and amalgamation of our troops with the British are those which make for mutual association.³⁶

Figure 5.1 British locals and American troops meet at the Dove Inn, Burton Bradstock, Dorset, 1944. © Imperial War Museum, IWM D 20142.

The timing of Eisenhower's request was auspicious. Osborn wanted data to convince High Command of the need for more information and orientation programming. A study of a representative sample of the army had already shown that large numbers were ignorant of world affairs. Half of those surveyed or interviewed were either complacent about the war or overly rosy in their expectations of victory. A quarter to half lacked a strong motivation to fight and wanted to avoid combat service full stop; the same percentage either doubted, or were cynical of, US war aims. No less than two-fifths distrusted the English as allies; the average enlisted man held British soldiers in low regard as fighters (below the Finns, though above the Japanese, Chinese, and Italians, who were considered the poorest).[37] That soldiers had so little regard for Japanese soldiers as fighters was a cause for alarm in its own right.

Osborn now folded all these concerns together to produce the European Theatre of Operations (ETO) Planning Survey I. The survey queried a cross-section of US troops in England about their backgrounds and time in the army, but also about their interactions with British civilians, British soldiers, and their knowledge of the country and its wartime sacrifices. It included questions (common to many of these surveys) about radio preferences and listening habits, books read, sports played, magazines they liked, and whether they drank beer or liquor (and how much), wrote letters, watched movies, and dated British women.[38]

The findings of the ETO Planning Survey I played an important role in altering the political calculus inside the War Department. It showed that US troops were appallingly uninformed about a great many matters. Brehon B. Somervell, the army's principal logistician and the second or third most powerful man in the organization after Marshall, was so concerned that he issued a capacious secret directive ordering additional troop surveys and broader dissemination of the research program's services and findings. Special Services was to continue "to employ to the fullest extent all media at its command," including shortwave radio programming, orientation and information films, publications, pamphlets, news maps, and posters.[39] Marshall concurred, while also encouraging the dissemination of materials to illustrate Japanese soldiers' tenacity and ferocity and the difficulty of the fight in the Pacific. The White House requested that it start receiving regular reports too.[40]

Osborn now had concurrences not only for his research activities, but for an entire information and education program.[41] Somervell's broad directive had finally opened the door. His team set to producing two-page summaries of their reports to be disseminated to time-pressed generals; on the left-hand side was a brief description of the conclusions reached from the data, on the right charts illustrating statistical findings. As word spread, more requests started to come in from the field, as well as from other government agencies. Consequently, 40 or so studies were undertaken in the first five months of 1943, covering topics as disparate as: job assignments, race relations, officers and leadership, officer selection, absence without leave and desertion, facilities, leisure time and entertainment, transportation, and the Women's Army Auxiliary Corps. In the spring of 1943, the branch was granted exclusive authority to conduct surveys in the field.[42] By the summer, researchers were not only working in the ETO and the US, but also in Australia and New Guinea, at the request of Douglas MacArthur, and in the Middle East, at the behest of Lewis Brereton.

THE SUCCESS OF THE MORALE PROGRAM

The success of the applied morale research program depended not only on the goodwill and cooperation of commanders, but on the willingness of citizen soldiers to divulge their experiences, opinions, predilections, fantasies, fears, hopes, and pains. To elicit this valuable information, research teams in the field promised personnel strict anonymity. Survey respondents were told not to sign their names or include their serial numbers; completed answer sheets were to be shuffled to ensure responses could not be traced. No one in the chain of command was to know who had written what, protecting soldiers, but also poorly performing commanding officers, from scrutiny. As one early research memorandum highlighted, the effect was an atmosphere of "frankness and enthusiastic cooperation."[43]

That first Planning Survey could have been completed in twenty minutes, but at the hour mark, all but one or two soldiers were still seated, and a half hour later around a quarter remained when the room had to be cleared. One enlisted man returned with the research staff to their temporary offices and continued to write until long after mess call. "Unlike many of my buddies, I am very concerned with the defeat of the Axis, as I don't think democracy has a chance of working itself out if the Axis wins in the rest of the world," he wrote. "Feeling as I do about the war it is very disheartening to see obvious faults ruining the efficiency of the Army and nullifying the efforts of so many. Many things that go on would be funny if they weren't serious."[44] This inductee was not one of a few thousand respondents, but one of many tens of thousands. Plenty may well have doubted their feedback mattered or that it would even be read. Yet the pain, humour, insights, and rage exhibited across page after handwritten page testified to the eagerness of many to avail themselves of these democratic instruments – to voice their thoughts unfettered. "This is the chance I've been waiting for ever since I got into the army," scrawled one citizen soldier in May 1942, "Nobody can tell me to shut up."[45]

The Morale Branch's work in providing US troops with an outlet for expressing themselves was one of the most important, and less well known, initiatives undertaken by the US Army during the Second World War. Whether troops appreciated what their input meant or how it was used, their responses led to corrective measures across the organization and informed a breadth of Army- and Navy-wide procedures, policies, and programming. Researchers worked closely with the Selective Service System, and later with the Surgeon General, to produce psychiatric screening techniques to identify recruits and soldiers believed most susceptible to combat psycho-neuroses or neuroses. The physical training program for all incoming enlistees was overhauled after comparative testing. Frank Capra's *Why We Fight* orientation films, shown serially to all US troops, were audience-tested.

The surveys led to efforts to increase pride in outfit, especially in the infantry, including the creation of special infantry badges. The Army Air Force continually updated its training program in light of feedback from surveys. They played a part in establishing a daily cable and radio news service; by the end of the war, the global Armed Forces Radio Service would be broadcasting from over 177 army or navy stations, 54 foreign government and commercial stations, and 149 sound systems. *Yank*, a military magazine with a worldwide circulation that reached 2.5 million, was widely tested by Osborn's team. United Service Organization camp shows, as well as other professional and amateur entertainments, were, like Capra's films, troop-tested. The demand for off-hours education was picked up in the reports, resulting in the planet's largest correspondence school. With a million enrolled students, the US Armed Force Institute educated troops stationed in England, Italy, Alaska, the Philippines, India, Puerto Rico, Panama, New Caledonia, and elsewhere. The announcement of the Allies' policy of "unconditional surrender" was okayed by Osborn after survey testing. Even the veteran's return to civilian life was, in some ways, determined by the work of Osborn and his researchers: the "point score" system that shaped demobilization priorities for all troops was based on what the soldiers themselves considered important, while various studies, one a worldwide cross-sectional survey, were conducted to help prepare for the veteran's readjustment post-conflict.

CONCLUSION

Beyond the efficacy of any one program or policy, these instruments in and of themselves helped military command to lead, manage, and unify through data, statistics, and easy to digest charts and graphs. A disparate, heterogenous, and sometimes blasé, displeased, and agitated force was turned into a war-winning tool. Osborn's research team never lost sight of who they served; their ultimate client was the high command. Osborn had the ears of Stimson, Marshall, and other high-ranking War Department officials. Nevertheless, he had to take great care in navigating the bureaucratic politics of the army. As he put it himself:

> While the directive which General Marshall wrote [authorizing research studies] personally stated that I was to report to General Marshall and to the Chiefs of the three forces on matters of policy, it was a matter of constant manoeuvring to do it in a way whereby I would not offend the Director of Personnel, Army Service Forces [ASF], and particularly the Control Division of the ASF, who were my bosses in the chart.[46]

To the chagrin of the team, the Research Branch never became part of the formal decision-making chain. Yet, by the final two years of the war, Osborn found himself "practically with no boss" and he was eventually elevated to the General Staff, thus becoming one of the twelve men leading the organization.

Even as his authority and responsibilities expanded, Osborn still had to contact commanding generals personally for his research team to carry out even a simple pre-test or a minor study on their posts.[47] As Richard V. Damms's chapter demonstrates, such frictions were not uncommon during America's war. Furthermore, the order that granted his division a monopoly on research was also a burden, as requests came in for studies tangential to or unrelated to morale. A refusal to engage with these demands, the branch's leadership feared, might put an end to the whole affair.[48] At the same time, it appeared that some in command conceived of their questionnaires as "an orientation medium rather than a fact finding tool." Many questions were deleted on the grounds that "they would start the men thinking,"[49] a "double error" in the eyes of the research team; the soldiers had opinions, the team constantly pointed out, whether they were asked about them or not.[50]

Command's control of the endeavour remained paramount throughout. The very first planning survey had revealed substantial animosity among enlisted personnel toward their commanding officers. Researchers continued to study leadership issues stateside, but in the more active overseas theatres they were forbidden from asking enlisted men what they thought of officer practices and privileges – the potential for a loss of control and authority was considered too great, making it impossible for the team to study an essential element of combat performance. The persistence and extension of segregationist

Jim Crow policies in the Army was another issue that Command showed little interest in tackling head on. One Black soldier wrote:

> Is Democracy suppose[d] to be for the White or Colored? It cant [sic] possibly be the later [sic]. What are we, am I, really fighting for? If its [sic] what the newspapers claim, I cant [sic] appreciate it, nor the fact I'm segregated on a so-called Negro post, the street cars, theatres, restaurants in a so-called democratic country. There must be a hidden reason … Has Germany treated the Jews more harshly than the Southern and Northern "cracker" treated the American Negro? Of course the answer is yes but they never claimed to be a true Democracy and we have … They have me in the army and there is very little I can do about it, but at least please advance some more logical and truthful slogan than "Fighting for Democracy." How can one fight for something one knows little or nothing about? Something that is the privilege of the chosen few?[51]

Offering troops the opportunity to articulate opinions, about leadership, segregation, and other matters, may not always have immediately changed realities on the ground. But it did help to shape perceptions and reassure the soldier "that somewhere the "brass" is interested in his welfare, [and] is making an effort to plan." In many cases, Command did act with alacrity to address the issues raised in the morale surveys. In others, it maintained its power to place other considerations above the morale of the troops. The evidence from the fighting performance of the US Army in the Second World War suggests that they got this balance right more often than they got it wrong.

NOTES

1 This chapter uses data generated via the Zooniverse.org platform, whose development is funded by generous support, including from the National Science Foundation, NASA, the Institute of Museum and Library Services, UKRI, a Global Impact Award from Google, and the Alfred P. Sloan Foundation. The American Philosophical Society and Rockefeller Archive Center provided the author additional research support. The author wishes to acknowledge research assistance provided by Ivan Snook and the Carnegie Collections archivist Jennifer S. Comins at Columbia University.

2 "Planning Survey 47," 5 February 1942, box 989, entry NM-12 93, RG 330, National Archives and Records Administration, College Park, MD (hereinafter NARA).
3 Anon. respondent 33-1046, Survey 106: Post-War Army Plans (Officers and EM): EM Pretest B4 Form, June 1944, directed by Samuel A. Stouffer for the Research Branch, Information and Education Division, War Department [producer]; Edward J.K. Gitre et al., *The American Soldier in World War II* [distributor], https://americansoldierww2.org/surveys/a/SP106EB4.Q63.F.15926722.
4 Anon. respondent 04-0979, Planning Survey V: Attitudes toward Civilians: Form A, Dec. 1942, https://americansoldierww2.org/surveys/a/PS5A.Q66.F.20729696.
5 In one survey of soldiers stationed in Alaska, 87 per cent responded that they believed that the survey would help win the war if the army heeded it (Samuel A. Stouffer, Edward A. Suchman, Leland C. DeVinney, Shirley A. Star, and Robin M. Williams, Jr, *The American Soldier: Adjustment During Army Life*, vol. 1 [Princeton: Princeton University Press], 5).
6 Special Service Division, *Research in Special Service: Textbook Prepared by the Faculty of the School for Special Research* (Washington DC: Army Service Forces, War Department, May 1943), 2.
7 Samuel E.M. Crocker to Rensis Likert, Quinn McNemar, and Samuel A. Stouffer [draft], 1 October 1941, fol. Psychiatry–Subcommittee on, box 60, entry NM-43 21, RG 225, NARA.
8 See among others, Benjamin Alpers, "This Is the Army: Imagining a Democratic Military in World War II," *Journal of American History* 85, no. 1 (June 1998), 129–63; George H. Roeder Jr, "Censoring Disorder: American Visual Imagery of World War II," in *The War in American Culture: Society and Consciousness during World War II*, ed. Lewis A. Erenberg and Susan E. Hirsch (Chicago: The University of Chicago Press, 1996), 46–70; and Andrew J. Huebner, *The Warrior Image: Soldiers in American Culture from the Second World War to the Vietnam Era* (Chapel Hill: The University of North Carolina Press, 2011), esp. chapter 2.
9 Frederick Osborn, draft memorandum for John C.H. Lee, Subject: Complete separation of Information and Education from Special Services in ETO, 5 March 1945, fol. Osborn, Maj. Gen. Frederick H., box 24, entry NM-43 18, RG 225, NARA.
10 Cf. James T. Sparrow, *Warfare State: World War II Americans and the Age of Big Government* (New York: Oxford University Press, 2011).

11 See Thomas Osborne and Nikolas Rose, "Do the Social Sciences Create Phenomena? The Example of Public Opinion Research," *British Journal of Sociology* 50, no. 3 (September 1999), 367–96.
12 Quoted in Herbert H. Lehman, "A Public Opinion Sustaining Democracy," *Public Opinion Quarterly* 2, no. 1, Special Supplement: Public Opinion in a Democracy (January 1938), 5.
13 George C. Marshall, memorandum for Gens Bryden, Moore, Arnold, 8 April 1941, Subject Files – Morale, reel 268, George C. Marshall Research Library, Lexington, Virginia (hereinafter GCM Library).
14 J.A. Ulio, memorandum for Assistant CoS (ACS), G-1, 18 April 1941, Subject: Public Opinion Survey in the Army, Subject Files – Morale, reel 268, GCM Library.
15 Wade H. Haislip, ACS, memorandum for the Chief of Staff, 25 April 1941, Subject: Public Opinion Survey in the Army, reel 268, GCM Library.
16 S.R. Michkelsen, memorandum for the AG, 23 May 1941, Subject Files: Morale, reel 268, GCM Library.
17 Frederick Osborn, "The Quality of Population," radio broadcast, 1940, fol. Osborn – Radio broadcast – "The Quality of Population," 1940, box Osb.-Papers, "T" – Osb.-Speeches, "D," Frederick Henry Osborn Papers, American Philosophical Society Library, Philadelphia, PA (hereinafter Osborn Papers); Frederick Osborn, "The Comprehensive Program of Eugenics and Its Social Implications," *Living* 1, nos. 2–3, Spring-Summer (May-August 1939), 33.
18 Frederick Osborn to Frederick Keppel, 23 December 1940, fol. 1, box 251, series III.A, Carnegie Corporation of New York Records, 1872–2000, Columbia University Libraries, Rare Book and Manuscript Library, New York, NY (hereinafter Carnegie Records).
19 Karl W. Marks, memorandum for the Director, Control Division, ASF, 15 July 1944, Subject: Subjects Draft of Morale Services Division section for Fiscal Year 1943–44 report of the Commanding General, Army Service Forces, fol. 330.11, 1 Nov 43–Section III (General), box 726, entry NM-12 88, RG 330, NARA.
20 Henry L. Stimson, memorandum for the Adjutant General, 8 March 1941, Subject: Reorganization of the Morale Division, of the Office of The Adjutant General, fol. History of Research Branch to 1946, box 969, RG 330, NARA.
21 Henry Stimson to Frederick Osborn, 12 June 1941, fol. General Frederick H. Osborn, Committee Correspondence from January–December 1941, box 60, entry NM-43 21, RG 225, NARA.
22 Frederick Osborn to Grenville Clark, 3 Sept. 1941, fol. MORALE – (Gen. Osborn), box 8, entry NM-43 21, RG 225, NARA.

23 "This Is What the Soldiers Complain About," LIFE, 18 August 1941, 16–17.
24 Kent Roberts Greenfield, memorandum for General Charles L. Bolte, Subject: Document Desired by the Secretary of War, 23 September 1946, Subject Files: Morale, reel 25, GCM Library.
25 Robert M. Lester to Samuel E.M. Crocker, 16 October 1941, fol. 1, box 192, series III.A, Carnegie Records.
26 Samuel A. Stouffer, memorandum for the Chief of Special Service, 9 June 1942, Subject: Some Reflections on the Program of the Research Division, fol. History of Research Branch to 1946, box 969, RG 330, NARA.
27 Samuel A. Stouffer to Frederick Osborn, 20 October 1941, fol. History of Research Branch to 1946, box 969, RG 330, NARA.
28 "Draft: Highlights of the Planning Survey," n.d., fol. Planning Survey I, Oct 41, box 2, entry A1 92, RG 330, NARA.
29 E.W. Burgess to Robert T. Crane, 17 December 1941, fol. 6128, Correspondence, 1941–1943, box 498, Series 1.82, RG 2, Accession 2, FA021, Social Science Research Council Records, Rockefeller Archive Center, Sleepy Hollow, NY.
30 Samuel A. Stouffer, "Notes to Brig. Gen. Osborn," n.d., fol. Planning Survey I, Oct 41, box 2, entry A1 92, RG 330, NARA.
31 Frank Keppel, "Study of Information and Education Activities in World War II," 6 April 1946, 18, fol. 1, Keppel, Frank – "Study of Information and Education Activities in World War II," box Co – L, Osborn Papers.
32 Frederick Osborn, memorandum for the Assistant Chief of Staff, G-1, 9 March 1941, Subject Conduct of Planning Surveys, fol. Planning Survey I, Oct 41, box 2, entry A1 92, RG 330, NARA.
33 See generally, John D. Millet, *The Organization and Role of the Army Service Forces* (1954; Washington, DC: Center of Military History United States Army, 1998).
34 Dwight D. Eisenhower, memorandum for the Adjutant General, 9 August 1942, Subject Files: Morale, reel 25, GCM Library.
35 Eisenhower to Frederick Osborn, "Paraphrase of Message, General Eisenhower to General Osborn," 5 August 1942, fol. "Plaudits" and "Testimonials," box 970, entry NM-12 89, RG 330, NARA.
36 Dwight D. Eisenhower, memorandum for the Adjutant General, 9 August 1942, Subject Files: Morale, reel 25, GCM Library.
37 Research Branch, Special Service Division, "Attitudes of Troops Toward the War: Based on Planning Surveys of Representative Cross Sections of Troops in the Army Ground Forces and Air Forces," Report no. 28, 8 September 1942, Subject Files – Morale, reel 25, GCM Library.

38 "History of the Research Branch, Information and Education Division, War Department Special Staff," 1 February 1946, 53, fol. History of Army Research to 1 Feb 46, box 970, entry NM-12 89, RG 330 NARA.

39 Breton Somervell, memorandum for General Marshall, 6 October 1942, Subject Files – Morale, reel 25, GCM Library.

40 George C. Marshall, memorandum for General Somervell, 6 October 1942, Subject Files – Morale, reel 25, GCM Library; Isador Lubin to Brehon Somervell, 6 November 1942, fol. "Plaudits" and "Testimonials," box 970, entry NM-12 89, RG 330, NARA.

41 "History of the Research Branch, Information and Education Division, War Department Special Staff," 19.

42 MR 1–10, 5 March 1943, superseding MR 1–10, 21 October 1941. See Charles Dollard, memorandum for the Director, Special Services Division, 21 May 1943, fol. History of Army Research to 1 Feb 46, box 969, entry NM-12 89, RG 330 NARA.

43 John B. Stanley, memorandum for the Officer in Charge of the Planning Division, Subject: Activities and Accomplishments of the Research Division, fol. Planning Survey Dr S.A. Stouffer (Semi-monthly reports), box 37, entry NM-43 18, RG 225, NARA.

44 "Planning Survey 47."

45 Anon. respondent 01-0304, Planning Survey II: Attitudes in Three Divisions: Form A-1, May 1942, https://americansoldierww2.org/surveys/a/PS2A1.QX.F.20722555.

46 A.M. Patch, et al., interview with Frederick Osborn, 8 October 1945, fol. 330.11, box 726, entry NM-12 88, RG 330, NARA.

47 "History of the Research Branch, Information and Education Division, War Department Special Staff," 15.

48 Dollard, memorandum for the Director, Special Services Division, 21 May 1943.

49 "History of the Research Branch, Information and Education Division, War Department Special Staff," 31; Harold F. Gosnell, interview with Donald Young, Consultant, Research Branch, SS 4/26/43, 27 April 1943, fol. War Information Services, War Dept., Special Services Division, Research Branch, 1943–45, box 23, The Papers of Harold F. Gosnell, Manuscript Division, Library of Congress, Washington, DC.

50 "History of the Research Branch, Information and Education Division, War Department Special Staff," 31.

51 Anon. respondent 11-1430, Survey 32: Attitudes of and toward Negroes, Negro Form, March 1943, https://americansoldierww2.org/surveys/a/S32N.Q78.F.15807235.

THEME THREE

"People's Wars" as Drivers of Change

6

Health Care and Disease in Italy's War, 1940–1945

Fabio De Ninno

During the Second World War, Italians experienced a crisis of continuously deteriorating health conditions, which led to a massive number of deaths among the civilian population. In many ways, the emergence of this crisis is understandable: civilians accounted for nearly two-thirds of global wartime deaths, and war is extremely toxic for public health, particularly so for women and children.[1] The effect of health problems on civilian life during the Second World War is a major factor in understanding the functioning and experience of societies during the conflict;[2] a growing body of research analyzes the health-care consequences for civilians and soldiers alike.[3] Research about the world wars and health care is continuously developing, with the responses of states to the health-care emergency caused by the First World War receiving particular scholarly attention.[4] Health-care scholarship for the Second World War is more nascent but it has established that the conflict was a watershed moment; it played a fundamental role in instituting European universal health-care systems post-1945.[5]

In spite of this growth in research, studies of health care in the Italian experience of the Second World War are limited. This is surprising given the country's status both as a major combatant and as the site of intense combat between 1943 and 1945. Instead, studies of health care are mainly limited to the First World War, when health-care difficulties related to the war (poor diet, distribution problems, limited access to medical treatments), induced a peak in the number of deaths caused by infectious diseases.[6] Discussion of aspects of health care during the Second World War only appears as an element of more general histories of Italian health care where coverage is characterized by the lack of archival research or statistical data.[7] Where it does exist, primary source-based analysis of the problems of wartime Italian health care has often emerged only in local histories of the conflict,[8] or studies dedicated to specific diseases, like malaria.[9]

This chapter rectifies the lack of rigorous assessment of Italian wartime health care, delivering an important contribution to our understanding of the effect of infectious diseases during the Second World War. By using previously neglected primary sources, the chapter demonstrates, for the first time, the interaction between fascist healthcare administration, regional differences, and the effect of military operations and enemy occupation on the civilian population. The lack of such a rigorous assessment of the effect of diseases on the Italian population between 1940 and 1945 until now has impeded historians' understanding of the civilian experience during the conflict; it has also hidden the real number of casualties caused by the war. This chapter demonstrates that the war had a considerable effect on the health of Italians. Dynamics relating to health care played an integral part in the way Italy navigated the war. They also drove a desire for fundamental post-war change in the state's approach to national health care.

THE SYSTEMIC WEAKNESSES OF ITALIAN HEALTH CARE

Wars trigger a series of complex mechanisms that directly affect the health of a population. They invite a plethora of social, physical, psychological, and environmental consequences, while contact between civilian populations and militaries increases the spread of infectious diseases.[10] Deteriorating economic conditions, the effects of occupation, and mass evacuations can all affect the health of the populace, leading to a higher incidence of death and disease and even the return of diseases that had previously been under control, such as tuberculosis.[11]

During the First World War, there were around 600,000 excess deaths in Italy compared with peacetime, with the effect of tuberculosis being particularly lethal, causing at least 73,000 deaths during the war.[12] The effect of diseases was so severe that it has retained an important place in the popular memory of the conflict.[13] After the war, the "Spanish flu" also affected a much weakened population, causing another 300,000 deaths and possibly the same number of indirect losses.[14] The high total of deaths during the Great War is evidence of a country heavily exposed to the problem of infectious diseases, due to the fragility of the national health-care system, poor hygienic conditions, and the poverty of its population.[15]

In 1940, Italian health care was still in the early stages of transforming into a welfare system and lacked a centralized and organic organization. During the interwar period, fascist eugenics had spurred a drive to create a stronger and healthier population, necessary to realize Mussolini's political projects. Greater attention was paid to maternal and child health, with the institution of the *Opera Nazionale maternità e infanzia* (National Institution for Maternity and Childhood) in 1925 and the *Enti Comunali di Assistenza* (ECA, Municipal Offices for Assistance) in 1937.[16] Nevertheless, health care remained a mixed system of public and private assistance, split into public and private hospitals and charitable foundations. At the central level, there was no specific agency for health care, which was controlled by the Ministry of the Interior (MoI), through the *Direzione generale della sanità pubblica* (General Directorate for Public Health), under which control of the Italian Red Cross also fell. Health administration was highly fragmented and controlled at the provincial level by the local prefectures.[17]

In July 1944, a report of the Allied Control Commission (ACC), the authority in charge of the civilian administration of occupied Italy, stated that the lack of a national agency for welfare was primarily responsible for the chaotic conditions of welfare and health-care assistance.[18] Indeed, the Italian health-care system did not provide universal assistance and hospitals, and clinical departments were not attached to a national structure capable of coordinating the provision of countrywide health care. As a result, the system was not prepared for the upcoming war and the subsequent deterioration in health-care conditions.[19] The lack of preparedness of Italian health care was part of the more general deficiencies of Italian civil defence.[20] It can thus be considered in the same context as the lack of preparedness for full-scale mobilization discussed in Nicoló Da Lio's chapter.[21]

High-ranking health-care officials were aware of the problems. On 29 May 1940, less than two weeks from entering into war, the Directorate of the Red Cross admitted that at least 400,000 beds were necessary for wartime, but that only 200,000 were available.[22] By 1942, the number of available beds had expanded to 335,000, but only by requisitioning spaces from psychiatric hospitals (74,000), orphanages (11,000), and those granted by municipal first aid stations (13,000). These improvised structures were usually inappropriate for the care of wartime diseases due to the lack of proper facilities.[23] The war also led to reduced financial resources available for health care. On 27 July 1940, the MoI issued a directive (n. 13012) urging cuts in expenditure for public assistance. As financial requirements increased for local administrations, they faced fiscal constraints rather than expansion. In September 1940, for example, the Prefecture of Genoa complained that local hospitals were already stopping the building of new departments. According to the local prefect, money could not be found by redirecting ordinary expenditures, because prices for consumables necessary for the everyday activity of hospitals continued to rise.[24]

During the following years, the financial situation worsened. The MoI's control over health-care expenditure became more restrictive; all work on infrastructure that was not considered urgent was blocked by Rome. On 15 April 1942, Law 432 was enacted, further restricting the financial autonomy of local administrations and blocking civilian fees for hospitalization and assistance, leading to further shortages of financial resources.[25] This left administrators in a very difficult position. To provide the necessary expansion of departments or increase the number of beds, or even to repair the damage done by bombing, local administrations were compelled to act in a way typical of fascist Italy's polycratic system: ask for direct help from a member of the Fascist Party hierarchy or appeal to Mussolini himself.[26] Nevertheless, such interventions were sporadic, and usually local authorities were on their own. The situation worsened with the growing difficulties of the Italian war economy, leading to shortages of materials even for hospitals that had financial resources and the authorization of the government to expand their infrastructure.[27]

With central authority determined to reduce expenditure, health-care effectiveness depended largely on the capacity and creativity of local administrations, creating regional divides in the efficiency of the system. For example, Bologna saw a rapid increase in the number of beds available for hospitalization, from 7,300 in 1939–40 to 10,000 in 1945, this during a period when the average population of the city fell by 2,000 inhabitants.[28] In contrast, during 1944 Milan experienced a chronic scarcity of available spaces for those wounded and sick recovering.[29]

Large cities, often subject to air raids, were the first to pay the price for the lack of finances and hospital places. In October 1941, the Prefecture of Naples organized a meeting to discuss child health care in the city, concluding that first aid stations were already insufficient and that the number of available paediatricians did not allow proper home care for children.[30] The city hospitals were already experiencing difficulties in buying medical supplies and drugs. Pellegrini Hospital reported that expenditure on these items had grown from 167,182 lire in 1937 to 201,348 in 1939 and 287,866 in 1941. Much of the growth was caused by inflated drug prices, which in some cases had increased tenfold.[31] Also, in rural areas assistance was poor, with small countryside villages usually relying on a single local doctor for basic assistance to the community. During the war, these doctors were often called up for armed service, leaving their community inadequately provided for. For example, in May 1943, the local doctor of Conca Campana, a small village north of Naples, was called up by the army. The local service was assigned to the doctor of Roccamonfina, a nearby village, but he was only able to visit Conca Campana twice a week. The municipality of Conca protested to the Naples Prefecture because his presence was insufficient to meet the health needs of the population.[32]

Another important aspect connected to the bombing was the need to evacuate hospitals. As air attacks increased in intensity in the autumn of 1942, Fascist authorities organized the mass evacuation of cities. But the process was chaotic and mismanaged.[33] Hospitals were often near Allied targets, so a top priority became evacuating medical departments to avoid precious equipment from being destroyed. The challenges involved in moving hospitals were significant. In early 1942, the Cotugno Hospital, the main site for the care of infectious diseases in Naples, was repeatedly hit by bombs because of its position near the strategic target of Capodichino's airport. The structure hosted nearly 200 patients, with a further capacity for 200 in case of possible epidemics. After taking note of the bomb damage, the prefect decided to evacuate the hospital.[34] In June, this move had still not been completed, because the owners of the Caputi Hospital, a private clinic designed to host the Cotugno's evacuated departments, opposed the transfer, fearing possible economic losses.[35] Finally, the hospital was moved into the psychiatric hospital of San Giorgio a Cremano, but the new place was inadequate because it lacked sterile environments and adequate sewers. Indeed, in January 1943, the carabinieri reported the risk that the existing cesspools of the hospital could soon transform into "a breeding ground for microbes dangerous for health."[36]

Evacuation was a complex and time-consuming activity that could result in long-term reductions of hospital efficiency. In 1944, the otolaryngology department of Vicenza Hospital was moved to Braganze and later to Montecchio Petraclino. Between 1940 and 1943, the hospital saw a constant increase in the number of patients and surgeries, but in 1944, according to the director of the department, evacuation caused the hospital's activity to diminish rapidly (see table 6.1).

Civilian evacuations also affected health conditions and the spread of disease. By May 1944, over 2.3 million refugees had left their homes in territories held by the German puppet state of the Italian Social Republic (*Repubblica Sociale Italiana* [RSI]), because of property damage and food scarcity.[37] This increased the burden on the health-care system of the areas into which refugees were evacuated, which often were not prepared for such a huge influx of people. In December 1941, Giovanni Petragni, chief of the *Direzione generale della sanità pubblica* (General Directorate for Public Health), after a visit to the recently bombed province of Brindisi, produced an alarming report on the health-care conditions in the area. Hygienic conditions were extremely precarious, because the civilians fleeing the city were moved into inadequate shelters. This was due to the primitive state of sanitation in the rural areas surrounding Brindisi, which left the refugees in dirty and overcrowded accommodation. The bombing had also destroyed the city's hospital, leaving the entire province without adequate medical infrastructure.[38] Incredibly, local authorities played down the sanitation problems, proposing to move the evacuees into improvised shacks.[39] In reality, worsening sanitary conditions remained a constant in the life of Italian refugees during the war, making them a persistent source of concerns for the local authorities. In April 1944, the podestà (chief magistrate of a commune) of Saletto, a small village in the province of Padua, reported the case of Anita V., a thirty-three-year-old woman evacuated from Pescara. Anita was infected by tuberculosis and was living in a two-room apartment with sixteen other refugees. According to Saletto's local doctor, she would have to immediately be sent to a clinic or she would infect her flatmates. Nevertheless, the municipal authorities did not have the necessary resources to allow her to be admitted to the local hospital.[40]

Table 6.1
Activity of the Vicenza Otolaryngology Department, 1939–45

Year	Patients	Days of hospital stay	Surgeries
1939	729	7,705	705
1940	646	6,828	567
1941	998	10,549	1,029
1942	1,330	11,524	1,203
1943	1,589	16,025	1,491
1944	939	11,114	893
1945	1,043	14,095	1,433

The effect of population movements on the diffusion of disease in wartime Italy was so significant that a post-war study on the diffusion of tuberculosis found that civilian evacuations were responsible for shifting infectious diseases from city to countryside. Indeed, families usually moved sick people to rural areas, to keep them away from the stress caused by enemy air raids. In the northern industrial cities of Genova, Milan, and Turin, accelerated evacuation during 1943 meant that fatalities from tuberculosis decreased while increasing in the surrounding provinces. In 1945, when refugees came back to the cities, there was an upsurge in deaths caused by tuberculosis: 32 per cent in Turin, 30 per cent in Milan, and 11 per cent for Padua.[41]

Refugees also paid the price for the administrative chaos that affected Italian civil defence. ECAs were responsible for financing health care for the citizens of their municipality. It was common, however, for local ECAs to refuse to pay for assistance once refugees had moved on to another city or town. The heavy economic pressures caused by the war were simply too great for many ECAs to handle. By 1943, the conflicts between different administrations were so widespread that the MoI had to issue a directive (n. 35878, 13 May 1943) ordering municipalities to pay for refugees' medical, midwifery, and pharmaceutical assistance. Nevertheless, local authorities continued to refuse financial support. For example, in September 1943, refugees from Palermo were unable to get a refund for health expenditure in Milan.[42]

In Allied-occupied areas, the situation improved, under the supervision of the ACC, which, during the occupation of Sicily, had overseen a reorganization of the health-care system. It shifted from a centralized to a decentralized administration, and also created *Uffici provinciali di sanità pubblica* (provincial public health offices), charged with governing all health-care aspects in their jurisdiction, putting an end to the polycratic chaos of the Fascist era. In 1944, when administration was transferred back to Italian authorities, the system was maintained and was used by the Italian government as a benchmark to study the structure of the local branches of the future ministry of health care.[43]

In contrast, in the territories held by the RSI these problems continued for the rest of the war. The "feudalization" of the administrative structure of the RSI made it impossible for the central authorities to fully control the welfare activities of provinces and municipalities. Still, at the end of 1944, despite repeated directives from the MoI,[44] municipalities continued to oppose payments for refugees' health services.[45] In one stark example from February 1945, Piera G., a pregnant woman from Rome, was hospitalized in Milan, but the municipality refused to pay the hospital for the service, because the expenditure had to be charged to the MoI.[46] Moreover, according to Italian law, expenditures for assistance had to be anticipated by hospitals and local administrations. However, often their budgets were insufficient to meet the rising costs caused by the war. The RSI administration was disarticulated by the civil war and German occupation, and the ministry proved unable to cope with the everyday communications to transfer money and authorize expenditures for recovery. At one point, a hospital in Reggio Emilia complained to the ministry that the financial situation was so precarious that it "can't wait until the end of war to obtain the refunds."[47]

A North-South divide also characterized access to medicinal drugs for Italian people. Before the war, the Italian pharmaceutical industry depended on imports. With the war ending supplies from Britain and America, many modern medicines like insulin and antibiotics were not available in Italy, at least until the Allied invasion. As a consequence, territories liberated by the Anglo-American forces could access a limited supply of modern drugs, while in German-occupied zones the scarcity of antibiotics was endemic, undermining attempts to cure infectious diseases.[48]

The scarcity of money, adequate hospital places, and medicines led to reduced services. By 1941, hospitals and clinics were reporting difficulties in distributing vaccines, even those that had been easy to access in pre-war years. For example, access to tuberculosis vaccines dramatically worsened in the province of Siena during 1940 in spite of the fact that vaccinations had been widely available during 1938–39. This was caused by the lack of transportation needed to distribute vaccines and the reduced availability of specialized personnel. Establishing proper coordination with the provincial clinics was also a problem because many doctors were away on military service. As a result, during 1940–41, vaccinations were limited to people capable of reaching the agency locations, thus reducing distribution significantly: in 1941, only 20 per cent of vaccines were distributed or available, compared with 1939.[49] By 1943, hospitals commonly did not have basic medications or even the materials (e.g., non-medical hospital supplies: dressings, bed linen, etc.) necessary for everyday activities. In July 1943, a report from the podestà of Sessa Aurunca, a small city north of Naples, complained that the local hospital had thirty beds, but only enough sanitized linen to cover ten of them. The lack of linen meant that the administration had to reject requests for hospitalization, and the empty spaces also resulted in a loss of income for the hospital.[50]

The armistice of 8 September 1943 represented a watershed. In German-occupied territories, financial and material means continued to diminish dramatically. A report of February 1944, from Gorizia Hospital to the MoI of the RSI, remarked that the structure was unable to meet the growing health-care difficulties, which saw an upsurge after the armistice, due to the intensified bombing campaign and the growing number of people injured by firearms incidents.[51] At the end of the war, nearly all Italian hospitals were bankrupt and lacked the basic materials they needed to function properly.[52]

THE IMPACT OF MILITARY OPERATIONS

Bombing raids were particularly relevant to the crisis of Italian health care; heavy damage started to occur almost immediately after the Italian declaration of war. On 17 June 1940, the French Air Force attacked Milan. During the raid, the local clinic of Vialba was mistaken for a barracks and hit by three bombs, which luckily did not explode. During 1943, Milan experienced the destruction of two major hospitals: Fatebenefratelli and Niguarda.[53] That year marked an intensification of the bombing and destruction of health-care infrastructure. Pellegrini Hospital, located in Naples city centre, was hit for the first time on 4 August 1943, resulting in the destruction of one recovery room and damage to a second, although there were no victims among the patients because they were evacuated in time. On 6 September, a second raid hit the hospital, and an entire section of the building collapsed, destroying two other recovery rooms and heavily damaging the emergency room, the surgery department, and the medical plaster room. As a result, activity in the hospital had to be suspended temporarily.[54] The same thing was happening in Turin. The major hospitals of Molinette and San Lazzaro were near the Fiat plant of Lingotto and were repeatedly hit during air attacks on the city.[55] On 8 November 1943, the San Lazzaro was heavily damaged by bombing, and its service interrupted. The day after the event, the chief of the hospital told the prefecture that he was unable to find the staff to restart activity, or even to take care of the surviving medical equipment.[56]

Due to the fear of enemy air raids, health workers in some cases started to refuse to work; local authorities experienced great difficulties in keeping even intact hospitals running. In June 1943, a report on the hospital of Pozzuoli noted that available local doctors preferred not to work continuously at the hospital, but to do so only after enemy air attacks despite the economic incentives offered by the fascist authorities. Consequently, the report acknowledged that it was difficult to organize emergency services and called for the prefecture to intervene to force doctors to work.[57]

The next stage in the destruction of the health-care infrastructure began with the Allied invasion of Sicily and the subsequent campaign that raged across the peninsula, in particular around the Gustav and Gothic German defence lines. Damage caused by front-line activity was concentrated south of the Gothic line, which was only breached by Anglo-American troops in the spring of 1945. Nevertheless, the destruction was considerable: between Sicily and Tuscany, 292 of the 930 hospitals active before the war (31.3 per cent) were damaged, costing a total of 758 million lire. This wave of destruction was not distributed evenly across the provinces, however; in Campania, 62 out of 111 hospitals were damaged (55.8 per cent); in Abruzzi and Molise, 19 out of 34 (55.8 per cent); in Lazio, 68 out of 138 (49.2 per cent); and in Tuscany, 59 out of 130 (45.3 per cent).[58]

The advance of the frontline through an area represented a cataclysmic event for regional health care. The destruction was particularly bad in the province of Naples, where 47 hospitals suffered a total of 270 million lire of damage, because of the combination of bombing and combat. In Tuscany, the greatest number of hospitals damaged (29 of 59) were in the province of Arezzo, because the provincial capital was a major railway junction and was subject to heavy fighting, leaving a third of the city destroyed. Between January and May 1944, the town of Terracina was caught between the rear of the Battle of Monte Cassino and the Anzio beachhead; it suffered accordingly. The local hospital was destroyed, and the nearest functioning alternative was in Rome. Meanwhile, civilians blamed the spread of malaria on flooding instigated by the retreating German forces.[59] By January 1945, the municipality was still unable to replace the hospital and had only activated an emergency service, insufficient to support a population that was 80 per cent infected by malaria and under threat of a typhus epidemic.[60] The destruction of the health-care infrastructure also directly affected preventive medicine. During early 1944, medical authorities in Campania and Puglia struggled to deal with an outbreak of smallpox. Much of the problem was because of the lack of proper facilities to distribute and conserve vaccines due to the collateral damage caused by ongoing combat.[61]

Behind the frontlines, Italians also had to coexist with two different occupation forces and their respective policies. In both cases, hospitals and clinics used by the civilian population were requisitioned, but the German occupation, which was underpinned by a massive exploitation and looting of Italian resources, was particularly problematic for public health. It further worsened the already precarious situation of RSI health care.[62] For example, in 1944, the Rizzoli Orthopaedic Institute of Bologna was requisitioned by the Germans; the number of patients was halved almost immediately, dropping from 6,450 in 1943 to 3,111 in 1944.[63] At the Careggi Hospital in Florence, the Germans initially requisitioned only part of the structure, but took over more of the structure as the occupation wore on. Even more important, they started to confiscate medicines, vaccines, ambulances, and even basic materials like gauze and disinfectant.[64] The German occupiers also had very little regard for local patients. On 2 July 1944, the hospital of Castelpulci, near Florence, was occupied by a German field hospital. The male section of the hospital was promptly ordered to evacuate; sixty children and fifty-three sick adults were forcibly moved to the psychiatric hospital of San Salvi in Florence, where they were left in precarious conditions. Immediately after their departure, the doctors were also evacuated, and the Germans razed the hospital.[65] The German requisitions exacerbated the general scarcity of drugs, already rare due to the deficits of Italian production. As a result, as a report from the prefecture of occupied Siena stated, "the lack of medical products is heavily resented in the hospitals, clinics and by the population."[66]

The Germans were also responsible for the destruction of the swamp reclamations in the province of Littoria. The goal was to cause an epidemic of malaria among Allied troops at the Anzio beachhead. These actions also affected the Italian provincial population, however. The number of cases of malaria in the province of Littoria reportedly grew from 1,217 in 1943 to 54,929 in 1944, dropping only slightly to 47,212 in 1945.[67] Allied forces during their passage through the area used dichlorodiphenyltrichloroethane (DDT) to disinfect the countryside, but the plague of infected mosquitoes spread again as soon as the spraying ceased. During the summer of 1944, people travelling in the area of Littoria risked certain contagion and serious illness.[68] Similar events blighted the province of Grosseto, where destruction inflicted by the Wehrmacht also caused a malaria outbreak. Even as late as autumn 1945, local authorities were struggling to contain the contagion; the lack of pesticides also meant that the plague spread to the city, infecting over 1,000 people.[69]

The use of DDT by the Allied forces is indicative of the completely different approach undertaken compared with that of the German forces. The Allied Military Government of Occupied Territories (AMGOT), as part of its government functions, had an entire division dedicated to public health. During the advance northwards, Allied forces faced numerous outbreaks of infectious diseases, especially malaria and smallpox and started massive vaccination campaigns. In July 1944, in the province of Naples alone, over 446,000 people were vaccinated against smallpox, and an air-spraying campaign was begun to address the mosquito situation.[70] Massive DDT deployment was conducted in the city, for the first time, to contain a possible typhus epidemic.[71] The same tactic was used to contain lice infestations: from February to March 1944, over 1,750,000 people were treated.[72] Finally, unlike the Germans, who usually requisitioned modes of transport, Allied forces put their ambulances at the service of Italian hospitals.[73] In 1944, the ACC also provided the first culture of *Penicillium notatum*, the bacteria required to produce penicillin, to the Italian health-care authorities.[74] Medicines were initially supplied directly by the Allied authorities, but in November 1944, with the transferring of powers from the ACC to the Italian government, the ENDIMEA (*Ente nazionale distibuzione medicinali alleati*/National agency for the distribution of allied medicines) was instituted. From that moment, Italian health care was able to provide adequate supplies in the liberated territories of central and southern Italy.[75]

During 1943–45, a major health-care problem faced by the occupying forces on both sides was the spread of venereal diseases. This was connected to widespread prostitution and the high number of rapes perpetrated against the civilian population.[76] Such contagion was particularly rife in the territories held by the Allied forces. Between October 1943 and December 1944, in Allied-held Italy, over 14,000 women suspected of prostitution were admitted to hospital to receive treatment for venereal diseases.[77] In Campania, where the number of prostitutes was particularly high, the spread of these diseases created a true health-care emergency.[78] According to a report of June 1945, more than 49 per cent of Neapolitan prostitutes were infected by venereal diseases.[79] In Livorno, a major logistical node for the Allied forces in Italy, over 8,000 women between 1944 and 1947 were treated for these types of diseases by the local hospitals.[80] Even in the RSI-held territories, the local authorities struggled to contain the outbreak of venereal diseases, because of the more general difficulties of local health care. The effect was so widespread that, even after the war, health-care authorities had difficulty coping with the diffusion of venereal diseases, which were more common than in pre-war years.[81]

To address the spread of infectious and venereal disease, the Allies instituted serious reforms and offered major support to compensate for the deficiencies of Italian health care and to keep both the civilian populace and their own troops safe. In June 1944, thanks to Allied support, the *Direzione generale della sanita pubblica* restarted its activity, with increased powers and effectiveness.[82] Indeed, already after the occupation of Sicily, the territorial organization of health care was restructured, creating autonomous provincial agencies, in charge of all sanitarian aspects, marking decisive progress in respect to the polycratic chaos of Fascist administration.[83] Allied occupation authorities established effective cooperation with local health-care agencies and worked closely with local doctors to prevent infectious and venereal diseases.[84] Furthermore, in October 1944, the United Nations Relief and Rehabilitation Administration (UNRRA) started a $9 million program for the acquisition and distribution of drugs, medications, and assistance, later expanded during the early post-war years.[85]

THE SPREAD AND MORTALITY OF DISEASES

The coming of the Allied occupation may not have resolved all the health-care problems of the Italian population, but it is plausible to claim that their arrival marked a watershed in the health-care experience of wartime Italy. Until the Anglo-American landings, the Italian population experienced a general decline of its health-care conditions. That trend continued in the German-occupied territories, while in Allied-controlled Italy the situation improved. Some diseases, like malaria, were connected to specific geographical and, as we have seen, military circumstances. To understand the general circumstances described previously, we will analyze the case of tuberculosis, probably the most dangerous infectious disease in wartime Italy.

The incidence of tuberculosis was perceived as a grave health-care threat during the conflict. In May 1942, the anti-tuberculosis agency of Siena described the spread of that disease as characterized by an "undeniable progressive growth of diffusion and mortality starting from 1941 and in the first months of this year." Indeed, infections in 1941 had jumped to 407, from 160 in 1940, and deaths increased from 155 to 180.[86] The situation was similar in Milan: during the war, deaths caused by tuberculosis increased by 33 per cent.[87]

Military, geographical, economic, and social conditions strongly influenced the spread of tuberculosis. According to a 1948 study, Turin reached the peak for tuberculosis mortality during 1942, with 10.12 deceased for every 10,000 inhabitants, against 9.27 during 1939. In the following years, the mortality per 10,000 decreased: 6.27 in 1943, 6.70 in 1944, and 8.42 in 1945. The author of the study concluded that the "challenges of wartime caused a worsened mortality that remained restricted to a few years."[88] In reality, much of this apparent decrease was caused by the fact that children, women, and the elderly proved more vulnerable to the circulating diseases, and were fleeing the city to avoid the threat of bombing. As a result, the number of people more vulnerable to infectious diseases increased in rural areas, where their condition as refugees further increased their vulnerability. Indeed, the small city of Novara, which was less than 100 kilometres from Turin and which was used by Milanese and Torinesi to escape the bombing, saw a 200 per cent increase in deaths among the local population. Between 1940 and 1945, the city hospital reported a total of 1,008 deaths from tuberculosis, with an acceleration in 1943, when the arrivals of refugees from larger cities increased.[89]

A very important location for the diffusion of tuberculosis was Rome. As the city was considered a safe haven from bombing, it was not evacuated until 1943. It thus became an attractive location for refugees from southern cities under air attack. By 1942–43, the population was experiencing a general scarcity of food supplies, with consequent detrimental effects on health. After the Anzio landing, the capital was just at the rear of the German frontline and was subject to intense air attacks; this made supplying the city difficult. Then, in 1944, more people from rural areas south of the city reached the capital; in many cases, these refugees brought diseases with them, such as malaria.[90] Worsened economic and living conditions led to an enormous increase in mortality rates from tuberculosis, in particular among the male population. According to a post-war survey, wartime tuberculosis caused 15,523 deaths in Rome and its mortality increase exceeded that of general mortality 2.6 times: by 1944, the harshest year of the war in the capital, the number of tuberculosis deaths had increased by 125 per cent compared with 1940, while general mortality increased by 48 per cent.[91] The death rates grew particularly during 1943 and 1944; in 1945, numbers began to fall because of the medical support provided by the Allied powers and the partial reactivation of hospitals and clinics.

These numbers are also relevant because they did not correspond with the official post-war statistics. Between 1940 and 1945, according to the Italian National Bureau of Statistics (ISTAT – *Istituto nazionale di statistica*), 10,687 total deaths during the war were caused by tuberculosis.[92] However, according to later research, 246,992 total deaths during the war were caused by tuberculosis. By comparing 1940, the last year of normal health-care conditions, with the period 1941–45, the increase in deaths caused by wartime conditions could be estimated at an average of 27.44 per cent, or 47,492, with a peak in 1942 (+37.02 per cent). These are raw estimates but are useful to understand the deep effect of tuberculosis on Italians during the Second World War.[93]

An analysis of the distribution of tuberculosis deaths in the largest Italian cities (over 100,000 inhabitants) may allow us to understand how the war affected health care in different ways along the peninsula. Southern cities (Naples, Bari, Taranto, Reggio C., Palermo, Catania, Messina, Cagliari) saw a peak in tuberculosis mortality between 1942

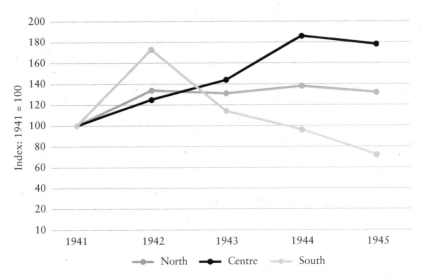

Figure 6.1 Tuberculosis death by geographical area of Italy, 1941–45. Calculations based on Giovanni L'Eltore, "La mortalità per tubercolosi durante la guerra alcune città italiane," *La Lotta contro la Tubercolosi* (May/June 1946), tab. 3.

and 1943, when they were subject to the bombing campaign and the consequences of the Anglo-American invasion. Later, during the Allied occupation, health care improved, leading to a rapid decrease in mortality. Naples, for example, jumped from 1,526 deaths in 1941 to 2,686 in 1942, then declined to 1,767 by 1943. The cities of Central Italy (Rome, Livorno, Florence) saw their peak during 1944, because of the combination of German occupation and Allied advances from the Gustav to the Gothic lines. Florence reached its peak in 1944 with 1,177 deaths, more than double the 557 losses of 1941. Northern Italian cities reached a stable number of deaths in 1942 and maintained about that level across the next three years. This occurred in spite of the massive evacuation of civilians. So, while in large cities the population decreased, the number of deaths remained roughly stable. Finally, Turin and Genoa represent specific cases, northern cities that experienced a mortality peak in 1941 and 1942. Turin, for example, had 1,530 tuberculosis deaths in 1941, declining to 542 in 1943. This drop reflected the more general trend of mortality in the city. Mortality per thousand in Turin jumped from 12.93 in 1940 to 14.42 in 1942; it then declined to 8.92 in 1943. But we must consider that over 160,000 people had left Turin by 1943, from an initial population of around 700,000. Women, children, and the elderly had priority during the evacuation, so many of those more vulnerable to tuberculosis had left by 1943, leaving the population less exposed to disease.[94] A presentation of the data by geographical area underlines these geographical differences (figure 6.1).

We lack reliable estimates of the total number of people infected and killed by infectious diseases during the war. Post-war statistical data on Italian deaths during the conflict is partially unreliable,[95] and health-care statistics are incomplete for the years 1942–46 because they lack information and data for the final three years of the war.[96] Despite the unreliability of available data, the number of recorded deaths clearly shows the rise in deaths caused by disease during the war. Table 6.3 shows the total deaths and their incidence per 10,000 people for the years 1941–46 while comparing them with the average data for the years 1938–40.

It is clear that the excess deaths during the war were caused by infectious diseases , with an average 10 per cent increase. Even more important, that growth was stronger than the general mortality increase for the same years. Indeed, during the war, while total deaths, including for all civilian victims of the war, increased by an average of 5.98 per cent per year, deaths caused by infectious diseases increased by an average of 9.98 per cent: nearly twice the general mortality.

CONCLUSION

During the Second World War, Italians experienced the consequences of total war, including the exacerbation of serious health-care problems. While current scholarship on the issue has concentrated on regional analysis and administrative problems,[97] this chapter has shown that health problems cannot be understood without considering the effect of bombing and land warfare. Also, while the estimates presented about the casualties caused by diseases are very conservative, it is evident that the effect of disease on the Italian population during the war grew and was much more consequential than previously considered. According to newly accessed source material, diseases claimed at least 38,672 more victims than in peacetime. This is far higher than official statistics, which give 153,147 total civilian deaths, of which just 99 were due to infectious diseases![98] This huge disparity between official data and the new research undertaken here shows just how deep the effect of the war on the health of Italians truly was.

Table 6.2
Tuberculosis deaths in Rome, 1939–45

	Males			Females		
Year	Total	Per 1,000 people	Index (1939 = 100)	Total	Per 1,000 people	Index (1939 = 100)
1939	788	1.25	100	747	1.11	100
1940	840	1.29	103	765	1.1	99
1941	991	1.48	118	887	1.23	111
1942	1,342	1.95	156	1,161	1.54	139
1943	1,720	2.44	195	1,239	1.58	142
1944	1,990	2.82	225	1,619	2.05	184
1945	1,475	2.09	167	1,221	1.54	193

Table 6.3
Reported deaths caused by infectious diseases in Italy, 1938–46

Year	1938–40 (average)	1941	1942	1943	1944	1945	1946
Total deaths	65,106	67,424	77,181	76,473	73,933	69,191	65,941
Deaths per 10,000 people	147.96	150.4	171	172.3	166.1	154.8	146.6

Table 6.4
Disease-induced mortality and general mortality growth in Italy, 1938–45

	1938–40 (average)	1941	1942	1943	1944	1945
Infectious diseases (1938–40 = 100)	100	101.3	115.57	116.24	112.19	104.6
General mortality (1938–40 = 100)	100	101.2	104.15	111.9	111.4	99.61

One key aspect remains constant. In the Italian "People's War," the performance of the health-care system and the increased rates of mortality caused by infectious diseases demonstrates how unprepared the fascist regime was for a major conflict. The statistics speak to the vulnerability of a society not entirely modernized and limited by an ineffective welfare system. The chapter, much like Nicolò Da Lio's, points to the importance of the civilian experience in understanding the prosecution and the consequences of Italy's war. Indeed, it is not a coincidence that the health-care difficulties experienced by the Italians fundamentally propelled their post-war requests to reform national health care.[99]

The war exposed the vulnerabilities and the limits of the Italian health-care system: an insufficient number of beds, ineffective assistance, and a considerable number of doctors called up for military service, all contributed to a decline in public health between 1940 and 1945.[100] Often left on their own, Italians shared the wartime sense of uncertainty that was common all over Europe during the Second World War. This experience propelled the construction of post-war welfare systems across Europe and paved the way for the creation of universal health-care systems.[101] The health-care reforms introduced by the Allied powers in Sicily showed a different model of administration, which Italian reformers attempted to introduce in Italy. The continuing influence of that model is testified by the reception of the British Beveridge Report and its influence on the construction of Britain's post-war health-care system, with the creation of the National Health Service (1948). This report had a profound impact on the Italian post-war political debate about the future of Italian welfare as well.[102]

After having established a republic (1946), early post-war governments (1946–48), characterized by the unity of all antifascist parties, conducted an intense debate about the possibility of introducing a universal free health-care system, to protect all social classes from the horrors that had emerged during the war.[103] Indeed, a series of parliamentary commissions of the newly born Italian democracy (the D'Aragona Commission in particular) proposed universal health care as a solution for the Italian system.[104] In this sense, the Second World War became a real driver for change immediately after the end of the conflict.

However, universal health care was not introduced. The existing continuity in the administrative apparatus between fascism and the republic stopped many reform projects, not only for health care but more generally for the Italian state and its social assistance.[105] Also, while the communist and socialist parties were in favour of universal assistance, the leading post-war party, the *Democrazia Cristiana* (Christian Democracy), was opposed to a universal welfare system, thinking that social assistance must be earned through work; otherwise, the risk was the rise of a dependency culture.[106] With the end of the constituent phase, the introduction of a new constitution, and the general election of 1948, the building of universal health care was put aside. Italy embraced a laissez-faire economic policy to encourage economic growth in a country still mostly poor and agricultural, and closed the possibility of reforming health care into a universal system.[107] Only in 1957 was a Ministry for Health instituted; a universal health-care system arrived in 1978, with the creation of the *Servizio Sanitario Nazionale* (National Health Service). The war could create the opportunity for change, but bureaucratic politics would ultimately determine the shape and timing of changes to the post-war Italian health-care system.[108]

NOTES

1 Barry S. Levy and Victor W. Sidel, "War and Public Health, An Overview," in *War and Public Health*, ed. Barry S. Levy and Victor W. Sidel (Oxford: Oxford University Press, 2009), 3–4.
2 See references in Nicholas Stargardt, *The German War: A Nation Under Arms, 1939–45* (London: Basic Books, 2017), 61–3, 206–8, 298, 308; Dan Todman, *Britain's War*, vol. I, *Into Battle, 1937–1941* (Oxford: Oxford University Press 2016), 86–91, 256–7, 486.
3 Some examples: Mary Schaeffer Conroy, *Medicines for the Soviet Masses During World War II* (Lanham: University Press of America, 2008); Sean Kennedy, *The Shock of War: Civilian Experiences, 1937–1945* (Toronto: Toronto University Press, 2011), 15, 29, 113; for example, on specific cases like refugees: Julian S. Torrie, *"For Their Own Good": Civilian Evacuations in Germany and France, 1939–1945* (New York: Berghan 2010), 40, 52; Mark Harrison, *Medicine and Victory: British Military Medicine in the Second World War* (Oxford University Press, 2004).
4 Some examples, Vincent Viet, *La santé en guerre, 1914–1918: Une politique pionnière en univers incertain* (Paris: Presses de Science Po, 2015); Jay Winter, *The Great War and the British People* (1985; repr., London and New York: Palgrave Macmillan, 2003), particularly the chapters "Civilian Health Britain" and "Medical Care Wartime," 103–213; Paul Windling, *Health, Race and German Politics Between National Unification and Nazism, 1870–1945* (Cambridge: Cambridge University Press, 1989), cit., 281–304.

5   See Virginia Berrige, *Health and Society Britain since 1939* (Cambridge: Cambridge University Press, 1999), especially 10; Daniel M. Fox, "The National Health Service and the Second World War: the elaboration of consensus," in *War and Social Change: British Society the Second World War,* ed. Harold L. Smith (Manchester: Manchester University Press, 1986), 32–57; John R. Watt, *Saving Lives Wartime China, How Medical Reformers built Modern Healthcare Systems amid War and Epidemics, 1928–1945* (Leida-Boston: Brill, 2014).
6   Tommaso Detti, "Stato, guerra e tubercolosi (1915–1922)," in *Storia d'Italia, Annali,* vol. 7, *Malattia e medicina,* ed. Ruggero Romano and Corrado Vivanti (Turin: Einaudi, 1984), 879–954; Giorgio Mortara, *La salute pubblica Italia durante e dopo la guerra* (Bari: Laterza, 1925); *Malattie e Medicina durante la Grande guerra* (Udine: Gaspari, 2009).
7   Giorgio Cosmacini, *Medicina e sanità in Italia nel 20 Secolo, Dalla Spagnola alla 2a guerra mondiale* (Rome and Bari: Laterza, 1989), 323–47.
8   Fiorenza Tarozzi, "Organizzazione Sanitaria e malattie," in *Bologna Guerra, 1940–1945,* ed. Brunella Dalla Casa and Alberto Preti (Milan: Franco Angeli, 1995), 273–89; Gian Luigi Agnoli, *Bologna e i suoi ospedali negli anni della guerra, 1940–1945* (Bologna: Giraldi, 2007); Orazio Barbieri, *Firenze: Guerra e resistenza nei servizi sanitari a Firenze* (Firenze: Vangelista, 1993).
9   Frank M. Snowden, *La conquista della malaria, Una modernizzazione italiana 1900–1962* (Turin: Einaudi, 2006), 251–330; Eugenia Tognotti, *Per una storia della malaria Italia. Il caso della Sardegna* (Milan: Franco Angeli, 2008).
10 M.R. Smallman-Raynor and Andrew D. Cliff, *War Epidemics, An Historical Geography of Infectious Disease, Military Conflict, and Civil Strife, 1850–2000* (Oxford: Oxford University Press, 2004), 4.
11 M.R. Smallman-Raynor and Andrew D. Cliff, "War and Disease: Some Perspectives on the Spatial and Temporal Occurrence of Tuberculosis in Wartime," in *The Return of the White Plague, Global Poverty and the "New" Tuberculosis,* ed. Matthew Gandy and Alimuddin Zumla (London: Verso, 2002), 70–92; Anne Rasmussen, "The Spanish Flu" in *The Cambridge History of the Great War,* vol. 3, ed. Jay Winter (Cambridge: Cambridge University Press, 2014), 334–57.
12 Pierluigi Scolè, "I morti," in *Dizionario storico della Prima guerra mondiale,* ed. Nicola Labanca (Rome and Bari: Laterza, 2014), 188; Giorgio Mortara, *La salute pubblica Italia durante e dopo la guerra* (Bari: Laterza, 1925); *Malattie e Medicina durante la Grande guerra* (Udine: Gaspari, 2009).

13 Giuliano Lenci, "Caduti dimenticati. I morti per malattie," in *La Grande Guerra. Esperienza, memoria, immagini*, ed. Diego Leoni and Camillo Zadra (Bologna: il Mulino, 1986), 231–6.
14 Eugenia Tognotti, *La "spagnola" Italia. Storia dell'influenza che fece temere la fine del mondo* (Milan: Franco Angeli, 2002).
15 Giovanni Montroni, *La società italiana dall'unificazione alla Grande guerra* (Rome and Bari: Laterza, 1995), 440–1.
16 Domenico Preti, "Per una storia sociale dell'Italia fascista: la tutela della salute nell'organizzazione dello stato corporativo," in *Salute e classi lavoratrici Italia dall'Unità al fascismo*, ed. Maria L. Betri and Ada Gigli Marchetti (Milan: Franco Angeli, 1982), 797–883; Silvia Inaudi, *A tutti indistintamente: l'Ente opere assistenziali nel periodo fascista* (Bologna: CLUEB, 2008).
17 Franco Silvano, *Legislazione e politica sanitaria del fascismo* (Rome: Apes, 2001).
18 Archivio Centrale dello Stato (ACS), Allied Control Commission (ACC), APO 394, Public Health Sub-Commission, Report for the month of July 1944, acc/3016/pm, 4.
19 Domenico Preti, "La questione ospedaliera nell'Italia fascista," in *Storia d'Italia, Annali 7, Malattie e medicina* (Turin: Einaudi, 1984), 380–1.
20 Claudia Baldoli and Andrew Knapp, *Forgotten Blitzes, France and Italy under Allied Air attack, 1940–1945* (London: Continumm, 2012), 83–109.
21 Nicoló Da Lio, "Fascist Warfare on the Home Front: War Mobilization and the Fragmentation of Italian Society, 1935–1943," chapter 2 of this book.
22 ACS, Ministero dell'Interno, Div. Gen. Amm. Civile, Divisione III, Ass. e Ben, 1940–42, b. 2f. 25100–33, Croce Rossa Italiana, Verbale del consiglio direttivo del 29 May 1940.
23 Alto commissariato per l'igiene e la sanità, *Relazione sull'attività svolta dalla sanità pubblica nel biennio 1944–45* (Rome: 1946), Rapporti con l'UNRRA, 15.
24 ACS, Div. Gen. Amm. Civ, Div. III, Assistenza e beneficienza, 1940–42, b. 2, Prot. N. 251000-35, Prefettura di Genova a Ministero dell'Interno, 11 September 1940; Similar reports from Leghorn: ACS, Div. Gen, Amm. Civ, Div. III, Assistenza e beneficienza, 1940–42, b. 2, Prot. N. 251000-35, Copia di lettera del presidente dell'Ospedale Civile di Livorno, Vittorio Emanuele III, October 1940.
25 ACS, Div. Gen, Amm. Civ, Div. III, Assistenza e beneficienza, 1940–42, b. 2, Prot. N. 251000-35, Ministero dell'Interno a tutte le prefetture 29 October 1942.
26 ACS, Segreteria particolare del duce, carteggio ordinario (SPD-CO), b. 2387, f. 550844, Revel a Mussolini, 15 February 1943: Other

examples: Trento: ACS, Div. Gen, Amm. Civ, Div. III, Assistenza e beneficienza, 1940–42, b. 2, Prot. N. 251000-35, Ministero dell'Interno a Prefetto di Trento, Mori, Infermeria, Lavori di sistemazione, Prot. 25299.84, 12 May 1942; Genoa: ACS, SPD-CO, b. 2387, f. 550843, Nicolò Cesare al Prefetto di Genova, 13 February 1943.
27 Archivio di Stato di Napoli (ASN), Prefettura, Gabinetto, II Versamento, Categoria V, b. 1061, f. V. 6.61, Ospedali riuniti di Napoli, segreteria generale, N. 4220, 15 July 1943.
28 Agnoli, "Bologna e i suoi ospedali," 169.
29 Massimiliano Paniga, *Welfare Ambrosiano, Storia, cultura e politiche dell'Eca di Milano (1937–1978)* (Milan: Franco Angeli, 2008), 81.
30 ASN, Prefettura, Gabinetto, II Versamento, Categoria V, b. 1061, f. V.6.69, Appunti manoscritti sulla riunione del 24 October 1941, 3.
31 ASN, Prefettura, Gabinetto, II versamento, Categoria III, b. 501, Relazione al prefetto sull'attività dell'augustissima arciconfraternita ed ospedali della SS. Trinità dei pellegrini e convalescenti, n. 3457, Napoli, 8 June 1941, 3.
32 ASN, Prefettura, Gabinetto, II Versamento, Categoria V, b. 1020, V.V.1688, Legione territoriale dei carabinieri reali di Napoli, gruppo di Caserta, Servizio sanitario del comune di Conca Campana, 7 May 1943.
33 Marco Gioannini and Giulio Massobrio, *Bombardate l'Italia, Storia della guerra di distruzione aerea* (Milan: Rizzoli, 2007), 386.
34 ASN, Prefettura, Gabinetto, II Versamento, Categoria V, b. 1061, f. V 6.46, Sgombero dell'ospedale Cotugno, Relazione del prefetto inviata a Celso Luciano, Capo di Gabinetto del Minculpo 20 February 1942.
35 ASN, Prefettura, Gabinetto, II Versamento, Categoria V, b. 1061, f. V. 6.46, Prefetto di Napoli a Gianni Petragni, Direttore generale della sanità pubblica, Roma, 28 June 1941.
36 ASN, Prefettura, Gabinetto, II Versamento, Categoria V, b. 1061, f. V.6.46, Legione territoriale dei carabinieri di Napoli a Prefetto, 15 January 1943.
37 Paola Cortesi, *L'odissea degli sfollati, Il Forlivese, il Riminese e il Cesenate di fronte allo sfollamento di massa* (Cesena: Il Ponte Vecchio, 2003), 92.
38 ACS, Ministero dell'Interno, Servizi Guerra, b. 75, Ministero dell'Interno, Direzione generale della sanità pubblica, Appunto per il gabinetto del Ministro, Il direttore della sanità pubblica, Petragni, 23 December 1941.
39 ACS, Ministero dell'Interno, Servizi Guerra, b. 75, Prefetto di Brindisi a Ministero dell'Interno, Sfollati Volontari, 13 February 1942.
40 ACS, Ministero dell'Interno, Servizi Guerra, b. 83, 182-2, Spedalità conseguenza dello stato di guerra, Padova, Prefettura di Padova al Consorzio Antitubercolare di Padova, Ricovero sanatorio di una sfollata affetta da t.b.c., 12 April 1944.

41 Giovanni L'Eltore, "La mortalità per tubercolosi durante la guerra in alcune città italiane," *La Lotta contro la Tubercolosi* (May/June 1946), 247.

42 ACS, Ministero dell'interno, Servizi guerra, b. 83, 182-2, Ministero dell'Interno, Direzione generale della sanità alla direzione generale per i servizi di guerra e per conoscenza alla direzione generale dell'Amm. Civile, Assistenza sanitaria agli sfollati, 24 September 1943, 1.

43 Alto commissariato per l'igiene e la sanità, Relazione sull'attività svolta dalla sanità pubblica nel biennio 1944–45 (Rome: 1946), Rapporti con fra la Sanità e l'organizzazione creata dagli alleati in Sicilia, 13.

44 ACS, Ministero dell'Interno, Servizi Guerra, b. 83, 182-2, Minstero dell'Interno, Direzione generale della Sanità Pubblica ai capi delle province, Assistenza medico-chirurgica farmaceutica ed ospedaliera agli sfollati, 21 July 1944.

45 ACS, Ministero dell'Interno, Servizi Guerra, b. 83, 182-2, Prefettura repubblicana di Piacenza a Ministero dell'Interno Direzione generale dei servizi di guerra, Direzione generale della sanità pubblica, 14 November 1944.

46 ACS, Ministero dell'Interno, Servizi Guerra, b. 83, 182-2-49, Ministero dell'interno a Direzione generale servizi guerra, Ricovero d'urgenza G. Piera, 9 February 1945.

47 ACS, Ministero dell'Interno, Servizi Guerra, b. 83, 182-2-69, Istituto psichiatrico S. Lazzaro di Reggio Emilia; rimborso spedalità per malati pertinenti comuni occupati dal nemico, 12 October 1944.

48 Vittorio A. Sironi, *Le officine della Salute, Storia del farmaco e della sua industria Italia* (Rome and Bari: Laterza, 1992), 152–4.

49 Archivio di Stato di Siena (ASS), Prefettura, 1941–1943, b. 53, 1.15.7-8-9, Consorzio provinciale antitubercolare, Vaccinazione preventive durante il 1941, 16 September 1942.

50 ASN, Prefettura, Gabinetto, II Versamento, Categoria V, b. 1061, f. V. 6.84, Il podestà di Sessa Aurunca nella provincia di Napoli, 24 July 1943.

51 ACS, Min. Int., Servizi Guerra, b. 83, 182-2, Ministero dell'Interno a Direzione generale servizi guerra, Ricovero feriti di guerra, 16 February 1944.

52 Alto commissariato per l'igiene e la sanità, *Relazione sull'attività svolta dalla sanità pubblica nel biennio 1944–45*, 135.

53 Maurizio De Filippis, *L'Ospedale Luigi Sacco nella Milano del Novecento* (Milan: Franco Angeli, 2003), 37; Giorgio Cosmacini, *Milano capitale sanitaria: modelli ideali, organizzativi, assistenziali, scientifici (1881–1950)* (Florence: Le Monnier, 2002), 123.

54 Augustissma arciconfraternita ed ospedali della SS. Trinità dei pellegrini e convalescenti, Napoli, *Relazione del Primicerio Gennaro Glado, all'assemblea generale dei confratelli 18 giugno 1944* (Naples: 1944), 19.
55 Gioannini and Massobrio, *Bombardate l'Italia*, 276.
56 Archivio di Stato di Torino (AST), Prefettura Torino, I versamento b. 134, Il presidente dell'ospedale S. Lazzaro, Camillo Rossotto al prefetto di Torino, 9 November 1943.
57 ASN, Prefettura, Gabinetto, II Versamento, Categoria V, b. 1061, f. V. 6.62, Prefettura di Napoli, Pozzuoli ospedale, servizio ispettivo, 26 June 1943.
58 Alto commissariato per l'igiene e la sanità, *Relazione sull'attività svolta dalla sanità pubblica nel biennio 1944–45*, 136; The number of active hospitals is for the year 1937, the last data available. Source: Annuario Statistico italiano, 1940 (Rome: Istituto poligrafico, 1941), Istituti ospitalieri al 30 June 1937, 57.
59 Franco Martinelli, Rossella Petrini, *Lo Sbarco di Anzio: una popolazione civile guerra*, (Rome: Aracne, 2007), 52–3.
60 ACS, Min. Int, Gab, 1944–46, b. 45, Comune di Terracina, Ufficio tecnico, relazione sullo stato attuale delle opere pubbliche, 9 January 1945, 3.
61 Bartolomeo Vezzoso, "Sei mesi con il governo di Salerno, Osservazioni ed esperienze," *Notiziario dell'Amministrazione sanitaria* (1944), 185–94.
62 The most comprehensive study of the German occupation is Lutz Klinkhammer, *L'occupazione tedesca Italia, 1943–1945* (Turin: Bollati Boringhieri, 1993); but the detailed material costs are documented in Nicola Labanca, ed., *Il nervo della guerra, Rapporti delle Militärkommandanturen e sottrazione nazista di risorse dall'Italia occupata (1943–1944)*, 3 volumes (Milan: 2020).
63 Tarozzi, *Organizzazione sanitaria e Malattie*, 277.
64 Barbieri, *Guerra e resistenza nei servizi sanitari a Firenze*, 300, 331, 373.
65 "Notizie," *Rivista sperimentale di Feniatria* 69 (1945), 290.
66 ASS, Prefettura, 1941–1943, b. 53, 1.1.57-8-9, appunti per la relazione economica, March 1944.
67 Snowden, *La conquista della malaria*, 270.
68 Luigi Ficacci, "L'epidemia malarica dell'anno 1944 e le sue caratteristiche cliniche," *Patologie del tempo di guerra, Malaria, Tubercolosi, Edemi da Fame* (Rome: Tipografia Guannella, 1945), 21–3.
69 ACS, Min. Int, Gab, 44–46, f. 17407, Prefetto di Grosseto, Avv. Amato Mati a Ministero agricoltura e foreste, Ministero dell'Interno, Gabinetto, port. 13104, 21 October 1945.
70 ACS, ACC, APO 394, ref/198/CA, Headquarter Allied control commission, Monthly Report for July, part 3, Administrative section, 25.

71 C.R.S. Harris, *History of the Second World War: Allied Administration of Italy, 1943–45* (London: HMSO, 1957), 419.
72 Harrison, *Medicine and Victory*, 137.
73 ASN, Prefettura, II Versamento, Categoria I, b. 55, Prefettura di Napoli, Divisione San. Prot. 11911, Malattie infettive 1/10 December 1944.
74 Per la produzione di medicina in Italia, *Il Policlinico*, Anno LI, n. 32–34, 504.
75 Alto commissariato per l'igiene e la sanità, *Relazione sull'attività svolta dalla sanità pubblica nel biennio 1944–45*, 170.
76 Michela Ponzani, *Guerra alle donne, Partigiane, vittime di stupro, amanti del nemico, 1940–45* (Turin: Einaudi, 2012), 238.
77 Gloria Chianese, *Italia, 1945–1950, Conflitti e trasformazioni sociali* (Milan: Franco Angeli, 1985), 101.
78 Paolo De Marco, *Polvere di piselli. La vita quotidiana a Napoli durante l'occupazione alleata (1943–44)* (Naples: Liguori, 1996) 40; According to Norman Lewis, *Napoli '44* (Milan: Adelphi, 1995), 136–7, in March 1944, over 42,000 women alone were operating in the city as prostitutes.
79 Maria Porzio, *Arrivano gli alleati, Amori e violenze nell'Italia liberata* (Rome and Bari: Laterza, 2007) 57–8.
80 Chiara Fantozzi, "L'Onore Violato: stupri, prostituzione e occupazione alleata (Livorno 1944–47)," *Passato e presente*, no. 99 (2016), 201, 97.
81 Saverio Luzzi, *Salute e sanità nell'Italia repubblicana* (Rome: Donzelli, 2004), 41.
82 Alto commissariato, *Relazione sull'attività svolta*, 1.
83 Ibid., 12.
84 Ibid., 14.
85 Ibid., 16.
86 ASS, Prefettura, 1941–1943, b. 53, 1.15.7-8-9, Consorzio provinciale antitubercolare, Raduno dei presidenti e dei direttori dei consorzi provinciali antitubercolari, Siena 13 May 1942.
87 Giorgio Cosmacini, "La dinamica della storia," Giorgio Cosmacini, Maurizio De Filippis, Patrizia Sanseverino, *La peste bianca: Milano e la lotta antitubercolare (1882–1945)* (Milan: Franco Angeli, 2004), 26.
88 Alberto Rocco, "Note sulla mortalità per tubercolosi Torino con particolare riferimento al periodo di guerra 1940–45," *Annali della sanità pubblica* 9, no. 1 (January/February 1950), 6.
89 Marcella Balconi and Giuseppe Giuffrida, "Mortalità per tubercolosi nel Comune di Novara durante la guerra," *L'Ospedale maggiore di Novara* 5–6 (1948), tab. 3, p. 11.
90 Giovanni L'Eltore and Mario Negri, "Mortalità tubercolare a Roma durante la guerra nei sessi, età e professioni," *Annali dell'Istituto Carlo Forlanini* (1946), 299.

91 Ibid., 301.
92 Istat, *Morti e dispersi per cause belliche negli anni 1940–45* (Rome: Istat, 1957), 26.
93 Luzzi, *Salute e sanità nell'Italia repubblicana*, 385.
94 *Annuario statistico Città di Torino, 1943*, Accame, Torino, 1945, Morti, Confronti mensili e annuali nel quinquennio 1939–1943, 66.
95 Giorgio Rochat, "Una ricerca impossibile, Le perdite italiane nella Seconda guerra mondiale," *Italia contemporanea*, no. 201 (1995), 687–700.
96 *Annuario Statistico Italiano*, Serie V, vol. I, 1944–48 (Istat: Rome, 1948), Igiene e Sanità, death causes, 58–60.
97 That limit of existing research about the impact of military operations on Italian civilians is underlined by Nicola Labanca, "Studiare le vittime civili di guerra," in *Città sotto le bombe, Per una storia delle vittime civili di guerra (1940–1945)*, ed. Nicola Labanca (Milan: Unicopli, 2018), 19.
98 Istat, *Morti e dispersi*, 28.
99 Cosmacini, *Dalla Spagnola alla II Guerra Mondiale*, 346–7.
100 Francesco Taroni, *Politiche sanitarie in Italia. Il futuro del SSN in prospettiva storica* (Rome: 2011), 19.
101 Gerard A. Ritter, *Storia dello stato sociale* (Rome and Bari: Laterza, 1996), 142.
102 Tony Judt, *Postwar: A History of Europe since 1945* (London: Penguin, 2005), 75–8.
103 Maurizio Ferrera, *Modelli di solidarietà: politica e riforme sociali nelle democrazie* (Bologna: Il Mulino, 1993), 84.
104 Leopoldo Di Nucci, "Alle origini dello stato sociale nell'Italia repubblicana. La ricezione del piano Beveridge e il dibattito nella Costituente," in *Cittadinanza. Individui, diritti sociali, collettività nella storia contemporanea*, ed. Carlotta Sorba (Rome: SISSCO, 2002) 153.
105 Guido Melis, *Storia dell'amministrazione italiana: 1881–1993* (Bologna: Il Mulino, 1996), 362; on the continuity of welfare policies Silvia Inaudi, "L'assistenza nel secondo dopoguerra tra continuità e mancate riforme. Note a margine del dibattito storiografico," *Storica* 46, no. 16 (2012), 1–21.
106 F. Taroni, *Politiche sanitarie in Italia*, 63.
107 Maurizio Ferrera, Valeria Fargion, and Matteo Jessoula, *Alle radici del welfare all'italiana, origini e futuro di un modello sociale squilibrato* (Venice: Marsilio, 2012), 111–12.
108 For more on the post-war period, see Chiara Giorgi and Ilaria Pavan, *Storia dello stato sociale in Italia* (Bologna: Il Mulino, 2021), 216–29.

7

The Second World War and the New Deal for American Science

Richard V. Damms

Given the prominent role of scientific research and development in the American war effort during the Second World War, and the manner in which this conflict concluded with the detonation of two atomic bombs, there was a degree of inevitability about the enhanced role of the state in post-war American science and technology. Nevertheless, while scientists, politicians, and military leaders shared a new-found consensus by the mid-1940s on the desirability for closer government-science relations, the actual terms of that partnership were contested and the eventual structures of what became the national security state were shaped by a combination of contingency and compromise. Ultimately, then, the war created the opportunity for change, but bureaucratic politics determined the shape of this change.

Among scientists, Vannevar Bush, who played a key role in orchestrating the mobilization of American science for war, probably developed the most comprehensive vision for what the post-war world of government-science relations should look like. Bush urged federal support of science and education through a single agency largely insulated from political control. This should be accompanied by greater support for science and technology within the armed forces, and the integration of civilian scientific expertise into national security planning, particularly in the area of new military technology. In all this, he anticipated a relatively autonomous role for civilian scientists in national policymaking. In a flurry of post-war state-building driven by pressing national and international considerations, however, his ideas were buffeted by a variety of forces. Ultimately, by the time of the Korean War, the essential patterns of the Cold War government-science relationship had been fairly well established and, to Bush's chagrin, with civilian scientists consigned to the role of very much junior partners.

The historiography of American science in the Second World War, rather like much of the scientific endeavour itself during the conflict, has tended to be compartmentalized by genre. Early semi-official accounts and participant histories presented generally positive assessments of how the marriage of scientists and the military had produced new weapons and techniques that contributed to ultimate victory, and implied that wartime administrative arrangements should be extended into the post-war period.[1] While the Manhattan Project, the atomic bomb, and the activities of the atomic scientists, such as J. Robert Oppenheimer, have spawned a plethora of excellent works, the principal wartime agency for scientific mobilization in which the atomic bomb enterprise was ostensibly subsumed, the Office of Scientific Research and Development (OSRD), has yet to receive a critical, in-depth analysis.[2] The larger narrative of the wartime mobilization of science therefore needs to be pieced together by consulting a variety of outstanding larger works on American physics, research universities, laboratories, and key personnel.[3] This chapter builds on and surpasses existing scholarship, drawing on the existing literature but also re-examining the contemporary record of principal actors. By doing so, it demonstrates how the post-war militarization of American science derived from the ideas and institutional innovations undertaken in the war years, as scientists, politicians, and military leaders negotiated the terms of their partnership.[4]

THE GREAT DEPRESSION CHALLENGES THE OLD ORTHODOXY

Until the 1930s, mutual aloofness generally characterized relations between the scientific community and political leaders. The scientific elite, as represented by the prestigious National Academy of Sciences (NAS), had long subscribed to the ideology of what one authority has called "best science elitism."[5] They espoused the view that society was beholden to science, particularly basic research conducted in private institutions, because it fostered the knowledge and ideas that would improve the human condition and hence advance civilization. They traditionally opposed any state direction or control of science for overt political purposes because such uninformed meddling would waste resources and result in inferior research. Only the best scientists deserved support, and only fellow scientists were qualified to judge the merits of research projects through the system of peer review. Given this prevailing philosophy, scientific leaders had typically eschewed close ties with the state.[6] Most political leaders, meanwhile, had embraced a similarly laissez-faire approach. Consequently, federal agencies usually only fostered mission-specific applied research. In short, the prevailing consensus was that basic research was best left to the universities and private foundations; government should only support limited research of direct utilitarian value; and research for commercial purposes was primarily the prerogative of private sector corporate laboratories.[7]

The onset of the Great Depression unleashed forces that finally fractured this laissez-faire consensus. Amid the economic catastrophe, scientists endured declining support as government, industry, foundations, and universities all engaged in fiscal retrenchment and curtailed research activities. Along with businessmen, scientists also found themselves hauled before the bar of public opinion for having caused mass unemployment through the practice of unregulated science and technology. Under such strains, some scientists moved tentatively into the public arena. In summer 1933, several Columbia University physicists, led by Nobel laureate Arthur Holly Compton, publicly petitioned President Franklin D. Roosevelt to restore federally-funded research projects.[8] Others embraced Secretary of Agriculture Henry A. Wallace's invitation for scientists to apply their unique skills to solving the nation's social and economic problems.[9] Significantly, the crisis also coincided with a generational changing of the guard among the nation's scientific elite. Yale geographer Isaiah Bowman, a founder of the Council on Foreign Relations, assumed the chairmanship of the Academy's National Research Council (NRC) in 1932. The same year, Princeton physicist Karl T. Compton, a founder of the American Institute of Physics, secured the presidency of the Massachusetts Institute of Technology (MIT).[10] Neither shared the older generation's paralytic fear of government, and both envisioned an enhanced public role and responsibility for scientific leaders. Rather like their contemporary "corporate liberals" in the business world, they envisioned a new partnership between science and government to ensure order, progress, and stability in the political economy of science.[11]

Although Bowman and Compton advocated a New Deal for science, they had limited success. They persuaded President Roosevelt to establish a short-lived Science Advisory Board (SAB) under the auspices of the 1933 National Industrial Recovery Act, chaired by Compton and comprising several Academy members.[12] Compton's major recommendation was for the creation of a national research administration with a budget of $100 million over five years to support fellowships and research projects in the universities, foundations, and trade associations. The new agency would secure a degree of insulation from political control of science by having a board of directors appointed by the president on the recommendation of the National Academy of Sciences, with the Academy president and NRC chair serving as ex officio members.[13]

Despite this public-private structure, conservative scientists on the SAB, led by Academy president W.W. Campbell and Frank B. Jewett of AT&T's Bell Labs, chafed at any federal support for science and the concomitant "bureaucratic control."[14] Under their influence, the SAB quietly expired in 1935. As Compton's grandiose plans came to naught, Bowman lamented that the Academy leadership comprised "men of technical or professional accomplishment who have no sense of organization, no sense of responsibility for science in government, and no breadth of outlook with respect to the relations and obligations of science to society."[15] Nevertheless, the reforming ideas of Bowman and Compton resonated among younger scientists. Some became overtly politicized through their participation in the American Association for the Advancement of Science's "Science and Society" conferences, or membership in the British-inspired and progressive-minded trade union, the American Association of Scientific Workers. The latter increasingly focused on the growing European crisis and the rising threat of Nazism.[16]

VANNEVAR BUSH AND THE WARTIME MOBILIZATION OF SCIENCE

One member of this younger group who would go on to become the most visible advocate for greater integration between science and the state, while safeguarding the principles of best science elitism, was Compton's protégé at MIT, Vannevar Bush. The son of a Universalist minister, Bush held an engineering doctorate awarded jointly by Harvard and MIT in 1916 and had worked on submarine detection for the Navy in the First World War. As a faculty member at MIT, he developed an improved vacuum tube and patented the differential analyzer, a forerunner of the electronic analogue computer. By the 1920s, his MIT department housed approximately one-third of the nation's electrical engineering graduate students. A skilled manager and master of external relations, under Compton's mentorship Bush became dean of the college of engineering at MIT and vice-president, and a member of one of the SAB's advisory panels. In 1939, Bush moved to the capital to assume the presidency of the Carnegie Institution of Washington and chair the National Advisory Committee for Aeronautics. In the latter capacity, he became increasingly aware of the woeful state of American military preparedness.[17]

As the European situation deteriorated, Bush gathered a coterie of elite, pro-interventionist scientists who quietly worked to gain the president's ear about the compelling need to harness science in the service of national security. Collectively, they represented the various estates of science. Jewett, recently elected to the presidency of the Academy, was a distinguished industrial researcher. Karl Compton, Bush's mentor, headed the nation's leading technical institution. James B. Conant, an accomplished chemist who had worked on chemical weapons in the First World War, presided over Harvard University. Together, they urged President Roosevelt to establish a new, temporary federal agency to contract out military research. By staffing the agency and its advisory groups with the nation's leading researchers, and by contracting with existing university and industrial facilities rather than creating new government laboratories, Bush and his associates believed that they could both bolster these blighted entities and secure the best scientific and technical expertise for military preparedness.[18]

After the outbreak of war in Europe, Bush secured the adoption of his group's plan in its entirety, essentially providing the organizational framework for the wartime mobilization of American science. In 1940, Roosevelt initially established the National Defense Research Committee (NDRC) by executive order as part of the Executive Office of the President. The following year, another presidential order created the OSRD as a wartime agency, subsuming the original NDRC and a new Committee on Medical Research.[19] The NDRC enjoyed broad authority to coordinate "scientific research on the mechanisms of warfare," to assist the research activities of the Army and the Navy, and to conduct its own military research through contracts with "individuals, educational or scientific institutions ... and industrial organizations."[20] Bush initially chaired the NDRC before handing the reins over to Conant to assume the directorship of OSRD and coordinate the entire defence research effort.

The wartime emergency and infusion of federal research funds came not a moment too soon for many leading universities. By 1939, at the University of California at Berkeley, a series of budgetary cutbacks had left the institution "at a critical point." At Columbia University, ten years of fiscal retrenchment led the provost, in early 1941, to predict "intellectual bankruptcy if financial restriction continues." At the University of Chicago, a decade of deficit financing had preserved faculty salaries, but the physical plant had been neglected.[21] Many universities therefore embraced the war effort, both out of a sense of patriotic duty but also self-interest. As one administrator at Chicago reported to the university president: "This government activity in research and training is the wave of the immediate future ... Our choice comes in whether at this time, impelled either by patriotism or by our financial needs, we should more aggressively seek government funding and training projects." His recommendation, of course, was in the affirmative. Dozens of other major universities quickly followed suit. By insisting that both companies and non-profit universities must "break even on contracts," moreover, Bush ensured that both the direct and indirect costs would be covered from government coffers, allowing universities to apply overhead toward long-neglected physical plant and other operating expenses. In very short order, "overhead," the calculation of indirect costs related to performing contracted research, became a major line item in university budgeting and long-term planning.[22]

Despite military leaders' early misgivings about civilian scientists directing military research, Bush's astute leadership, coupled with the tangible products of OSRD contracts, converted many of these sceptics to the idea of a closer partnership with civilian researchers. Although the atomic bomb project managed by the Army's Manhattan Engineer District represented the prime example of wartime collaboration between scientists, industry, and the military, the OSRD-funded Radiation Laboratory (Rad Lab) at MIT made arguably an equally significant contribution to the Allied war effort. Directed by Lee A. DuBridge, chair of physics at Rochester University, the Rad Lab pioneered the development of microwave radar. By war's end, it employed some 4,000 people, almost 500 of whom were trained physicists, and had spent some $1.5 billion. Its gadgets included airborne interception devices for night fighters, radar bomb-aiming systems, and long-range navigation devices. Exceeded in scale only by the Manhattan Project, DuBridge and his staff later liked to quip that the atomic bomb ended the war, but radar won it.[23]

ALTERNATIVE VISIONS FOR POST-WAR SCIENCE

Even before war's end, the mobilization of science fostered a greater appreciation of the centrality of science to the national welfare among military leaders, politicians, and even scientists, and raised questions about future institutional arrangements. Only a handful of laissez-faire diehards, such as Academy president Frank B. Jewett, cautioned that any continuing federal support or direction of science would entail scientists becoming "intellectual slaves" of the state.[24] Most believed that the changing nature of the scientific enterprise and the increasing importance of scientific expertise to national security and economic well-being necessitated a closer partnership between science and the state. As early as 1942, freshman Democrat Senator Harley M. Kilgore of West Virginia had begun drafting legislation to establish a permanent national science agency to promote centrally planned and socially responsive research. Such a prospect disconcerted elite scientists, but Kilgore persisted. Eventually, by 1944, Bush began formulating his own plans to apply the lessons learned during wartime to establish a permanent civilian federal agency to support research broadly in the natural sciences, medicine, and national defence under the guidance of elite scientists insulated from direct political control. Bush believed that the wartime experience of OSRD had demonstrated that only a civilian body with congressional authority, independent funding, and guided by scientists could ensure the "freshness of approach and independence of mind" essential for innovative research, including military research.[25]

Bush presented his blueprint in his famous report to the president, *Science: The Endless Frontier*. Drawing upon his mentor Compton's stillborn New Deal initiative, and in keeping with the philosophy of "best science elitism," Bush proposed a National Research Foundation, governed by a nine-member, part-time board of leading academic and industrial researchers, appointed by the president. The foundation's director, however, would be appointed by the board, in consultation with the National Academy of Sciences, rather than the president.

National science policy would thus be determined by elite scientists rather than politicians. Moreover, Bush intended much of the federally funded research to be performed in private institutions rather than government laboratories, where researchers would be free of stifling bureaucracy or burdensome security restrictions that inhibited the free flow of ideas essential to scientific progress. Bush's plan formed the basis of enabling legislation drafted within OSRD and introduced by Democrat Senator Warren G. Magnuson of Washington in July 1945, timed to coincide with the release of Bush's report.[26]

Early passage of national science legislation, however, ran afoul of philosophical divisions within the scientific community and also between Bush and the new Harry S. Truman administration. Bush's elitist approach initially commanded the support of most OSRD veterans, representatives of the leading private research universities, industrial researchers, and the armed forces. Corporate researchers and the military particularly liked his flexible patent provisions that would provide an incentive for industry to engage in government-sponsored research. On the other hand, more liberal-minded scientists, especially at the working level, and representatives of land-grant universities, which had largely lost out on wartime research contracts, backed Kilgore's alternative legislation.[27] In Kilgore's scheme, what he now called the National Science Foundation (NSF) would support a broad-based program of utilitarian research in both the natural sciences and the social sciences and be responsive to elected leaders. Kilgore advocated a presidentially appointed foundation director, advised by a presidentially appointed board of experts drawn from government, industry, labour, and the public at large. Any patents arising from federally funded research would become public property and be subject to non-exclusive licensing arrangements, which Truman heartily approved.[28] He also called for some research funding to be allocated according to a geographical formula.

While the differences between the two approaches were not insuperable, compromise legislation failed to clear the House of Representatives in 1946 when Bush urged his supporters to hold fast to his original plan. The Truman administration privately considered that Bush had "reneged" on a compromise deal, and the executive secretary of the American Association for the Advancement of Science accused Bush and his friends of the "homicide" of the foundation. For the next five years, competing science foundation bills fell victim to partisan bickering.[29] Only in May 1950 did Truman sign into law a compromise

National Science Foundation Act. By then, it was a greatly circumscribed institution, and the hoped-for levels of integration had been significantly scaled down. Gone were the provisions for a broad-based program of national research, replaced by a more limited mission of promoting basic research and science education only. Similarly, the final bill omitted a division of military research. Frustrated over the delay and anxious to build upon the productive wartime relationship with academic researchers, the armed services had already taken matters into their own hands.

THE ARMED FORCES FILL THE VOID

The Second World War emphasized to defence planners the importance of science and technology to national security. Testifying in support of a science foundation, Secretary of War Robert Patterson declared that laboratories were now "our first line of defense."[30] Not only did the military value the practical technologies developed but they also understood the importance of continued access to academic scientists at the cutting edge of basic research. Familiarity with the state of the art in various fields could have a direct bearing on applied research for military purposes. Civilian scientists could bring their expertise to bear in a variety of part-time, advisory roles. The universities and educational foundations also represented an important source of scientific manpower ready to be mobilized for the next great emergency. Finally, defence agencies wanted to steer academic researchers toward fields and problems that might have direct military applications. As the proposed science foundation legislation stalled, the armed services filled the void.[31]

The Navy's initiative was a new Office of Naval Research (ONR), established by statute in 1946, "to maintain the interest of civilian scientists in the Navy's problems."[32] With the Navy anxious to secure a firm foothold in nuclear physics, the ONR adopted a strategy and structure designed to allay scientists' and university administrators' concerns about undertaking military research. In addition to conducting applied research in the Navy's own facilities, the ONR funded basic research in the universities, allowed scholars to initiate their own projects, subjected them to peer review, and adopted a liberal policy toward publishing results. Moreover, ONR drew expert advice from a part-time committee of civilians "preeminent in the fields of science, research, and development work." Significantly, Chief of Naval

Research Admiral Harold G. Bowen selected a Yale physicist and OSRD veteran, Alan T. Waterman, as his first chief scientist.

Within a few months of its activation, the transformative ONR approved over $24 million in research contracts to universities for 602 academic research projects employing over 4,000 scientists and students.[33] In the period before the establishment of the NSF, the chair of ONR's civilian advisory group declared, with only slight exaggeration, that: "As the only Federal agency now supporting a broad program of basic research, *the Navy is in the position of temporary trustee of a great national asset*" [emphasis in original].[34] At MIT, the ONR established the Laboratory for Nuclear Science and Engineering. As Karl Compton put it, such funding served "a double-barrelled purpose," in this case advancing the state of the art in nuclear power reactors and providing a cadre of trained personnel to build and operate them.[35]

Not to be outdone, the Army attempted to establish similarly intimate ties with the civilian research community. Following the advice of Bush and MIT electrical engineer Edward L. Bowles, Army Chief of Staff Dwight D. Eisenhower asserted, in April 1946, that the Army had "a duty to support broad research programs in educational institutions, in industry, and in whatever field might be of importance." Not only would such programs directly benefit the Army, but they would also prepare civilians for mobilization in another national emergency.[36] To that end, Eisenhower established a new Research and Development Division within the General Staff with responsibility for the "initiation, allocation, coordination and progress" of all research and development programs. The director, assisted by a civilian scientist, would also advise the chief of staff and secretary of war on research and development matters and liaise with civilian scientists.[37]

In practice, Eisenhower's new division proved to be short-lived, undermined by the creation of an independent US Air Force branch in 1947 and the resistance of the Army Technical Services and their long-established arsenals to what they considered unwarranted encroachment on their prerogatives in the research and development field.[38] Nevertheless, Army Ordnance contracted out research on guided missiles to the California Institute of Technology's Jet Propulsion Lab, and the Air Force established its own basic research unit. A Joint Services contract in 1946 provided open-ended support for MIT's Research Laboratory for Electronics and the next year all three armed services provided a grant to initiate what became the

Electronics Research Lab at Stanford University.[39] Collectively, these initiatives by the armed forces to secure direct access to civilian scientific talent short-circuited Bush's original notion that military research and development would be subsumed within an overarching civilian agency such as the National Science Foundation. Indeed, as the NSF legislation floundered, congressional leaders recognized the new reality and dropped the concept entirely.

Even as Bush's designs for a relatively autonomous civilian role in performing military research stalled, his efforts to deploy civilian scientific expertise to rationalize the overall military research and development program ran aground on the shoals of military opposition and inter-service rivalries. In 1946, at Bush's urging, the service secretaries established the Joint Research and Development Board to assume OSRD's wartime mandate of "coordinating all research and development programs of joint interest to the armed services" and establishing a "strong, unified, integrated and complete research and development program in the field of national defense."[40] Bush chaired the group, which also comprised two members of each service. Under the 1947 National Security Act, this group morphed into the Research and Development Board and expanded to include Air Force representatives. Bush and his board set up over a dozen committees and 76 technical panels; employed over 250 staff and some 2,000 part-time consultants from academia, industry, and the armed forces; and supposedly had the ear of the Secretary of Defence. Yet it quickly became apparent that it lacked either the ability or the authority to develop a unitary approach to military research and development. The service members of the various committees merely replicated inter-service feuds over roles, missions, and weapons systems.[41] The board could do little more than make recommendations. When Bush attempted to review each service's research budget and advise on priorities, he was shut out by the Joint Chiefs of Staff.[42]

Before departing government service, Bush attempted unsuccessfully to integrate civilian scientists into long-range military planning through the creation of a support agency attached to the Joint Chiefs, the Weapons Systems Evaluation Group (WSEG). He and Secretary of Defense James V. Forrestal intended to cut through some of the controversies over roles and missions by having the WSEG provide "rigorous, unprejudiced and independent analyses and evaluations of present and future weapons systems under probable combat conditions." MIT physicist and operations research specialist Philip M.

Morse served as deputy director and chief scientist, backed up by fifty civilian scientists and military officers.[43] Nevertheless, the WSEG could not cut the Gordian knot of inter-service rivalry and duplication of effort in research and development. In 1949, when new Secretary of Defense, Louis A. Johnson, turned to the WSEG for a technical study on the feasibility of strategic bombing, its pessimistic assessment of the viability of a sustained air-atomic offensive and the efficacy of the new B-36 bomber had no appreciable effect either on the preferred air-atomic strategy or procurement of the aircraft. Characteristically, the report spurred the Air Force to seek the dissolution of the WSEG.[44] By 1950, much to the chagrin of Bush, the armed services had become deeply entrenched in military research and development on their own terms, operating research laboratories, subsidizing university research and facilities, and contracting civilian scientific expertise.

MANAGING THE ATOM

While the armed forces moved in piecemeal fashion over the course of several years to assert authority over certain areas of American science, the debate over the establishment and structure of a new federal agency to control and promote the development of atomic energy occurred in a much more highly charged political atmosphere. The dramatic culmination of the war with the atomic bombing of Japan, emerging difficulties among the former wartime allies, and mounting concerns about a potential international nuclear arms race provided the context. Amid the heated discussion, the spectacle of working-level scientists taking up political cudgels undermined Bush's vision of scientists as apolitical technical experts quietly influencing decision making in partnership with political and military elites. The final outcome represented a further step along the road to science as a servant of the national security state.

As with the science foundation, Bush initially helped to set the terms of the debate but then saw his handiwork reshaped by competing forces. A year before Hiroshima, Bush had sketched out a proposal for an atomic energy commission with broad authority over all nuclear materials and research in which elite civilian scientists would exercise predominant influence. While the commission would include both military officers and civilians appointed by the president, a plurality of commissioners would be nominated by the National Academy of Sciences. Shortly after the Trinity atomic test in July 1945, however, the War Department drafted a bill establishing military autonomy over atomic energy affairs. It expanded the military representation on the proposed commission, which would exercise a monopoly over all raw materials, plants, facilities, equipment, technical information, and patents related to atomic research. It also empowered the commission to conduct all atomic energy research, either in federal facilities or under contract, with the exception of military research that would remain in the hands of the armed forces.[45] Democrats Andrew J. May of Kentucky and Edwin C. Johnson of Colorado introduced the bill in October 1945. Although only loosely based on his original scheme, Bush reluctantly endorsed the May-Johnson legislation. Like other wartime scientific leaders, such as Ernest O. Lawrence and J. Robert Oppenheimer, he now considered swiftly establishing a domestic commission a necessary precondition for any international control of atomic energy.[46]

Somewhat to the consternation of Bush and his associates, the proposed legislation immediately aroused a broad-based coalition in opposition, with rank-and-file atomic scientists in the vanguard. Following the atomic bombings, scientists' organizations had sprung up at the various Manhattan Project sites, inspired by a sense of responsibility to educate the public to the realities of atomic energy, primarily the necessity of international control measures. Moreover, having chafed at the army's wartime security restrictions, they championed "the spirit of free inquiry and free interchange of information" necessary for science to prosper.[47] Coalescing as the Federation of American Scientists in late 1945, they embarked on a concerted lobbying campaign against what they perceived as the May-Johnson Bill's militarization of atomic energy.[48] Belatedly, some science administrators, such as MIT Rad Lab director Lee A. DuBridge, also entered the fray to contest the "threat to the freedom of science" posed by a commission with "dictatorial powers."[49]

With the militarized atomic energy bill hamstrung, those who preferred a more socially responsive approach to atomic energy development, analogous to Senator Kilgore's philosophy regarding the science foundation, seized the opportunity to craft an alternative bill. Significantly, President Truman and his inner circle welcomed the idea of a single overarching agency establishing a monopoly in the atomic energy field, but they insisted upon the principle of civilian control and appropriate legislative oversight, and urged that greater attention be paid to non-military applications of atomic energy, such as the possibility of generating cheap electrical power.[50] Together, they helped freshman Democratic Senator Brien McMahon of Connecticut craft a bill providing for an exclusively civilian commission. While the commission would produce atomic weapons, retain custody of the atomic stockpile, and conduct research and development in the military applications of atomic power, it would also promote research in atomic energy either in-house or in private institutions. Civilian scientists would be assured a voice in the commission through a nine-member General Advisory Committee appointed by the president.

The McMahon bill ultimately formed the basis for the 1946 Atomic Energy Act, but political horse-trading resulted in an Atomic Energy Commission (AEC) that favoured military interests and completely jettisoned Bush's original organizational design. Truman and McMahon held steadfast to the principle of civilian control but acquiesced to a military liaison committee that would assume responsibility for military applications of atomic energy and answer to the service secretaries. The atomic scientists denounced this "administrative monstrosity."[51] They also bridled at restrictions on the dissemination of technical information, enacted amid growing fears of espionage.[52] Moreover, given the woeful state of the American atomic weapons arsenal, scarce budgetary resources in a period of post-war retrenchment, and the apparent impracticability of nuclear power reactors, the new AEC quickly prioritized weapons development.[53] Much like his organizational ideas, Bush found himself jettisoned, both by the atomic scientists who now mistrusted his cosiness with the armed forces, and by the Truman administration inner circle, who considered him politically unreliable.[54] Indeed, by 1950, as the Cold War deepened and the atomic arms race escalated, even Bush's friend and wartime partner in OSRD, James Conant, concluded that the AEC should be reconstituted as a purely military agency.[55]

CONCLUSION

The extent to which American science was distorted or stimulated by this emerging pattern of post-war patronage by the national security state has been debated among historians of science, but after the wartime experience many university administrators and researchers unequivocally embraced the new relationship. Some subscribed to what Michael Sherry has called a "preparedness mentality," best articulated by MIT president James Killian, a protégé of Compton and Bush. Killian asserted that the nation's leading research institutions constituted "a powerful fleet in being" ready to be "thrown instantly into action if needed." Dynamic, free universities could provide the technical expertise to "outwit an enemy in the design of weapons and countermeasures, and ... beat an enemy to the draw." They would be the source of "invincible battalions" of scientists and engineers.[56] True to his word, when China intervened in the Korean War, Killian quickly accepted an Air Force request to establish a new, off-campus research facility, the Lincoln Laboratory, devoted to technical problems of air defence in part because "the Institute owed a major duty to the country."[57]

Moreover, scientists and academic administrators recognized that university partnerships with the national security state could be mutually beneficial, helping to build advanced research facilities and secure top-flight scientists and engineers. During the Second World War, state funding for defence-related research had caused many American scientists, especially physicists, to experience a revolution of rising expectations. Paul Klopsteg recalled that demobilized scientists

> had become accustomed to large funds, easily acquired ...
> they felt the need for paid assistants because the military jobs
> furnished them with paid assistants. Many were convinced
> that team research was the new order ... In many instances their
> university administrations were easily persuaded to adopt the
> same view.[58]

As Paul Foreman has shown, Ernest Lawrence's thinking about the Radiation Laboratory at Berkeley exemplifies this point. When drawing up post-war plans in early 1944, he anticipated that the lab would downsize and be reintegrated into the physics department with an annual budget of $85,000. By the spring of 1945, as the Manhattan Project was nearing its successful conclusion, he expected to retain a staff of 239 technicians and scientists at an annual budget of $7 to $10 million supplied by the Army.[59] Even some of the most prominent scientists who waxed lyrical in public about the necessity of pursuing science for its own sake, free of political or military considerations, like Columbia University physicist and 1944 Nobel Prize winner Isidor I. Rabi, became promoters and lobbyists for their respective institutions.[60] During the war, Rabi tried to mitigate the loss of key personnel Enrico Fermi and Harold Urey to the Manhattan Project at the University of Chicago by negotiating the establishment of a Rad Lab satellite laboratory at Columbia. At war's end, Rabi had no compunction about securing contracts from the military services and the AEC to sustain the Columbia Radiation Laboratory and, by extension, the physics department.[61]

For American science and scientists, therefore, the experience of the Second World War represented a major catalyst for change. Unlike the case with Italian health care (see chapter 6), post-war change proved to be rapid, even if the final shape of that change was largely determined by bureaucratic politics. Wartime mobilization, primarily under the auspices of Bush's OSRD, demonstrated that state-directed research could have a significant and even decisive impact on the technology and techniques of war. The contracts, institutional partnerships, and personal and professional relationships forged by war also put paid to older laissez-faire notions about the relationship between science and the state. In the cauldron of war, Bush, Kilgore, and other forward-thinking military and political leaders began to consider how the lessons of war for American science might be applied in the post-war period. Above all, science and technology came to be viewed as vital assets for long-term national well-being, especially for defence purposes. In a sense, Bush was perhaps too successful evangelizing in this regard. Buffeted by various political forces, his program for American science, in which elite scientists would exercise a relatively autonomous role in shaping military research and development and oversee a national research program balanced between civilian and military needs, became flipped. In the new and dangerous era of nuclear weapons and deepening Cold War tensions, many political and military leaders considered science and technology too important to be left to academic scientists alone. As the sinews of the new relationship between science and the national security state evolved in the late 1940s, military interests predominated. Indeed, by the time of the Korean War, the military and the Atomic Energy Commission accounted for over 90 per cent of federally funded university research, and an estimated two-thirds of the nation's scientists were actively engaged in defence-related research.[62] Significantly, however, most scientists and university administrators, especially those who recalled the austerity of the pre-war years, readily acceded to their role as junior partners, reaping the academic, professional, and institutional benefits of federal largesse. Some even posited that the expanding and diverse nature of federal research support provided by the armed services, the AEC, and the NSF now provided the best guarantee of high-quality research and academic freedom.[63]

NOTES

1 James Phinney Baxter III, *Scientists Against Time* (Boston: Little, Brown, 1946); Irvin Stewart, *Organizing Scientific Research for War: The Administrative History of the Office of Scientific Research and Development* (Boston: Little, Brown, 1948); Vannevar Bush, *Modern Arms and Free Men: A Discussion of the Role of Science in Preserving Democracy* (New York: Simon and Schuster, 1949); James B. Conant, *Modern Science and Modern Man* (New York: Columbia University Press, 1952).

2 Two important exceptions that hone in specifically on OSRD are Carroll Pursell, "Science Agencies in World War II: The OSRD and its Challengers," in *The Sciences in the American Context: New Perspectives*, ed. Nathan Reingold (Washington, DC: Smithsonian Institution Press, 1979), and Larry Owens, "The Counterproductive Management of Science in the Second World War: Vannevar Bush and the Office of Scientific Research and Development," *Business History Review* 68 (Winter 1994): 515–76. Among the best works on atomic energy and the atomic scientists are Richard G. Hewlett and Oscar A. Anderson, Jr, *The New World, 1939–1946*, vol. 1, *A History of the United States Atomic Energy Commission* (University Park: Pennsylvania State University Press, 1962); Alice Kimball Smith, *A Peril and a Hope: The Scientists' Movement in America, 1945–1947* (Cambridge, MA: MIT Press, 1971); Richard Rhodes, *The Making of the Atomic Bomb* (New York: Simon and Schuster, 1986); Barton J. Bernstein, "Four Physicists and the Bomb: The Early Years," *Historical Studies in the Physical and Biological Sciences* 18 (1988): 231–63; Gregg Herken, *Brotherhood of the Bomb: The Tangled Lives and Loyalties of Robert Oppenheimer, Ernest Lawrence, and Edward Teller* (New York: Henry Holt, 2002); Kai Bird and Martin J. Sherwin, *American Prometheus: The Triumph and Tragedy of J. Robert Oppenheimer* (New York: Alfred A. Knopf, 2005); David C. Cassidy, *J. Robert Oppenheimer and the American Century* (New York: Pi Press, 2005); Priscilla J. McMillan, *The Ruin of J. Robert Oppenheimer and the Birth of the Modern Arms Race* (New York: Viking, 2005).

3 See Daniel J. Kevles, *The Physicists: The History of a Scientific Community in Modern America*, 2nd edition (Cambridge, MA: Harvard University Press, 1987); Paul K. Hoch, "The Crystallization of a Strategic Alliance: The American Physics Elite and the Military in the 1940s," and Peter Galison, "Physics between War and Peace," both in *Science, Technology and the Military*, ed. Everett Mendelsohn, Merritt Roe Smith,

and Peter Weingart (Dordrecht, NL: Kluwer Academic Publishers, 1987); Paul Forman, "Behind Quantum Electronics: National Security as a Basis for Physical Research in the United States, 1940–1960," *Historical Studies in the Physical and Biological Sciences* 18 (1987): 149–229; Paul Forman, "Into Quantum Electronics: The Maser as 'Gadget' in Cold War America," in *National Military Establishments and the Advancement of Science and Technology*, ed. Paul Forman and Jose M. Sanchez-Ron (Dordrecht, NL: Kluwer Academic Publishers, 1996); Roger Geiger, *Research and Relevant Knowledge: American Research Universities since World War II* (New York: Oxford University Press, 1993); Stuart W. Leslie, *The Cold War and American Science: The Military-Industrial-Academic Complex at MIT and Stanford* (New York: Columbia University Press, 1993); Rebecca S. Lowen, *Creating the Cold War University: The Transformation of Stanford* (Berkeley: University of California Press, 1997); Christophe Lecuyer, "The Making of a Science-Based Technological University: Karl Compton, James Killian, and the Reform of MIT, 1930–1957," *Historical Studies in the Physical and Biological Sciences* 23 (1992): 153–80; James G. Hershberg, *James B. Conant: from Harvard to Hiroshima* (New York: Alfred A. Knopf, 1993); and G. Pascal Zachary, *Endless Frontier: Vannevar Bush, Engineer of the American Century* (New York: Free Press, 1997).

4 For examples of works that seek to situate scientists and their institutional preferences within the larger political economy, see Robert Kargon and Elizabeth Hodes, "Karl Compton, Isaiah Bowman, and the Politics of Science in the Great Depression," *Isis* 76 (September 1985): 301–18; Nathan Reingold, "Vannevar Bush's New Deal for Research: Or, the Triumph of the Old Order," *Historical Studies in the Physical and Biological Sciences* 17 (1987): 299–344; David M. Hart, *Forged Consensus: Science, Technology, and Economic Policy in the United States, 1921–1953* (Princeton, NJ: Princeton University Press, 1998); Patrick J. McGrath, *Scientists, Business and the State, 1890–1960* (Chapel Hill: University of North Carolina Press, 2002).

5 For a fuller discussion of "best science elitism," see Kevles, *The Physicists*, passim.

6 Useful surveys of government-science relations include the classic A. Hunter Dupree, *Science in the Federal Government: A History of Policies and Activities* (Baltimore: Johns Hopkins University Press, 1986), which takes the story up to 1941; Daniel S. Greenberg, *The Politics of Pure Science*, revised edition (New York: Plume Books, 1970); Bruce L.R. Smith, *American Science Policy since World War II* (Washington, DC:

Brookings Institution, 1990); and Alan I. Marcus and Amy Sue Bix, *The Future is Now: Science and Technology Policy in America since 1950* (Amherst, NY: Humanity Books, 2007).

7 Greenberg, *Politics of Pure Science*, 22–30; Smith, *American Science Policy*, 19–22.

8 Peter L Kuznick, *Beyond the Laboratory: Scientists as Political Activists in 1930s America* (Chicago: University of Chicago Press, 1987), 25–32; Dupree, *Science in the Federal Government*, 344–6.

9 Henry A. Wallace, "The Social Advantages and Disadvantages of a Scientific-Engineering Approach to Civilization," *Science* 79 (5 January 1934): 1–5; Kuznick, *Beyond the Laboratory*, 15, 18–24.

10 Kargon and Hodes, "Karl Compton, Isaiah Bowman, and the Politics of Science in the Great Depression," 304–8.

11 For the ideology of Bowman and Compton, see Kargon and Hodes, "Karl Compton," 308–11. On corporate liberalism, see Ellis W. Hawley, "The Discovery and Study of a 'Corporate Liberalism,'" *Business History Review* 52 (Autumn 1978): 309–30; Louis P. Galambos, "Technology, Political Economy, and Professionalization: Central Themes of the Organizational Synthesis," *Business History Review* 57 (Winter 1983): 471–93; and Thomas Ferguson, "From Normalcy to New Deal: Industrial Structure, Party Competition, and American Public Policy in the Great Depression," *International Organization* (Winter 1984): 51–94.

12 For a full discussion of the SAB, see, Lewis E. Auerbach, "Scientists in the New Deal: A Pre-war Episode in the Relations between Science and Government in the United States," *Minerva* 3 (Summer 1965): 457–2; and Carroll W. Pursell, "The Anatomy of a Failure: The Science Advisory Board, 1933–1935," *Proceedings of the American Philosophical Society* 109 (December 1965): 342–51.

13 *Second Report of the Science Advisory Board: September 1, 1934 to August 31, 1935* (Washington, DC: no publisher, 1935), 81–4; Karl T. Compton, "Science Still Holds a Great Promise: An Answer to Those Who Contend that Ills of Today Can Be Blamed on Technology," *New York Times Magazine*, 16 December 1934, 17.

14 Jewett to Compton, 6 December 1934, cited in Kargon and Hodes, "Karl Compton," 316.

15 Bowman to Frank Lillie, 21 October 1935, cited in Kargon and Hodes, "Karl Compton," 310.

16 Kuznick, *Beyond the Laboratory*, chapters 7–8; William McGucken, *Scientists, Society and the State: The Social Relations of Science Movement*

in Great Britain, 1931–1947 (Columbus: Ohio State University Press, 1984).
17 Vannevar Bush, *Modern Arms and Free Men*, 17–26; *Current Biography, 1947* (New York: H.W. Wilson, 1947), 80–2; Kevles, *The Physicists*, 293–6.
18 Vannevar Bush, *Pieces of the Action* (London: Cassell, 1970), 32–3, 38; James B. Conant, *My Several Lies: Memoirs of a Social Inventor* (New York: Harper and Row, 1970), 234–6; James Phinney Baxter III, *Scientists Against Time*, 13–15; Nathan S. Reingold, "Vannevar Bush's New Deal for Research," 307–11.
19 Bush, *Pieces of the Action*, 35–6; Conant, *My Several Lives*, 235.
20 The executive orders are in Baxter, *Scientists Against Time*, 451–5.
21 Verne F. Stadtman, *The University of California, 1868–1968* (New York, 1970), 259–61; Carol Gruber, "The Overhead System in Government-Sponsored Academic Science: Origins and Early Development," *Historical Studies in the Physical and Biological Sciences* (HSPBS) 25 (1995): 246.
22 Gruber, "The Overhead System," 243–4, 249.
23 Baxter, *Scientists Against Time*, 137–57; Kevles, *The Physicists*, 305–8; James R. Killian, Jr, *The Education of a College President: A Memoir* (Cambridge: MIT Press, 1985), 22–7; Isidor I. Rabi, *Science: The Center of Culture* (Cleveland, OH: World Publishing, 1970), 66–70; Owens, "Counterproductive Management of Science," 527, 554–6.
24 For Jewett's views, see US Congress, Senate, Subcommittee on War Mobilization of the Committee on Military Affairs, *Hearings on Science Legislation*, 79th Cong., 1st sess., 1945, 427–47, and 1116–18.
25 US Congress, House, Committee on Military Affairs, *Hearings, Research and Development*, 79th Cong., 1st sess., 1945, 5–7; Vannevar Bush, *Science: The Endless Frontier. A Report to the President by Vannevar Bush, Director, OSRD, July 1945* (Washington, DC: Government Printing Office, 1945), 27–8.
26 The Magnuson and Kilgore bills are summarized in *Hearings, Research and Development*, 2–8.
27 Ibid., 52–66, 91–3, 786–7, 967–8; *Science* 104 (4 January 1946), 11.
28 Truman memo for Secretary of War and Secretary of the Navy, 23 January 1946, Harry S. Truman Papers, Official File, Box 1523, OF 692 (1945–47), Harry S. Truman Library (HSTL), Independence, MO.
29 Howard A. Meyerhoff, "Obituary: National Science Foundation," *Science* 104 (2 August 1946): 97; J. Donald Kingsley memo to Dr John R. Steelman, Issues Involved in Proposed Legislation for a National Science Foundation, 31 December 1946, Truman Papers, Official File, Box 681,

OF 192-E, National Science Foundation (1945–47), HSTL; J. Merton England, *A Patron for Pure Science: The National Science Foundation's Formative Years, 1950–57* (Washington, DC: National Science Foundation, 1983), 48–59.

30 Patterson in *Hearings on Science Legislation*, 228; Michael Aaron Dennis, "'Our First Line of Defense': Two University Laboratories in the Postwar American State," *Isis* 85 (1994): 427.

31 Daniel J. Kevles, "Scientists, the Military, and the Control of Postwar Defense Research: The Case of the Research Board for National Security, 1944–46," *Technology and Culture* 16 (January 1975): 20–31, 35–44.

32 US Congress, House, Select Committee on Postwar Military Policy, *Hearings, Surplus Material – Research and Development*, 78th Cong., 2d sess., 1944–45, 179.

33 Roger L. Geiger, "Science, Universities, and National Defense, 1945–1970," *Osiris* 7 (1992): 26–48, esp. 35–7; Harvey M. Sapolsky, *Science and the Navy* (Princeton, NJ: Princeton University Press, 1990), 132; Richard V. Damms, *Scientists and Statesmen: Eisenhower's Science Advisers and National Security Policy* (Dordrecht, NL: Republic of Letters Publishing, 2015), 45–6.

34 Warren Weaver to Secretary of the Navy James V. Forrestal, 3 January 1947, Harry S. Truman Papers, Official File, Box 677, OF 192 (1945–August 1947), HSTL.

35 Compton to John R. Steelman, 26 September 1947, Harry S. Truman Papers, Official File, Box 678, OF 192 (October 1947), HSTL; Damms, *Scientists and Statesmen*, 46, 59–60.

36 Eisenhower to Directors and Chiefs of War Department, 30 April 1946, in Louis Galambos, ed., *The Papers of Dwight D. Eisenhower*, vol. 7, *The Chief of Staff* (Baltimore, MD: Johns Hopkins University Press, 1978), 1046–49; Vannevar Bush memo to scientists and engineers now or formerly associated with the Office of Scientific Research and Development, no date, Isidor I. Rabi Papers, Box 38, Columbia University Office File, Folder: Navy Department Research and Development, 1942–1948, Manuscripts Division, Library of Congress (LC), Washington, DC.

37 Eisenhower to Secretary of War Patterson, 27 April 1946, *Eisenhower Papers*, 7:1045–6.

38 Thomas C. Lassman, "Putting the Military Back into the History of the Military-Industrial Complex: The Management of Technological Innovation in the U.S. Army, 1945–1960," *Isis* 106 (2015): 94–120, esp. 101–7.

39 Leslie, *The Cold War and American Science*, 27–8.

40 Eisenhower to Joint Chiefs of Staff, Memoranda Regarding Army-Navy Research and Development, 31 December 1945, note 5, *Eisenhower Papers* 7:707–8.
41 Damms, *Scientists and Statesmen*, 47–8; Steven L. Rearden, *A History of the Office of the Secretary of Defense*, vol. 1, *The Formative Years, 1947–1950* (Washington, DC: Office of the secretary of Defense Historical Office, 1984), 96–101, 385–401; Golden memo of conversation with William Webster, chair RDB, on 29 November 1950, 4 December 1950, William T. Golden Papers, box 1, folder: Government Military Scientific Research Review 2, HSTL.
42 Michael J. Hogan, *A Cross of Iron: Harry S. Truman and the Origins of the National Security State, 1945–1954* (New York: Cambridge University Press, 1998), 231–2.
43 Philip M. Morse, *In at the Beginnings: A Physicist's Life* (Cambridge, MA: MIT Press, 1977), 244–50.
44 Damms, *Scientists and Statesmen*, 48–9; David A. Rosenberg, "American Atomic Strategy and the Hydrogen Bomb Decision," *Journal of American History* 66 (June 1979): 83–4; US Congress, House, Committee on Armed Services, *Hearings on the National Defense Program – Unification and Strategy*, 81st Cong., 1st sess., 1949, 52, 259, 350–1, 451–8, 472–4, 515–41.
45 Hewlett and Anderson, *The New World*, 408–13; Kevles, *The Physicists*, 349.
46 US Congress, House, Committee on Military Affairs, *Atomic Energy, Hearings*, 79th Cong., 1st sess., 1945, 35–9, 51–2. During hearings on the NSF bills on 17 October 1945, Oppenheimer remarked: "The Johnson Bill, I don't know much about." See US Congress, Senate, Subcommittee on War Mobilization of the Committee on Military Affairs, *Hearings on Science Legislation*, 79th Cong., 1st sess., 1945, 306.
47 Survey of the Federation of American Scientists, 17 January 1946, J. Robert Oppenheimer Papers, Membership File, Box 120, Folder: FAS, 1943–June 1946, LC.
48 Hewlett and Anderson, *New World*, 436–9; *Bulletin of the Atomic Scientists* 1 (24 December 1945): 5.
49 Lee A. DuBridge telegram to Hon. Leroy Johnson, n.d., Rabi Papers, Box 15, Columbia University Office File, Folder Atomic Bomb, 1945–85, LC.
50 Truman memo for the Secretary of War and the Secretary of the Navy, 23 January 1946, Truman Papers, Official File, Box 1523, OF 692 (1945–47), HSTL.
51 FAS press release, 27 March 1946, Oppenheimer Papers, Membership File, Box 120, Folder: FAS, 1943–June 1946, LC.

52 Eisenhower to Patterson, 4 June 1946, *Eisenhower Papers* 7:1101–2; Damms, *Scientists and Statesmen*, 33–4; Alice Kimball Smith, *A Peril and a Hope*, 312–18.
53 Hart, *Forged Consensus*, 189–91.
54 Zachary, *Endless Frontier*, 309.
55 Golden memo for file of conversation with Dr James B. Conant, 14 December 1950, William T. Golden Papers, box 1, folder: Government Military Scientific Review 2, HSTL.
56 James R. Killian, Jr, "Obligations and Ideals of an Institute of Technology," *Technology Review* 51 (May 1949): 429–31; "The Universities in a Period of Armed Truce," *Vital Speeches* 19 (1949–50): 252–6; and "Military Research in the Universities," *Proceedings of the American Society for Engineering Education* 60 (1952–53): 13–17; Geiger, "Science, Universities, and National Defense," 35–6; Michael Sherry, *Preparing for the Next War: American Plans for Postwar Defense* (New Haven, CT: Yale University Press, 1977), chapter 5, passim.
57 James R. Killian, Jr, *The Education of a College President: A Memoir* (Cambridge, MA: MIT Press, 1985), 71–3.
58 Paul Klopsteg, "University responsibilities and government money," *Science* 124 (1956): 919–22; Paul Forman, "Into Quantum Electronics," 262–3.
59 Forman, "Into Quantum Electronics," 262.
60 Isidor I. Rabi, "The Physicist Returns from the War," *Atlantic Monthly* 176 (1945): 107–14.
61 Forman, "Into Quantum Electronics," 265–9.
62 Memo of conversation with Robert F. Bacher on 3 February 1951, 6 February 1951, William T. Golden Papers, box 1, folder: Government Military Scientific Review 2, HSTL.
63 DuBridge to ODM Director Arthur Flemming, 12 August 1953, and DuBridge to Waterman, 18 August 1953, both in Karl Compton-James Killian Papers as Institute President, AC-4, Box 213, Institute Archives and Special Collections, MIT, Cambridge, MA; England, *Patron for Pure Science*, 197–201.

8

Edward Murrow and the "Little People" of the Blitz

A Study in American Idealism

Sean Dettman

I'm standing on a rooftop looking out over London. At the moment everything is quiet ... Off to my left, far away anti-aircraft bursts against the steel sky, but the guns are so far away that it's impossible for me to hear them from this location.

Edward Murrow, *This Is London*[1]

The Second World War had a profound effect on all aspects of British life. Since its end, historians have tried to determine what the conflict meant to different people. Although the arguments have evolved to reflect the political mood of the time, most studies seek to define what it meant to be British during the Second World War, including concepts of citizenship, national identity, and unity, as well as the collective experience of ordinary Britons as it relates to class, race, and gender. This chapter examines three main points communicated by US journalist Ed Murrow and concludes that the importance of his efforts to draw out the more ideological elements of Britain's war effort for a stronger US commitment toward halting Nazi aggression deserve greater recognition than it has received to date.

First, the evacuations of Dunkirk, the Battle of Britain, and the bombings of London and other British cities during the winter of 1940–41 evoked a sense of sacrifice and national unity among its population, feeding the narrative of the "People's War." This issue is covered comprehensively in a number of scholarly studies. Angus Calder's pioneering work *The People's War* challenges the language coming from British leadership that the people came together as a nation of "unknown warriors" to defend their island against invasion and attack. Instead, Calder concludes, the people surged forward led not by their normal leaders, but rather the "willing brains and hearts" of the most "vigorous elements in the community."[2] Sonya Rose agrees, claiming that a populist and utopian construction of national identity projected a unitary Britain that was conveyed through government propaganda and progressive commentary. However, the cultural construction of "equality of sacrifice" that was crucial to wartime unity failed to produce a single national identity of "the people." Nevertheless, this did not prevent them from being unified in their quest to redefine their experiences along the popular public discourse of "we-ness."[3]

Second, the "People's War" transformed social and political attitudes in Britain. Throughout most of the 1930s, unemployment remained at 2 million people (14 per cent) and the traditional industries of iron, steel, coal, and shipbuilding in northern England and Wales were hit particularly hard. Failure to solve the "social problem" of poverty and mass unemployment affected the perceptions of state legitimacy, alienating those who were needed to ensure the nation's survival. Therefore, if the British people were to engage in "equality of sacrifice," the state had to offer them something in return.[4] Geoffrey Field argues that by 1940 national survival rested upon the active participation of Britain's "little people." This played a major role in shaping the nation's political, social, and cultural development during the early years of the war, bringing about a pronounced shift in the sociopolitical discourse that emphasized "wartime egalitarianism," while promising a fairer post-war Britain. The "People's War effect" had a positive effect on the status of many ordinary Britons, creating a more united country and helping to heal old wounds between state and society.[5]

Last, the shift in the nation's sociopolitical discourse, particularly during the Blitz, was driven by a range of cultural meanings and social behaviours. Central to this concept are the emblematic phrases "taking it" and "carrying on" aimed at boosting morale. Dan Todman suggests that the bombings of London failed to produce any greater sense of national unity, but the Blitz was an event "to which national meaning was ascribed" and that by far the most important meaning was that the country could take it. Of course, these images did not represent everybody's experience, but they did help people who were in the thick of the bombings cope with the situation and build self-confidence.[6] Indeed, morale was "the woolliest and most muddled concept of the war" that often left government officials looking to American journalists to bolster British resolve.[7] Angus Calder's *The Myth of the Blitz* goes a long way to demonstrate how "taking it" was an American expression, and therefore all the more believable because it came from American and therefore neutral sources.[8] Yet a closer review of the historical record shows that US journalists rushed to Britain in summer 1940 not as "chaperoned scribes" but as adventure seekers with strong convictions, voicing their support for the "People's War" through a particular worldview that was ideologically aligned with US democratic values and principles.[9]

Certainly, these conversations were not confined to British voices only, but reflected a wider understanding of social democratic values.[10] By summer 1940, there were well over one hundred US journalists reporting on the Battle of Britain and then the Blitz. These individuals were key architects of the "People's War" narrative; they positioned a new national solidarity at the centre of their stories and thus habituated global audiences to viewing the war as a dynamic moment of change. Yet there has been little research highlighting their motivations for travelling to London and for rearticulating the major themes of the "People's War" back to the United States. This chapter argues that a core group of ideologically charged American broadcasters, journalists, and correspondents were excited by reports showcasing the transformative effects of the "People's War" and the movement in language that created conditions for a "social revolution."

Evidence for these arguments can be found in the published accounts of American journalists during this period and their private papers. The former is often overlooked in the historiography of the Blitz, while the latter is a rich source of their true motivations for supporting Britain's war effort. These trade publications are a mixture of personal accounts and recorded broadcasts, full of emotive language and strong ideology that laid bare the conditions of the "People's War." Ed Murrow's *This is London* (1941) holds a special place in the Blitz canon. If not the most important period of his prolific life, Murrow had certainly mastered his powerful technique and gave support to the "little people" of the world in his broadcasts during these events. This would have a profound effect on how he viewed Britain's mobilization to defend its country against attack, and the nature of the British people's demands for a fairer and more equal post-war society.

The sheer volume of material covering Murrow's fertile career has produced a range of interpretations. A common view is that Murrow was a man of integrity, whose balanced reporting of the Blitz has come to define his legacy during this period, leaving most historians to emphasize his contributions to the newly emerging field of broadcast journalism.[11] Such characterizations miss an important point: that Murrow's advocacy of democratic values and principles informed much of his style. For Murrow, the new technologies of radio and then television were less about standards, and more about using the mediums to push the boundaries of popular public consciousness, particularly during the winter of 1940–41. What emerged was a rich tapestry of ideology, cooperation, and a utopian vision of a more inclusive post-war world.

In practice, of course, this proved more difficult than Murrow hoped. The "People's War" unleashed the revolutionary language of the young for the purpose of bringing about social change that Murrow and other US journalists looked to articulate through "New World thinking." Although he largely followed the rhetorical framework of his British colleagues and friends by showcasing the "little people" of the Blitz with regard to sacrifice, heroism, and class to promote national unity, a significant body of evidence suggests that Murrow communicated these themes back to the American people, particularly the idea that Britain was undergoing a "social revolution," through a distinct American mindset. This was done largely as proof that the "little people" were pushing the nation toward becoming more democratic in look and feel, and they deserved a stronger commitment from the American people to deal more effectively with Nazi aggression. By 1941, there was an observable correlation between Murrow's broadcasts and the United States' pledge to act as the "arsenal of democracy." Yet the extent to which they laid the foundations for a more equal and fairer society, both in Britain and the United States, is the subject of intense historical debate.

"THIS IS LONDON"

On the eve of the Second World War, the British government was facing a crisis of confidence that threatened its ability to defend the nation against a Nazi attack. The economic dislocation of the 1930s and the failure of the "just reward" system in Britain resulted in a "distinct disconnect" between government "rhetoric and reality," leaving many citizens apathetic and less than enthusiastic about fighting. As Jonathan Fennell notes, democracies that fail to manage narratives regarding structural inequalities and social justice cannot expect a "passionate commitment" from citizens to defend its position. Thus, by 1939, the British government was left scrambling to devise a strategy of national survival that depended on everyone, both on the battle front and the home front.[12] To help disseminate this message, senior government officials enlisted the support of US journalists to bolster claims that the nation was united in its aims and purpose, ready to meet the enemy head on.[13] By 1940, officers at the British Broadcasting Corporation and the Ministry of Information were regularly supplying US journalists with special viewing facilities to "reinforce their objectivity." Most of the correspondents responded with a steady flow of "good stories" that demonstrated Britain's "energy and determination" for the purpose of boosting morale in both Britain and the United States.[14]

However, the fall of France in June 1940 signalled that the European balance had been radically upset and that a single aggressive power now dominated the whole continent, leaving Britain's ability to survive in doubt.[15] As the Battle of Britain played out in the skies over the southeast of England and the Channel, a core group of American journalists working in London began to echo the popular public sentiments coming from scores of progressive British commentators who were attempting to alter public discourse about class, tradition, and democratic values and norms. This type of reporting by the small but ideologically charged cluster of American correspondents and broadcasters is a good example of the "People's War effect." As Geoffrey Fields reminds us, it is easy to forget how deeply divided Britain was along class lines in the interwar period.[16] However, the sacrifice of the British people, and the shared dangers along class-based lines during the events of summer and autumn 1940, helped erode social distinctions, linking the shared experiences of the "People's War" directly with the undertakings of the "People's Peace."[17] Over the course of the next 10 months, these US journalists reported the emerging concepts of the "People's War" with great enthusiasm and excitement, with the aim of showcasing the British people at war for the purpose of a stronger US commitment against Nazi aggression in Europe.

More than any other US journalist working in Britain during this period, Ed Murrow looked to report the "People's War" not as a neutral reporter but as an active participant. No doubt this influenced his selection of material, such as courage, class, and tradition as it related to civilian defence, and the extent to which his reporting of the "People's War" was shaped by his own understanding of American democratic principles. Central to Murrow's broadcasts of the Blitz were the everyday people of Britain, who, he prophesied, would sacrifice the most during the bombings. On 18 August, Murrow stated that it was the "little people" he wanted to discuss, "who live in those little houses who have no uniforms and get no decorations for bravery." According to Murrow, "there was no bravado, no loud voices" coming from the common people who were now tasked with undertaking the bulk of the fighting that lay ahead, only a "quiet acceptance of the situation."[18] Weeks later, he told his audience that life in Britain was very different than before the war, and that the courage of the British people "must be experienced to be understood."[19] Enthused by what he was witnessing, Murrow wrote to his parents in September that it was this section of British society that had provided the majority of resilience and energy, and that those who had "appeared strong are weak and others have found strength from strange backgrounds."[20]

Similar to the progressive commentary undertaken by the likes of J.B. Priestley, E.H. Carr, and Ritchie Calder, Murrow looked to explain how these levels of sacrifice would alter the status of the "little people" by articulating their position through the rhetoric of class and tradition. Most historians agree that 7 September 1940 marks the opening of the Blitz, when the Luftwaffe dropped thousands of one-kilogram incendiary bombs on the East End. Bombs hit the wharfs and factories, where the curve of the Thames made them an easy target for German raiders. Subsequent fires then quickly spread through the closely packed neighbourhoods on both sides of the river.[21] Over the course of the next two months, these targets were bombed repeatedly, with little reprieve. Almost immediately, Murrow began broadcasting the conditions of the working-class districts of the East End where "cheap, flimsy houses jammed one against the other" were under attack by Nazi bombers.[22] Two days after the Blitz began, on 9 September, Murrow reported that these communities "where disaster is always just around the corner" were handling the attacks better "than the more fashionable districts in the West End."[23] Analysis of these remarks suggests that Murrow quickly moved beyond the scripted narrative of unity and courage once the bombings accelerated, and toward challenging what he viewed as the more uneven aspects of British society.

The mounting criticism in Murrow's broadcasts was leveraged by statements aimed at boosting morale with promises of a more democratic post-war Britain. Days after the bombings began, Murrow addressed the prospect of a collapse in national confidence and a negotiated peace by the British government. He told his audiences in both the United States and Britain that Hitler and his people "believe Londoners, after a while, will rise up and demand a new government, one that will make peace with Germany." Yet according to Murrow, the "little people" of Britain were more interested in defending their island for the purpose of a fairer and more egalitarian society than pursuing a negotiated peace and living in muted liberties under a fascist regime. "The politicians who called this a 'People's War' were right," he argued, "probably more right than they knew at times. I have seen some horrible sights in this city during these days and nights, but not once have I heard man, woman, or child suggest that Britain should throw in her hand." Murrow concluded that after four days and four nights, the British people were rapidly becoming hardened veterans in the battle for London, with a view to first defeating Nazi aggression and then winning the minds of British leadership.[24] According to Angus Calder, Murrow's assessment was all the more believable because it came from an American and therefore neutral source.[25] Yet there was very little neutrality in his evaluation of the situation and advocacy for extending rights and representation to the "little people" of the Blitz.

For Murrow, the reorganization of British society during the Blitz was more than a national defence effort to repel invasion; it was the very basis on which egalitarian change could occur. In July 1940, Britain's new coalition government brought in emergency measures that enabled it to seize public property, levy harsh taxes, implement strict rationing, and impose a curfew, as well as other national controls.[26] According to Murrow, these emergency powers were some of the most sweeping changes Britain had ever experienced, and the speed with which the government had implemented these rules over life and property, he argued "will probably be surprising to the British who are accustomed to a cumbersome, slow-moving government machine bound in red-tape, formality, and tradition."[27] He continued by stating that the changes to the social and political culture encompassing the nation would have been "called revolutionary" in peacetime, while guessing that there would be more "sweeping changes in this war." Central to his message was that Britain was now tasked to devise a workable solution to stem the rise of authoritarian regimes on the continent, with a renewed commitment to "social justice" without "smashing the unity of the nation" or restricting individual liberties. Borrowing an analogy he had heard from J.B. Priestley only days before, Murrow closed his broadcast by stating that "this ferment of change" was a revolt against the "long rule by old men whose ideal for their country was a comfortable old age."[28] Indeed, this view reflected a radical shift in the nation's thinking and provided Murrow a platform to espouse his own ideas on political and social reform.

Nowhere was this type of change more obvious in Murrow's broadcasts than in his reporting of non-democratic structures and institutions. According to Sonya Rose, the media was instrumental in portraying the political elite and royalty as equal participants in the "People's War."[29] Undeniably, Murrow also presented the king and queen as working side-by-side with the British people. On 9 September, he explained how the king and queen, long-standing symbols of class in Britain, spent the day visiting heavily bombed areas of East London. According to his broadcast, the "little people" displayed a "calm and quiet" manner among the royal couple, demonstrating "that they are all in this thing together."[30] Yet when Buckingham Palace was bombed five days later, Murrow sought to expose the underlying conditions of their support for the royal family, stating that the bombing of the iconic London palace went relatively unnoticed by the "little people" and, according to one Londoner, "wouldn't seriously have damaged the nation's war effort." It is true that the king and queen had earned the "respect and admiration of the nation," he claimed, but so "have tens of thousands of humble folk who are much less well protected." Murrow used his editorial privileges not to provoke class resentment during a time of national emergency, but rather to contextualize how "this war has no relation with the last one, so far as symbols and civilians are concerned." According to Murrow, the world of privilege and status "is dying," and the "old values, the old prejudices, and the old bases of power and prestige are gone." Taking its place, he concluded, was something more inclusive and, overall, a lot better.[31]

Murrow's language advocating the shift in political and social dynamics away from established elite positions aligned with his proletarian roots and support for the historically marginalized and under-represented.[32] Throughout the opening weeks of the air attacks, he stated that if the ruling class trusted the defence of the nation with "the people who work with their hands," then the defence of Britain "will be something of which men will speak with awe and admiration as long as the English language survives."[33] As the bombings intensified, he refined this message that the nation's new workman mentality dominated the rescue efforts, reporting that the labourers working "down here on the ground" paid little attention to the bursts of anti-aircraft fire overhead "as they bent their backs and carried away basketfuls of mortar and brick."[34] Key to these efforts, he continued, was the American concept that the bombings had created a "frontier atmosphere," and that for some Londoners "action seems to drive out fear."[35] Clearly these concepts of work, community, and courage were not confined to a strictly American understanding, but also reflected a larger conversation brought about by the conditions of a nation at war. However, Murrow communicated the events of autumn 1940 through democratic language that was symptomatic of New World thinking, mainly vitality, class, and tradition. The effect he had on his audiences, both in Britain and the United States, was instrumental in generating further enthusiasm for the regeneration of a "new England."

"LONDON CAN TAKE IT"

A significant aspect of the "People's War" was the British cultural construct of "taking it," which produced new ways of thinking and acting that became politically mobilized during summer 1940.[36] By October, more American journalists began arriving to see if London, in fact, could take it. Reports on this started to appear in Ralph Ingersoll's popular leftist American publication *PM*, prompting him first to send Ben Robertson to find out how well British morale was holding up, before arriving in Britain himself in late autumn 1940. Ingersoll concluded that there was no reason not to believe that "London can take it if it continues to want to, and it certainly was prepared to when I was there."[37] In November, the original roving reporter, Ernie Pyle, insisted that "London's amazing ability to take it" was obvious in the "attitude of the people ... the casual way folks talk" and "just by looking around and seeing people going about their business."[38] Other American journalists argued that the "People's War" rested solely on how far Britain "can resist the Blitzkrieg."[39] These endorsements by popular American media personalities had a massive effect on US public opinion, while strengthening Anglo-American efforts to keep Hitler confined to the European continent.

This level of transatlantic cooperation reached its apogee in late 1940 with the release of a ten-minute documentary titled *London Can Take It!* Later renamed *Britain Can Take It* to reflect the shift in Nazi bombing tactics to include other British cities, the Ministry of Information's Crown Film Unit hired famed US journalist Quentin Reynolds to convey the rhetorical framework of Britain's resolve and stoic ability to "carry on."[40] "I am a neutral reporter," he concludes, and although "It is true that the Nazis will be over again tomorrow night and the night after that and every night. They will drop thousands of bombs and they'll destroy hundreds of buildings, and they'll kill thousands of people … But they cannot kill the unconquerable spirit and courage of the people of London. London can take it."[41] The significance of Reynolds framing the "taking it" narrative as a neutral reporter, like Murrow, masked his support for the "little people" of the Blitz, while confirming in the United States Britain's growing sense of national resilience. The documentary was a resounding success and the term "taking it" was quickly absorbed into the national lexicon, indicating how "strong the desire for American approval of its spirit was in the country."[42]

The image of Londoners standing up to German bombs portrayed by Murrow and his colleagues was directly linked with the notion that Britain was undergoing a social revolution.[43] Perhaps more than any other wartime change, this transformation was communicated as distinctly American in character. Writing soon after he returned to the US in early 1941, Murrow's colleague at CBS Eric Sevareid observed that "a wonderful thing was happening to the British people, some kind of moral revolution was underway, and out of it would come the regeneration of a people."[44] He continued:

> And so it was at this point that a new conception of the war
> began to take root in the minds of the imaginative and articulate:
> the idea that Hitler's pressure was accomplishing rapidly
> what the long struggle of organized working-class British people
> had been approaching only very slowly. Perhaps we confused the
> wish with the fact, but we caught sight of a new England: men
> who had so suffered and achieved in common would no longer

fear one another's clothes, accents or manners ... Men and women who sacrificed their chill and ugly dwellings for the absorption of the enemy's explosives would demand to return to something better than the slums ... All the men of social conscience and vision had always insisted could be done was now being done. It was being done to make the nation safe; it could – and would, we thought – be done later to make the people happy. For the first time the war seemed to have taken on a positive meaning.[45]

The suggestion that the "little people" of Britain were trading in their meagre dwellings for a stake in a new and more dynamic Britain excited many American journalists, who hurried there to tell the story. Elmer Davis joined Murrow in a tour of bombed-out Britain in early 1941. An early sceptic of Britain's position, Davis quickly reversed his views, writing soon after his visit that "you'll see a tougher, leaner, poorer England; more egalitarian, and probably on the whole very much better."[46] This suggests that Sevareid, like Davis, believed the bombings were finally achieving what decades of progressive mobilization had not – the bringing together of all people of social consciousness, including the "little people," for the purpose of a more democratic society.

The levels of enthusiasm demonstrated by this core group of headstrong American journalists for a more "positive meaning" of the war is best captured in their support for Britain's "swing to the left." According to Ralph Ingersoll, the worst thing that could happen to Britain was "to have Germans stop bombing it." As long as the bombs don't kill too many people, he continued, "England will continue to change, and for what we in America will think for the better." He concluded:

Class snobbery, so offensive to us whether in lords and ladies or truck drivers or scullery maids, is forcibly breaking down. A nation cannot sleep wherever it finds itself at night and with whomever happens to lie down next to it and not have things happen to its class distinction. A nation cannot be in such desperate need of skill and so deeply indebted to whoever has it regardless of class without things happening to it. A nation cannot go bankrupt cheerfully as England is going bankrupt within the next six months without things happening to social relations based on capital and property.[47]

When Ingersoll returned to the United States, a friend asked him "Do you believe there is a social revolution in England? And if so, in what direction?" – to which he quickly answered "Yes. To the Left."[48] Whether this indicates Ingersoll's own understanding of what Americans believed a better Britain would look like or reflected popular sentiments regarding US democratic values and principles is unknown. Yet there is no doubt that Ingersoll, like Davis and Sevareid, communicated his support for the "People's War" by showing how a post-war Britain might more closely resemble the United States in scope and feel.

Again, the energy for Britain's "swing to the left" and shift in the sociopolitical landscape was part of a wider effort of progressive commentators "whose appeal spanned all classes and regions."[49] Whether their efforts to inspire a "revolution by consent" signalled a more radical shift in Britain's political culture or reflected a more negative rejection of the "comfortable old age" of the Conservative Party is often debated. Geoffrey Field suggests that the destruction of British cities, battlefield defeats, and growing anxiety over the direction of the war in the early years precipitated the public discourse that focused almost entirely on radical change. The outbreak of war and the participation of the "little people" in the defence of Britain brought further changes in the "arena of public debate" which moved popular opinion further to the left.[50] The "growing terrain" of shared cultural references such as "fair shares" and "equality of sacrifice" accelerated the call for a new social contract.[51] Labour was the unquestionable beneficiary of this new public discourse and party hardliners such as Harold Laski shared Murrow's views (Laski and Murrow were good friends) that conditions for social reform were looming.[52]

Key to Laski's argument was that the progressive movement was no longer bargaining as the supplicant and therefore should leverage its position for a post-war vision aligned with party ideology.[53] In several instances, this included direct references to democratic values and structures in the United States. In addition to Murrow, Laski was also friendly with US president Franklin Roosevelt, the architect of US social and economic reforms brought about by the New Deal. The two friends had been communicating for several years, mostly discussing the plight of the common man and the extent to which New Deal thinking could cure the world of social injustices. In late October, Laski wrote to Roosevelt offering a glimpse of what it was like for the British people during the bombings, stating that his "heart goes out to these grand people" who had faced adversity with dignity and honour. Yet Laski pushed further, telling the president that "the condition of a real victory is a New Deal for Britain," and that if its leaders could tell "the homeless docker and the evacuated mother" that the "New Deal begins for them and their children even while our national existence is at stake," British leadership would not only commit the nation to an "unbreakable resolution," but also serve notice to the Nazi powers "that the world we envisage is better than any they can offer and is being made even while bombs fall. That England and FDR's America in conjunction," Laski concluded, "can take over the leadership of the masses throughout the world. There is the best revolution by consent in world-history in this approach."[54]

Laski's enthusiasm for a British New Deal was matched only by Murrow's efforts to push for a clear set of British war aims. At about the same time that Laski was writing to Roosevelt, Murrow broadcast that there was "occurring in this country a revolution by consent," which called for more public services and shelters, reducing unemployment, and expanding opportunity for everyone. Equally, argued Murrow, there needed to be a more workable solution for a post-war Britain other than the "long rule by old men" that had paralyzed European democracies for the past twenty years. He stated that more than anything else, it was these issues that over the past several weeks "of the air blitz of this country" the British people had debated and discussed, and that only the political system that "best provides for the defence and decency of the little man will win."[55]

There is every reason to believe that Murrow's comments were genuine. Days later, he told his parents that "this war will end in revolution and bloodshed such as the world has never seen before," and although there will be "rough days ahead for anyone who is interested in truth ... I have no desire to escape it."[56] No doubt Murrow and his colleagues reported the events of the Blitz with an imperfect sense of US democratic values and how they related to the "People's War." But it is clear that he perceived the "little people" of Britain as being proactive in the defence of the nation and part of a wider movement to change the public discourse about their position within society – a project that encouraged a new type of mentality and language.[57] In mid-November, Murrow told his parents that "there is no chance of going back to the old ways and the old life," and although "an entire world is going down in ruins," he had no regrets as "maybe something better will be born of it all."[58]

"UNNEUTRAL REPORTING"

Murrow's goal, then, was to communicate the more ideological aspects of the "People's War," and the promise of a more democratic Britain for the purpose of a stronger US commitment to combat the spread of fascism in Europe. In particular, Murrow and his colleagues advocated full-scale mobilization of US industry to a war footing and an accelerated US policy of aid to Britain. In December, Murrow suggested that "no definition of democracy's objectives can be made until it comes from Washington," or, at the very least, in the form of a "joint declaration" from Britain and the United States. Only then, he concluded, can the Anglo-American post-war world establish the universal basic principles of personal liberties, freedom, and the "restoration of peace and happiness to man." The theory that the United States could serve as an effective check on Nazi Germany as a non-belligerent rather than a fully fledged ally had "perished," argued Murrow, and nothing short of US participation in the war would guarantee a stable and liberal post-war order.[59]

By the end of 1940, Murrow had all but abandoned the veneer of neutral reporting, while accelerating his language linking the themes of the "People's War" in Britain with US participation in the war. During his Christmas Eve broadcast, Murrow told the American people that "This is not a merry Christmas in London ... for the people who spend tonight and tomorrow night by their firesides in their own homes realize that they have bought this Christmas with their nerves, their bodies, and their old buildings." Although the painful year of 1940 was coming to an end, Murrow concluded, the space "between now and next Christmas" will only bring "increased toil and sacrifice," a period when "Britishers will live hard." Yet most of the "little people" were thinking about the future rather than the "aftermath of hardship" sustained over the past year.[60]

Murrow's broadcasts suggesting that nothing less than the fate of the British nation was at stake had a widespread effect, making them attractive ornaments for Roosevelt's pro-aid policies in the United States. Fully aware of his position and growing bolder in his assessment, Murrow reminded his audience on 29 December that Britain and its democracy "is in mortal danger." He stated that although few people in Britain would have admitted in December 1939 that "American action would determine the outcome of the war," as it stood in December 1940 the "realization is widespread" that decisions taken in Washington "will determine the course of the war during the coming year or years." Murrow finished his broadcast by arguing that the "little people" of the Blitz "have seen a powerful enemy advance almost to their homes" as well as the "beginning of great social changes," yet they have never failed to face "death in the streets and by their fireside."[61] These words were particularly relevant on this night, as London underwent one of the worst raids of the entire Blitz: historic monuments were destroyed, St Paul's Cathedral was damaged, warehouses and slums destroyed – hundreds of years of British history, and to some extent, the history of "the Western world," had gone up in smoke.[62] Thousands of miles away, almost at the exact same time, Roosevelt was telling the American people of his plans for the United Sates to act as the "arsenal of democracy."

Murrow's last broadcast of 1940, only days after Roosevelt's announcement, brought the events of the past 12 months into focus, while attempting to explain what they meant to the American and British people. On 31 December, he reminded his audience in the United States that as they celebrated the New Year, Britain was under siege: "[Y]ou will have no dawn raid as we shall probably have if the weather is light. You will walk this night in the light. Your families are not scattered by the winds of war." Yet it was the opinion of nearly every "informed observer over here that the decisions you take will overshadow all else during this year that opened an hour ago in London."[63] It was fitting, in acknowledging that 1940 brought very different experiences for the two countries, that Murrow used the occasion to mobilize popular opinion in the United States, with very little sense of neutrality. Only weeks before, Murrow admitted that he was ready to use his influence to "preach from a powerful pulpit" for "the eternal verities of living and dying."[64] Not willing to let the opportunity pass him by, Murrow declared that he had spent the last three years cultivating his audience, and now had every intention of using it "for all it's worth."[65]

CONCLUSION: "THE STORY OF WAR"

In 1959, Ed Murrow returned to a London "in peace," where he "once told a listening world the story of war." The picture that emerges from the documentary confirmed his view that the "People's Peace" was being forged by the same "little people" of the "People's War." To reinforce his position, Murrow read from a pamphlet titled *War Aims*

(1939) written by the British political theorist George Douglas Howard Cole that was circulating in Britain during those "dark days and darker nights." The passage that Murrow read focused exclusively on the points that he hoped to help realize during the second half of 1940, including the idea that Britain did not "fight to restore, but to rebuild." He concluded that the "little people" were determined that Britain after the war would not be the same Britain as before the war – "the equality of sacrifice obtained during the war would replace the inequality of opportunity. In short, fair shares for all."[66]

Few rival Murrow's legacy as a journalist. The record of his achievements includes a long list of awards, accolades, and honours bestowed upon him by the highest holders of British and American leadership. According to his biographer, Joseph Persico, Murrow "infected his people with his religion," bringing them to the mountaintop of broadcast journalism and then television.[67] Yet it was in the opening years of the war, particularly the events of 1940, that leave little doubt as to where his own priorities lay. The war to Murrow was not solely about defeating the evils of Nazism but defeating the pervasive social and economic injustices of the pre-war world. To achieve this end, he stayed true to his proletarian roots, while developing a reputation as an unrelenting stinging critic of "unearned privilege, a champion of the underdog and advocate of a new social order." The Blitz made him a household name, in both Britain and the United States; he employed his new power in the service of his democratic convictions.[68]

Murrow elaborated on this doctrine in his reporting of the "People's War" in three main ways. First, he looked to alter the status of the "little people" of the Blitz by challenging the long-standing language of class and tradition, while drawing the American people's attention to their energy to defend the nation against attack. Although he may have played a smaller role than British commentators in the effort to bring about revolutionary change, his contribution had a profound effect. By echoing the idea that the "little people" of the Blitz played an active role in the defence of the British nation against Nazi air attacks, he helped instigate new conversations on both sides of the Atlantic, about the energy of Britain's war effort. Evidence for this can be found in his many broadcasts that sought to highlight the shift in the sociopolitical discourse to help establish a "new Britain."

Second, the lessons of the "People's War," widely drawn from the broadcasts and accounts by a core group of ideologically charged US journalists, was that the fate of democracy in Britain was irrevocably tied to the outcome of a social revolution gripping the nation; no longer could the champions of democratic values and principles wait for the "old ferment of change;" rather, they should seize the moment with power and determination. Often, these transformations were communicated through an American temperament. Finally, Murrow and his colleagues advocated their support for the "little people" of the Blitz and the revolutionary spirit that they were forging as justification for a stronger US commitment against Nazi bombs falling on British cities. By the end of 1940, Murrow had abandoned any sense of impartiality, instead using his editorial privileges to link, often explicitly, the survival of the British nation and democracy in Europe with full-scale US belligerency. Only then, he argued, would the United States be in a position to secure an Anglo-American post-war liberal order forged by the common man.

But with how much certainty can we take this narrative at face value? Unsurprisingly, both British and American commentators made considerable use of these convenient images of the British people at war. Popular descriptions of the "People's War" sought to portray a once divided nation ready to unite as one country and defend its position against Nazi attacks. This functioned particularly well for the Labour Party, which was unquestionably a beneficiary of these discussions, by highlighting the failures of the interwar years and portraying Labour largely as the vanguard for change.[69]

Both Murrow and his British colleagues fused the historic and contemporary in their analysis of the "People's War," demonstrating the continuity of themes brought about by a nation at war, the behaviour of the "little people" of the Blitz ultimately justifying a fairer, more egalitarian Britain. Yet Murrow's contribution to this assessment is different; in his relationship with the "little people" of the Blitz, Murrow spoke under the auspices of a neutral reporter. But, as this chapter has demonstrated, Murrow's worldview pervaded his reporting. Nevertheless, in the summer, autumn, and winter of 1940, there was little doubt that his reports carried a sense of authority that transcended national barriers. As a result, Murrow and his colleagues were able to add another layer to the "People's War" narrative, one that was distinctly American in character, and play their part in the sociopolitical changes that would accompany the war. It is these aspects of his reporting of the "little people" of the Blitz that have largely been left out of the historical record.

NOTES

1. Edward R. Murrow, *This Is London* (Simon and Shuster), 179.
2. Angus Calder, *The People's War: Britain 1939–1945* (Jonathan Cape, 1969), 17–18.
3. Sonya Rose, *Which People's War? National Identity and Citizenship in Wartime Britain 1939–1945* (Oxford University Press, 2003), 288.
4. Jonathan Fennell, *Fighting the People's War: The British and Commonwealth Armies and the Second World War* (Cambridge University Press, 2019), 681.
5. Geoffrey Field, *Blood, Sweat and Toil: Remaking the British Working Class, 1939–1945* (Oxford University Press, 2011), 374.
6. Dan Todman, *Britain's War: Into Battle 1937–1941* (Penguin, 2016), 522.
7. Paul Addison, *The Road to 1945: British Politics and the Second World War* (Jonathan Cape, 1975), 121; Amy Helen Bell, *London was Ours: Diaries and Memories of the London Blitz* (I.B. Tauris), 52–3.
8. Angus Calder, *The Myth of the Blitz* (Pimlico, 1989), 212.
9. Stephen Casey, *War Beat, Europe: The American Media at War Against Nazi Germany* (Oxford University Press, 2017), 5.
10. Field, *Blood, Sweat and Toil*, 37.
11. Edward Bliss Jr, *In Search of Light: The Broadcasts of Edward R Murrow 1938–1961*, (Palgrave Macmillan, 1968); Alexander Kendrick, *Prime Time: Life of Edward R Murrow* (Littlehampton Books, 1970); A.M Sperber, *Murrow, His Life and Times*, (Freundlich Books, 1986); Joseph E. Persico, *Edward R. Murrow: An American Original*, (Doubleday, 1988); Philip Seib, *Broadcasts of the Blitz: How Edward R Murrow Helped Lead American to War* (Potomac, 2007).
12. Fennell, *Fighting the People's War*, 85, 92.
13. Nicolas Cull, *Selling War: The British Propaganda Campaign Against American "Neutrality" in World War II* (Oxford University Press, 1995), 68.
14. BBC Written Archives Centre, Reading, United Kingdom, R61/3/2, "Facilities for American Broadcasting," 25 January 1940.
15. Todman, *Britain's War*, 361–2.
16. Field, *Blood, Sweat and Toil*, 5.
17. Ibid., 2–3.
18. Murrow, *This is London*, 144–5.
19. Ibid., 177–8.
20. Edward R. Murrow (ERM) letter to Mother and Dad, 20 September 1940, Edward R. and Janet Brewster Murrow Papers,

Mount Holyoake College Archives and Special Collections (MHC), South Hadley, Massachusetts.
21 Todman, *Britain's War*, 474.
22 Murrow, *This is London*, 142.
23 Ibid., 160.
24 Ibid., 163.
25 Calder, *The Myth of the Blitz*, 212.
26 Todman, *Britain's War*, 410–11.
27 Murrow, *This is London*, 105.
28 Ibid., 135–6.
29 Rose, *Which People's War?*, 31–2.
30 Murrow, *This is London*, 173–4.
31 Ibid., 175–7.
32 Persico, *Murrow: An American Original*, 20–1.
33 Murrow, *This London*, 146.
34 Ibid., 197.
35 Ibid., 183–4.
36 Field, *Blood, Sweat and Toil*, 76.
37 Ingersoll, *Report on England* (Simon & Schuster, 1940), 80–1.
38 James Torbin, *Ernie Pyle's War: America's Eyewitness to World War II* (The Free Press, 1997), 55.
39 "Depression Sets in For Business of East England," *Chicago Tribune*, 22 October 1940, 3.
40 Jo Fox, *Film Propaganda in Britain and Nazi Germany* (Berg Publishing, 2007), 109–10.
41 *London Can Take It*, directed by Humphrey Jennings and Harry Watt (1940; Crown Film Unit).
42 Calder, *The Myth of the Blitz*, 215.
43 Todman, *Britain's War*, 488.
44 Eric Sevareid, *Not So Wild a Dream* (University of Missouri Press, 1976), 166.
45 Ibid., 173–5.
46 Elmer Davis, "Journey to England, 1941," *Harper's Magazine* 183 (August 1941), 235.
47 Ingersoll, *Report on England*, 188.
48 Ibid., 188.
49 Field, *Blood, Sweat and Toil*, 303.
50 Ibid., 299.
51 Fennell, *Fighting the People's War*, 89–91.
52 Persico, *Murrow: An American Original*, 120–1.

53 Field, *Blood, Sweat and Toil*, 303.
54 Harold Laski to Franklin Roosevelt, 20 October 1940; Folder: Great Britain, Harold Laski; Papers of Franklin D. Roosevelt; Franklin D. Roosevelt Library, Hyde Park, New York.
55 Murrow, *This is London*, 196.
56 ERM to Mother and Dad, 11 October 1940, MHC, Murrow Papers.
57 Field, *Blood, Sweat and Toil*, 73.
58 ERM to Mother and Dad, 18 November 1940, MHC, Murrow Papers.
59 Murrow, *This is London*, 218–19.
60 Ibid., 222.
61 Murrow, *This is London*, 228.
62 Sperber, *Murrow: His Life and Times*, 182.
63 Murrow, *This is London*, 230.
64 ERM to Janet Brewster Murrow (JBM), 5 December 1940, MHC, Murrow Papers.
65 ERM to JBM, undated, MHC, Murrow Papers.
66 Murrow, *This is London*, 230.
67 Persico, *Murrow: An American Original*, 162.
68 Ibid., 192.
69 Murrow, *This is London*, 218.

… THEME FOUR

Wars among the People

9

German Anti-partisan Warfare

The Spectrum of Ruthlessness to Restraint

Ben H. Shepherd

INTRODUCTION

Between 1941 and 1944, the German armed forces (*Wehrmacht*) inflicted brutal anti-partisan measures across vast swaths of eastern and southern Europe. To place these activities in perspective, it is estimated that in the central sector of the occupied Soviet Union alone, German forces destroyed 5,000 villages and killed 300,000 people, the great majority of whom were non-combatants rather than partisans.[1] This chapter presents a comparative analysis of the anti-partisan warfare practised by the German army in the Soviet Union and Yugoslavia. Although the chapter identifies commonalities in the German approach to anti-partisan operations, its primary aim is to discuss what caused variations in this picture, leading some anti-partisan units to follow ruthless orders unquestioningly, some less severely, and others more severely than ordered. Only by differentiating the picture can the diverse, evolving influences that shaped anti-partisan warfare on the ground be properly understood. It will thus be possible to illuminate how far officers and their units in the field were active agents of brutality, rather than merely – as is widely perceived – passive recipients of brutal higher-level orders. It is also possible to illuminate how much less ruthlessly some officers and units behaved than higher command expected of them. This latter undertaking reflects an anti-partisan campaign whose brutality, though damning, extensive, and heavily intertwined with Nazi ideology, was not entirely uniform and wholesale.

The main command level upon which the chapter focuses is the divisional level, though division-level conduct was also shaped by influences from above and below. This approach seeks to distill the essence of the German approach to anti-partisan operations. It interrogates the extent to which immediate factors, such as pragmatism, personal experience, and frustration might dictate practice over policy or politically inspired ideologies. Consequently, this chapter contributes toward the broader themes of the volume by adding nuance to the issue of individual agency within the "People's War" paradigm, which has too often stressed national homogeneity in beliefs and behaviour.

Questions of agency, responsibility, and restraint are central to comprehending German involvement in the Second World War. However, the answers have long been clouded by post-war expedients. Like so much of the public, political, and scholarly debate surrounding the culpability of the Wehrmacht in Nazi crimes, the German army's conduct of anti-partisan warfare was, for several decades in the West, depicted in sanitized, indeed whitewashed terms. This suited the self-image of the federal German army (the *Bundeswehr*), of its political masters, and of a post-war civilian society that itself, in large part, comprised former soldiers. It also suited the agenda of a western alliance that sought to integrate the new West German armed forces into NATO as a reliable anti-communist ally.[2] Not until the 1980s and 1990s was the full horror of the army's anti-partisan warfare uncovered, though to some extent the newly critical scholarship of that period built on credible earlier work by East German historians.[3] During the 1990s, the German army's anti-partisan campaigns were a major focus of the groundbreaking, controversial Wehrmacht Exhibition, which toured German cities displaying extensive evidence of the army's involvement in an array of war crimes.[4] Their ongoing potential for engendering bitter controversy was highlighted more recently in calls by the far-right Alternative für Deutschland party for Germans to feel national pride and spurn any sense of national shame over Germany's military conduct during the world wars.[5]

Though the actual degree of culpability of ordinary soldiers remains contested, the anti-partisan warfare the German army waged in southern and eastern Europe went well beyond the dictates of military necessity. It was driven by a combination of National Socialist ideology, economic calculation, and ruthless careerism, fused with the German army's unusually severe, long-standing aversion to irregular warfare.[6] Nor was it restricted to compartmentalized sections of the army, such as the small number of security divisions that operated across the Army Group Rear Areas of the occupied Soviet Union. Front-line divisions were also frequently employed in anti-partisan operations, albeit temporarily; indeed, their generally superior equipment, training, and overall standards often better suited them to such operations than the substandard German formations most commonly committed to security or the Germans' indigenous collaborationist forces.[7]

THE INFLUENCE OF GEOGRAPHIC OR NATIONAL SETTING ON BRUTALITY OR RESTRAINT

The particular focus of this chapter is the execution of individuals in grossly disproportionate reprisals and large-scale mobile operations – *Grossunternehmen* – activities that collectively accounted for the vast majority of civilian deaths. Analysis of these activities comprises an effective barometer of brutality. The scale of civilian reprisals was set by orders such as a Wehrmacht High Command directive of 16 September 1941 stipulating the execution of 50 civilians for every German wounded by partisan action, and of 100 civilians for every German killed.[8] Grossunternehmen, meanwhile, saw army units, often with cooperation from collaborationist auxiliaries and/or SS and police personnel, comb large areas supposedly inhabited by pro-partisan populations, or "pro-bandit" populations in the Wehrmacht parlance of 1942 onward.[9] Grossunternehmen varied in form, but the basic concept was that the Germans isolated a suspected partisan-supporting area with a cordon of troops, before mobile troops "cleansed" the surrounded area. However, most victims of Grossunternehmen were civilians, because partisans were often able to elude German forces, leaving German units to conceal their failure through inflated body counts, or to mete out their frustrations on local communities (whom they often viewed with racially tinged disdain, or blamed for aiding partisan groups). By contrast, German forces usually suffered disproportionately minor losses during such operations, indicating that few clashes with armed partisans occurred. As Germany's war worsened, Grossunternehmen also increasingly resembled large-scale plunder operations. They swept up vast amounts of crops and livestock, and redirected labour, aiming to deny resources to the partisans and exploit them for the Germans' own ends.[10]

These methods were applied at different times within the Soviet Union and Yugoslavia. Both territories possessed one or more of the types of terrain, such as mountains, swamps, or forests, within which irregular forces operate most effectively. They were populated by peoples who, sooner or later, were subjected to the brutal, exploitative treatment that Nazi doctrine and its associated beliefs reserved for "inferior races." They also shared a historical tradition of violent resistance toward foreign occupiers. For all these reasons, it was highly probable that partisan warfare would arise within these territories.

The bulk of army security forces in the occupied Soviet Union were stationed in the army-administered occupation zones.[11] How ruthlessly or rapaciously the populations of these regions were treated could depend on a range of pragmatic circumstances, including how far the German war effort coveted their economic resources and on the position of their peoples in the Nazi racial hierarchy. Lowest of all in Nazi eyes, in the Soviet Union as elsewhere, was the Jewish population. More generally, the numerous Soviet regions whose populations Nazi ideology derided and exploited accordingly saw greater levels of partisan activity. These included Russia, the Ukraine, and the area of present-day Belarus. The least extensive anti-German partisan action in the occupied Soviet Union occurred in the Baltic states.

In 1941, German "anti-partisan" measures in the occupied Soviet Union predominantly comprised hunting down purportedly dangerous elements roaming the rural areas. Such elements included, among others, civilian refugees, Red Army soldiers trapped behind the German advance, and "Jew-Bolsheviks." Indeed, the first wave of anti-partisan terror that the Germans unleashed in the Soviet Union saw the army disproportionately target Jews as reprisal victims, and collude in the round-up and mass shooting of Jews by the *Einsatzgruppen* (task forces) of the SS and police.[12] From 1942 onward, the ferocity of German countermeasures, particularly Grossunternehmen, increased in tandem not just with the Reich's increasingly pressing economic needs, but also with the growth of an increasingly well-resourced, well-organized partisan movement. For instance, the Germans estimated that the partisan movement in Byelorussia grew from 57,000 in January 1943 to 103,600 by September.[13]

From 1941 onward, occupied Yugoslavia comprised jurisdictions under not just the Germans, but also Germany's Axis allies and regional proxies. The three main regions in which the Germans operated in this theatre were: the Independent State of Croatia, or NDH, governed brutally, but increasingly ineffectively, by the extreme fascist Ustasha regime; a puppet Serbian state; and part of Slovenia. The Germans took on further territory when Italy left the Axis in September 1943. All these regions were the setting for ferocious German anti-partisan measures at different times. During 1941, Wehrmacht forces faced particularly alarming conditions in Serbia, thus adopting mass reprisals as their main anti-partisan measure. They targeted reprisals disproportionately at Serbian Jews, seeking to make them a *Demonstrationsobjekt*, for example, designed to scare the majority Serb population into submission. From 1942 to 1944, the Germans transferred the bulk of their anti-partisan effort to the mountainous territory of the NDH, particularly Bosnia. Here, facing a burgeoning communist partisan movement, the progressive disintegration of Axis control and, from 1943, the threat of an opportunistic Allied invasion, they unleashed successive waves of indiscriminate Grossunternehmen. These operations, as elsewhere, exacted an enormous civilian death toll while failing to destroy the partisans themselves. By the spring of 1943, communist partisans numbered 150,000 in the NDH alone.[14] Partisan strength was boosted further by Italy's departure from the Axis, which brought copious Italian weaponry under partisan control, not to mention significant numbers of fugitive Italian soldiers under partisan command.[15]

THE INFLUENCE OF HERITAGE AND IDEOLOGY ON BRUTALITY AND RESTRAINT

The oldest brutalizing influence was the German army's counterinsurgency tradition. Regular armed forces often face frustration when confronted by asymmetric adversaries applying insurgent methods.[16] However, while the point is debatable, there is much to suggest that German counterinsurgency traditions were unusually harsh. This was apparent in the remarkable ferocity with which German colonial troops sometimes comported themselves, and in the widespread violence German forces meted out to supposedly hostile Belgian and French civilians during the opening weeks of the First World War.[17] The latter killings dovetailed into that war's wider destructive impact on civilians, including, from the German side, the economic plunder of occupied territories, and scorched earth measures executed during the fighting retreat through northern France and Belgium during the late summer and autumn of 1918. German troops were far from alone in ruthlessly instrumentalizing civilian populations. But, as this chapter will argue, the experience impressed itself upon German officers who, in many cases, would go on to become senior commanders during the Second World War. It also lowered the threshold of what they themselves were prepared to inflict upon civilians in the cause of "military necessity."[18]

Experience of front-line life during the First World War also had profoundly brutalizing potential. On the Western Front, brutalization came predominantly via soldiers' experience of the industrialized mass slaughter that characterized that theatre of war. On the Eastern Front, a much larger theatre, encompassing at various times Poland, the Baltic region, and Ukraine, soldiers could be brutalized not just by the fighting, but also by the stereotypes that already prejudiced officers and men might have imbibed of the "primitive" East and its "backward" peoples.[19] This, of course, formed a bedrock of contempt upon which National Socialist ideology would later build.

Anti-Bolshevism also originated during the First World War, yet was more significant still in its potential to radicalize future warfare. The most obdurate irregular opponents the Germans faced in the Soviet Union and Yugoslavia during the Second World War were communist partisans. In part, the Germans' anti-communist ruthlessness stemmed from situational factors, including the highly ruthless methods communist partisans often employed themselves. However, long-term loathing also contributed. The German right and the German officer corps despised Bolshevism from the Russian Revolution onward. Hatred of Bolshevism, of Jews, and of irregular warfare all combined to particularly ferocious effect during 1918–20, when Germany's defeat at the hands of the Allies was succeeded by a period of domestic chaos in which radical left-wing forces sought, unsuccessfully, to foment revolution in Germany itself. This period, which became known on the German right as the *Kampfzeit* (time of struggle), saw army units and *Freikorps* (Free Corps) militias clash with the left in bloody urban battles.[20]

With the advent of the Third Reich and the growth of the Wehrmacht from the mid-1930s, the German army leadership increasingly subordinated itself to the Nazi regime. Among other things, it intensified its indoctrination of officers and men. The confluence of National Socialist ideology and the army leadership's harsh perception of military necessity reached its apogee in the planning and prosecution of the invasion of the Soviet Union in 1941. From the start, the invasion was envisaged not as an ordinary military campaign, but as a crusade to annihilate "Jewish Bolshevism" and decimate and subjugate the Soviet Union's Slavic population. Hitler invoked the supposed backwardness and savagery of the enemy the Germans would be facing to justify any brutal lengths in the cause of breaking their resistance. "The war against Russia," he declared, "is one of ideologies and racial differences and will have to be conducted with unprecedented, merciless, and unrelenting harshness."[21] Implementing this pitiless vision was bound to engender both fierce resistance across occupied Soviet territory and a ferocious German counter-reaction. Thus, the Wehrmacht came, almost universally within occupied Soviet territory, to believe in the existence of a putative "Jew-Bolshevik" partisan menace.[22]

The occupation of Yugoslavia, in contrast, saw ideology shape the treatment of the occupied less fundamentally. Hitler had, after all, not originally intended to conquer the country. Rather, he had felt compelled by strategic necessity to conquer Yugoslavia, together with Greece, during the spring of 1941. Eventually, however, Serbs and others were subjected to brutal measures steeped in the kind of contempt that National Socialist ideology reserved for "inferior peoples." Field commanders expressed themselves in particularly vexed terms concerning the allegedly criminal disposition of south-east European peoples. Field Marshal Wilhelm List, Wehrmacht Commander South-East from the summer of 1941 to the summer of 1942, condemned the "passionate, hot-blooded and cruel" nature that the Serbs had supposedly displayed throughout their history.[23] By 1943, as cases from German-occupied Greece and Italy in particular show, the potential for brutality in anti-partisan warfare was heightened further by the fact that many officers and men were of an age to have undergone extensive National Socialist indoctrination at school and in the Hitler Youth.[24] Moreover, across most of southern and eastern Europe, German occupation grew increasingly rapacious as the needs of the German war economy grew increasingly acute. More exploitation fuelled more partisan resistance, fuelling still harsher German countermeasures.[25] A final important change over time was the ever more brutalizing effect of the war itself. This could affect officers and men, not just through their own experiences, but also through their knowledge of the war's wider destructiveness. In particular, the Allied bombing of German cities inflicted a death toll on civilians that German troops in the occupied territories saw as justifying the brutal measures they themselves were dealing out against "enemy" civilians.[26] Such, then, were the ingredients for potential German brutality on an enormous scale.

THE INFLUENCE OF ORGANIZATIONAL CULTURE ON BRUTALITY AND RESTRAINT

Analyzing the immediate context in which brutality occurred provides answers to the central question of what caused *variations* in brutality. Accordingly, the following sections address numerous relevant institutional, situational, and personal factors. Opening with institutional factors, it is, first, important to recognize that not every precedent of German military tradition was necessarily brutal. The German military had a tradition of flexible orders, founded on the principle of *Auftragstaktik* (mission tactics). In accordance with Auftragstaktik, broad orders were set from above, but officers on the ground had discretion as to how best to carry them out, responding to battlefield conditions in a flexible, rapidly reactive manner.[27] As a result, the orders that German army anti-partisan formations received from above, and the orders they went on to disseminate, were often not so much specific orders as broad guidelines for action, with considerable discretion left to officers on the ground. Historical precedents show that this could lead to de-escalation. The German army's conduct in occupied Ukraine in 1918, for example, saw its units often place more emphasis on cultivating the local population and its leaders than on exercising terror.[28] Thus, the effect in the context of anti-partisan warfare could certainly radicalize behaviour, but might also restrain it.

The predominant effect, during the Second World War, was to fuel radicalization. Auftragstaktik proved a perfect partner for the Nazi "leadership principle." According to this principle, the key to personal advancement was to be seen to implement the Führer's will more radically than one's rivals. This required displaying not just ideological belief, but also resourcefulness and determination – qualities synonymous with the effective application of Auftragstaktik – together with the kind of ruthlessness that anti-partisan warfare was likely to bring forth.[29]

The command culture engendered by Auftragstaktik ensured that orders from above often set the tone within which local actions occurred and could exert significant influence over brutality or restraint. Among the most infamous examples of higher-level orders designed to harness the brutalizing potential inherent in this combination were the "Barbarossa Decree" and the "Guidelines for the Conduct of the Troops in Russia." Both directives were issued across the army before the invasion of the Soviet Union. They encouraged the troops to comport themselves ruthlessly toward the occupied civilian population, the better to cow it into submission. That the directives were designed with this aim was intended partly to compensate for the relative paucity of troops whom the army was committing to security duty, in regions whose expanse and terrain would lend themselves well to partisan warfare. The "Guidelines for the Conduct of the Troops" declared that

> Bolshevism is the mortal enemy of the National Socialist German people ... It is against this subversive worldview and its carriers that Germany is fighting. This battle demands ruthless and energetic measures against Bolshevik agitators, irregulars, saboteurs and Jews, and the total eradication of any active or passive resistance.[30]

The Barbarossa Decree was even more directly designed with pacification and security in mind. It ordered the routine seizure of hostages, to be executed in the event of attacks by partisans or saboteurs. Article 50 of the "Regulations Respecting the Laws and Customs of War on Land" in the 1907 Hague Convention did not expressly forbid the execution of hostages. However, it did stress the importance of establishing guilt among those upon whom reprisals were to be inflicted, and placed more emphasis on financial penalties.[31] Thus, whether in their commonplace failure to confirm that the civilian population of a particular locality was genuinely responsible for a specific partisan attack, in the grossly disproportionate numbers of hostages they would so often execute, or in the lack of provision for giving irregulars a proper trial, German troops in the Soviet Union were permitted to diverge radically from internationally recognized practice.[32] The Barbarossa Decree further augmented their freedom of action by stipulating that "acts committed by *Wehrmacht* personnel or followers against enemy civilians, even if the act is a military crime or offence, may go unpunished."[33]

Examples from the rear area of Army Group Centre during the autumn of 1941 demonstrate the destructive potential of such directives. This was the first period in which German security forces operating in this jurisdiction faced noticeable levels of partisan activity and wider unrest. Actual partisan activity was as yet poorly organized and sporadic. This partly reflected the immaturity of Soviet efforts to lay the groundwork for post-invasion partisan warfare. It also reflected the fact that most people whom the Germans were labelling partisans in their after-action reports were the aforementioned Red Army soldiers caught behind the German advance, dislocated civilians bereft of food or shelter amid the fighting, or Jews fleeing for their very lives. Nevertheless, fear of even the possibility of resistance or unrest, and a singularly harsh interpretation of military necessity, led army security divisions to escalate the violence in their pacification efforts. Thus, for instance, the 403rd Security Division killed 1,093 "partisans" at no significant loss to itself during the month of October alone.[34] The 286th Security Division reported killing 715 partisans during the same period, losing eight dead in the process.[35] It is clear from these disparities that such "partisan" body counts comprised far more non-combatants than actual partisans.

High-level orders issued for the recently conquered territories of Yugoslavia during the late summer and autumn of 1941 precipitated an even more brutal campaign. The catalyst was a national revolt in Serbia, which erupted largely in response to the mass murder, deportation, and terrorizing of ethnic Serbs by the Ustasha regime in the NDH. The reins of the revolt were rapidly taken by the Yugoslav communist partisan movement, at one point in temporary alliance with their Serb nationalist Chetnik rivals. This prompted Wehrmacht High Command to rush reinforcements to Serbia to crush the revolt. Commanding these reinforcements was the newly appointed Plenipotentiary Commanding General in Serbia, the Austrian-born General Franz Boehme. Boehme wasted no time in issuing a major directive, combining Auftragstaktik and the Nazi leadership principle with an appeal to the historical prejudices of his troops. It sought particularly to appeal to those Austrian-born soldiers whose resentment of Serbs was likely to be most acute because of their collective historical memory of the First World War.[36] A further order of Boehme's on 10 October repeated the Wehrmacht General Order that one hundred hostages be executed for every German killed in the insurgency, fifty for every German wounded.[37] A disproportionate number of the hostages who went on to perish were Jews, with more than a quarter of Serbia's 23,000-strong Jewish population falling victim.[38]

During the second half of 1942, Wehrmacht High Command issued a series of directives with the potential to further radicalize the conduct of operations against partisans and other irregulars. Two such examples were the Commando Order of October 1942 and a further

Wehrmacht High Command directive of 16 December. The former decreed that

> only where the struggle against the partisan nuisance was begun and carried out with ruthless brutality have successes been achieved ... Throughout the eastern territories, the war against the partisans is therefore a struggle of total annihilation of one side or the other.[39]

The latter ordered "the most brutal means ... against women and children also," declaring that to display any scruples in the matter was to commit treason against the German people. It exceeded even the Barbarossa Decree for severity; while that earlier directive had granted officers the discretion not to punish soldiers for excesses committed against the population, this directive *forbade* such punishment.[40]

The spirit of such decrees was disseminated downward and could be radicalized still further in the process. In late October 1942, General Alexander Löhr, Field Marshal List's recently appointed successor as Wehrmacht Commander Southeast, augmented the Commando Order with further ruthless specifics:

> All visible enemy groups are, under all circumstances, to be exterminated to the last man. Only when every rebel realises that he will not escape with his life under any circumstances can the occupation troops expect to master the rebel movement ... I expect every commander to commit his entire person to ensuring that this order, without exception and in a brutally harsh spirit, is executed by the troops. I will investigate every transgression and bring those responsible to account.[41]

The conduct of units on the ground could be influenced not just by brutal guidelines from above, but also by more measured ones. These were, however, relatively few and far between, and often fudged the conflict between the perceived imperative to brutality and the need for a more moderate, hearts-and-minds-oriented counterinsurgency doctrine. Wehrmacht High Command's "Combat Directive for Anti-Partisan Warfare in the East," issued in November 1942, stated that "unjust punishment shakes the confidence of the population and creates new partisans," but also that "the severity of our measures and the fear of expected punishment must restrain the population from aid or support of the partisans."[42] In an effort to woo partisans rather than simply terrorize them, a Wehrmacht High Command order of August 1943 stipulated better treatment for partisan deserters, but it came too late to significantly affect partisan strength in any European theatre.[43]

More generally, however, the fact that high-level orders were worded somewhat ambiguously did provide a degree of freedom to commanders seeking to prosecute anti-partisan warfare with greater restraint. The 221st Security Division, serving in the rear area of Army Group Centre for most of the period from 1941 to 1944, was ahead of Wehrmacht High Command by a year when in August 1942 it directed that, while partisans captured in battle should be shot as irregulars, potential deserters should be offered promises of treatment "not only better than that which POWs normally receive, but [which] also improves on their previous experiences in the Red Army." Even more important, it recognized that "if such propaganda is to work, then deserters must actually receive better treatment."[44] In Yugoslavia that same year, the 718th Infantry Division issued orders for a sequence of anti-partisan operations in the NDH that were relatively restrained by the standards of German units serving in that theatre. During Operation Southeast Croatia, the 718th relayed orders declaring that "women and children will not be shot or carried off, unless they demonstrably have taken part in combat or message-carrying."[45] In a later operation, the division directed that Chetniks be treated as prisoners of war, rather than shot, if they surrendered with their weapons.[46]

Officers did not need to be particularly dovish in their approach to anti-partisan warfare to issue such orders. Many feared that allowing their troops leeway for brutality might endanger their discipline, to the extent that they might cease to be a cohesive fighting force or needlessly exacerbate tensions with the population to a point that might significantly fuel partisan support. The 342nd Infantry Division, General Boehme's principal weapon in his effort to crush the Serb uprising of 1941, attacked its task with murderous enthusiasm. But at different times that autumn, the division forbade its troops to plunder, destroy churches, shoot prisoners who might be carrying useful information, shoot dogs or livestock, seize livestock except on the highest authority, or execute persons outside the domain of the proper legal offices.[47] Conversely, some commanders saw in flexible higher-level orders a freedom of action to behave even more ruthlessly than directed. The 342nd Infantry Division also provides a stark example of this. During the course of the Serb uprising, it ordered that one hundred hostages should be shot for every German wounded, doubling the number stipulated by Wehrmacht High Command.[48]

THE INFLUENCE OF IMMEDIATE CONDITIONS ON BRUTALITY AND RESTRAINT

Practical conditions provided an even more immediate determinant of how much ruthlessness or restraint an anti-partisan unit might exercise. These factors included the scale and nature of the environment in which the army's security forces operated, levels of pressure exerted by partisan activity, and the quantity and quality of German forces involved. In the latter regard, many anti-partisan units were qualitatively inferior, and their capability had a bearing on their behaviour. Senior commanders frequently entreated their security formations to deploy *Jagdkommandos*, or hunter units, envisaged as relatively mobile, flexible, and well-equipped, and with a better chance of locating and destroy partisan groups. But the German army's security forces generally lacked the standard and resources necessary to use Jagdkommandos ubiquitously.[49] For example, during the spring of 1941, the four German army divisions that were assigned to occupation duty in Yugoslavia were "Category Fifteen" divisions, each possessing only two infantry regiments, in contrast with the three allocated to each front-line division at that time. The troops were mainly reservists drawn from older age groups and their equipment was inferior to that of frontline divisions, and when they arrived in Yugoslavia their training was incomplete.[50] The frustration such conditions caused could contribute to brutalizing both the troops and their commanders. It made the former more likely to lash out against the civilian population, and the latter more likely to resort more systematically to greater harshness to compensate for their men's shortcomings.

An example of this phenomenon from the Eastern Front is Security Battalion 242. In July 1943, the 221st Security Division identified this battalion as its weakest unit, commenting on an incident in which the unit lost a strongpoint that "the average age of other security regiments may not be so high, or the signs of strain so clear, as they are in the case of Security Battalion 242."[51] The following month, the battalion killed or wounded over 350 "partisans" in two separate engagements, losing just 15 dead and 13 wounded in the process – a further indication of the mass killing of non-combatants by troops in an increasingly brutalizing state of desperation.[52] Indeed, the battalion itself gave the game away, reporting a few weeks later that its "troops' pride and confidence are suffering, because their paltry numbers, inadequate weaponry and low mobility prevent them from delivering the bandits a powerful blow."[53]

The manner in which the pressure of circumstances might exert a brutalizing effect are illustrated by the contrasting cases of the 201st and 221st Security Divisions, within their adjacent sectors of Army Group Centre's rear area of the Eastern Front, during late 1942. Both were substandard security divisions. However, the 201st was posted to the strategically critical Vibtesk-Polotsk sector, a hotbed of partisan activity, whereas the 221st operated within the quieter Gomel sector, known to be both less strategically significant and more quiescent. Disparities in their casualty data reveal how activity within each environment conspired to influence divisional behaviour. Despite operating in a less pressurized sector, the 221st Division reported that it killed 687 "partisans," for a loss of 182 dead and 207 wounded during the five months from the start of July to the end of November 1942.[54] While such a disparity indicates that the total number of "partisan" dead probably included large numbers of civilians, the 221st itself had at least suffered considerable losses.

Conversely, during September 1942 alone, the 201st Security Division claimed to have killed 864 "partisans," and sent another 245 to a likely death at the hands of the Wehrmacht's Secret Field Police. For the 1,100-plus casualties inflicted, the division suffered just eight killed and 25 wounded, and captured a meagre 99 firearms.[55] The disparity between these statistics attests to the likelihood that the division meted out extreme punishment to the civilian population. Two linked circumstances, befitting the higher incidence of partisan activity within the 201st's sector, seem to have conspired toward this outcome. The 201st was itself reinforced, and elements of the Waffen-SS and Himmler's militarized Order Police fought in close proximity to it.[56] The division's greater numbers were insufficient to allow it to establish an effective long-term presence within its zone, but did enable it to conduct more of the kind of large-scale operation that killed civilians in large numbers. Meanwhile, the proximity of ideologically charged formations may have driven the 201st Division's officers to further excesses, so that they might compare favourably with their peers in the eyes of their superiors.

INDIVIDUAL EXPERIENCE AND AGENCY AS INFLUENCES OVER BRUTALITY OR RESTRAINT

Of all the factors that might influence an anti-partisan unit's propensity for brutality or restraint, local commanders' personal influence remains hardest to dissect. This section considers further cases to determine how the implications of differences in socioeconomic background, age, geographical origin, and formative life experiences might all play a role.[57]

As its policy over the execution of hostages has demonstrated, the 342nd Infantry Division comported itself with unusual severity in its role as General Boehme's principal bludgeon against the Serb uprising of 1941. The background of the divisional commander, General Walter Hinghofer, offers two clues as to what lay behind this. First, Hinghofer was Austrian, and may have harboured the long-standing resentment toward Serbs alluded to earlier in this chapter. Second, Hinghofer spent considerable time on the Eastern Front during the First World War, including fighting Bolshevik insurgents during 1918.[58]

The second example lies within the contrasting actions of the 221st Security Division's regimental commanders during the late 1942 operations in the Gomel area, outlined above. Colonel Hans Wiemann, commanding the division's 45th Security Regiment, issued the following orders for a pacification operation around Novosybkov in late June: "Partisan suspects and any civilians who are possibly in contact with the partisans are to be dealt with using the utmost harshness. If the population does not voluntarily participate in the anti-partisan effort [through information and reconnaissance], it is to be treated as suspect."[59] No directive issued by any of the 221st's other subordinate regiments during 1942 displayed such blanket suspicion and severity. This directive also jarred with the more nuanced treatment that the 221st's division-level command itself had begun to order from the summer of 1942 onward, through such measures as its aforementioned stipulation for the treatment of deserters from August 1942. Between September and December 1942, the 45th killed civilians and burned down villages on a scale exceeding anything committed by the 221st's other subordinate regiments, despite the fact that all such formations were operating under similar degrees of strain at this time. An even worse example was a particularly savage anti-partisan operation in April 1943, grotesquely code-named "Easter Bunny" (*Osterhase*), in which the 45th reported killing 250 "partisans" in combat with only 34 small arms captured, at a cost to itself of five dead. These disparities considerably exceeded equivalent figures across all the 221st's other mobile operations of 1943.[60]

Wiemann's biography goes some way to explain his exceptional ruthlessness. During the First World War, he spent three years fighting on the Eastern Front, experiencing "primitive" eastern living conditions during a formative time in his life. His participation in the bloody suppression of left-wing uprisings on German soil during the period 1918–20 was significant; in 1919, he was a battalion commander in the government security forces in Bremen, and eight months later was working for the security police. During the 1920s and early 1930s, Wiemann managed a building firm that was liquidated in 1932 at the height of the economic crisis that heralded the collapse of the Weimar Republic.[61] At virtually every stage over a period of nearly twenty years, then, Wiemann was subjected to influences likely to harden his ideological convictions beyond the point experienced by his fellow regimental commanders. One such individual, Colonel Joachim von Geldern-Crispendorff, of old-school aristocratic stock, had yet to get around to joining the Nazi Party as late as 1935;[62] indeed, in January 1943 his superiors described his approach to anti-partisan warfare as "not yet harsh enough."[63] Hailing from relatively old-fashioned conservative stock did not preclude treating occupied Soviet civilians severely,[64] but was more likely to preclude treating them, as Wiemann did, with such unusual severity.

CONCLUSION

Only by breaking down the picture of brutality, then, is it possible to explain accurately the diverse, evolving range of influences that shaped how the German army conducted anti-partisan warfare on the ground. Consequently, levels of brutality and restraint varied considerably both between and within geographical regions, in a manner that has some resonance to that shown in Emanuele Sica's chapter on Italian methods. A range of factors accounts for the general tendency toward brutality as well as for degrees of nuance within the application of violence. Broad influences do emerge. These include: a National Socialist ideological underpinning heightened by the experiences of many officers during the First World War and its aftermath; a German tradition of counterinsurgency that had been hardened through various earlier conflicts; stereotypical responses toward different subject populations; and, increasingly, an economic impetus for more rapacious anti-partisan warfare. These influences do not comprise the complete picture, however, and were not the only drivers of belligerents' behaviour.

Organizational culture, coupling Auftragstaktik with the Nazi leadership principle, provided a framework within which individual commanders were often accorded flexibility to determine operating methods within their local areas of responsibility. They possessed significant freedom of action to behave with greater ruthlessness or restraint, depending on the circumstances they faced, and on how their personal influences filtered their perceptions of those circumstances. All too often, the pressure of circumstances, such as vast distances, inhospitable terrain, high levels of partisan activity, the often-substandard quality of German troops, or any combination of those factors, hardened commanders' pre-existing proclivities to ruthlessness. Combined with racial, ideological, and organizational influences, such circumstances were likely to push commanders and their units to act with greater brutality. So too was the brutalizing impact of the war itself, whether directly in the field, or indirectly through such things as the knowledge that countless German civilians were perishing because of Allied bombing.

Yet, as foreshadowed by the German counterinsurgency in Ukraine in 1918, some commanders exercised freedom of action with more restraint. Birthplace, generational influences, social and professional background, and other individual life experiences could all play a role here. In the broadest sense, however, such influences also drove some commanders to interpret higher-level guidelines with unusual ferocity.

Here, then, we see anti-partisan units and their commanders as active, thinking agents of their own still all-too-often brutal conduct, rather than as uniformly obedient recipients of higher-level orders. We need, therefore, to view them within this context, and to eschew notions of the "clean," untainted soldiery of unjustified post-war reputation.

NOTES

1 Christian Gerlach, *Kalkulierte Morde: Die deutsche Wirtschafts- und Vernichtungspolitik in Weißrußland 1941 bis 1944* (Hamburg: Hamburger Edition, 1999), 870; Timothy P. Mulligan, "Reckoning

the Cost of People's War: The German Experience in the Central USSR," *Russian History* 9, no. 1 (1982), 45, 47.
2. On the *Wehrmachtsdebatte* up to the end of the 1980s, see Theo J. Schulte, *The German Army and Nazi Policies in Occupied Russia* (Oxford: Berg, 1989), introduction.
3. See for example Norbert Müller, ed., *Deutsche Besatzungspolitik in der UDSSR 1941–1944: Dokumente* (Cologne: Pahl-Rugenstein, 1980).
4. In 2000, the *Wehrmachtausstellung* underwent significant revision following the revelation that it had unintentionally misattributed massacres depicted in a small number of exhibition photographs to the Wehrmacht, when it transpired that they had been perpetrated by the Soviet secret police. See Kristin Semmens' review of Hannes Heer, *Vom Verschwinden der Täter* (Berlin: Aufbau Verlag, 2004), www.h-net.org/reviews/showrev.php?id=11538.
5. Justin Huggler, "Co-founder of far-Right AfD party says Germany should be proud of its Second World War soldiers," *The Telegraph*, 15 September 2017, www.telegraph.co.uk/news/2017/09/15/co-founder-far-right-afd-says-germany-should-proud-second-world.
6. Introductions to themes relating to German counterinsurgency, including pointers to further literature, include Lutz Klinkhammer, "Der Partisanenkrieg der Wehrmacht 1941–1944," in *Die Wehrmacht: Mythos und Realität*, ed. Rolf-Dieter Müller and Hans-Erich Volkmann (Munich: Oldenbourg, 1999), 815–36; Peter Lieb, "Few Carrots and a Lot of Sticks: German Anti-partisan Warfare in World War Two," in *Counterinsurgency in Modern Warfare*, ed. Daniel Marston and Carter Malkasian (Oxford: Osprey Publishing, 2008), 70–90; Ben H. Shepherd, "Guerrilla Warfare and Counter-insurgency," in *The Cambridge History of the Second World War*, vol. 1, *Strategies, Operations, Armed Forces*, ed. John Ferris and Evan Mawdsley (Cambridge: Cambridge University Press, 2015), 190–215.
7. See, for example, Truman O. Anderson, "Incident at Baranivka: German Reprisals and the Soviet Partisan Movement in Ukraine, October–December 1941," *Journal of Modern History* 71, no. 3 (1999), 585–623; Hermann Frank Meyer, *Blutiges Edelweiss: Die 1. Gebirgs-Division im Zweiten Weltkrieg* (Berlin: Ch. Links Verlag, 2008); Jeff Rutherford, *Combat and Genocide on the Eastern Front: The German Infantry's War* (Cambridge: Cambridge University Press, 2014).
8. Gerlach, *Kalkulierte Morde*, 802.
9. The chapter refers to the German army as "the German army," not as the Wehrmacht. "Wehrmacht" translates as Armed Forces, and is used accordingly in this chapter.

10 See for example Gerlach, *Kalkulierte Morde*, 899–906; Tomislav Dulić, *Utopias of Nation: Local Mass Killing in Bosnia and Herzegovina, 1941–42* (Uppsala: Uppsala University Library, 2005), chapter 13.

11 Christian Hartmann, *Wehrmacht im Ostkrieg: Front und militärisches Hinterland 1941/42* (Munich: Oldenbourg, 2010), 231–57.

12 Jürgen Förster, "Die Sicherung des 'Lebensraumes,'" in *Der Angriff auf die Sowjetunion*, ed. Horst Boog, Jürgen Förster, Ernst Klink, Rolf- Dieter Müller, and Gerd R. Ueberschär (Frankfurt: Fischer, 1991), 1227–87.

13 Erich Hesse, *Der Sowjetrussische Partisanenkrieg 1941–1944 im Spiegel deutscher Kampfanweisungen und Befehle*, 2nd ed. (Göttingen: Musterschmidt Verlag, 1993), 207–8.

14 Jozo Tomasevich, *War and Revolution in Yugoslavia, 1941–1945: Occupation and Collaboration* (Stanford, CA: Stanford University Press, 2001), 658–9, 711.

15 See Klaus Schmider, *Partisanenkrieg in Jugoslawien 1941 bis 1944* (Hamburg: E.S. Mittler, 2002).

16 General surveys include John Ellis, *From the Barrel of a Gun: A History of Guerrilla, Revolutionary, and Civil Warfare from the Romans to the Present* (London: Greenhill, 1995); Ian F.W. Beckett, *Modern Insurgencies and Counter-Insurgencies* (London: Routledge, 2001); Gregory Fremont-Barnes, ed., *A History of Counterinsurgency* (Santa Barbara, CA: Praeger, 2015).

17 Trutz von Trotha, "'The Fellows Can Just Starve': On Wars of 'Pacification' in the African Colonies of Imperial Germany and the Concept of 'Total War,'" in *Anticipating Total War: The German and American Experiences 1871–1914*, ed. Manfred F. Boemke, Roger Chickering, and Stig Förster (Cambridge: Cambridge University Press, 1999), 415–36; Sabine Dabringhaus, "An Army on Vacation? The German War in China," in *Anticipating Total War: The German and American Experiences 1871–1914*, ed. Manfred F. Boemke, Roger Chickering, and Stig Förster (Cambridge: Cambridge University Press, 1999), 459–76; Isabel V. Hull, *Absolute Destruction: Military Culture and the Practice of War in Imperial Germany* (Ithaca, NY: Cornell University Press, 2006); Susanne Kuss and Andrew Smith, *German Colonial Wars and the Context of Military Violence* (Cambridge, MA: Harvard University Press, 2017). On German conduct in 1914, see John Horne and Alan Kramer, *German Atrocities 1914: A History of Denial* (New Haven: Yale University Press, 2001); the counterargument of Ulrich Keller, *Schuldfragen: Belgischer Untergrundkrieg und deutsche Vergeltung im August 1914* (Paderborn: Schöningh, 2017), and the related 2017

conference at the University of Potsdam, www.hsozkult.de/conference report/id/tagungsberichte-7409.

18 Johannes Hürter, *Hitlers Heerführer: Die deutschen Oberbefehlshaber im Krieg gegen die Sowjetunion 1941/42* (Munich: Oldenbourg, 2006), part 1, chapter 2; Ben H. Shepherd, *Terror in the Balkans: German Armies and Partisan Warfare* (Cambridge, MA: Harvard University Press, 2012), chapter 2.

19 Vejas Gabriel Liulevicius, *War Land on the Eastern Front: Culture, National Identity, and German Occupation in World War I* (Cambridge: Cambridge University Press, 2000); Shepherd, *Terror in the Balkans*, 39–45.

20 Nigel H. Jones, *Hitler's Heralds: The Story of the Freikorps 1918–1923* (London: John Murray, 1987); Robert Gerwarth, "The Central European Counter-Revolution: Paramilitary Violence in Germany, Austria and Hungary after the Great War," *Past and Present* 200, no. 1 (2008), 175–207.

21 Alan Bullock, *Hitler: A Study in Tyranny* (London: Penguin, 1990), quotation from 640–1.

22 Christian Streit, *Keine Kameraden: Die Wehrmacht und die sowjetischen Kriegsgefangenen*, 2nd ed. (Bonn: Dietz, 1997), 50–9; Christian Streit, "Ostkrieg, Antibolschewismus, und 'Endlösung,'" *Geschichte und Gesellschaft* 17, no. 2 (1991), 242–55.

23 Christopher R. Browning, "Wehrmacht Reprisal Policy and the Mass Murder of Jews in Serbia," *Militärgeschichtliche Zeitschrift* 33, no. 1 (1983), 31–47, quotation from 34–5.

24 Carlo Gentile, *Wehrmacht und Waffen-SS im Partisanenkrieg: Italien 1943–1945* (Paderborn: Schöningh, 2012), 389.

25 The best recent survey of Nazi occupation policy is Mark Mazower, *Hitler's Empire: Nazi Rule in Occupied Europe* (London: Penguin, 2009).

26 Meyer, *Blutiges Edelweiss*, 211; Mungo Melvin, *Manstein: Hitler's Greatest General* (London: Weidenfeld & Nicolson, 2010), 396; Walter Manoschek and Hans Safrian, "717./117. ID. Eine Infanterie-Division auf dem Balkan," in *Vernichtungskrieg: Verbrechen der Wehrmacht 1941 bis 1944*, ed. Hannes Heer and Klaus Naumann (Hamburg: Hamburger Edition, 1995), 359–73, here 369.

27 See Marco Sigg, *Der Unterführer als Feldherr im Taschenformat: Theorie und Praxis der Auftragstaktik im deutschen Heer 1869 bis 1945* (Paderborn: Schöningh, 2014).

28 Peter Lieb, "Aufstandsbekämpfung im Strategischen Dilemma: Die deutsche Besatzung in der Ukraine 1918," in *Die Besatzung der Ukraine 1918*,

ed. Wolfram Dornik and Stefan Karner (Graz: Ludwig Boltzmann-Institut, 2008), 111–40.
29 On the leadership principle, see Ian Kershaw, *The Nazi Dictatorship: Problems and Perspectives of Interpretation*, 4th ed. (London: Edward Arnold, 2000), chapter 4. On rear area security directives as guidelines rather than clear orders, see Hannes Heer, "The Logic of the War of Extermination: The Wehrmacht and the Anti-Partisan War," in *War of Extermination: The German Military in World War II 1941–1944*, ed. Hannes Heer and Klaus Naumann (Oxford: Berghahn, 2000), 99–103. Heer arguably overstates how far "leadership principle"–type directives brutalized Wehrmacht anti-partisan warfare, but his observations as to *how* they worked are illuminating.
30 Both documents are reproduced in Wolfram Wette and Gerd R. Ueberschär, *Der deutsche Überfall auf die Sowjetunion 1941: Berichte, Analysen, Dokumente* (Fischer: Frankfurt am Main, 1991), 258–9.
31 *Convention IV respecting the Laws and Customs of War on Land and its annex: Regulations concerning the Laws and Customs of War on Land*, The Hague, 18 October 1907, https://ihl-databases.icrc.org/applic/ihl/ihl.nsf/Article.xsp?action=openDocument&documentId=B2D5C9BD27F0DC51C12563CD005168FB.
32 Felix Römer, "'Im alten Deutschland wäre solcher Befehl nicht möglich gewesen.' Rezeption, Adaption und Umsetzung des Kriegsgerichtbarkeitserlasses im Osther 1941/42," *Vierteljahreshefte für Zeitgeschichte* 56, no. 1 (2008), 53–98; Jürgen Förster, *Die Wehrmacht im NS-Staat: Eine strukturgeschichtliche Analyse* (Munich: Oldenbourg, 2007), 59.
33 Reproduced in Wette and Ueberschär, *Der deutsche Überfall auf die Sowjetunion*, 258–9.
34 Gerlach, *Kalkulierte Morde*, 604; Ben H. Shepherd, *War in the Wild East: The German Army and Soviet Partisans* (Cambridge, MA: Harvard University Press, 2004), 84.
35 Shepherd, *War in the Wild East*, 84.
36 Walter Manoschek, "The Extermination of the Jews in Serbia," in *National Socialist Extermination Policies: Contemporary German Perspectives and Controversies*, ed. Ulrich Herbert (Oxford: Berghahn, 2000), 163–85, 170.
37 Shepherd, *Terror in the Balkans*, 121.
38 Walter Manoschek, *"Serbien ist judenfrei:" Militärische Besatzungspolitik und Judenvernichtung in Serbien 1941/42* (Munich: Oldenbourg, 1995), 11.
39 Timothy P. Mulligan, *The Politics of Illusion and Empire: German Occupation Policy in the Soviet Union, 1942–1943* (New York: Praeger, 1988), quotation from 139.

40 Reproduced in Müller, *Deutsche Besatzungspolitik*, 139–40.
41 Shepherd, *Terror in the Balkans*, quotation from 201.
42 Mulligan, *The Politics of Illusion and Empire*, quotation from 139–40.
43 Hans Umbreit, "Das unbewältigte Problem: Der Partisanenkrieg im Rücken der Ostfront," in *Stalingrad: Ereignis – Wirkung – Symbol*, ed. Jürgen Förster (Zurich: Piper, 1992), 145.
44 Bundesarchiv-Militärarchiv (hereafter BA-MA), Freiburg-im-Breisgau, RH 26-221/34. 221. Sich.-Div. Ic, 4.8.42. Betr.: "Behandlung von Kriegsgefangenen, Partisanen und Bevölkerung," 2.
45 BA-MA, film MFB4/56155, file 28326/2, frame 1037. 718. Inf.-Div. Ia, 1.9.42. Kampfanweisung (zur Belehrung der Truppe), 2.
46 BA-MA, MFB4/56155, 28326/5, 630. Anlage 2 zur Nr. 718. Inf.-Div. 310/42 geheim vom 25.1.42. Kampfanweisung (zur Belehrung der Truppe).
47 Shepherd, *Terror in the Balkans*, 133.
48 BA-MA, MFB4/72334, 15365/9, 188. 342. Inf.-Div. Ia, 11.11.41. Betr.: Meldungen über Erschießungen, Festnahmen und Sühnemaßnahmen.
49 BA-MA, MFB4/72351, 20294/4, 179. I/JR 724, 27.8.41. Meldung über den Einsatz des I/JR 724 bei Miskovici am 25.8.41; MFB4/72350, 20294/3, 1110. Höheres Kommando LXV, 14.6.41; Charles D. Melson, "German Counter-Insurgency Revisited," *Journal of Slavic Military Studies* 24, no. 1 (2011), 115–46, here 129–32.
50 Klaus Schmider, "Der jugoslawische Kriegsschauplatz," in Karl-Heinz Frieser, Klaus Schmider, Klaus Schönherr, Gerhard Schreiber, Krisztián Ungváry, and Bernd Wegner, *Das deutsche Reich und der Zweite Weltkrieg, Band Acht: Die Ostfront 1943/44. Der Krieg im Osten und an den Nebenfronten* (Munich: Deutsche Verlags-Anstalt 2007), 1013.
51 National Archives and Records Administration (hereafter NARA), College Park, Maryland, film T-315/1683, file 36509/5. Sich.-Div. 221 Ia, 6.7.43. Monatsbericht, 3–4.
52 NARA, T-315/1682, file 36509/1. Sich.-Div. 221 Ia, 17.5., 29.8.43. Kriegstagebuch, 1.5.-31.8.43. See also Shepherd, *War in the Wild East*, 240–2.
53 NARA, T-315/1684, file 36509/8. Sich.-Btl. 242, 10.5.43. Betr.: Bandenlage im Bereich des Sich.-Batl. 242, 2.
54 NARA, T-315/1681, files 35408/1 and /2. Sich.-Div. 221 Ia. Monatsberichte, Juli – November 1942.
55 NARA, T-315/1584, file 29196/2. Sich.-Div. 201 Ia, 17.9.42. Abschlußbericht, Unternehmen Luchs, Anlage 1; Sich.-Div. 201 Ia, 5.10.42. Abschlußbericht, Unternehmen Blitz, Anlage 1.

56 Gerlach, *Kalkulierte Morde*, 899–902.
57 See also Hartmann, *Wehrmacht im Ostkrieg*, chapter 2; Manoschek, "The Extermination of the Jews in Serbia"; Meyer, *Blutiges Edelweiss*, 207–39; Rutherford, *Combat and Genocide on the Eastern Front*, chapter 1; Shepherd, *War in the Wild East*, chapter 7; Shepherd, *Terror in the Balkans*, chapters 1–3; Gentile, *Wehrmacht und Waffen-SS im Partisanenkrieg*, 346–89; Jorn Hasenclever, *Wehrmacht und Besatzungspolitik in der Sowjetunion: Die Befehlshaber der rückwärtigen Heeresgebiete 1941–1943* (Paderborn: Schöningh, 2009), 206–15; Mark Mazower, "Military Violence and the National Socialist Consensus: The Wehrmacht in Greece, 1941–44," in *War of Extermination: The German Military in World War II*, ed. Hannes Heer and Klaus Naumann (Oxford: Berghahn, 2000), 146–74.
58 Shepherd, *Terror in the Balkans*, 138–9; Manoschek, "The Extermination of the Jews in Serbia," 170; Wolfram Dornik, "Die Besatzung der Ukraine 1918 durch österreichisch-ungarische Truppen," in *Die Besatzung der Ukraine 1918*, ed. Wolfram Dornik and Stefan Karner (Graz: Ludwig Boltzmann-Institut, 2008), 141–82, here 179–80.
59 NARA, T-315/1679, file 29380/5. Sich.-Rgt. 45, 6/23/42. "Befehl für die Sicherung und Aufklärung im Raum um Nowosybkoff," 2.
60 Shepherd, *War in the Wild East*, 209–13.
61 Ibid., 213–15.
62 BA-MA, Pers 6. File on Joachim von Geldern-Crispendorff. Abw. IIIc, 5/3/35.
63 BA-MA, Pers 6. File on Joachim von Geldern-Crispendorff. 286. Sich.-Div., 1.3.43. Beurteilung.
64 Hasenclever, *Wehrmacht und Besatzungspolitik in der Sowjetunion*, 206–15.

10

Italian Occupation Policies and Counterinsurgency Campaigns in France and in the Balkans, 1940–1943

Emanuele Sica

In 1944, a report by the French Vichy government noted that there was no evidence that Italian forces had executed inhabitants in the eight occupied French departments during the Second World War.[1] These conclusions were corroborated in a French post-war paper, which concluded that no known executions had taken place inside occupied Nice.[2] By comparison, Italian forces occupying the Balkans accrued a body count in the thousands, often brutalizing local populations instead of their elusive partisan targets.[3] Male civilians deemed to be *favoreggiatori* (accomplices) of the partisans were executed, while women, children, and the elderly were confined within camps. As historian James Burgwyn argues, "[T]he behavior of the Italian army in Yugoslavia was at times as beastly as the Wehrmacht's toward the occupied peoples in that country."[4] Why, therefore, did the experience and practice of concurrent Italian occupations differ so starkly? And what drove Italian practitioners of counterinsurgency toward brutality or restraint?

This chapter reveals a fundamentally inconsistent approach to Italian counterinsurgency operations. It highlights the different characteristics of Italian military occupations during the Second World War and thus deepens our understanding of Axis-occupation policies. Although the hackneyed myth of the *Italiani, brava gente* (the good Italians) has not stood the test of time, other aspects should be taken into account in explaining the different occupation policies.[5] While both occupations suffered from a lack of an overarching strategic plan, owing in part to a flawed counterinsurgency doctrine,[6] these inherent shortcomings were more evident in the Balkan context than in Mediterranean France. If the dysfunctionality of the Italian Army was forgivable in the relatively insurgency-free Côte d'Azur, it proved problematic in a region deeply riven with ethnic hatred and political chaos. This chapter advances a three-tiered analysis, which contends that the drivers of divergence are multiple, though they can be broadly split into situational, ideological, and institutional trends. The first theme evaluates the extent to which local conditions had the potential to trigger escalating cycles of reciprocal violence between Italian forces and elements within local populations. The second explores whether assumptions instilled from colonial experience or fascist ideology predisposed Italian practitioners toward directing different behaviour toward the French and Yugoslav peoples. The third theme questions the extent to which differences in Italian institutional identity really exerted a demonstrable influence over policy and practice. The answers shed light on both the practical business of counterinsurgency, as well as the degree to which fascist thinking pervaded the Royal Italian Army.

RESTRAINED OCCUPATION: THE ITALIANS IN FRANCE

The Italian occupation of French territory never degenerated into the levels of brutality displayed in occupied regions of the Balkans. To understand why this was so, this section charts the chronology of the Italian military presence in French territory, emphasizing why mutual antipathy never quite developed into widespread violence of the type encountered further east. Low-level antipathies arose, in large measure, from the circumstances in which Italy entered the Second World War. Although France and Italy shared long-standing cultural connections, the rise of Italy's Fascist regime tested the relationship between the "Latin Sisters." Italy's strategic ambitions in the Mediterranean included revanchist claims over French-governed territory, including the County of Nice and the Savoy region, formerly possessions of the Kingdom of Piedmont-Sardinia. The manner in which Italy sought to regain these territories during June 1940 sowed resentment that would last throughout the occupation. With France distracted by the German blitzkrieg in the north, Italy initiated the four-day Battle of the Alps. While the tangible gains from this campaign were modest, amounting to the Italian seizure of only the medium-sized town of Menton and some Alpine pastures, the effect was to toxify the Franco-Italian relationship. Indeed, French commentators came to describe the episode as a *coup de poignard dans le dos* (stab in the back).[7] Following the Allied invasion of French North Africa, the Italian occupation was extended to include eight departments of the former *Zone Libre*. This was intended to bolster the defence of the Mediterranean coastline; from 11 November 1942, over 150,000 soldiers of General Mario Vercellino's Italian Fourth Army entered the Côte D'Azur, Savoy, and Corsica. This triggered a ten-month occupation that lasted until the Italian-Allied Armistice of 8 September 1943.

Local French reaction to this occupation was equivocal, notwithstanding the existence of low-level antipathy. On the one hand, although officials of the collaborationist Vichy government were required to cooperate with Axis authorities, French resentment, arising from the clashes of 1940, ensured that attitudes toward the Italians were often much cooler, if not downright hostile. However, such underlying antipathy rarely gave rise to open acts of resistance. In part, this stemmed from the enduring apathy of the French engendered by the shock of France's collapse in 1940. It also arose from regard for the Vichy leader Maréchal Philippe Pétain, the *Héro de Verdun*, whose policy of sincere collaboration was reinforced by Vichy propaganda, which depicted the Maréchal as a benevolent father shielding France from the fate that had befallen other occupied territories. Pétain certainly bore a share of personal responsibility for the lack of resistance; he ordered the *Armée d'Armistice*, the skeletal remains of the French Army of 1940, not to oppose Italian occupation.[8]

Perhaps more surprisingly, grassroots resistance was also restrained across south-eastern France. Modest centres of resistance emerged immediately after the defeat of 1940, though initially they were mainly confined to urban working-class centres such as Marseille and Lyon, away from enclaves occupied by Italian forces.[9] The expanded occupation of November 1942 broadened the scope for resistance activity, though actual instances took time to emerge. Among the first to act were the *fuoriusciti*, an exiled diaspora of Italian political opponents of fascism, living in the formerly French-controlled County of

Nice. Although their activities began after November 1942, they employed non-violent means, such as spreading anti-Axis propaganda to Italian soldiers, and obtained limited results.[10] French military resistance activity to the Italian occupation began during January 1943, operating under the umbrella of *Mouvements unis de Résistance* (MUR). The attacks initially concentrated on rail sabotage or bombing Vichy offices. Actions against Italian forces escalated to a limited extent from mid-1943, emboldened by news of Axis defeats on other fronts. On 11 April, French activists gunned down an Italian officer in Nice, ambushed a patrol a month later, then bombed a restaurant packed with Italian soldiers and officials on 20 July.[11] It was only in parts of the remote territories of Corsica and Savoy that the Italians encountered anything approaching open confrontation with the local population.[12]

It is, thus, noteworthy that the Italians were never confronted with a full-scale insurgency, as was the case in the Balkans. This was ostensibly caused by a complex combination of situational factors that include the timing of the Italian occupation. The occupation ended during September 1943, before the German policy of STO (*Service de travail obligatoire*), swelled the ranks of resistance units with youthful evaders of compulsory labour in Germany.[13] As the membership figures for the Alpes-Maritimes region demonstrate, STO evaders bolstered the ranks of the resistance by more than 20 per cent.[14] Luckily for the Italians, the effect of STO was only felt in late 1943, when the Italian occupation was already almost over.

The effect of the Italian occupation in France was also tempered by accommodations with the local population. These arose, in large measure, from a pragmatic realization that, after a share of the Italian Fourth Army's strength was diverted to reinforce Russia, North Africa, and to defend the homeland, the remaining forces were too weak to both defend the French coastline and enact widespread repression inland.[15] The strategic situation thus drove the Italian military authorities toward softer occupation policies. This effect is illustrated by contrasting the harsher policies applied in Menton in the early years of the occupation (when local Italian commanders believed the war to be running in favour of the Axis) with the more conciliatory tone adopted during the extension of the occupation in November 1942. The latter occurred at a time of deep soul-searching for Italian commanders, with military defeat on the horizon. Short-term strategic motivations then prevailed over long-term dreams of annexation. That is not to say that the Italians did not occasionally employ harsh measures to curtail political or military opposition;[16] in fact, curfews, mass round-ups, and waves of arrests took place throughout the occupation. However, the situation never quite degenerated into open confrontation with the local population.

THE CONTRASTING EXPERIENCE OF OCCUPATION IN THE BALKANS

After the successful invasion on 6 April 1941, the Germans and Italians carved out two spheres of influence in the Balkans: Germany annexed northern and eastern Slovenia, occupied the Serb Banat (which contained an important ethnic German minority), and established a military protectorate in Serbia, based in Belgrade, where it created a puppet state headed by General Milan Nedić.[17] The Italian Fascist regime incorporated part of Dalmatia (Split, Kotor, and the province of Zadar) into Italy as the Governorate of Dalmatia, and the western part of Slovenia as the Italian Province of Ljubljana.[18] Further south, the Italians sponsored the creation of the Kingdom of Montenegro, extending their control by instituting the Italian Governorate of Montenegro during October 1941. In contrast to the meagre numbers posted later to southeastern France, this occupation eventually billeted 100,000 Italian troops among a civilian population of fewer than 400,000 Montenegrins within a territory of 15,000 square kilometres.[19] All told, more than 200,000 soldiers of General Vittorio Ambrosio's Italian Second Army were stationed on former Yugoslavian soil, illustrating both the importance of the area for Fascist expansionist plans as well as the difficulties that arose from attempts at pacification.

In stark contrast to France, the Italian Army was confronted with a widespread insurgency in the Balkans almost from the outset of the occupation. The Balkans had once been a contested region at the crossroads of the multi-ethnic Austro-Hungarian and Ottoman empires. It thus had a strong tradition of fighting foreign occupiers.[20] Moreover, pre-existing animosities confounded Italian efforts to establish effective relationships with local intermediary authorities, as they had done with the Vichy regime. Instead, Axis forces became quickly embroiled in a complicated game of unsteady partnerships, revolving door alliances, and convoluted power politics in a climate of ruthless brutality. Take, for example, the Croatian Ustasha movement, which, under the leadership of Ante Pavelić, governed the Independent State of Croatia (NDH). Between 1941 and 1945, the Ustasha murdered 500,000 Serbs, 25,000 Jews, and 20,000 Roma in a campaign of "ethnic cleansing" that horrified Italian commanders and severely disrupted the stability of the region.[21]

The resulting resistance activity was severe. Insurgents first coalesced into the monarchist national Serb movement, the Chetniks,[22] and non-political groups, but later on they swelled the ranks of the Communist partisans under the leadership of Josef Broz Tito, a long-time apparatchik of the Communist Party of Yugoslavia (KPJ). The KPJ, along with all Communist parties across Europe, spread the banner of anti-Axis resistance after the beginning of Operation Barbarossa on 22 June 1941. The KPJ relied on delivering a simple message: among the imbroglio of faltering coalitions in the Balkans, the Communists were those who never compromised with the occupiers. While this emphasis isolated the Communist partisan movement in the first months of the occupation, over time it attracted a wide number of individuals who also admired the organization's multi-ethnic composition.[23] By the end of 1941, these partisans numbered 80,000, and by 1942 they had reached 150,000 mustered into organized battalions, spreading resistance from Serbia to Bosnia-Herzegovina and Montenegro.[24] Thus, the Italians faced in the Balkans perhaps the most organized and militarily adept insurgency in Europe.

These structural circumstances differentiated the Italian experience in the Balkans from that in France by increasing the potential for organized violence. In Montenegro, a combined Communist and Chetnik uprising began on 13 July 1941, only to be crushed mercilessly by the Italian Fourteenth Army.[25] The situation was also severe in Slovenia where General Mario Robotti's Eleventh Army was required to thwart resistance around the capital, Ljubljana.[26] Spring 1942 was, however, a watershed in fascist counterinsurgency operations as Italian commanders stiffened their attitude toward the resistance. General Mario Roatta had replaced Ambrosio at the head of the Italian Second Army during January, and his infamous *Circolare* 3C was influential in developing this new approach.[27] In this circular, published on 1 March 1942, Roatta laid out precise instructions for dealing with the insurgency movement in the Balkans.[28] He criticized the supposedly soft mentality of Italian soldiers (the *bono italiano* or good Italian), and gave comprehensive tactical instructions for counterinsurgency conditions, including raids on villages or outpost fortifications. More important, the circular decreed toughening the occupation policy by using reprisals, epitomized in the slogan "not a tooth for a tooth, but a head for a tooth." However, the directive did admittedly temper more emphatic instructions with guidance that wanton retaliations could prove counterproductive and might conceivably push the population to side with the partisans. To that effect, for instance, churches, schools, hospitals, and public works were not to be destroyed under any circumstances, and mass executions were still considered justified only rarely.[29] Overall, however, the directive's nefarious effects should not be underestimated, because it was widely circulated to all Italian units in the Balkans, to whom the document clearly legitimized violence against civilians.[30] These effects manifested in Slovenia, for instance, in repressive measures, such as the shooting of hostages from 1942.[31] Elsewhere, Italian units engaged in partisan sweeps, destroyed villages, and executed hostages in response to attacks.[32] This cycle of reciprocal violence is well described by Don Pietro Brignoli, a military chaplain in the Granatieri di Sardegna in his book *Santa Messa per i miei fucilati* (Holy Mass for the Executed).[33] Moreover, the Italians also deported over 100,000 civilians to concentration camps, where the internees were incarcerated in atrocious conditions. These included the infamous Arbe (Rab) camp, administered by Second Army personnel, which became notorious for inmate mortality rates that were higher than in Buchenwald.[34]

These harsh repressive measures should be placed within the context of a long-running counterinsurgency campaign that for two years pitted Italian forces and their Axis allies against Communist *partizani*. After some serious setbacks at the end of 1941, when isolated outposts were overwhelmed by partisan incursions, Roatta decided to consolidate the Italian Army garrisons by regrouping the Italian defensive network into a few strongly fortified garrisons, which would act as operating bases from which to coordinate concentrated attacks on partisan-infested areas.[35] The three ensuing Axis anti-partisan operations, Operations "Trio" (April to May 1942), "Weiss" (January to March 1943), and "Schwartz" (May to June 1943), all had the same strategy: to coordinate encircling actions against known centres of partisan activity. However, all the results were underwhelming, because they never succeeded in eradicating the partisan movement from the areas of operations or in eliminating partisan higher command.

Axis political wrangling underpinned these underwhelming results. During Operation "Trio," for instance, the German commander in Serbia, General Paul Bader, notwithstanding the Italian leadership of the operation, decided unilaterally to start the manoeuvre on 15 April without waiting for Italian units. While Bader asserted that the operation, which was already three days late, should have started as soon as possible to avoid possible intelligence leaking to partisans, the Italians suspected that their Axis partners had rushed it to avoid Italian troops occupying parts of Bosnia that were within the German sphere of influence.[36]

From a purely tactical standpoint, Operation "Weiss" also fell wide of its mark and degenerated into a bloody string of civilian reprisals. Despite drawing in a total of 90,000 Axis troops and auxiliaries (50,000 Germans from four divisions, 25,000 Italians, 10,000 Croat Ustasha and Drobomani, and 5,000 from Chetnik groups and the Milizia Volontaria Anti Comunista [MVAC]), the operation still failed in its ambition to eliminate partisans within the Bihac sanctuary in northwestern Bosnia. Indeed, the partisans slipped away via the Nerevta Valley, eliminating most of the Italian 154th Infantry Division (Murge) in the process.[37] The reasons behind this reverse are complex and play to many of the perennial problems that Italian forces faced in their occupation of the Balkan territories. Axis commanders again struggled to engender coordination within their multinational force. Moreover, the morale of Italian forces, already exhausted by years of asymmetric warfare, collapsed when news of Allied bombing raids on Italy reached operational units.[38] The decline in the mood of the Italian units shifted the burden of attaining operational success to other national contingents. However, this exposed qualitative differences within the Axis forces. Croat forces proved too unreliable, while Chetnik auxiliaries lacked combat capability, often failing to implement orders to attack, and sometimes surrendering without fighting.[39] Conversely, the Germans, perhaps inspired by the fierce anti-Bolshevism and anti-Slavism outlined by Ben H. Shepherd in the previous chapter, implemented an extremely destructive campaign against civilians that only exacerbated local resentment.[40]

These efforts ended with the 8 September armistice. Subsequent Axis activity diminished when entire Italian units, such as the Division Venezia and part of the Taurinense Division, joined the partisans in their fight against the Germans, uniting during December 1943 to form the Garibaldi Division.[41]

THE INFLUENCE OF COLONIAL EXPERIENCE AND FASCIST IDEOLOGY ON OPPRESSION

Whereas the previous sections have emphasized the significance of situational factors and the presence (or absence) of cyclical violence in influencing differing levels of brutality within Italian occupations, this section argues that underlying ideological factors also shaped occupation policy. In particular, the Italian Army had extensive recent experience of mounting occupations in Africa, and it has been contended that elements of the Balkan occupations adhered to these precedents, whereas the same logic was never applied within occupied France. The Italian colonial experience of occupation dated back to the nineteenth century, acquiring extra impetus under the fascist regime.[42] Mussolini authorized the pacification of Libya from 1923 to 1932, leveraging Eritrean colonial troops, a scorched earth policy, and massed deportations to attain starkly effective results.[43] The subsequent Italian invasion of Abyssinia, initiated during October 1935, showed how hardline totalitarian mindsets could augment established colonialist goals. Mussolini spared no expense to realize his desire of crushing Abyssinian military resistance, drawing over 500,000 soldiers into the campaign during the first year of the conflict, and empowering commanders like Pietro Badoglio and Rodolfo Graziani to use chemical warfare and indiscriminate bombing against civilians.[44] Mussolini cast the invasion of Abyssinia as a fascist war to attain his linked ambitions of destroying the Versailles system and radically overhauling the Abyssinian political and social order; the colonial "other" was incessantly vilified and portrayed as an impediment to Italian imperialist dreams.[45] The ensuing military occupation degraded swiftly into a fierce counterinsurgency campaign leading to abject war crimes such as the massacre of Debre Libanos in which more than 2,000 monks were executed between 20 and 29 May 1937, in reprisal for a bombing attack on Graziani.[46]

Opinion remains split over the extent to which Italian colonial experience informed European occupations during the Second World War. On the one hand, historians such as Isabel Hull find comparable precedents within German military culture. Hull traces coherent connections between early-twentieth-century colonial massacres of the Herero in German South West Africa and the contempt for life displayed during the war four decades later.[47] Despite much closer temporal linkages between Italian colonial experience and wartime practice, historians have been more tentative in articulating connections. Eric Gobetti downplays this link, arguing that different tactical methods (such as the non-employment of poison gas in Europe) illustrates significant differences in the way Italians viewed occupied populations.[48] Giorgio Rochat stresses the differences between the organization of the Abyssinian and Yugoslavian resistance, but his conclusions, that a sense of Italian cultural and racial superiority pervaded both examples, merit further investigation.[49] Both explanations dwell upon the ostensible, rather than identifying the more subtle transfer of ideas and perspectives.

Rather than looking for repetition in the minutiae of tactics, influence might still be transferred across time and space through experience and ideas. Historian Cristiana Pipitone downplays these links, noting that the African colonial campaigns were mostly waged by Indigenous troops, foremost among them the Eritrean Askari, while European anti-partisan activity was typically conducted by metropolitan Italian troops.[50] However, these arguments overlook the wealth of crossover experience of the commanders of both operations. A plethora of Italian officers responsible for running the occupation of the Balkans brought significant experience of colonial campaigning. These included the future governor of Montenegro, Alessandro Pirzio Biroli, whose tenure as governor of the Amhara province in 1936–37 had already been tainted by war crimes, including the hanging of civilians. Moreover, much of the Italian Fourth Army's senior leadership also boasted African experience, including Sandro Piazzoni (commanding VI Corpo d'Armata [Army Corps]), Gastone Gambara (VIII Corpo d'Armata), Renzo Dalmazzo (IX Army in Albania) and Quirino Armellini (XVIII Corpo d'Armata).[51] It would, thus, seem fair to reopen the question of whether colonial experience informed their behaviour during the Second World War.

Ideas by other prominent proponents of colonial warfare flowed reasonably freely across geography and time. As David Rodogno notes, Graziani, a major player in both the wars in Libya and Abyssinia, wrote a book ominously titled *The Roman Peace in Libya*. In this book, he set an intellectual precedent for wartime Italian occupation methods, by asserting that to quell any rebellion, one should not be too shy to use deportation policies, euphemistically called "resettlement," to sever close connections between the insurgents and the population. Unencumbered by any moral qualms in fighting non-European populations, Graziani also advocated the application of indiscriminate terror, such as razing villages and indiscriminatly shooting civilians.[52] Given the prominence that Graziani attained as an Italian wartime commander, his work undoubtedly carried some impact. Other Italian scholars, such as Teodoro Sala, have concentrated on the more practical similarities between such occupations, emphasizing commonalities in the ways in which Italian authorities sought to apply colonial-style extractive frameworks to leverage resources from occupied European territories to further the interests of the Italian metropolitan nation.[53]

This chapter augments these findings by comparatively analyzing Italian attitudes in the Balkans and France to reveal that "racial" attitudes, informed by colonial experience and fascist thinking, were prominent in driving difference in occupational policy. Beyond the situational differences outlined above, these form the predominant underlying explanation as to why the occupation of France was characterized by restraint, whereas the occupation of the Balkans involved more bloodshed. Issues of "race" were of immediate significance to the Italian fascist regime. The *Manifesto della razza* (the Manifesto of Race), which was published in the summer of 1938, not only ushered in the antisemitic legislation of the fascist regime, but also proclaimed that, in light of the supposed Aryan nature of the Italian "race," "it [was] necessary to make a clear distinction between Mediterranean peoples of Europe (westerners) on the one hand and Africans and "easterners" on the other."[54] This provided the Fascist regime with the pseudo-intellectual justification to impose their self-declared superior civilization on lands that they considered to be on the fringe of the western world. This New Mediterranean Order (*Nuovo Ordine Mediterraneo*) was clearly trying to emulate ancient Roman conquests. However, it deviated in one significant way: while the Romans had aimed to co-opt local elites whose loyalty, not ethnicity, was the prime criterion for their inclusion into the Roman Empire, Fascist panegyrists repeatedly asserted that no mixing of the "New Italian Man" with supposedly inferior "races" would be permitted. Italian fascist ideology was "racially" determinist, some "races" being deemed inherently superior to others.[55] The "racial" scale, which placed the Italic "race" at the top, and Slavs and Africans at the bottom, explains why, unlike the ancient Romans, the Fascists failed to assimilate "locals" into the Italian social fabric.[56]

This "racial" prejudice against Indigenous inhabitants translated into the forceful Italianization of annexed provinces where the Italians were a minority.⁵⁷ In the mindset of the Italian occupiers, the Italianization process was carried out first by the detention, and possibly later the deportation, of "undesirable" elements living in the new provinces, starting with those who were involved in the former Indigenous administration. Practices, such as the governor of Dalmatia Bastianini's dismissal of ex-Yugoslavian officials on 18 July 1941, followed colonial precedents. Moreover, Italian commanders and military authorities were equally adamant that the Italians were bringing the light of a new era into the annexed lands by imposing a new civilization. The prefect of Fiume (Rijeka), Temistocle Testa, a committed fascist who had participated in the March on Rome, declared that the Italian occupation was "the most efficient example of industrial colonisation of the Empire [against] a population that more and more every day is showing what it has always been, that is an inferior race that should be treated as such and not as equal to equal."⁵⁸ The contempt for the local population trickled down to the rank-and-file, who characterized the Balkans as "a world where everything is precarious, loyalty and friendship, alliance and strife," and cast its inhabitants as "cold and distant" if not outright "beasts."⁵⁹ The language used in military reports in the Balkans in fact disturbingly harkened back to a colonial vision of war fought in frontier lands at the fringe of "civilization," with the same exhilarating effect on Italian commanders casting themselves as the vanguard for the new Italian empire.⁶⁰ Both the message and tone of these pronouncements closely echoed the language in publications such as Graziani's *The Roman Peace in Libya*.

However, while this discourse was dominant in the Balkans, it was almost entirely absent from Italian-occupied France. France was, after all, a metropolitan power of a magnitude greater than Italy. Moreover, the eight occupied departments contained a significant number of ethnic Italian economic migrants.⁶¹ The exodus of these impoverished Italians to a sophisticated French society diminished the credibility of the claim that occupying Italian armies formed the vanguard of a civilizing nation. Perhaps unsurprisingly, therefore, the Italian Fourth Army's messages throughout their 10-month sojourn in southeastern France are devoid of colonialist undertones. Even at its most radical, during the three-year occupation of Menton, Italian endeavours appeared limited to excluding former representatives of the French state (such as municipal officials, policemen, and firemen) from government employment, and encouraging muted linguistic change by imposing Italian education in schools and erasing non-Italian road signs and street names.[62] Thus, colonial experience and fascist ideology produced clear differences in the ways in which the Italians understood their interactions with French civilians, compared with their Yugoslav counterparts. When taken alongside the relative lack of organized resistance that obviated the requirement for reciprocal violence, this largely explains why Italian soldiers were loath to enact repressive measures on individuals they considered equals. Perhaps, then, Italian armed forces went further than what Giorgio Rochat has dubbed the "alliance" between monarchy and fascist establishment,[63] by actively incorporating and promoting the fascist imperialist discourse and allowing it to influence their occupational policies and tactical actions.[64]

THE INFLUENCE OF INDIVIDUAL AGENCY AND INSTITUTIONAL CULTURES ON OPPRESSION

This chapter has demonstrated that differences in ideology, experience, and the structural conditions of violence drove brutality and restraint within different Italian occupations. Another prominent facet of the experience of occupation was the clash between Italian civil and military authorities, which occurred in all occupied regions. Thus, this section questions the extent to which distinctions in Italian institutional cultures can really be claimed to comprise a significant driver of difference.

Overwhelmingly, local military commanders prevailed. The CIAF (Italian Armistice Commission with France) operated in France from July 1940 and drew many of its officials from the diplomatic service. While it achieved some impact within Menton, its members were increasingly sidelined by the commanders of the Italian Fourth Army after the November 1942 invasion.[65] They especially resented being ousted from their role as paladins of the Italian community in France. The same scenario occurred in the Balkans, with even more profound consequences. Local commanders decried civilian interference in the occupation policy within openly rebellious regions and resisted Rome's imposition of civil servants. For instance, General Alessandro Pirzio Biroli, commander of the Italian Ninth Army, eventually became the governor of Montenegro after lambasting the civil commissar, Serafino Mazzolini, for not being able to quell the partisan groups' uprising of July 1941.[66]

Conversely, other instances emerged in which civilian officials leveraged their superior political connections to sideline local military commanders. Perhaps the main dispute between civilian and military officials erupted in Dalmatia with the opposition between Mussolini's plenipotentiary in Yugoslavia, Giuseppe Bastianini, and the commander of the Second Army, Roatta. A rising star in the Fascist firmament, Bastianini was part of il Duce's inner circle as a member of the Fascist Grand Council. Thus, with his appointment as governor of Dalmatia on 20 May 1941, Rome sent a message that Dalmatia, a territory formerly claimed by the Italians at the end of the First World War, would be considered fully Italian land.[67] The governor did not hide his contempt for the military leaders in the Balkans whom he lambasted as "mediocre generals,"[68] not least in his dispute with General Quirino Armellini, the commander of the Eighteenth Army quartered in Dalmatia. Armellini's preference was for short-term pragmatism over long-term political plans, as he sought to pacify the region. He urged that only a unified military command, free from civilian interference, could prevail over the mounting insurgency he faced. By contrast, Bastianini and the civil officials, such as the Italian prefects and police forces, toed the ideological line in deeming the province to be a part of the Kingdom of Italy, to be administered and defended accordingly.[69] Indeed, the Bastianini-Armellini quarrel is almost unique in demonstrating how civilian authorities could exert their will over military commanders' preferences.

However, for all the heat generated by these squabbles, it is important not to overstate the effect of institutional rivalries in driving varying levels of repression. Civil and military authorities may have differed in outlook, but officials still strove for results that worked for both parties. Take, for instance, the Province of Ljubljana, where the civil high commissioner, Emilio Grazioli, a Fascist Party notable who came from a city bordering Slovenia (Trieste), sought to forcefully Italianize his domain in anticipation of future annexation. Grazioli failed to produce any significant result and in fact fuelled the resistance movement further in the region, living up to an earlier assessment that characterized him as a "man of modest value (*figura di modesto rilievo*) with ... little education and no administrative skill."[70] This failure paved the way for the commander of the Italian Eleventh Army, Mario Robotti, to take over command of the region.[71] The way in which both parties handled this awkward series of events exemplifies the mutual cooperation that more often prevailed between these parties. Robotti did not criticize Grazioli for his overarching goal (annexing the Slovenian territory to Italy), but only for failing to provide law and order in the region with the police forces at his disposal. What differed here were the methods, not the ends. Thus, differences in institutional culture can only be claimed to exert a minimal impact upon the actual experience of populations under the Italian fascist yoke.[72]

CONCLUSION

As this chapter has established, the character of the Italian occupations of France and the Balkans differed significantly. Whereas the style of the occupation of southeastern France was overwhelmingly defined by restraint, brutality formed a far greater aspect of concurrent practice in the east. This chapter advances two arguments to explain this pattern and discounts a third. First and foremost, conditions "on the ground" served to create structural circumstances within which brutality arose (or did not occur). Conditions in France were defined by Italy's strategic priorities, numerical weakness, and cordial relations with the leadership of the Vichy regime. This reduced the drive toward brutality Italian forces did face resistance, but it was infrequent and was confined to a handful of open attacks. Italian behaviour was not wholly benign, belying their reputation as "Italiano brava gente." However, compared with the Balkans, instances of excessive repression were few and far between. Thus, in occupied French territory, there arose a limited impetus for cycles of reciprocal violence to emerge.

Structural conditions differed markedly in the Balkans, where Italian forces encountered less compliant local authorities and faced far higher levels of organized resistance. This manifested in the emergence of cycles of violence as Italian forces lashed out in reprisals against partisan attacks. Such behaviour was influenced by colonial experience and fascist ideology. These conspired collectively to colour Italian attitudes toward different subject populations in Europe. Through these lenses, the French population was viewed as being broadly equal to metropolitan Italians, whereas the Indigenous peoples of the Balkans were perceived more pejoratively in perspectives redolent of Italian attitudes toward the inhabitants of their African colonies. Thus, Italian cultural colonization within France tended to be limited to minor linguistic adaptation, holding back violence for targeted reprisals, whereas those occupying the Balkans employed more radical methods that displaced populations and destroyed ways of life. Occupations in both theatres were accompanied by high-level power struggles between civil and military representatives of the fascist state. However, this chapter argues that these episodes generated more drama than difference in the substance of occupations. Civil and military institutional culture ran subordinate to structural circumstances and ideology in determining brutality or restraint.

NOTES

1 AN, AJ41, 329, "Statistique Générale," 27 February 1944, cited in Alan Mitchell, *Nazi Paris: The History of an Occupation, 1940–1944* (New York: Berghahn, 2008), 107–8.
2 Archives départementales des Alpes-Maritimes (hereafter ADAM) 169 W 3, "Occupation et Libération de la Commune de Nice, Guerre 1939–1945," Mairie de Nice, 7 May 1949.
3 Overall figures are hard to determine, as are distinctions between partisan and civilian casualties. By way of example, between April and May 1942 alone 1,646 alleged partisans were killed in Italian counterinsurgency operations: see table 48, "Axis and rebel losses in Croatia, Montenegro and Bosnia from 20 April to 13 May 1942," in Davide Rodogno, *Fascism's European Empire: Italian Occupation during the Second World War* (Cambridge: Cambridge University Press), 442.
4 James Burgwyn, *Empire on the Adriatic: Mussolini's conquest of Yugoslavia 1941–1943* (New York: Enigma, 2005), 301.
5 For representational memoirs advancing the idea of a good-natured Italian soldier, see Mario Roatta, *Otto milioni di baionette* (Milan: Mondadori 1946); Salvatore Loi, *Jugoslavia 1941* (Turin: Il Nastro Azzurro 1953); Giuseppe Angelini, *Fuochi di Bivacco in Croazia* (Roma: Tipografia Regionale, 1946) and Giacomo Zanussi, *Guerra e catastrofe d'Italia*, vol. 1 (Rome: Corso, 1945); For revisionist challenge, see Filippo Focardi, *Il cattivo tedesco e il bravo italiano: la rimozione delle colpe della seconda Guerra mondiale* (Rome-Bari: Laterza, 2014); and Filippo Focardi and Lutz Klinkhammer, "The Question of Fascist Italy's War Crimes: The Construction of a Self-Acquitting Myth (1943–1948)," *Journal of Modern Italian Studies* 9, no. 3 (2004): 330–48.
6 The Italian army as most armies at the outset of the Second World War lacked a coherent counterinsurgency doctrine, Filippo Cappellano, "La 2a Armata e le operazioni di controguerriglia in Jugoslavia (1941–1943),"

in Federica Saini Fasanotti, Basilio di Martino, Andrea Crescenzi and Alessandro Gionfrida, *L'esercito alla macchia, Controguerriglia italiana 1860–1943, L'esperienza italiana di controguerriglia dal Brigantaggio alla Seconda Guerra Mondiale* (Roma: Stato maggiore della Difesa, Ufficio storico, 2015), 209.

7 On the Battle of the Alps, Emanuele Sica, "The Italian Army and the Battle of the Alps," *Canadian Journal of History* 47, no. 2 (2012): 355–78.

8 Henri Amoroux, *La vie Française sous l'Occupation* (Paris: Fayard, 1961), 279–90.

9 Olivier Wieviorka, *Histoire de la Résistance* (Paris: Perrin, 2013) 74–86.

10 Jean-Louis Panicacci, "Les Communistes italiens dans les Alpes-Maritimes (1939–45)," *Annali della Fondazione Giangiacomo Feltrinelli* 24 (1985): 155–80; Jean-Louis Panicacci, *L'Occupation italienne, Sud-Est de la France, juin 1940–septembre 1943* (Rennes: Presses Universitaires de Rennes, 2010), 146–51.

11 Emanuele Sica, *Mussolini's Army in the French Riviera, Italy's Occupation of France* (Urbana: University of Illinois Press, 2017), 138–43.

12 Corsica: Jean-Paul Pellegrinetti and Ange Rovere, *La Corse et la République, La vie politique de la fin du Second Empire au début du XXIe siècle* (Paris: Seuil, 2004), 312–27; Karine Varley, "Between Vichy France and Fascist Italy: redefining identity and the enemy in Corsica during the Second World War," *Journal of Contemporary History* 47, no. 3 (2012), 505–27. For the occupation of Savoy, Christian Villermet, Pierre Guillen, and Pierre Milza, *A noi Savoia: histoire de l'occupation italienne en Savoie: novembre 1942–septembre 1943* (Montmélian: La Fontaine de Siloé, 1999).

13 Richard Vinen, *The Unfree French: Life under the Occupation* (New Haven: Yale University Press, 2006), 247–79.

14 Wieviorka, *Histoire de la Résistance*, 222.

15 Domenico Schipsi, *L'occupazione italiana dei territori metropolitani francesi (1940–1943)* (Roma: Ufficio storico, Stato Maggiore Esercito), 106–7; AUSSME, N-I-11, DS SMRE 2079, Lettera n° 21260, 7 December 1942; MacGregor Knox, *Dictatorship, Foreign Policy, and War in Fascist Italy and Nazi Germany* (Cambridge: Cambridge University Press, 2000), 156.

16 AUSSME, N-I-11, DS 1320, Rapporto n° 6824/I di prot., "Epurazione della città di Nizza," Diario Storico Quarta Armata, 1 May 1943; ARC, T-821, Roll 265, IT 3099, Rapporto n° 1244/o di prot., "Epurazione della città di Nizza," Comando 223° Divisione Costiera, 6 May 1943.

17 Vjeran Pavlaković, "Yugoslavia," in *Hitler's Europe Ablaze, Occupation, Resistance and Rebellion during World War II*, ed. Philip Cooke and Ben H. Shepherd (New York: Skyhorse Publishing, 2014), 216–17.

18 On the Italian occupation of Slovenia, Marco Cuzzi, *L'occupazione italiana della Slovenia* (Roma: Stato Maggiore dell'Esercito, Ufficio storico, 1998); Amedeo Osti Guerrazzi, *Italian Army in Slovenia: Strategies of Antipartisan Repression 1941–1943* (London: Palgrave Macmillan, 2016); Gregor Joseph Kranjc, *To Walk with the Devil, Slovene Collaboration and Axis Occupation, 1941–1945* (Toronto: Toronto University Press, 2013).

19 Federico Goddi, *Fronte Montenegro, L'occupazione militare italiana 1941–1943* (Gorizia: LEG, 2016), 28–33. See also Francesco Caccamo, "l'Occupazione del Montenegro: dai progetti indipendentisti alla collaborazione con i Četnici," in *L'occupazione italiana della Iugoslavia (1941–1943)*, ed. Francesco Caccamo and Luciano Monzali (Firenze: Le Lettere, 2008), 133–219.

20 Ten. Col. Angelo Ravenni, *Cenni sulla guerriglia*, Rivista Militare, 1930/XI.

21 Comando 2° Armata a SMRE, Prot. n° 529/A.C., "Milizia ustacia," 10 June 1941, in Talpo, *Dalmazia, Una Cronaca per la Storia (1941)*, 468–71.

22 Paolo Formiconi, "I rapporti con l'alleato tedesco," in *La Quinta Sponda, Una storia dell'occupazione italiana della Croazia. 1941–1943*, ed. Alberto Becherelli and Paolo Formiconi (Roma: Stato maggiore della Difesa, Ufficio storico, 2015), 95.

23 Marko Attila Hoare, *Genocide and Resistance in Hitler's Bosnia: The Partisans and the Chetniks 1941–1943* (Oxford: Oxford University Press, 2006), 39–67.

24 Pavlaković, "Yugoslavia," 223–8.

25 Goddi, *Fronte Montenegro*, 101–17.

26 Osti Guerrazzi, *Italian army in Slovenia*, 32–9.

27 Paolo Formiconi, "I rapporti con l'alleato tedesco," 89.

28 The Circolare 3C can be found in Gianni Oliva, "*Si ammazza troppo poco*," *I Crimini di guerra italiani, 1940–1943* (Milano: Mondadori, 2006), 173–201. A summarized version can be found in http://www.criminidiguerra.it (accessed 24 June 2019).

29 Eric Gobetti, *Alleati del nemico: l'occupazione Italiana in Jugoslavia (1941–1943)* (Rome and Bari: Laterza, 2013), 83–4.

30 H. James Burgwyn, *Mussolini Warlord, Failed Dreams of Empire, 1940-1943* (New York: Enigma Books, 2012) 162–3.

31 Tone Ferenc, "There is not Enough Killing," *Condemned to Death – Hostages –Shot in the Ljubljana Province 1941–1943 documents* (Ljubljana: Institute for Contemporary History, Society of the Writers of the History of Liberation War in Slovenia, 1999), 19–21.

32 Italians were often referred by the Slavs as *palikuća* or "incendiary" (house-burner): Davide Conti, *L'occupazione italiana dei Balcani, Crimini di guerra e mito della "brava gente" (1940–1943)* (Rome: Odradek, 2008), 1.
33 Pietro Brignoli, *Santa Messa per i Fucilati: le spietate rappresaglie italiane contro i partigiani in Croazia dal diario di un cappellano* (Milan: Longanesi, 1973).
34 Carlo Spartaco Capogreco, *I Campi del duce, l'internamento civile nell'Italia fascista (1940–1943)* (Turin: Einaudi, 2006), 136–147; Eric Gobetti, *L'occupazione allegra, gli italiani in Jugoslavia (1941–1943)* (Rome: Carocci, 2007), 177. Alessandra Kersevan, *Lager italiani* (Rome: Nutrimenti, 2008), 267; Capogreco, *I Campi del duce*, 271.
35 Gobetti, *Alleati del nemico*, 67.
36 Alberto Becherelli, "La lotta antipartigiana," in *La Quinta Sponda, Una storia dell'occupazione italiana della Croazia. 1941–1943*, ed. Alberto Becherelli and Paolo Formiconi (Roma: Stato maggiore della Difesa, Ufficio storico, 2015), 70–3; Filippo Cappellano, "La 2ª Armata e le operazioni di controguerriglia in Jugoslavia (1941–1943)," 248–50.
37 Alberto Becherelli, "Jugoslavia 1943: L'operazione Weiss nei documenti dell'Ufficio Storico dello Stato Maggiore dell'Esercito italiano," *Historia* 10, Studia Universitatis 'Petru Maior' (2010), 148–60; Oddone Talpo, *Dalmazia, Una cronaca per la storia (1943–1944)* (Stato Maggiore dell'Esercito, Ufficio storico, 1994), 89–117; Gobetti, *L'occupazione allegra*, 215–20.
38 Talpo, *Dalmazia, Una cronaca per la storia (1943–1944)*, 119.
39 Ben Shepherd, *Terror in the Balkans, German Armies and Partisan Warfare* (Boston: Harvard University Press, 2012), 155; Gobetti, *Alleati del nemico*, 138–9.
40 Shepherd, *Terror in the Balkans*, 215–28.
41 Elena Aga-Rossi and Maria Teresa Giusti, *Una guerra a parte, I militari italiani nei Balcani, 1940–1945* (Bologna: Il Mulino, 2011), 190–5.
42 Nicola Labanca, *Oltremare, Storia dell'espansione coloniale italiana* (Bologna: Il Mulino, 2002).
43 Giorgio Rochat, "Le guerre coloniali dell'Italia fascista," in *Le guerre coloniali del fascismo*, ed. Angelo Del Boca (Rome and Bari: Laterza, 2008), 176–82; Giorgio Rochat, *Le guerre italiane in Libia e in Etiopia dal 1896 al 1939* (Udine: Gaspari, 2009); Federica Saini Fasanotti, *Libia 1922–1931, le operazioni militari italiane* (Rome: Stato Maggiore dell'Esercito, Ufficio Storico, 2012).
44 Angelo Del Boca, *I gas di Mussolini: il fascismo e la guerra d'Etiopia*, Roma: Riuniti, 1996; Alberto Sbacchi, "Poison Gas and Atrocities in

the Italo-Ethiopian War (1935–1936)," in *Italian Colonialism*, ed. Ruth Ben-Ghiat and Mia Fuller (Basingstoke: Palgrave Macmillan), 47–56.
45 Nicola Labanca, *La guerra d'Etiopia, 1935–1941* (Bologna: Il Mulino, 2015), 84–7.
46 Paolo Borruso, *Debre Libanos 1937, Il più grave crimine di guerra dell'Italia* (Rome and Bari: Laterza, 2020); Federica Saini Fasanotti, *Etiopia 1936–1940, Le operazioni di polizia coloniale nelle fonti dell'esercito italiano* (Rome: Stato Maggiore dell'Esercito, Ufficio Storico, 2010).
47 Isabel Hull, *Absolute Destruction: Military Culture and the Practices of War in Imperial Germany* (Ithaca, NY: Cornell University Press, 2006).
48 Eric Gobetti, "Allied with the Enemy: the Italian Occupation of Yugoslavia (1941–1943)," in *Italy and the Second World War, Alternative Perspectives*, ed. Emanuele Sica and Richard Carrier (Leiden: Brill Publishing, 2018), 26–7.
49 Giorgio Rochat, *Le guerre italiane, 1935–1943. Dall'imperio d'Etiopia alla disfatta* (Turin: Einaudi, 2005), 367.
50 Cristiana Pipitone, "Dall'Africa all'Europa: pratiche italiane di occupazione militare," in Istituto romano per la storia d'Italia dal fascismo alla Resistenza, *Politiche di occupazione dell'Italia fascista, l'Annale Irsifar* (Milan: Franco Angeli, 2008), 32.
51 Angelo Del Boca, *Italiani, Brava Gente?* (Vicenza: Neri Pozza, 2005), 241.
52 Rodogno, *Fascism's European Empire*, 57–63.
53 Teodoro Sala, "Guerra ed amministrazione in Jugoslavia 1941–1943, un'ipotesi coloniale," in *Annali della Fondazione Micheletti*, vol. 5, ed. Bruna Micheletti and Pier Paolo Poggio (Brescia: Fondazione Luigi Micheletti, 1990), 87.
54 Sandro Servi, "Building a Racial State: Images of the Jew in the Illustrated Fascist Magazine, *La Difesa della Razza*, 1938–1943," in *The Jews in Italy under Fascist and Nazi rule*, ed. Joshua D. Zimmerman (Cambridge: Cambridge University Press, 2005), 119–20.
55 Aaron Gillette, *Racial Theories in Fascist Italy* (London and New York: Routledge, 2000).
56 Rodogno, *Fascism's European Empire*, 63–7.
57 Italians made up only 1 per cent of the population in the province of Ljubljana and 9 per cent of the Governorate of Dalmatia, Gobetti, *Alleati del nemico*, 12–15.
58 Conti, *L'occupazione italiana nei Balcani*, 18.
59 All citations in Gobetti, *L'occupazione allegra*, 181.

60 Nicholas Virtue, "Royal Army, Fascist Empire: The Regio Esercito on Occupation Duty, 1936–1943," PhD thesis, University of Western Ontario, 2016, 582–3.
61 Pierre Milza, *Voyage en Ritalie* (Paris: Payot, 2004), 113–60.
62 Pascal Molinari and Jean-Louis Panicacci, *Menton dans la tourmente* (Menton: Société d'art et d'histoire du Mentonnais, 1984), 58; Claude Barneaud, *Les Mentonnais et la Résistance* (Menton: Société d'Art et d'Histoire du Mentonnais, 1992), 34; Rodogno, *Fascism's European Empire*, 265; ADAM 616 W 260, "Conférence pour l'étude des problèmes posés par l'occupation et la propagande italiennes tenue à Vichy le 16 décembre 1940," 8–9.
63 Rochat, *Le guerre italiane*, 147.
64 For a view on the low ideologization of the Italian army, Bastian Matteo Scianna, *The Italian War on the Eastern Front, 1941–1943: Operations, Myths and Memories* (Cham: Palgrave Macmillan, 2019), 258–9.
65 Niall MacGalloway, "Italian Governing Apparatuses in Occupied France, 1940–1943," in *Italy and the Second World War, Alternative Perspectives*, ed. Emanuele Sica and Richard Carrier (Leiden: Brill Publishing, 2018), 88–90.
66 Goddi, *Fronte Montenegro*, 26.
67 Frank P. Verna, "Notes on Italian Rule in Dalmatia under Bastianini, 1941–1943," *The International History Review* 12, no. 3 (August 1990), 530.
68 Rodogno, *Fascism's European Empire*, 139.
69 For a comprehensive analysis on the conflict, Oddone Talpo, *Dalmazia, una cronaca per la storia*, vol. 2 (Rome: Stato maggiore dell'Esercito, Ufficio storico, 2000), 210–376.
70 According to the 1929 police report, cited by Cuzzi, *L'occupazione della Slovenia*, 32.
71 Marco Cuzzi, "La Slovenia italiana," in *L'occupazione italiana della Iugoslavia (1941–1943)*, ed. Francesco Caccamo and Luciano Monzali (Firenze: Le Lettere, 2008), 243–6; Osti Guerrazzi, *Italian Army in Slovenia*, 31–9.
72 Rodogno, *Fascism's European Empire*, chapter 4, "Mussolini, the civil and military authorities and the co-ordination of occupation policies," 109–43.

11

Divided Loyalties

Indian Prisoners of War in Singapore, February 1942 to May 1943

Kevin Noles

After a series of catastrophic defeats in 1942, 67,000 Indian troops belonging to the British and Commonwealth forces in Southeast Asia found themselves in Japanese captivity. Their history continues to be highly contested.[1] Much of the controversy focuses on the creation and activities of the Indian National Army (INA), a force allied to the Imperial Japanese Army (IJA) that made use of Indian prisoners of war (POW) to fight against the British. The INA was formed to further the cause of Indian nationalism. Its historiography has been shaped by differing interpretations with, broadly speaking, western military historians typically dismissing its military effectiveness and emphasizing the use of coercion to recruit its members, whereas accounts written from an Indian nationalist perspective tend to emphasize its political significance in the run-up to Indian independence.

This chapter addresses the period from the surrender of Singapore in February 1942 to the arrival of the Indian revolutionary leader Subhas Chandra Bose in Asia in May 1943, a period during which Singapore acted as the main hub of the Indian prisoner experience. The chapter addresses the question: who volunteered for the INA, who resisted recruitment, and why? With previous scholarship emphasizing factors such as coercion, following the lead of officers, and the draw of Indian nationalism, this chapter will argue that newly available primary sources indicate that other factors were also involved in driving volunteering. These included a competition for status between different categories of Indian officer, and the employment of nationalist concert parties to deliver political propaganda in the guise of entertainment. This chapter therefore provides an insight into the distinctive features of captivity as experienced by Indian colonial troops.

The first significant contribution to the historiography on the INA was from Hugh Toye, who had served during the Second World War as an officer in the Combined Services Detailed Interrogation Centre (India) (CSDIC(I)), the British Military Intelligence unit that interrogated captured INA personnel. Toye interrogated Captain Mohan Singh, the first commander of the INA, although Toye's book *The Springing Tiger* is focused primarily on events after the arrival of Subhas Chandra Bose in the middle of 1943.[2] Toye later published an article examining events during 1942, although it concentrates on the small Indian elite that worked closely with the Japanese.[3] Toye also donated CSDIC(I) material to the British Library, an important primary source for this chapter. Subsequent contributions included Kalyan Ghosh's *The Indian National Army*, which contains a detailed discussion of the Mohan Singh era, and the work of Joyce Lebra, who drew heavily on Japanese sources.[4] But it is Peter Fay's *The Forgotten Army*, published in 1993, that has become the nearest thing to a standard text for the INA; the title of Fay's final chapter, "The Triumph of the INA," is indicative of his verdict on the organization.[5] An author critical of Fay is Chandar Sundaram, although his article "Paper Tiger" largely addresses the later rather than early combat performance of the INA in Burma.[6] Another notable article is G.J. Douds's "The Men Who Never Were: Indian POWs in the Second World War."[7] Ambitious in scope, it highlights the suffering of those who resisted volunteering for forces such as the INA. More recently, Daniel Marston devoted a chapter of *The Indian Army and the End of the Raj* to the INA. His less than positive stance is representative of the current consensus among western military historians.[8] Srinath Raghavan's impressively wide-ranging monograph, *India's War*, includes a chapter with a balanced discussion of the Mohan Singh era, although it concentrates on the later impact of Subhas Chandra Bose rather than the period before his arrival.[9]

The historiography suggests that a variety of factors drove recruitment into the INA, with the role of nationalism emphasized by Ghosh,

Fay, Douds, and Raghavan.[10] The role of officers in promoting recruitment is prominent in Marston, Douds, and Ghosh, while Douds and Raghavan mention the lure of promotion as an important factor for viceroy's commissioned officers (VCOs).[11] Coercion is prominent in Toye, although Fay highlights the arguably misleading use of the emotive term "Concentration Camp" to describe the INA detention camp.[12] Concern for the Indian civilian population under Japanese occupation is a factor in Ghosh and Marston.[13] Marston mentions that recruitment often proceeded on a communal basis, although some authors, such as Ghosh, ignore this as a factor.[14] It is worth noting that INA soldiers' cooperation with the Japanese is normally presented in simple binary terms: either join the INA or not, with those resisting remaining "true to their salt."[15] Gajendra Singh has demonstrated that resistance was a more nuanced process. This aspect of Indian prisoner experience deserves greater attention.[16] Also, books such as Fay's were published before the release of the CSDIC(I) archives, while material at the British Library is only rarely cited.[17] In addition, recent research by Rajesh Rai on the Indian civilian community provides new insights into the events in Singapore.[18] In summary, with much of the writing on the INA dominated by the later career of Subhas Chandra Bose, the experiences of Indian POWs before his arrival in mid-1943 is a neglected subject.

Although Fay described the primary INA sources as "beggarly," recent decades have seen a number of new sources become available.[19] This chapter uses CSDIC(I) material held at the British Library and also at the National Archives at Kew to transform our understanding of the INA's membership.[20] The CSDIC(I) interrogations follow a standardized format, with the longest over 130 pages, although a typical length is around 10. The text is full of jargon and abbreviations, with phrases such as "a Bat of the Flittermouse B party" being sometimes difficult to decipher when first encountered (a "Bat" is a parachutist).[21] When interpreting the texts, it needs to be remembered that these are interrogations rather than interviews. While there is no evidence of physical abuse of detainees by CSDIC(I), they would have been under intense psychological pressure, often believing they faced long periods of imprisonment or even execution. At a minimum, one CSDIC(I) detainee suffered a mental breakdown and two appear to have committed suicide.[22] Another factor is the evidence of "orientalist" attitudes among interrogators, in other words a tendency to typecast individuals on the basis of their religion or caste, with one example being "he has the usual Sikh gift for intrigue, highly developed and that he cannot be trusted."[23] There is also a sampling bias in the CSDIC(I) material, in that only Indian POWs who were thought to have joined the INA were interrogated. Nonetheless, despite the challenges of interpretation, the CSDIC(I) interrogations provide extraordinary insight into the experiences in captivity of hundreds of Indian troops of all ranks. Unlike the interrogations, CSDIC(I) reports come in a variety of forms, with one particularly valuable example providing a concise history of the force.[24] There is also other relevant material, including weekly intelligence summaries, as well as other sources.[25]

Memoirs are also a valuable source of material, with two INA officers tending to dominate in secondary sources: Shah Nawaz Khan and Mohan Singh.[26] Fay has described Shah Nawaz's memoir as "a narrative incomplete in substance," although he rated it as "the fullest report by any of the participants."[27] Mohan Singh's memoir is also essential reading, although it is decidedly self-serving.[28] Other INA officer memoirs include those by Mohammad Kiani and Naranjan Gill.[29] Memoirs of officers who resisted the INA include that of Gurbakhsh Singh,[30] while the only account from an ordinary soldier, John Baptist Crasta, is also from someone who resisted.[31] There is also an excellent oral history from an officer who resisted the INA.[32] Of Japanese memoirs, Iwaichi Fujiwara's is essential reading.[33] Other sources include a documentary study by Tilak Sareen.[34] While Fay lamented the lack of primary sources in the early 1990s, today a wide range is available.

PRISONERS IN SINGAPORE

The Indian POWs captured at the fall of Singapore had been trained for a variety of roles, including those of infantry, artillery, engineers, and medical. The British colonial practice of recruiting the army from a variety of "classes," to prevent one becoming dominant, meant that the Indian POWs were a heterogeneous group drawn from varied religious and ethnic backgrounds. The term "class" was a contemporary British term covering a complex combination of religion, ethnicity, language, caste, and region, but was typically synonymous with the "martial races" from which the Army attempted to recruit the majority of Indian *jawans* (meaning a "heroic or martial young man").[35] Examples included Sikhs, Punjabi Muslims, Jats, Dogras, and Gurkhas, with most battalions containing multiple "classes."[36]

Many of the officers within these units were British, but the Indian officers among them held two broad types of commission, Indian commissioned officers (ICOs) and viceroy's commissioned officers (VCOs). ICO is used in this chapter as shorthand for officers who had attended military academies, often as a result of the pre-war "Indianization" process, which entailed replacing some British officers with Indian ones. ICOs held various types of commission, the most prestigious being the King's commissioned Indian officer (KCIO), granted to those who had attended the Royal Military College at Sandhurst in England, although most had graduated from training academies in India, such as the Indian Military Academy at Dehra Dun. VCOs were promoted from the ranks and traditionally acted as intermediaries between British officers and jawans, although a British pre-war "Indianization" policy of replacing VCOs with ICOs led to discontent within some units, a legacy that would later assist their recruitment into the INA.[37]

The experiences of Indian POWs during 1942 and early 1943 were framed by a dramatic series of events. The surrender of Singapore on 15 February 1942 was the culmination of a rapid military campaign.[38] During it, Major Fujiwara of Japanese Military Intelligence and his F. Kikan organization successfully subverted captured Indian personnel of the British Indian Army with the help of an Indian revolutionary from Bangkok named Pritam Singh, who headed an organization called the Indian Independence League (IIL).[39] One of the first ICOs captured was Captain Mohan Singh of the 1/14th Punjab Battalion, and he quickly proved a willing and capable collaborator.[40] After the surrender of Singapore, all British officers were removed from Indian units and some 45,000 Indian POWs proceeded to Farrer Park, where they were handed over by Fujiwara en masse to Mohan Singh.[41] Throughout the rest of 1942, Mohan Singh would remain the dominant personality in the lives of Indian POWs.[42]

Dispersed into camps across Singapore Island, the Indian POWs settled into a routine of performing fatigues for the Japanese.[43] From Mohan Singh's perspective, the next six months were framed by two conferences. The first, in Tokyo in March, was marred by an air crash that killed Pritam Singh, among others, while the second, in Bangkok in June, culminated in Mohan Singh being promoted to general amid concerns among some civilian delegates that he wanted to dispense with civilian leadership.[44] Although propaganda and coercion to persuade Indian POWs to volunteer for the INA were present throughout, they intensified after the Bangkok conference and were given extra impetus when Gandhi's "Quit India" movement began in August 1942.[45] The First Division of the INA, some 16,000 strong, was officially formed in September and represented the high point of Mohan Singh's career.[46] Thereafter, increasing tensions between him, the Japanese, and factions within the Indian civilian leadership, culminated in a crisis in December that led to his arrest by the Japanese. Singh's final act was to order the dissolution of the INA, although he was only partially successful.[47] After a few months of uncertainty, the news that Subhas Chandra Bose was en route to Asia revived the INA under a new military leadership, although some previous volunteers refused to rejoin it.[48] Those who refused were sent to the Southwest Pacific in May 1943, where they suffered a high mortality rate.[49] The period relevant to the current chapter was therefore a dramatic one.

The lived experience of most Indian POWs was driven by factors that were similar to those of British and Australian POWs: work fatigues for the Japanese, inadequate and poor-quality food, and the debilitating effects of disease, particularly dysentery and malaria. A dominant factor was Singapore's tropical climate, with its high humidity and rainfall. The Indian POWs were dispersed across half a dozen main camps. In late February 1942, the camp at Nee Soon held over 20,000 men, with some "forming supra-regimental groups and parties by classes which took no orders from their officers."[50] The overcrowding and a damaged water supply led to a major outbreak of dysentery at Nee Soon that by June 1942 had killed 700 prisoners from 7,000 cases.[51] Conditions were similar at Bidadari camp, which held 22,000 prisoners in February 1942.[52] Even those with the best food and medical help could suffer badly. Mohan Singh had both malaria and dysentery, and had lost twenty pounds by March.[53] Performing work fatigues for the Japanese brought its own dangers. In one example, a party of sixty Indian POWs was caught in a large explosion while stacking ammunition, killing forty.[54] The Japanese also sought to identify Indian POWs with specialist skills and came to view the Indian POWs as a critical source of labour. One example was electricians and fitters, who were sent to Borneo in May 1942 "in order to work in the Japanese oil fields."[55]

For the civilian population of Singapore, the Japanese occupation would be remembered as "an era of darkness."[56] Soon after the surrender, the Japanese began a "pacification" program, or *sook ching*, that involved the killing of up to 50,000 ethnic Chinese civilians, an event that shocked Indian civilians.[57] The last available census figures show some 53,000 Indians in a population of 567,000, over 400,000 of whom were ethnic Chinese.[58] The Indian POWs therefore found themselves among a large civilian population with a substantial Indian minority organized through the IIL, whose political activity tended "to parallel developments in India," most notably during Gandhi's "Quit India" campaign.[59] The radio broadcasts of both sides were the main medium across which news travelled. Indian POWs in Singapore were therefore individually isolated from home, but collectively were part of a wider Indian community that suddenly found itself within the Japanese Empire. Subject to divided loyalties, including religion, regiment, rank, and class, the divisions among them would play an important role in shaping their reactions to recruitment for the INA. The remainder of this chapter reviews statistical evidence, before examining the creation of the INA, its temporary dissolution in late 1942, and its re-establishment in early 1943.

QUANTIFYING PARTICIPATION

As Ashley Jackson has noted, when it comes to INA volunteering rates, "statistics vary."[60] For officers, Marston states that 50 ICOs were captured, with 35 joining the INA.[61] Other figures quoted by Douds and Raghavan talk of "400 Indian officers" joining the INA, of whom 250 were medical personnel and 100 were VCOs.[62] Fay talks of "less than 250" officers, although it is unclear whether this includes medical personnel or VCOs.[63] In contrast, there is broad agreement that 20,000 Indian troops joined the INA, although this includes those who joined after May 1943.[64] CSDIC(I) sources provide an opportunity to review the statistics.[65] Two datasets have been created: a listing of ICOs based on a report, and information captured from all interrogations. The ICO dataset lists 416 ICOs, comprising 181 doctors and 235 combatant ICOs, a much higher figure than typically found in the historiography.[66] INA volunteering rates show differences between doctors and combatant officers, with 68 of 181 doctors (38 per cent) volunteering compared with 125 of 235 combatant officers (53 per cent). Accurate numbers are essential for a meaningful discussion of volunteering rates, and these figures represent a significant revision to the combatant ICO figures found in the work of Marston and elsewhere, increasing the number having been captured almost five-fold, while reducing the proportion of combatant ICOs joining the INA to just over half.

The second dataset is derived from all CSDIC(I) interrogations of Indian personnel available in London archives. It contains 561 interrogations, with 423 military personnel (of whom 79 were ICOs) and 138 civilians; although this represents less than 5 per cent of the total number of Indian troops who joined the INA, it is nonetheless large enough to provide useful evidence. As an example, the date of joining is presented in figure 11.1.

The underlying frequency distribution represents a total of 318 military personnel, lower than the total number of military interrogations (423) because the remainder either joined after May 1943, or not at all. This is the first time such a time-based analysis of INA recruitment has been possible. A distinct pattern is evident, with an initial surge during the Malayan campaign (shown for context), slow recruitment until June, and then building to a peak in September. The peak coincides with Gandhi's "Quit India" movement and the formal establishment of the INA shortly afterwards.

Another question is how many Indian POWs were in Singapore, with the British official history stating that 67,000 were captured during the Malayan campaign.[67] A CSDIC(I) report suggests that this figure is for the whole Far East, with 45,000 in Singapore and 10,000 in Malaya, to give a total of 55,000 covered by this study.[68] The same report states that 40,000 of the 45,000 Indian POWs in Singapore, or eight out of nine, volunteered to serve, with the 10,000 in Malaya being "accidental non-volunteers."[69] This suggests that many more Indian POWs were willing to serve in the INA than actually did so.[70] Also, volunteering rates for Indian POWs were much higher than for ICOs, suggesting that different factors were at work for the two groups. It is worth noting that CSDIC(I) categorized interrogated Indian POWs as "Black," "Grey," or "White," with "Black" being the worst from a British perspective, but as these designations mostly relate to activities that took place after the period of this study, they have been ignored.[71] In summary, the datasets provide a framework within which to address who volunteered for the INA and who resisted joining it.

DIVIDED LOYALTIES

The surrender of Singapore was probably the worst defeat in British military history. As one Indian officer put it: "The ease and speed with which the Japanese defeated the British forces in the Far East broke the legend of British power."[72] Fay has suggested that it seemed to

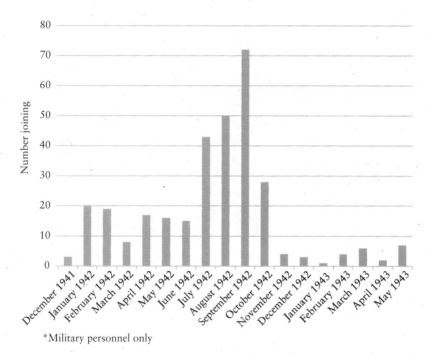

*Military personnel only

Figure 11.1 INA Monthly Recruitment Profile, December 1941 to May 1943. British Library, AAS, Mss Eur F275/2, F275/3, F275/4, F275/5, F275/6, F275/7, F275/8, F275/12, F275/14, F275/15, F275/16, F275/17, F275/18, F275/21, F275/23; National Archives, WO 106/5881, WO 325/51.

many that "the world of the Raj was finished."[73] In the immediate aftermath of the surrender, two factors began to divide Indian POWs in Singapore. The first involved the disruption of the traditional military hierarchy through the promotion to ICO rank of VCOs and others who supported Mohan Singh. In one case, a Naik (corporal) was promoted to second lieutenant. The second involved the development of schisms along ethno-cultural lines, with this initial phase dominated by a Sikh military and political leadership.[74] As one officer put it, "[M]ost officers were apprehensive, but most suspicious of this Jap-Sikh alliance were the Muslims – especially the senior ones," with their concerns relating to the domestic politics of India, and in particular communal tensions in the Punjab.[75] When one Muslim officer visited Mohan Singh's headquarters in March, the preponderance of Sikhs caused him to remark to one of the few other Muslims there, "Is this a Sikh Raj?"[76] It was a question that many were asking.

A neglected aspect of Indian POW experience, is the way some were directly incorporated into the Imperial Japanese Army, fulfilling roles that included manning anti-aircraft (AA) guns. According to Mohan Singh, "about a thousand" AA gunners were provided to the Japanese by the beginning of March 1942 "for the defence of the island" of Singapore.[77] A similar category of Indian personnel was motor transport (MT) drivers; in one example from March 1942, some 60 drivers were transferred to the Japanese.[78] It is apparent that service in the Japanese-commanded units was unpopular, not least because of the harsh discipline, but the Indian POWs seem to have had little choice but to accept the fait accompli with which they were presented.

For the remaining Indian POWs, the differences in conditions between those who cooperated with the Japanese, and those who did not, quickly became apparent. For example, at Bidadari, within days of the surrender, a separate "Free Army Camp" had been established where "the officers had bungalows to live in and Chinese girls to serve them."[79] But for one Muslim officer, Major M.Z. Kiani, there were also personal rivalries at work.[80] Kiani was from the same battalion as Mohan Singh and therefore knew him well. A promising officer, Kiani had won the Sword of Honour as best officer cadet during his training, and had served as a staff officer during the Malayan Campaign.[81] Appointed as commander of Nee Soon POW Camp, he quickly became worried that Mohan Singh might use his new power to exact revenge on him, or even murder him, because he had been promoted above him.[82] At this point, he considered him "a Sikh officer with no standing either inside or outside India, a mere Japanese marionette."[83] But Kiani's cousin, Captain I.J. Kiani, had joined Mohan Singh during the Malayan Campaign and now worked to "clarify the situation between the two men."[84] Simultaneously, Kiani came into contact with leading members of the Indian civilian community who had joined the IIL.[85]

Despite his concerns about Mohan Singh, Kiani clearly had Indian nationalist sympathies, and was worried about what a Sikh-dominated INA would mean for the Muslim community. Soon his cousin had "managed to reassure him and persuaded him of the expediency of joining hands with Mohan Singh," a volte face that came as a shock to other officers.[86] As a senior Punjabi Muslim ICO, his decision influenced other Muslim officers, who otherwise "would never have joined the movement."[87] Kiani's decision process illustrates a number of common factors: the significance of family connections where they existed; the importance of professional rivalries, often framed in terms of erstwhile Indian Army seniority; the influence of the wider Indian community; and the importance of ethno-cultural identity for Indian POWs. CSDIC(I) certainly believed that the reason Punjabi Muslim officers were joining at this early stage was "to preserve Muslim influence which was threatened by the line of action taken by Mohan Singh."[88] A similar dynamic was also at work for Hindu Dogras and Jats.[89]

Other officers remained opponents of the INA and its propaganda. Japanese demands for labour parties away from Singapore provided an escape from the propaganda, with the most successful example being a party led by Lieutenant Colonel Gurbakhsh Singh. His battalion, the Jind Infantry, was a Sikh battalion with a strong esprit de corps, its cadre of Sikh ICOs potentially invaluable to the INA. In June 1942, with most senior INA personnel at the conference in Bangkok, Gurbakhsh Singh used contacts within the remaining INA administration to get himself and his men sent as the core of a 3,000 strong fatigue party to Malaya.[90] Although he and his men would spend the rest of the war in Malaya doing fatigues for the Japanese, often under very trying conditions, he had successfully managed to extract a large number of troops from the influence of the INA. The majority of Indian POWs, however, remained in Singapore, where the intensity of propaganda and coercion was about to increase dramatically.

In June 1942, a major conference in Bangkok brought together Indian nationalists from across Japanese-controlled Asia, against a backdrop of growing political unrest in India.[91] Mohan Singh was at the height of his oratorical powers, making a speech that lasted a full day, an extract of which gives a sense of its tone: "The responsibility of deciding the fate of 400 million brothers has now finally been put on our shoulders. Indians inside India are a bird in a cage and decreed not to sing. The world has great hopes in us and our country men are staring in askance."[92]

The conference established a "Council of Action," with a civilian president and four other members, including Mohan Singh.[93] It sanctioned the raising of the INA and promoted Mohan Singh to the rank of general, while emphasizing that the army would only be used "in conformity with the express or implied wishes of the Indian National Congress."[94] Mohan Singh's promotion from captain to general was the ultimate example of the subversion of Indian Army seniority. Before the conference, Singh had increased the tempo of propaganda and had gathered 25,000 volunteer names, although he had doubts about how enthusiastic some were.[95] Some were, however, genuinely committed, one example being 200 men from the 5/11th Sikh, who had been armed and trained in jungle warfare in Malaya under Japanese instructors.[96] When Mohan Singh returned to Singapore in the middle of July, the propaganda and recruitment reached a crescendo, driven by what CSDIC(I) considered his "magnetic and compelling personality."[97] Singh also persuaded "senior and elderly VCOs" to establish a "welfare committee" that bolstered his standing among the jawans by touring the POW camps and hospitals, and reporting issues back to him.[98] The INA was formally established in September 1942, the timing reflected in the recruitment profile seen in figure 11.1.

RECRUITING AN ARMY

A variety of methods were used to recruit Indian POWs into the INA. Propaganda lectures were the foundation of recruitment, particularly as most jawans were illiterate, with Mohan Singh claiming that he could "make anyone in those days volunteer by lecturing."[99] Other officers also delivered lectures, including M.Z. Kiani and Lieutenant-Colonel Chatterjee, one of several senior medical officers who joined the movement.[100] The themes in Mohan Singh's lectures included calls for the liberation of India from British rule. He "abused those Indians who still remained loyal in spite of the British handing them over unconditionally to the Japanese,"[101] and he encouraged Gurkhas to enlist because, as he put it, if the Japanese arrived in India without the INA "they would surely violate the modesty of the Indian and Gurkha women."[102]

Another vehicle for propaganda was concert parties, which combined nationalistic storylines with musical entertainment. A central figure was a Hindu VCO, Subedar Bhandari, who, as well as writing plays, was in charge of the INA Dramatic Party, a unit that in the view of CSDIC(I) "did much to condition the minds of the Indian P[O]W into accepting the ideology of the renegade movement."[103] Bhandari's first play was *Dukhia Bharat* (Distressed India) and featured a plot with a "young graduate" called Ramesh as its hero, who "is living a very expensive life" due to his western education, but who then joins the Indian National Congress, before being imprisoned for trying to help Indian villages who are resisting British taxes. His sacrifice prompts the suicide of other students and leaves "the headman of the village determined to marry his daughter to Ramesh on release." After independence, Ramesh and other students are "garlanded" and offered good government jobs. The message was clear: sacrificing now for the nationalist cause would bring rewards later. The play was followed by a "comic act" that showed "how corruption amongst the Indian ladies is increasing as a result of the Western education."[104] Bhandari would write and organize the performance of several plays over the following months. Their plot lines share a number of features: their civilian setting; a hero who is invariably a young male student; and women who need to be protected, proxies for India herself. While what they delivered was entertainment as much as propaganda, with saris and musical instruments obtained locally, CSDIC(I) considered them a key part of the propaganda effort of the INA.[105]

The propaganda may have drawn men to the INA, but they were also driven toward it by a variety of coercive methods, ranging from performing heavy fatigues for the Japanese, to being sent to the concentration camp. One senior VCO, who was resisting the INA's attempts to recruit his men, found that heavy fatigues at Tengah Air Base soon resulted in defections.[106] The INA was able to satisfy constant Japanese demands for fatigue parties, while simultaneously putting pressure on non-volunteers. At the same time, Mohan Singh established a hierarchy of informants within each camp, typically headed by a VCO, whose job was "to move amongst the men and listen for any one speaking against Mohan Singh or the movement."[107] Those denounced were often sent to the concentration camp, one repeated victim being a Major Sardana.[108]

The operation of the informant network is a clear example of how Mohan Singh's power was founded on the support of VCOs rather than ICOs. The concentration camp was run by two VCOs, whose staff included a "sweeper" called Nimbu, who would become notorious for his cruelty (sweepers were non-combatants, recruited from the Dalit or "untouchable" community, who were attached to battalions to perform menial work).[109] Inmates were regularly flogged, normally by Nimbu.[110] Other "special" punishments were used, including "ducking individuals through manholes into sewers" and forcing men to stand while their testicles were squeezed, a manoeuvre that became known as a "Nimbu."[111] Nimbu's identity as a Dalit, and therefore a member of the lowest caste within the Hindu caste system, added an additional frisson of humiliation to the power over inmates that Singh enjoyed. Humiliation also featured in other ways, with what CSDIC(I) described as "the quite unnecessary public humiliation of Major Sardana," while a Lieutenant Chowdry was beaten for not saluting a jawan who was an INA guard.[112]

Nonetheless, CSDIC(I) was sometimes sceptical of the stories it was told about the camp. Toye, following a visit to the site of the camp in 1945, stated that "the physical nature of the camps show clearly that these stories have far outstripped the truth," putting the discrepancy down to the attempts of those being interrogated to explain why they had volunteered for the INA.[113] Away from the camp, one story involved a murder plot against an Indian lieutenant-colonel, allegedly motivated by his resistance to joining the INA, although CSDIC(I) knew that the plot had originated when he "and one of his Subedars [a VCO] quarrelled over the ownership of a male prostitute."[114] Another common trope encountered by CSDIC(I) was that a volunteer had only joined to escape to British lines at the first opportunity. Evidence of scepticism by CSDIC(I) does not mean that coercive methods were not used, just that those being interrogated were overwhelmingly those who had joined the INA, a sampling bias in the CSDIC(I) material that needs to be taken into consideration.

However, sometimes INA violence could take an extreme form, with two shooting incidents involving non-volunteers. The first involved Gurkha troops at Bidadari Camp in August 1942, and arose when an INA propaganda party started beating a Gurkha who had told them "to go away and not worry" the POWs. Four Gurkhas were wounded by rifle fire in the fracas that followed.[115] The second was more violent, involving Muslim troops at Kranji Camp in September, with at least two Muslims killed and others wounded by rifle fire, but not before one of the INA guards was beaten to death.[116] A distinctive feature of both these groups of POWs is that they appear to have been led from below with little or no regard to military hierarchy. The Gurkhas had rejected the leadership of their VCOs, many of whom had joined the INA, while the Muslim troops at Kranji were led by a group of five men whose only claim to authority was that they were "Hafiz-i-Quran," men who had memorized the Koran.[117] The incidents demonstrate that resistance to the INA did not always require the leadership of officers, but could draw on ethno-cultural loyalties, with jawan POWs capable of acting independently of officers.

While events in the camps dominated the lived experience of Indian POWs, the political context changed dramatically in early August thanks to the "Quit India" declaration by the Indian National Congress.[118] The arrest of Gandhi and Congress activists by the British authorities resulted in the IIL organizing mass rallies in Singapore, including the "Great Indian Independence Rally" held at Farrer Park on 12 August 1942, attended by "tens of thousands of Indians."[119] There was clearly "public indignation" regarding events in India and this also affected Indian POWs, with ICOs such as Captain Sahgal citing political developments in India as the reason that they joined the INA at this time.[120] The surge in INA recruitment seen in figure 11.1 in September 1942 was also driven by the practical impact of the official establishment of the INA in September.[121]

An interesting aspect is that those joining made a personal oath of loyalty to Mohan Singh rather than to the IIL "for the purpose of serving the real interests of India."[122] Toye has stated that the attraction of this approach for the 40,000 who gave the pledge was that it "would enable their leader to release them if things went wrong."[123] But it also acted as a substitute for the personal loyalty that many had shown previously toward their British officers.[124] There was certainly no lack of volunteers for the INA, with many civilians also wanting to join, although, much to Mohan Singh's frustration, the Japanese would only give permission to raise a single division of 16,000 men.[125] One factor in INA recruitment emphasized in the historiography is the lead shown by the Indian officers, whether the few ICOs or the many VCOs. One ICO explained: "I told the men under my command that I was going to join the INA and that they must join too."[126] In the case of a VCO, CSDIC(I) noted: "[I]t was undoubtedly through the bad example set by him and by other senior Gurkha VCOs that about 650 Gurkha [other ranks] enlisted."[127]

Nonetheless, the situation was often more complex. In one incident, junior medical ICOs refused to follow the example of more senior medical officers in joining the INA, although many of the medical VCOs agreed after being offered "better terms of service and promotion."[128] In the case of the 2/10th Baluch Regiment, the men stayed out of the INA despite their senior ICOs joining it. One was Captain Thimayya, the elder brother of a future head of the Indian Army, K.S. Thimayya.[129] In another case, CSDIC(I) believed that a Sandhurst-trained officer had, in effect, been led by his men, joining for the "reason that nearly all the Dogras had already volunteered and that he, as senior Dogra officer, could not but follow suit."[130] The simple notion of jawans following officers was often more nuanced in practice, although the leadership of ICOs and VCOs could still be decisive.

Gandhi's birthday on 2 October 1942 provided the opportunity for "a propaganda occasion," with the whole INA parading in Singapore and being inspected by Japanese officers.[131] It was the high point of Mohan Singh's career, the culmination of all he had worked for during 1942. While the INA saluted the flag of the Indian National Congress and wore new badges of rank, in practice it resembled the old Indian Army, wearing British uniforms and using captured British equipment.[132] Its main units comprised three "guerrilla" regiments named after the Congress leaders, Gandhi, Nehru, and Azad, and a "field force group" that was meant to be the "regular" part of the army.[133] Preference was given to volunteers from infantry battalions, while thousands of civilian volunteers were excluded entirely.[134]

By joining the INA, the jawans could serve as soldiers with men they knew, while avoiding being under direct Japanese command.[135] The Japanese restricted the size of the INA for two reasons: the limited number of Japanese troops in Singapore available to handle any emergency relating to the INA, and the need to satisfy requirements for labour parties across Southeast Asia.[136] Some of the surplus INA volunteers approached the Japanese directly; Subedar Barkat Ali suggested the idea of forming a motor transport unit so that his men could avoid "more strenuous fatigues," and by October 1942 the unit had been established.[137] It is unclear how representative this attitude was among the many hundreds of Indian drivers employed by the Japanese throughout Southeast Asia.[138]

Although the INA had now been established, the "concentration camp" continued to operate. In October 1942, a jawan was hospitalized "with septic and almost gangrenous ankles, which bore marks of having been shackled," and died soon afterwards.[139] Two Sikhs also died in November after being beaten for having "killed a pig and cooked the pork in the lines in contravention of INA Standing Orders," treatment that was later justified by Mohan Singh to senior INA officers.[140] The episode shows how seriously the INA took any incident that could increase communal tension, but it also demonstrates that not all incidents of cruelty at the camp related to coercing men to join the INA.

THE CRISIS AND ITS CONSEQUENCES

The crisis that led to the downfall of Mohan Singh has been described by many authors.[141] Originating in suspicions about Japanese intentions toward the INA, the situation was exacerbated by a power struggle between him and the civilian leadership of the IIL. When some ICOs close to Mohan Singh escaped to India, it was a major blow to his prestige in the eyes of the Japanese, who were "losing confidence in him."[142] By December, Singh was briefing INA troops on the possible need to dissolve the INA, and "his audiences were profoundly moved and many," including Mohan Singh, "wept."[143] The crisis reached a climax with his arrest on 29 December 1942, an event that triggered the dissolution of the INA, according to pre-arranged orders.[144] Mohan Singh would spend the rest of the war under house arrest. His stand against the Japanese may explain why, despite all he had done, he was never put on trial by British authorities after the war.

The crisis came as a shock to many in the INA where "a feeling of despair prevailed among the rank and file," and also in the Indian civilian community, particularly the Sikhs.[145] The removal of Mohan Singh created a power vacuum among the POWs as a variety of interests competed for influence. Groupings emerged, often based on ethno-cultural affiliations. These were headed typically by particular ICOs, including Dogras under Major Prakash Chand, some Sikhs under Captain Brar, Muslims under Lieutenant Colonel Gilani, and Jats under Captain Dilsukh Man. As CSDIC(I) put it, "various Indian Communities were struggling for communal supremacy, or failing that, for alliance with the Japanese under separate flags."[146] But it was Major Bhonsle who was appointed as head of a new INA administrative committee in January 1943, with the aim of uniting everyone under the civilian leadership of the IIL.[147] Establishing the committee was an important step in reconstituting the INA, although it was not supported by everyone. Major Fujiwara, the Japanese officer who had placed Mohan Singh in charge of all Indian POWs in early 1942, made a speech at this time in which he said: "Mohan Singh was not empowered to break the INA. I am the father and Mohan Singh was the mother of this; your mother is dead and your father will now look after you," to which some Indian officers "replied that the child was too young to be looked after by its father."[148] It was a sign that not all would be rejoining.

The early months of 1943 saw Indian POWs again being subjected to a variety of pro-INA propaganda, given added impetus by Gandhi's protest fast against British policy in India in February 1943.[149] Written propaganda came in a variety of forms, including pamphlets and the *Azad Hind* newspaper.[150] The INA Dramatic Party also continued to operate, with a new play themed on the importance of communal harmony.[151] With the INA now under the civilian control of the IIL, a pledge that recruitment would henceforth be purely voluntary, and with Bhonsle's administrative committee running it, most of its former troops rejoined it.[152] One CSDIC(I) assessment of those who did not was that they stayed out because they believed that "the Japanese had no intention of using the INA to liberate India" rather than "any reborn sense of loyalty."[153] The 4,500 former INA personnel who refused to rejoin (many of whom were Sikhs) were shipped to the Southwest Pacific in May 1943.[154] They were sent both to fulfill Japanese labour needs and "to limit their influence on those who had volunteered."[155] Douds appears to confuse these men with Indian POWs who had never been INA volunteers and had been sent to the same area.[156] The departure of the ex-volunteers from Singapore in May 1943 marked the end of the first phase of the history of the INA.

The arrival of the Indian political leader Subhas Chandra Bose in Singapore ushered in a period that Rai has described as "the zenith of Indian nationalist fervour amongst Indians in Singapore."[157] The subsequent history of the INA from its first engagements against British forces in Burma, to its ultimate defeat, has been examined by numerous authors, a striking contrast to the relative lack of work on its early history.[158] The later INA would be expanded using civilian volunteers, although its core would always remain the Indian POWs captured at the fall of Singapore.

CONCLUSION

The Indian POWs in Singapore in 1942 and early 1943 found themselves in a situation different from their erstwhile British and Australian counterparts, situated among a large Indian civilian community and pressured to switch allegiance by joining the INA. That many chose to switch sides has been explained in the historiography as being due to a variety of reasons, including coercion, following the lead of officers, and Indian nationalism. CSDIC(I) sources indicate that there were more ICOs captured than previously thought, with roughly half volunteering for the INA, while an analysis of the joining date for INA volunteers reveals a recruitment peak in the middle of 1942. Eventually, some 20,000 joined the INA, although this understates the number willing to join because the Japanese limited its size. Two factors that helped drive recruitment had their origins in the organizational structure of the British Indian Army. First, Mohan Singh proved adept at exploiting the perceived lower status of VCOs vis-à-vis ICOs, by offering to promote them to ICO rank in return for their support. Second, the ethno-cultural recruitment policies of the army, embodied in the recruitment of multiple "classes" of troops, created the conditions for a competitive dynamic between them in captivity.

All Indian POWs were subject to INA propaganda at some point, whether in the form of speeches, written material, or concert parties. CSDIC(I) emphasized the effectiveness of Mohan Singh's speeches, although they also rated the concert parties highly. Central to the propaganda was the notional alignment of the INA with the Indian National Congress, the "Quit India" declaration of August 1942 providing a huge fillip to the INA recruitment drive. But it is also clear that some Indian POWs were coerced into volunteering, whether through heavy fatigues, or periods in the so-called concentration camp. The estimated dozen or so deaths in the camp and in shooting incidents elsewhere, represents a serious indictment of the Mohan Singh regime.[159] Much of the historiography has focused on the small Indian elite that interacted closely with senior Japanese, but this chapter has also sought to highlight the experience of VCOs and jawans. The CSDIC(I) material reveals that jawans did not always follow their ICOs or VCOs, and were certainly not the "almost child-like" figures found in some British descriptions.[160] They sometimes rejected the direction of their superiors, whether to join the INA or to resist it, although, overall, more volunteered for the INA than did ICOs, amounting to eight out of nine jawans in Singapore, compared with just half of ICOs.[161]

The extraordinary circumstances of the mass surrender at the fall of Singapore left Indian POWs with divided loyalties: of nationalism, community, and their identities as soldiers. With the British Empire apparently collapsing around them, many volunteered for the INA, although only a minority actually served in it. The history of Indian POWs before the arrival of Subhas Chandra Bose in May 1943 has often been treated in the historiography as little more than a prologue to later developments. It was, however, a period of dramatic events, although it remains a history of largely forgotten men.

NOTES

1. S. Woodburn Kirby, *The War Against Japan*, vol. 1, *The Loss of Singapore* (London: HMSO, 1957), 473.
2. Hugh Toye, *Subhash Chandra Bose (The Springing Tiger): A Study of a Revolution* (Bombay: Jaico Publishing, 1959).
3. Hugh Toye, "The First Indian National Army, 1941–42," *Journal of Southeast Asian Studies* 15, no. 2 (1984), 365–81.
4. Kalyan Ghosh, *The Indian National Army: second front of the Indian independence movement* (Meerut: Meenakshi Prakashan, 1969); Joyce Lebra, *Jungle Alliance, Japan and the Indian National Army* (Singapore: Asia Pacific Press, 1971).
5. Peter Ward Fay, *The Forgotten Army: India's Armed Struggle for Independence, 1942–1945* (Ann Arbor: University of Michigan Press, 1993).
6. Chandar S. Sundaram, "A Paper Tiger: The Indian National Army in Battle, 1944–1945," *War & Society* 13, no. 1 (1995), 35–59.
7. G.J. Douds, "The Men Who Never Were: Indian POWs in the Second World War," *South Asia: Journal of South Asian Studies* 27, no. 2 (2004), 183–216.
8. Daniel Marston, *The Indian Army and the End of the Raj: Decolonising the Subcontinent* (Cambridge: Cambridge University Press, 2014).
9. See chapter 12 in Srinath Raghavan, *India's war: The Making of Modern South Asia, 1939–1945* (London: Allen Lane, 2016).
10. Ghosh, *Indian National Army*, 70; Douds, "The Men Who Never Were," 199; Raghavan, *India's war*, 284.
11. Marston, *Indian Army*, 120; Douds, "The men who never were," 197–9; Ghosh, *Indian National Army*, 60; Raghavan, *India's War*, 286.
12. Toye, *The Springing Tiger*, 9; Fay, *Forgotten Army*, 101.
13. Ghosh, *Indian National Army*, 69; Marston, *Indian Army*, 120.
14. Ibid., 121.
15. Douds, "The Men Who Never Were," 215.
16. Gajendra Singh, *The Testimonies of Indian Soldiers and the Two World Wars: Between Self and Sepoy* (London: Bloomsbury, 2014), 190.
17. Kevin Noles, "Renegades in Malaya: Indian Volunteers of the Japanese, F. Kikan," *British Journal for Military History* 3, no. 2 (2017), 100–18.

18 Rajesh Rai, *Indians in Singapore, 1819–1945: Diaspora in the Colonial Port City* (New Delhi: Oxford University Press, 2014).
19 Fay, *Forgotten Army*, 563.
20 British Library, London, Asian and African Studies collection (hereafter, AAS), Mss Eur F275, *Selected papers of the CSDIC(I)*. Note that F275 contains over 500 interrogations and reports; The National Archives at Kew (hereafter, TNA), WO 325/51, *Captain Mohan Singh*.
21 AAS, Mss Eur F275/2, 112.
22 AAS, L/I/1/1040, *File 462/80(e)vii INA trials*, 1.
23 AAS, Mss Eur F275/6, 230. *Captain Tehl Singh*.
24 AAS, L/WS/2/45, *CSDIC(I): A Brief Chronological and Factual Account of the INA*.
25 Including: AAS, L/WS/1/1433, *Intelligence summaries*.; AAS, L/WS/1/1576, *Indian National Army and Free Burma Army*, vol. 1; AAS, L/WS/1/1711, *Indian National Army*; TNA, WO 203/6314, *F Kikan report*.
26 Shah Nawaz Khan, *My Memories of INA & Its Netaji* (Delhi: Rajkamal Publications, 1946)
27 Fay, *Forgotten Army*, 553.
28 Mohan Singh, *Soldiers' Contribution to Indian Independence: The Epic of the Indian National Army* (New Delhi: Army Educational Stores, 1974).
29 Mohammad Zaman Kiani, *India's Freedom Struggle and the Great INA: Memoirs of Maj. Gen. Mohammad Zaman Kiani* (New Delhi: Reliance Publishing House, 1994); Naranjan Singh Gill, *Story of the INA* (New Delhi, India: Ministry of Information and Broadcasting, 2001).
30 Gurbakhsh Singh, *Indelible Reminiscences: Memoirs of Major General Gurbakhsh Singh* (New Delhi: Lancer, 2013).
31 John Baptist Crasta, *Eaten by the Japanese: The Memoir of an Unknown Indian Prisoner of War* (New York: CreateSpace, 2012).
32 Imperial War Museum (hereafter, IWM), sound recording 80011491, 2nd Lt. Ismail Khan
33 Iwaichi Fujiwara, *F. Kikan: Japanese Army Intelligence Operations in Southeast Asia during World War II*, trans. by Akashi Yoji (Hong Kong: Heinemann Asia, 1983).
34 *Indian National Army: A Documentary Study*, ed. Tilak Raj Sareen, 5 vols (New Delhi: Gyan, 2004).
35 Philip Mason, *A Matter of Honour: An Account of the Indian Army, Its Officers and Men* (London: Jonathan Cape, 1974), 315.
36 Kaushik Roy, *The Army in British India: From Colonial Warfare to Total War 1857–1947* (London: Bloomsbury, 2013), 127.

37 Alan Jeffreys, *Approach to Battle: Training the Indian Army during the Second World War* (Solihull: Helion & Company, 2017), 36–7.
38 The extensive historiography includes: Louis Allen, *Singapore, 1941–1942* (London: Cass, 1993); Malcolm H. Murfett, *Between Two Oceans: A Military History of Singapore from First Settlement to Final British Withdrawal* (Oxford: Oxford University Press, 1999); Brian Farrell, *The Defence and Fall of Singapore 1941–1942* (Stroud: Tempus, 2005).
39 Noles, *Renegades in Malaya*, 100; The IIL had its roots in the Ghadar movement of the First World War.
40 TNA, WO 325/51, *Mohan Singh CSDIC(I) interrogation*, 9.
41 Ghosh, *Indian National Army*, 35.
42 AAS, L/WS/2/45, 10.
43 Ghosh, *Indian National Army*, 36.
44 AAS, L/WS/2/45, 5.; Rai, *Indians in Singapore*, 212.
45 Fay, *Forgotten Army*, 134.
46 AAS, L/WS/2/45, 6.
47 Ghosh, *Indian National Army*, 121.
48 Rai, *Indians in Singapore*, 227.
49 AAS, L/WS/2/45, 14.
50 AAS, F275/16, 185. *Captain Kiani*.
51 AAS, F275/18, 230. *Lt. Col Chatterji*.
52 AAS, F275/7, 196. *Major Bhonsle*.
53 AAS, F275/5, 129. *Major Raju*.
54 AAS, F275/15, 128. *Major Nagar*.
55 AAS, F275/5, 50. *CSDIC(I) Report no. 698*.
56 Rai, *Indians in Singapore*, 203.
57 Ibid., 211.
58 Ibid., 112. (Note: census figures from 1931.) The proportion of Indian males to females was 5:1.
59 Ibid., 218.
60 Ashley Jackson, *The British Empire and the Second World War* (London: Hambledon, 2006), 371.
61 Marston, *Indian Army*, 120.
62 Douds, "The Men Who Never Were," 199; Raghavan, *India's War*, 283.
63 Fay, *Forgotten Army*, 81.
64 For example: Raghavan, *India's War*, 283.
65 Based largely on AAS, Mss Eur F275, *Selected papers of the CSDIC(I)*.
66 AAS, Mss Eur F275/9, 282, *Information report no. 19, dated 27th June 1946*.
67 Kirby, *The War Against Japan*, 1:473.

68 AAS, L/WS/2/45, 14. (Identical to: Fay, *Forgotten Army*, 81.)
69 Ibid., 13.
70 See also: Fujiwara, *F Kikan*, 186; Mohan Singh, *Soldiers' Contribution*, 112.
71 Marston, *Indian Army*, 128.
72 Khan, *INA & Its Netaji*, 11.
73 Fay, *Forgotten Army*, 84.
74 AAS, Mss Eur F275/5, 342. *Captain Hussain.*
75 AAS, Mss Eur F275/16, 185. *Major Kiani.*
76 AAS, Mss Eur F275/5, 123. *Captain Burhan Ud Din.*
77 Singh, *Soldiers' Contribution*, 113.
78 AAS, Mss Eur F275/16, 158. *Subedar Lal Din.*
79 Gurbakhsh Singh, *Indelible Reminiscences*, 92.
80 Kiani, *India's Freedom Struggle*, 51.
81 AAS, Mss Eur F275/16, 183. *Major Kiani.*
82 AAS, Mss Eur F275/6, 130. *Captain Shah Nawaz Khan.*
83 AAS, Mss Eur F275/16, 185. *Major Kiani.*
84 Ibid., 186.
85 Ibid.
86 AAS, Mss Eur F275/6, 130. *Captain Shah Nawaz Khan.*
87 AAS, Mss Eur F275/16, 186. *Major Kiani.*
88 AAS, Mss Eur F275/6, 131. *Captain Shah Nawaz Khan.*
89 AAS, Mss Eur Photo Eur 397, 80.
90 Gurbakhsh Singh, *Indelible Reminiscences*, 99.
91 Ghosh, *Indian National Army*, 56.
92 AAS, Mss Eur F275/11, 65. *Extract from Bangkok Times, 16 June 1942.*
93 TNA, WO 325/51, 34. *Captain Mohan Singh.*
94 Toye, *The Springing Tiger*, 9.
95 TNA, WO 325/51, 30. *Captain Mohan Singh.*
96 AAS, Mss Eur F275/3, 48. *CSDIC(I) report no. 698.*
97 TNA, WO 325/51, 66. *Captain Mohan Singh.*
98 AAS, Mss Eur F275/17, 17. *Subedar Major Ghufran Khan.*
99 TNA, WO 325/51, 65. *Captain Mohan Singh.*
100 AAS, L/WS/2/45, 10.
101 AAS, Mss Eur F275/7, 136. *Lieutenant Safi Ullah.*
102 Ibid., 32. *Subedar Thapa.*
103 AAS, Mss Eur F275/7, 4. *Subedar Dharam Chand Bhandari.*
104 Ibid., 14.
105 Ibid., 18.
106 AAS, Mss Eur F275/8, 79. *Subedar Major Bakhtawar Singh* MBE.
107 AAS, Mss Eur F275/5, 9. *Captain Rodrigues.*

108 AAS, Mss Eur F275/9, 139. *INA Administration Report*.
109 AAS, Mss Eur F275/7, 251. *Jemadar Fateh Khan*.
110 Ibid., 252.
111 AAS, Mss Eur F275/5, 161. *Lieutenant Colonel Loganadan*.
112 TNA, WO 325/51, 61. *Captain Mohan Singh*.; AAS, Mss Eur F275/15, 79. *Subedar Ali Haider*.
113 TNA, WO 325/51, 63. *Captain Mohan Singh*.
114 AAS, Mss Eur F275/3, 75. *Captain Das*.
115 AAS, Mss Eur F275/4, 194. *Havildar Chettri*.; AAS, Mss Eur F275/5, 131. *Major Raju*.
116 AAS, Mss Eur F275/4, 274. CSDIC(I) report no. 770.
117 AAS, L/WS/2/45, 15.; AAS, Mss Eur F275/4, 274. CSDIC(I) report no. 770.
118 Fay, *Forgotten Army*, 113–35.
119 Rai, *Indians in Singapore*, 218.
120 Fay, *Forgotten Army*, 135.
121 TNA, WO 325/51, 37. *Captain Mohan Singh*.
122 AAS, Mss Eur F275/7, 18. *Major Gill*.
123 Toye, *The Springing Tiger*, 9.
124 Marston, *Indian Army*, 120n18.
125 TNA, WO 325/51, 67. *Captain Mohan Singh*.
126 Singh, *Testimonies of Indian Soldiers*, 177.
127 AAS, Mss Eur F275/7, 45. *Subedar Thapa*.
128 AAS, Mss Eur F275/18, 270. *Captain Joseph*.
129 AAS, Mss Eur F275/5, 145. *Major Thimayya*.
130 AAS, Mss Eur F275/15, 96. *Major Chand*.
131 TNA, WO 325/51, 40. *Captain Mohan Singh*.
132 Fay, *Forgotten Army*, 141.
133 Ibid., 140.
134 TNA, WO 325/51, 37. *Captain Mohan Singh*.
135 Ghosh, *Indian National Army*, 69.
136 Toye, *The First Indian National Army*, 376.
137 AAS, Mss Eur F275/7, 116. *Subedar Barkat Ali*.
138 AAS, Mss Eur F275/21, 91. *Captain Shah Nawaz Khan*.
139 AAS, Mss Eur F275/5, 161. *Lieutenant Colonel Loganadan*.
140 AAS, Mss Eur F275/6, 180. *Major Ahmed*.
141 Including: Ghosh, *Indian National Army*, 93–121; Fay, *Forgotten Army*, 148–51; Rai, *Indians in Singapore*, 222–5.
142 AAS, Mss Eur F275/5, 143. *Major Raju*.
143 TNA, WO 325/51, 52. *Captain Mohan Singh*.

144 Ibid., 54.
145 Ghosh, *Indian National Army*, 122; Rai, *Indians in Singapore*, 225.
146 AAS, Mss Eur F275/6, 290. *Captain Ehsan Qadir.*
147 AAS, L/WS/2/45, 6; AAS, Mss Eur F275/6, 290. *Captain Ehsan Qadir.*
148 AAS, Mss Eur F275/14, 147. *Lieutenant Jaswant Singh.*
149 Ghosh, *Indian National Army*, 124.
150 AAS, Mss Eur F275/16, 216. *Subedar Major Bahadur.*
151 AAS, Mss Eur F275/7, 15. *Subedar Bhandari.*
152 Rai, *Indians in Singapore*, 227.
153 AAS, L/WS/2/45, 14.
154 TNA, WO 106/5881, *CSDIC(I) Report no. 804*, 7.
155 Rai, *Indians in Singapore*, 227.
156 Douds, "The Men Who Never Were," 205. See also note 116.
157 Rai, *Indians in Singapore*, 239.
158 For example, see: Sundaram, "Paper Tiger."
159 AAS, Mss Eur Photo Eur 397, 53.
160 AAS, Mss Eur F274/95, 3. *Typewritten Minute from General Auchinleck.*
161 AAS, L/WS/2/45, 13.

12

Spawning Fratricide

Occupation and Resistance in Greece, 1941–1944

Christina J.M. Goulter

The Axis invasion and occupation of Greece during the Second World War caused the death of 8 per cent of the Greek population (around 360,000 people).[1] Some of these casualties were the result of the fighting in 1940–41, but the remainder were caused by an occupation that led to the brutalization of the population, famine, disease, and a series of civil wars.[2] Some of the internecine strife occurred between collaborationist auxiliary units and the Greek resistance; some arose away from mainland Greece within the ranks of the Greek armed forces in the Middle East. The principal civil war, however, resulted from the attempt by the Greek Communist Party, best known by its Greek acronym KKE (Κομμουνιστικό Κόμμα Ελλάδας), to control all resistance activity in occupied Greece and thus be the only political force at the end of occupation.[3]

The chief protagonists in this struggle were the communist-controlled ELAS (Greek Popular Liberation Army)[4] and the Republican EDES (National Democratic Greek League)[5] resistance groups. Several phases of the civil war can be identified. The first bid by the communists to take power spanned the period 1943–44, a second more serious attempt occurred in December 1944, and there was a third phase in what is usually referred to as the Greek Civil War proper, from 1946 to 1949. It is easier to view the period 1943 to 1949 as a continuum because the third communist bid for power cannot be understood without referring to the two earlier phases. The subject is made more complex by a polarization in the Greek historiography, which has largely been replicated in English-language works.[6] The left claims that the civil war started in 1946 as a direct result of the so-called White Terror, a period of lawlessness in 1945 during which right-wing gangs hunted down left-wing resistance members in revenge for communist atrocities committed during the occupation. Most other interpretations argue that the Greek Communist Party had every intention of taking power, and that during the occupation the communists deliberately targeted other resistance groups to destroy more moderate political parties, hence the first two "rounds" or phases.

Similar to Kevin Noles's chapter on the Indian National Army, international and domestic trends also exacerbated schisms within Greek society during the interwar years and the Second World War; Axis occupation merely served to deepen these inherent fault lines and make civil war more likely. This chapter explores these schisms and how Britain navigated the fault lines when it became involved in Greece. British actions, especially in the early stages of the conflict, often demonstrated a lack of understanding of the situation inside Greece and the way in which it was morphing under the pressure of occupation. But the Greeks themselves found the politics of occupation and resistance difficult to disentangle. As a result, it took Greek and British personnel alike time to understand the nature of the communist threat. By the mid-war point, both Britain and the Greek government in exile found themselves having to balance wartime imperatives and post-war political interests. This chapter also shows how this balancing act put Mediterranean strategy at risk, and led to intra-service and intra-departmental disagreements over the management of the resistance.

PRELUDE TO CIVIL WAR: THE NATIONAL SCHISM

The seeds of civil war were planted first by the so-called national schism of 1915–17, a period that undermined the credibility of the regular political parties. The national schism was brought about by the opposition of King Constantine I to the foreign policy direction of Prime Minister Venizelos, over the issue of Greece's involvement in the First World War and was at the root of the Greek military defeat in Asia Minor in 1922 at the hands of a revitalized Turkish state.[7] This military defeat was not just "a lost war ... but was a huge military, political and social disaster"[8] that brought about a sustained period of political upheavals, principally between Venizelists (liberal republicans) and anti-Venizelists (monarchists).[9] Relative political stability while Greece was a republic came to an abrupt end when the Venizelist party lost the elections in 1933. Fears over a return of the exiled monarchy generated two unsuccessful pro-Venizelist coups (in 1933 and 1935), and a reawakening of the national schism, leading to the purging of the armed forces.[10] After a rigged plebiscite, the monarchy was restored.[11] A period of political turmoil ensued, resulting in a hung parliament in 1936 and a caretaker government under Konstantinos Demertzis. Demertzis died shortly after taking office, and was replaced by the right-wing monarchist Ioannis Metaxas. With the tacit support of the king, Metaxas took advantage of a wave of labour unrest to declare martial law, with the stated aim of preventing a communist revolution.[12] Metaxas's administration froze political development in Greece. However, the old schisms remained, and joining the fray was the KKE. The Liberals and Metaxas alike had tried to suppress the KKE, with varying degrees of success, but the Axis occupation in 1941 provided the KKE with an opportunity to emerge from the shadows and mobilize society in its favour.

From April 1941, Greece was occupied by Germany, Italy, and Bulgaria. Each had differing objectives. Italy and Bulgaria, in particular, exacerbated minority issues in the regions they occupied. Bulgaria annexed Thrace, conducted "ethnic cleansing," and won the loyalties of segments of the population in western Macedonia.[13] The KKE proved adept at capitalizing on the population's fears and separatist sentiment among ethnic minorities (including Vlach, Slav, and Turkish-speaking communities), especially in northern Greece. The KKE had a largely free hand during the occupation because the legitimate Greek government under the Liberal prime minister, Emmanuel Tsouderos, had been forced into exile in 1941 and now resided in Egypt. Therefore, the KKE was in an ideal position to dominate the resistance movement.[14] It created the National Liberation Front (EAM)[15] in September 1941, although it was careful not to publicize the connection, and then established EAM's military arm, ELAS, in 1942. Its membership grew exponentially; estimates vary from 50,000 to 85,000 people by 1944.[16] The long-term KKE agenda – the creation of a communist state after liberation – was not broadcast, and it took the Greeks and the British Special Operations Executive (SOE) personnel in the country some time to understand that this was its intent. The KKE also exerted influence outside of Greece, and communist agitators within the Greek forces who had escaped to the Middle East after the Axis invasion sparked several mutinies (the first in 1943 and a more serious one in 1944).

In contrast, the Republican EDES resistance was very open about its political agenda: the creation of a democratic government along socialist lines and the permanent exiling of the Greek monarchy. EDES began at the same time as EAM. With SOE support, its head, Colonel Napoleon Zervas, established a guerrilla army in the northwestern province of Epirus.[17]

EARLY RESISTANCE

Although ELAS and EDES became the dominant resistance movements during the occupation, it is worth noting that a multiplicity of groups existed, and, contrary to accepted wisdom, the first resistance movements were not communist.[18] The earliest resistance organizations were located either in Macedonia or Thrace. Among the very first were the Pan-Hellenic Resistance Organization (PAO)[19] and Defenders of Northern Greece (YVE).[20] Both were non-communist resistance movements and both were targeted by the Axis and ELAS, very often at the same time. The most serious threat to ELAS in northern Greece was PAO because of its size (numbering several thousand members), and ELAS singled it out for destruction early in the occupation. Not only was PAO destroyed by ELAS but it also suffered the double ignominy of being branded a collaborationist force by the Allies simply because it was involved in skirmishes with ELAS.[21] This misconception over PAO arose because many of the SOE liaison officers embedded in ELAS units could not speak fluent Greek and accepted at face value information on other resistance groups passed on to them.[22]

One of the earliest urban resistance groups was created by a Greek colonel, Dimitris Psarros, in the spring of 1941.[23] He gathered like-minded Venizelist army officers around him, and several acts of sabotage were undertaken in Athens during the summer of 1941. In November 1942, Psarros created the resistance movement EKKA (National and Social Liberation),[24] and a military wing the following April, operating mainly in the south of the country. Psarros was captured by ELAS in the spring of 1944 and murdered, along with his subordinate leadership. EKKA was the third significant resistance movement to be targeted by ELAS, and ceased to exist after May 1944. However, resistance groups that remained in the cities usually escaped the attention of EAM/ELAS, at least initially; their main threat for most of the occupation period came from the Axis internal security apparatus. Another Athens-based resistance group was PEAN (Pan Hellenic Union of Fighting Youths), which succeeded in spectacular attacks against German units and collaborationists in the capital.[25] Because it attracted the attention of the German security apparatus, it came under attack increasingly from 1942 onwards.[26] Although PEAN reduced its sabotage activity, it continued to exist as a source of intelligence for the Allies. However, PEAN eventually went the same way as EKKA. During the fighting in Athens in December 1944, ELAS targeted PEAN because it sided with the Greek government and British forces. It lost half its members to ELAS attacks.[27]

There were other urban resistance movements like PEAN that provided intelligence to the Allies. The speed of the German invasion in 1941 afforded few opportunities for British intelligence to establish permanent stations in Greece; most military intelligence and Secret Intelligence Service (SIS) operatives were evacuated to Cairo. However, it soon became apparent that there was a requirement for an intelligence effort from Greece.[28] When the British Army continued to suffer reversals in North Africa, it became imperative for the Allies to cut Rommel's supply lines.[29] The principal sea line of communication for the Afrika Korps was via the Greek port of Piraeus, and information on Axis shipping was vital if the Royal Navy and the RAF were to have any chance of intercepting German supplies. The intelligence provided by Greek resistance groups was critical for building an accurate picture of German capability because there was no high-grade signals intelligence (SIGINT) for the Mediterranean at this point in the war.

However, this early dependence on contacts in the Greek resistance proved to be dangerous for both SOE and Greeks. Because very few SOE personnel were experienced in undercover work, they often unwittingly put themselves and their Greek contacts at risk. A number of politically moderate resistance groups in Athens were compromised, and control of the resistance in the capital passed to more revolutionary organizations that were either extreme left or staunchly anti-monarchical.[30] The loss of the moderate resistance in Athens had far-reaching consequences that could not be appreciated at the time. On one level, Britain lost important intelligence networks at a critical juncture in the Western Desert campaign. The Axis launched an offensive in January 1942, ultimately reaching El Alamein by July; and there was now an urgent requirement to know the scale of Axis logistics via Greece. However, the compromising of networks also served to exacerbate tensions within SOE headquarters in Cairo and between that HQ and the British diplomatic legation in Cairo. These tensions ultimately affected how Britain managed the resistance in Greece, which had serious implications in the mid-war period, when the communists made their first significant bid for power.

SOE headquarters was divided into two main directorates, one operational and one political. The former comprised mainly service personnel and the latter were drawn from the Foreign Office or SIS. Because several of the Greek resistance networks had been compromised as a result of SOE operatives making elementary mistakes in intelligence tradecraft, relations between the operational and political wings of SOE deteriorated sharply. Throughout much of 1942, guerrilla activity in Greece and in the Balkans occurred without any input from SOE's political directorate.[31] For SOE operatives to have had no political briefings at all in most cases caused misconceptions and misunderstandings between the Greeks and their SOE liaison officers.

The complex political developments in Greece before 1941 and the morphing political scenery under occupation were largely unknown to the main body of SOE personnel when they arrived in Greece in October 1942 as part of the Harling Mission to undertake the first major sabotage operation against the Gorgopotamos railway viaduct. This was despite the fact that other British organizations, such as SIS, were already operating in mainland Greece.[32] However, the information that was shaping views about the resistance movements in Greece was based largely on anti-monarchist sources, and some were favourably disposed toward the communists, if not necessarily toward individual communists themselves.[33] One SOE liaison officer, Rufus Sheppard, wrote that ELAS had "no political aims whatsoever" and it was "purely a resistance movement."[34] Reports of this type were common in the latter stages of 1942 and helped to convince SOE HQ that ELAS was trustworthy. Because of the urgent operational requirement to do as much damage as possible to the German war machine, such reports were often accepted at SOE HQ without additional verification. However, the head of the main SOE mission in Greece,

Brigadier Eddie Myers, and his second in command, Colonel Monty Woodhouse, had changed their opinions of EAM-ELAS by 1943. They both noticed that EAM-ELAS was increasingly open about its affiliations, and remarked on how it was Soviet in flavour, including the use of political commissars in each unit, Soviet methods of saluting, etc. But without a detailed intelligence picture before their arrival in Greece, it was inevitable that the SOE team would take some time to piece together an accurate understanding of the resistance. Myers and Woodhouse had the benefit of working alongside a Greek Army officer, Lieutenant Themis Marinos, who eventually helped them to disentangle the various political threads, but even Marinos was unaware of all the loyalties at play.[35] In January 1943, Myers warned Cairo that EAM-ELAS was controlled by the KKE, and that EAM-ELAS saw British supplies as crucial for them to gain control over Greece at the point of liberation, and only secondarily to contribute to the victory over the Axis occupiers. Myers advised SOE HQ to switch its support to Zervas and EDES.[36]

This was the point at which immediate wartime imperatives ran headlong into Britain's wider political interests. In March 1943, ELAS launched an offensive against other resistance movements. Its main focus was on EDES, but by the summer, it was targeting the monarchist stronghold in the Peloponnese and other resistance groups in central Greece. Fearing all-out civil war, Myers switched his focus from the prime SOE mission (undermining the Axis war machine) to keeping ELAS in line.[37] Intelligence gathered by SOE from mid-1943 onwards was dominated by Greek politics.[38] SOE became so concerned about the threat of civil war that at least one SOE mission was despatched to Greece with the sole objective of reporting on the political situation, with a view to orchestrating a modus vivendi between ELAS and EDES.[39] This was when the Allies were planning the invasion of Sicily (Operation Husky), and SOE and the guerrilla bands in Greece were to provide a diversionary feint to mislead the Germans into thinking that the invasion of southern Europe would come via Greece, and not Italy. A plan of guerrilla activity, codenamed Operation Animals, was drawn up, but first Myers had to ensure that ELAS and EDES ceased fighting each other. He succeeded in getting both groups to agree that they were to operate only with British authority. The National Bands Agreement, as it was known, had the desired effect, and Operation Animals was carried out between 21 June and 14 July 1943. The ruse proved successful; SIGINT showed that the German High Command believed that the guerrilla activity in western Greece was a prelude to an Allied invasion via the Balkans. The number of German divisions in Greece and the Balkans rose from 8 to 18, and no reinforcement of Italy occurred.[40]

By the middle of 1943, therefore, the most important role that the Greek resistance had was to draw off and tie down enemy forces that would otherwise be deployed against the Allies on the frontline. However, the resistance leaders were also aware of this fact, and this led to ELAS, in particular, exerting more leverage over Britain. It also placed British foreign policy in an invidious position because Britain was supporting groups that had an anti-monarchical agenda, while also calling for the return of George II, the Greek king, once the country was liberated. The oscillation between short-term military necessity and longer-term political interests created confusion and distrust of the British among many of the guerrillas (in both ELAS and EDES, although Zervas himself continued to support Britain without hesitation).

The National Bands Agreement held for several months, because KKE was keen to see EAM-ELAS gaining international respectability. However, fighting broke out again between ELAS and EDES. Desperate to pre-empt all-out civil war, Myers organized a deputation of resistance leaders for a meeting in Cairo, who were flown out by SOE. Thanks to some adept manoeuvring by KKE, the communists managed to have a disproportionate representation at the Cairo meeting. This meant that demands to block the Greek king's return were more insistent than would otherwise have been the case, but this merely entrenched the position that Churchill and the Foreign Office had adopted. The latter communicated thus with the Foreign Secretary, Anthony Eden: "Greece is and always has been a vital British interest and ... the King is entitled to look to us for support, in return for the gallant role he played in the early part of the war."[41] In contrast to the First World War, when Greece remained neutral until mid-1917, the Greek monarchy ensured that the country entered the Second World War on the Allies' side from the outset, and Churchill, in particular, was determined to see that the Greek king's support was acknowledged. The Greek delegation left Cairo empty-handed; no agreement was reached on the king's position once Greece was liberated. However, as ever, perceptions mattered, and, in this case, the communist contingent came away from the Cairo meeting believing that Britain intended to restore the Greek monarchy. Meanwhile, the British Foreign Office believed that Myers was going beyond his brief and was interfering with foreign policy. The British ambassador to the Greek government in exile, Reginald Leeper, and Churchill, were both of the opinion that SOE needed to be controlled by the Foreign Office and, as far as the latter was concerned, possibly even dissolved.

In October 1943, ELAS launched several major attacks on EDES in northwestern Greece, prompting Leeper to advocate the withdrawal of British personnel, with SOE missions being the first to go.[42] Eden felt that this option was too radical, but he did advocate severing contact with EAM-ELAS and used the fallout from Myer's Cairo delegation meeting and the return of internecine violence as justification. However, the Supreme Allied Commander in the Mediterranean, General Sir Henry Maitland Wilson, rejected this idea, arguing that ELAS was the only guerrilla group capable of killing Germans in any numbers.[43] He appears to have made this judgment on the basis of ELAS's estimated size at that time, some 15,000 to 20,000 personnel, about three times the size of EDES.[44] Wilson rebuked the Foreign Office for its support of the Greek king, which he believed was alienating many of the more moderate EAM-ELAS personnel, who would otherwise be prepared to support British operations. Wilson's views prevailed, SOE was kept in Greece, and ELAS continued to receive material support from Britain, but at a reduced level.

The requirement to continue supporting EAM-ELAS put Britain in a challenging position. The Foreign Office was compelled to address the civil-war issue head on, and it believed the best solution was to have EAM represented in a new coalition government. In January 1944, the Foreign Office indicated to the Greek government in exile in Cairo that it wanted to hold talks with EAM-ELAS. The latter were told that talks could occur only when the fighting between ELAS and EDES came to an end.[45] After a series of meetings between the guerrilla groups, brokered by Monty Woodhouse, the first round of the civil war came to an end on 29 February 1944 with the signing of the Plaka Agreement. By the terms of the agreement, hostilities between the resistance groups would cease; each would retain its existing territorial span; fighting would be limited to action against Axis forces; ELAS and EDES HQs would engage in joint planning for operations; and political prisoners would be released.[46] For its part, the Allied Mission agreed to maintain material support to all the resistance groups. To have done otherwise would have caused a breakdown in reconciliation efforts.

The fact that ELAS was prepared to sign the Plaka Agreement demonstrates a degree of self-awareness; a campaign to eliminate all its rivals had not succeeded, and more time was required to prepare for the post-liberation battle ahead. It also realized that its popularity was waning in many parts of Greece. The internecine warfare since the spring of 1943 disgusted many Greeks, and word was spreading about the relative inactivity of ELAS against the Germans, compared with EDES. Contrary to General Wilson's view of ELAS as the most potent of the resistance groups, its activity had inflicted little damage on the occupation forces, but the German reprisals against the population had been severe. This was particularly the case in the Peloponnese during December 1943, when at least 1,000 civilians were executed by the Germans in response to resistance activity.[47]

While the Plaka Agreement brought about a truce between ELAS and EDES, many of the political issues were sidestepped. KKE wanted some of the most significant portfolios in a new coalition government, but when these did not materialize, EAM-ELAS formed its own government, the Political Committee of National Liberation (PEEA), at ELAS's HQ in the Pindus Mountains, northwest of Athens. PEEA claimed to be the body best able to provide a transitional government at the time of Greece's liberation. Although it called itself a committee, PEEA very quickly adopted the trappings of a rival to the Greek government in exile. It issued a statement on 16 March 1944 to the effect that its role was to co-ordinate the "national liberation struggle by the side of the Allies" and the "safeguarding" of political life throughout the country after liberation.[48] PEEA established a cabinet, ensuring that its personnel were made "ministers" of the Interior, Justice, and Agriculture. Local elections were held in ELAS-controlled areas, and a "National Assembly" was called in May. While representatives from EDES and local politicians were invited, most declined, citing their allegiance to the Greek government in exile.

THE GREEK MUTINIES

The establishment of PEEA and ongoing uncertainty over the constitutional position of the Greek king reignited tensions not only within the Greek government in Cairo but also within the Greek armed forces. The Greek forces in exile were created from the remnants of air force and naval units that had withdrawn from Greece in May 1941, and army personnel started to arrive in Egypt via the

Middle East in the late summer of 1941.[49] Many officers and men of the early arrivals were from the eastern Aegean islands, areas that were traditionally against the monarchy, and recruitment from among the Greek diaspora in Egypt also injected a large number of anti-monarchists.[50] The desire for revenge for the perceived injustices of the past (often related to the events of 1935) and professional jealousies among personnel led to general discord within the services. Such issues could have been dealt with had the Greek government and military high command in exile been strong and decisive. However, the former chose a course of action that accommodated all perspectives, and the resultant divisions opened the way for the creation of communist cells in the armed forces, especially in the army and navy.

In the autumn of 1941, several communist organizations germinated within the Greek forces in exile. The first was the Communist Military Organization Middle East (KSOMA). This body later changed its name to the Anti-Fascist Military Organization (ASO).[51] In 1942, ASO spawned an Anti-Fascist Navy Organization (AON)[52] and an Anti-Fascist Air Force Organization (AOA).[53] ASO created cells of three, and later of five, members and by the end of 1942 it had developed into what one author described as the "nervous system of the Army."[54] Units were commanded by committees and operated on the basis of consent among rank and file.[55] This made the British High Command in the Middle East sceptical of the fighting capacity of the Greek units, in spite of their good performance earlier on in the war at Alamein.[56] By late 1943, Greek Army personnel found themselves in constant training or idle in Egypt, and, with loose discipline, the units were easy prey for political manipulation. Mutinous behaviour toward officers became increasingly commonplace, and the Greek Brigade, which had spent several months training and equipping for deployment to Italy, was particularly badly affected.[57] The mutineers were convinced that they could force the prime minister in exile, Emmanuel Tsouderos, and the Greek king to address the constitutional question. After two weeks of refusing orders, the Greek Brigade was issued with an ultimatum by the British commander-in-chief (C-in-C) Middle East, General Paget, to the effect that unless the mutineers surrendered their weapons and complied with orders, British troops would surround their barracks. Those found to be guilty of insubordination would be arrested.[58] This threat was sufficient to bring most of the mutineers in line by 24 April, but at a cost of one British officer's life, after an exchange of small-arms fire.

The mutiny of the Hellenic Navy's personnel was in some respects even more serious, both in terms of its scale and in its immediate consequences for the war in the Mediterranean, and it took the longest to quell. The crews of at least a dozen Greek ships were involved in the mutiny, including that of the Hellenic Navy's flagship, the *Averoff*. Of a ship's company of some 900 personnel, over half mutinied. The British C-in-C Mediterranean, Admiral Sir John Cunningham, expressed grave concern that he was having to tie up precious Royal Navy assets just to deal with mutinous Greeks, rather than employing them in their usual escort duties. So frustrated was Cunningham that he tasked his staff with drawing up plans to seize the mutinous ships, and he also considered the idea put forward by loyal Greek officers that the ship containing the ringleaders be sunk by Greek demolition teams.[59] The Admiralty added to the debate, and proposed that Royal Navy torpedo boats should sink the vessel (the *Hephaistos*) if the mutiny dragged on.[60] This proved unnecessary, as loyal Greeks managed to take over the mutinous warships on 23 April.[61] This was facilitated by a change in the Hellenic Navy's C-in-C (from Admiral Alexandris to Admiral Voulgaris) and the desire to form a new Greek government in exile to deal with the situation.

Although the mutiny among Greek army and navy personnel had been suppressed by the end of April, some mutinous behaviour persisted well into May.[62] Of the Greek services, only the Hellenic Air Force remained relatively mutiny-free, although there were EAM sympathizers poised to act.[63] The difference between the air force and the other two services can be explained by the fact that aircrews had been on almost constant operations since they arrived in North Africa. There had been no lengthy periods of inactivity, and the air force units were also based far away from Cairo and Alexandria, the main centres of communist agitation.[64]

Although the mutinies were brought to an end, the consequences were serious.[65] Questions were raised in the House of Commons as to why the UK was getting involved in Greece's internal politics, and criticism of Churchill mounted.[66] The mutinies and the creation of PEEA, combined, compelled Greeks to take sides, and the political fallout was particularly grave for the Greek government in exile. Tsouderos was forced by his cabinet to resign, and was succeeded by the Minister for Marine Affairs, Sophocles Venizelos. His government lasted less than two weeks, and he was replaced by George

Papandreou, described by Reginald Leeper as "a breath of fresh air in the overcharged atmosphere of Greek Cairo."[67] Although Papandreou had liberal republican credentials, having founded the Social Democratic Party during the 1930s, he deferred the issue of the Greek king's return to Greece and prioritized national unity and the liberation of Greece. This endeared him to the king, who offered his support, but led to a "sit-down strike" by most of his cabinet, because the issue of the king's return to Greece was inextricably linked to national unity.[68] As a result, Papandreou effectively presided alone over a government in exile for the first few days.

Meanwhile, the Greek armed forces put in place vetting measures to root out EAM sympathizers. All personnel were interviewed to ascertain their political sympathies. Those considered to be irreconcilable EAM supporters were detained, and those expressing leftist sympathies were kept under close watch. The ringleaders of the mutinies were incarcerated in various prisons in Egypt, Libya, and Eritrea, and subjected to courts martial, and hardliners were put on trial for treason.[69] While these measures dealt with the problem of communist agitation in the Greek armed forces, the immediate consequences for the Allied war effort were serious. All Greek units were effectively taken out of the frontline for several months. The Greek Brigade, which was in the process of embarking for Italy, was delayed by several months. Once reformed, it became known as the 3rd Brigade, and went on to serve with distinction in the Italian campaign.[70] Vetting in the Greek Navy was done on a ship-by-ship basis, and vessels were placed under the command of officers loyal to the Greek government in exile. Similar processes occurred in Hellenic air force squadrons based in North Africa. In the longer term, the vetting procedures put in place by the Greek armed forces prevented any subsequent mutinies, including during the main civil war period, 1946–49.[71]

Papandreou pursued most of the policies set in train by his predecessors, Tsouderos and Venizelos. The most pressing was the desire to gather resistance leaders at a conference in Lebanon to achieve consensus on an "all party" government. The decision to hold the conference in Lebanon was deliberate; Cairo was considered too febrile an atmosphere to allow for reasoned debates. All the resistance group leaders and politicians were invited, as was Reginald Leeper. The agenda for the conference in the third week of May covered five main areas: reorganizing the Greek armed forces and establishing discipline; unifying all resistance groups and adhering to the orders of a single Greek government; establishing personal security and liberty in "Free Greece"; supplying food and medicine to Greece; and maintaining order and political liberty following the country's liberation.[72] Not included on the agenda, but perhaps one of the most significant issues addressed by the conference, was the issue of the king's constitutional position. It was agreed that a decision would be made shortly after liberation, but that the king would have to wait for a national consensus. A declaration to this effect was issued the following month, and the matter was left there. Greater progress was made on other topics, however. Agreement was reached on: the reorganization of the Greek armed forces, both inside and outside Greece; an end to internecine violence between the resistance groups; restoration of law and order; humanitarian relief, and Greece's economic and territorial stability.[73] Believing that he had achieved a consensus among conference delegates, Papandreou drew up a coalition government, including representatives from KKE, EAM, and PEEA. What he had not anticipated, however, was the influence exerted by the hardline communist leadership remaining in Greece, including Giorgis Siantos, the head of KKE. Although the KKE, EAM, and PEEA representatives signed the Lebanon Charter, as it would become known, EAM (directed behind the scenes by the KKE) started to impose additional demands, including a call for more cabinet posts. EAM wanted control over at least four of the thirteen to fifteen cabinet posts on offer, including the Ministry of the Interior.[74] Over the next few months, more qualifications and concerns were raised.[75]

The mounting number of demands put forward by KKE during the summer of 1944 reflected the communists' anxiety over the extent of their political influence and control relative to their competitors. Although EAM/ELAS now controlled over half of Greece's territory, much of that was achieved through coercive measures. The KKE was also alarmed by the various anti-communist vetting measures introduced in the armed forces after the mutinies. At the same time, the Soviets were putting pressure on KKE to focus on winning through the ballot box. All these factors served to unnerve the KKE, and fissures started to appear in its senior leadership. Siantos and many in EAM were prepared to negotiate with Papandreou, but others, such as the leader of ELAS, Aris Velouchiotis, pressed for armed conflict the minute the German and Bulgarian forces left the country.[76]

RE-ENTRY INTO GREECE

On 26 August, Papandreou moved his government from Cairo to Caserta in Italy, where the Allied HQ was in the process of formulating plans for Greece as part of a wider Mediterranean strategy. The rationale for the move was twofold: for Papandreou to have input into the planning for Greece, but also to get the Greek government away from the hotbed of intrigue in Cairo. British forces were given three main tasks: to occupy the mainland and significant islands at the point of a German and Bulgarian surrender or withdrawal; to facilitate the return of the exiled Greek government; and, finally, to organize humanitarian relief. The first two tasks were purely British affairs, and the latter was to be done in conjunction with Allies and international relief agencies, such as the Red Cross. For the British-only operations, three brigades were to be despatched to Greece: an armoured brigade, supported by British and Greek special forces; a British parachute brigade; and the Greek Brigade, then serving in the Italian campaign.[77] In addition to these forces, some 3,500 Greeks with military experience residing in the Athens area were also placed under British authority. General Wilson nominated Lieutenant-General Ronald Scobie as the senior British commander, Greece, with an HQ in Athens.[78]

General Wilson had two scenarios under consideration for the liberation of Greece. The first was a rapid withdrawal of Axis forces, which would require a harassing British force to ensure that the Germans, in particular, suffered as many losses as possible. The second envisaged a more direct confrontation with German forces. Either way, it was decided that Britain had to send a credible force to Greece, which would then act as a deterrent to any Greek group intent on taking power. The same force could also be swung into organizing relief operations for the whole country on behalf of the Greek government returning from exile. What is particularly noteworthy about the planning is that a Greek military mission was embedded in the Athens headquarters, and Scobie was instructed to make full use of the advice and assistance of the Greek officers.[79] In other words, the Greeks were considered to be equal partners in the mission. This was important to reinforce the fact that Britain was supporting the return of the Greek government.

The British chiefs of staff approved the plans for Greece, although reservations were expressed over the size of the force that could be spared from the Italian campaign.[80] However, as August gave way to

September, planning became more detailed and more urgent. At the end of August, the first intelligence reports were received to indicate that a German withdrawal from Greece was imminent. Given D-Day and Soviet advances on the Eastern Front, this was later than anticipated.[81] During September, the German Order of Battle in Greece fell by some 44,000 men, although an estimated 15,000 to 20,000 remained in Attica and in the Corinth Canal zone.[82] The rapid German withdrawal from Greece caused the Anglo-Greek planning staffs to rework some of their assumptions about the liberation of the country. By this point, there was little doubt in the minds of most SOE personnel in Greece as to what ELAS's intentions were. As soon as German forces withdrew from a region, ELAS took the opportunity to attack anyone they suspected as anti-communist. Reports of ELAS atrocities were increasing. This had already caused alarm in Allied HQ in Italy. Back in July, the Foreign Office had sent one of its liaison officers, Major David Wallace, to Greece to provide information on EDES and ELAS. He reported that a massacre of "nationalists" by ELAS had occurred in two towns, Amfilokhia and Kardhitsa, in central Greece, and that this was just "a foretaste" of what was to come. He was correct.[83] In the town of Pyrgos in the northern Peloponnese, the massacre of civilians lasted 48 hours, and the local SOE officer signalled back to Cairo, begging HQ to intervene.[84] Another report, also from the second week of September, seems to have caught the attention of the Foreign Office and the Allied HQ. A British liaison officer in Roumeli recounted in graphic detail: "[O]ver 500 have been executed within the last few weeks … Lying unburied on the ground are naked corpses with their heads severed."[85] By this point, the Foreign Office was taking very seriously rumours of an ELAS advance on Athens and their threats to kill 60,000 in the capital.[86]

Planning readjustments were made and British re-entry into Greece was to be undertaken in stages. Scobie's UK III Corps comprised two main components: the 2nd Independent Parachute Brigade and the 23rd Armoured Brigade Group. The former landed to the north of Athens on 14 October.[87] Four days later, Prime Minister Papandreou, accompanied by Reginald Leeper, disembarked in Piraeus Harbour (see figure 12.1). Leeper observed how their route to the centre of Athens was flanked on all sides by KKE flags and slogans daubed with red paint.[88] He and the Greek prime minister were left in no doubt that the communists were omnipotent. Over the next few weeks, the HQ staff were tasked with a variety of responsibilities, including

Figure 12.1 A crowd in the main square of Athens greets the new government led by Prime Minister George Papandreou, 18 October 1944. © Imperial War Museum, IWM TR 2500.

co-ordinating humanitarian relief; re-establishing basic infrastructure (water, electricity, sewerage, road, and rail communications, etc.); and rounding up enemy aliens. But what was originally conceived of as a "liberation and stabilization" operation very quickly developed into a major, mainly urban, counterinsurgency campaign during December.[89] After a month of attritional fighting against ELAS, British forces prevailed.[90] The second phase of the Greek civil war was over.

CONCLUSION

In the period following the cessation of violence, Churchill concluded that there would have been a wholesale massacre in Athens had Anglo-Greek forces not intervened. Details of the atrocities committed by ELAS were published in a government White Paper on 31 January 1945, and further reinforced by the report of a British Trades Union Congress (TUC) delegation that had visited Athens on 22 January on a fact-finding mission. The TUC report was clear as to who had perpetrated the atrocities.[91] EAM/ELAS lost much of its international support as a consequence. Some writers have suggested that this was only a "victory of a sort" because the communists made a final bid for power between 1946 and 1949, but such criticism overlooks a number of factors.[92] First, Britain did not have the person-power to commit more forces to Greece at that point in the war. Second, the events of 1944–45 caused insecurity within KKE, not least because ELAS had lost upwards of 3,000 personnel in the fighting in Athens.[93] This level of attrition was one of the factors that contributed to re-assessing communist strategy, and, ultimately, their failure during the "third round." The KKE's leadership concluded that it needed to move away from guerrilla warfare and develop a regular army. This played into the hands of the rebuilt and reformed Greek National Army, allowing it to prevail between 1946 and 1949.

Throughout its intervention in Greece during the Second World War, Britain faced dilemmas posed by having to balance operational priorities and longer-term strategic objectives. As the war dragged on, it became clear that by prioritizing immediate operational objectives (i.e., the defeat of the Axis), there would be unintended consequences, which would damage Britain's long-term strategic interests in the region. What was not expected was the speed with which these unintended consequences manifested themselves at the end of 1944, causing Britain to divert valuable resources to secure both British interests and Greece's freedom from communist domination. However, it is also true that SOE's arrival in mainland Greece in October 1942 as part of the Harling Mission ensured the survival of the non-communist resistance movement. This in turn prevented ELAS from becoming the only resistance group in Greece at the time of liberation and monopolizing political power. Competing visions and the fragmentation of the resistance movement in Greece had made the conflict anything but a classically defined "People's War."

NOTES

1 Sources vary on the precise figure. The author uses figures from the Greek government's Reconstruction Unit at the end of the Second World War. Hoover Archive, Stanford University, Hellenic Department for Reconstruction, GR WWII 46 "Rise in Mortality during Occupation"; GR WWII 47, "Deaths Listed According to Age and Sex." See also P. Papastratis, *British Policy Towards Greece During the Second World War, 1941–1944* (Cambridge: Cambridge University Press, 1984), 114–15, and 84n4.

2 The concept of multiple civil wars is analyzed by Stathis Kalyvas and Nikos Marantzides in their work, *Εμφύλια Πάθη – 23 Ερωτήσεις και απαντήσεις για τον Εμφύλιο (Civil Passions)* (Athens: Μεταίχμιο, 2015), 191–4.
3 For an analysis of the KKE, see Kalyvas and Marantzides, *Civil Passions*, 135–63.
4 Acronym for Ελληνικός Λαϊκός Απελευθερωτικός Στρατός – Greek Popular Liberation Army.
5 Acronym for Εθνικός Δημοκρατικός Ελληνικός Σύνδεσμος – National Democratic Greek League.
6 For a discussion of polarization, see N. Marantzides and G. Antoniou, "The Axis Occupation and Greek Civil War: Changing Trends in Greek Historiography, 1941–2002," *Journal of Peace Research* 41, no. 2 (2004): 223–31. Works in English have typically used translated sources without offering radically different interpretations or perspectives.
7 For a succinct treatment, see Stathis Kalyvas, *Modern Greece: What Everyone Needs to Know* (Oxford: Oxford University Press, 2015), 69–71. See also Michael Llewellyn-Smith, *Ionian Vision – Greece in Asia Minor 1919–1922* (London: Hurst, 1998), 35–61; Thanos Veremis, *Ελευθέριος Βενιζέλος Ο οραματιστής του εφικτού* (Athens: Μεταίχμιο, 2017), 71–102.
8 Kalyvas and Marantzides, *Civil Passions*, 73.
9 Thanos Veremis, *The Military in Greek Politics – From Independence to Democracy* (London: Hurst, 1997), 50–69.
10 Thanos Veremis, *Οι επεμβάσεις του στρατού στην ελληνική πολιτική 1916–1936* (Athens: Αλεξανδρεια, 2018), 229–75. Veremis demonstrates the nexus between political parties and factions in the officer corps.
11 This undermined the legitimacy of the monarchy and was an argument used against the return of King George II to Greece after occupation. Richard Clogg, *Parties and Elections in Greece* (London: Hurst, 1987), 11–12.
12 J. Loulis, *The Greek Communist Party, 1940–1944* (London: Croom Helm 1982), 17; A. Gerolymatos, *An International Civil War: Greece, 1943–1949* (New Haven: Yale University Press, 2016), 1–26.
13 The best discussion of the Occupation's impact on this region is John Koliopoulos, *Plundered Loyalties: World War II and Civil War in Greek West Macedonia* (New York: New York University Press, 1999).
14 Loulis, *The Greek Communist Party*, 14–20, 62–5, 83–8. See also: C.M. Woodhouse, *Apple of Discord: A Survey of Recent Greek Politics in Their International Setting* (London: Hutchinson, 1948), 9–98.
15 Acronym for Εθνικό Απελευθερωτικό Μέτωπο.

16 L.S. Stavrianos, "The Greek National Liberation Front (EAM): A Study in Resistance Organization and Administration," *Journal of Modern History* 24, no. 3 (1952): 42–55.
17 Woodhouse, *Apple of Discord*, 72–5; C.M. Woodhouse, *Struggle for Greece, 1941–1949* (London: Hurst, 2018), 29–30; H. Gardner, *Guerrilla and Counter-Guerrilla Warfare in Greece, 1941–1945* (Washington: Office of the Chief of Military History 1962), 12–14.
18 The Left claims that ELAS was the first Resistance organization in Greece during the occupation. See, for example, Thanasis Hajis, "EAM–ELAS: Resistance or National Liberation Movement?" in *Greece: From Resistance to Civil War*, ed. Marion Sarafis (Nottingham: Spokesman, 1980), 63–74. See also: Woodhouse Papers, Liddell Hart Centre, King's College London, File 1/5. Note on Greek Resistance groups, 1943.
19 PAO: acronym for Πανελλήνια Απελευθερωτική Οργάνωση.
20 YVE: Greek acronym for Υπερασπισταί Βορείου Ελλάδος.
21 Several works address the resistance movements in Macedonia and Thrace. Koliopoulos' *Plundered Loyalties* concentrates on Western Macedonia. Vaios Kalogrias, *Το αντίπαλο δέος* (Thessaloniki: University Studio Press, 2012), describes the non-communist resistance movements throughout Macedonia. Nikos Marantzidis et al., eds., *Οι άλλοι Καπετάνιοι* (Athens: Εστία, 2005), catalogued the non-communist groups in both Macedonia and Thrace.
22 C. Goulter-Zervoudakis, "The Politicisation of Intelligence: The British Experience in Greece, 1941–1944," in *Knowing Your Friends: Intelligence Inside Alliances and Coalitions from 1914 to the Cold War*, ed. Martin Alexander (London: Frank Cass, 1998), 170–4. The importance of being able to understand the political nuances in spoken and written Greek is explained in Nicholas Hammond, *Venture into Greece: With the Guerrillas, 1943–1944* (William Kimber & Co., 1983), 24.
23 Liddell Hart Centre, King's College London, Woodhouse Papers, File 1/5. Note on Greek Resistance groups, 1943. See also: Loulis, *The Greek Communist Party*, 18–19.
24 Acronym for Εθνική Και Κοινωνική Απελευθέρωση.
25 E. Hatzivassiliou, *ΠΕΑΝ (1941–1945) Πανελλήνιος Ένωσις Αγωνιζόμενων Νέων* (Athens: Society for the Dissemination of Useful Books, 2005).
26 Ibid., 123–36.
27 Ibid., 145–53, 183–96, 353. For an account of a PEAN member's experiences, see Georgis Maratos, *Ο κόκκινος σταυρός* (Athens: Εστια, 2004), 123.
28 Goulter-Zervoudakis, "The Politicisation of Intelligence," 165–94.

29 Benaki Museum, Athens. SOE Archive, SOE Reports, "Report on SOE Activities in Greece and the Islands of the Aegean," Appendix II.
30 Goulter-Zervoudakis, "The Politicisation of Intelligence," 168.
31 Ibid., 169–73.
32 SOE was already operating in Crete.
33 Hammond, *Venture Into Greece*, 30–1; Petros Makris-Staikos, *Ο Άγγλος Πρόξενος* (Athens: Ωκεανίδα, 2011). The latter discusses the types of personnel recruited by British intelligence.
34 E. Myers, *A Greek Entanglement* (London: Cassell, 1955), 127.
35 Themis Marinos, *Θέμης Μαρίνος Ο Εφιάλτης της Εθνικής Αντίστασης*, vol. 1 (Athens: Εκδόσεις Παπαζήση, 2003), 143–12.
36 Myers, *A Greek Entanglement*, 108, 126–9. See also Woodhouse, *Struggle for Greece*, 31–2.
37 Myers, *A Greek Entanglement*, 130–2.
38 Benaki Museum, SOE Report, App. X, 1–2, 10.
39 Lars Baerentzen, ed., *British Reports on Greece, 1943–44* (Copenhagen: Museum Tusculanum, 1982), 1–46.
40 Benaki Museum, Peltekis Archive, File 4, Sig 25 to Smyrna, 1943 (circa end of July); H. Hinsley et al., *British Intelligence in the Second World War*, vol. 3, part 1 (London: HMSO, 1984), 78–80; C.M. Woodhouse, "Summer 1943: the Critical Months" in *British Policy Towards Wartime Resistance in Yugoslavia and Greece*, ed. Phyllis Auty and Richard Clogg (London: MacMillan, 1975), 125.
41 The National Archives [hereafter TNA], FO 371/37198, Sargent to Eden (20 August 1943). See also: Myers, *A Greek Entanglement*, 228–65.
42 TNA, FO 371/37209. Leeper to Foreign Office, 18 December 1943.
43 TNA, WO 204/1984. Wilson to Chiefs of Staff, 27 January 1944; WO 202/974. See also Air Ministry for British Chiefs of Staff, from Wilson, 2 February 1944. See FO 371/43677 for discussions regarding support to ELAS.
44 L. Woodward, *British Foreign Policy in the Second World War*, vol. 3 (HMSO, 1971), 394. See also: WO 201/1598. C-in-C, MEF, to AFHQ, 6 May 44, Appendix B.
45 R. Leeper, *When Greek Meets Greek* (London: Chatto and Windus, 1950), 36–7.
46 Woodhouse, *Struggle for Greece*, 65–6; Woodward, *British Foreign Policy*, 403–05; WO 204/1984. MIDEAST to FREEDOM, 4 March 1944.
47 Woodhouse, *Struggle for Greece*, 62. See also: Tom Evans, *With SOE in Greece: The Wartime Experiences of Captain Pat Evans* (Barnsley, UK: Pen and Sword, 2018), 34–5.

48 Quoted in J. Iatrides, *Revolt in Athens: The Greek Communist Second Round, 1944–45* (Princeton: Princeton University Press, 1972), 44.
49 Georgios Beldekos, *Ιστορία της Ελληνικής Πολεμικής Αεροπορίας Τόμος Δ 1941–1944* (ΥΙΠΑ, 1997), 64; Dimitris Katsikostas, *Ο Ελληνικός Στρατός στην Εξορία 1941–1944* (Athens: Αλφειός, 2015), 40.
50 Katsikostas, *Ο Ελληνικός Στρατός στην Εξορία*, 45–50, 86–97.
51 Ibid., 186–7. ASO: acronym for Αντιφασιστική Στρατιωτική Οργάνωση.
52 Acronym for Αντιφασιστική Οργάνωση Ναυτικού.
53 Acronym for Αντιφασιστική Οργάνωση Αεροπορίας.
54 Katsikostas, *Ο Ελληνικός Στρατός στην Εξορία*, 187.
55 Sakis Moundzis, *Η Κοκκινη βια, 1943–1946* (Athens: Επικεντρο, 2013), 100–9. For an account by a Communist participant in the 1943 mutiny, see Vasilis Nefeloudis *Η Εθνική Αντίσταση στη Μέση Ανατολή* (Athens: Θεμέλιο, 1981), vol. 1.
56 Katiskostas, *Ο Ελληνικός Στρατός στην Εξορία*, 135–46.
57 TNA WO 204/1984. C-in-C MED, General Sir Bernard Paget, to Air Ministry, 9 April 1944. See also: Woodward, *British Foreign Policy in the Second World War*, 3:408n.
58 TNA WO 204/1984. C-in-C MED to Admiralty, 23 April 1944. The second volume of Nefeloudis's book (see note 55) provides an account of the 1944 mutinies, exposing the contradictions in the thinking of the mutineers, as well as the political and ideological reasons behind the mutinies.
59 TNA WO 204/1984. C-in-C MED to Admiralty, copied Wilson, 17 April 1944; C-in-C MED to Admiralty, 16 April 1944, 3.
60 TNA WO 204/1984. Admiralty to C-in-C MED, 22 April 1944.
61 *Έκθεσις επι της δράσεως του Βασιλικού Ναυτικού κατά τον πόλεμον, 1940–1944 Τόμος Β* (Athens: Ιστορική Υπηρεσία ΒΝ, 1954), 440–70.
62 E. Spyropoulos, *The Greek Military (1909–1941) and the Greek Mutinies in the Middle East (1941–1944)* (Columbia: Columbia University Press, 1993), 374.
63 TNA WO 204/1984. MIDEAST to Air Ministry, 8 April 1944.
64 Beldekos, *Ιστορία της Ελληνικής Πολεμικής Αεροπορίας*, 275–85.
65 During the suppression of the mutiny, thirty Greek navy personnel were wounded and six were killed. Of those wounded, nine were mutineers. Dimitrios Fokas, *Έκθεσις επι της δράσεως του Βασιλικού Ναυτικού κατά τον πόλεμον, 1940–1944 Τόμος Β* (Athens: Ιστορική Υπηρεσία ΒΝ, 1954), 442–4.
66 Hansard, House of Commons, vol. 400, MP for Romford, 14 June 1944. This suggests that a total of one hundred Greek personnel lost their lives in the mutinies.
67 Leeper, *When Greek Meets Greek*, 47.

68 Ibid. See also Iatrides, *Revolt in Athens*, 58–9.
69 Iatrides, *Revolt in Athens*, 54.
70 Greek Historical Service, Athens. *Ο Ελληνικος Στρατος στη Μεση Ανατολη (1941–1945)* (ΓΕΣ/ΔΙΣ, 1995), 102–43.
71 However, fears over communist infiltration of the military persisted and led to the creation of several secret organizations, and these created a climate which facilitated the military dictatorship, 1967–74.
72 Woodward, *British Foreign Policy in the Second World War*, 408–9.
73 Woodhouse, *Struggle for Greece*, 88. See also Leeper, *When Greek Meets Greek*, 57; and Iatrides, *Revolt in Athens*, 69.
74 Loulis, *The Greek Communist Party*, 132. The number of posts was debated at the time, ranging from thirteen to fifteen.
75 Iatrides, *Revolt in Athens*, 72–4.
76 Woodhouse, *Struggle for Greece*, 94–9; Leeper, *When Greek Meets Greek*, 56–8. Bulgarian forces left Greece in September after the change to a pro-Soviet government in that country.
77 TNA WO 106/3199. British Forces for Greece, vol. 2, AMSSO to JSM, 19 September 1944; TNA WO 32/12264. *Report by the Supreme Allied Commander, Mediterranean, to the Combined Chiefs of Staff on Greece, 12th December 1944 to 9th May 1945* (London: HMSO, 1949), 7. See also: TNA WO 106/3171. Plan for Operation in Greece, September 1944; Woodward, *British Foreign Policy in the Second World War*, 396–7.
78 TNA WO 106/3199. British Forces for Greece, vol. 2, Alexander to Churchill, 12 December 1944.
79 TNA WO 106/3199. British Forces for Greece, vol. 2, Minutes, COS meeting, 27 September 1944; TNA WO 106/3171. Note for Plan of Operations in Greece, September 1944.
80 TNA WO 106/3199. TNA WO 106/3199. British Forces for Greece, vol. 2, Minute D 314/4, n.d. 81 Hinsley et al., *British Intelligence* D 314/4, n.d.
81 Hinsley et al., *British Intelligence in the Second World War*, vol. 3, part 2, 288–94.
82 TNA WO 170/4410. 2nd Independent Parachute Brigade, Information Summary 8, 4 October 1944, 3.
83 I. Baerentzen, ed., *Reports on Greece, 1943–44*, Report by Major Wallace, 140.
84 TNA WO 204/1985. Message MIDEAST to Freedom, 11 September 1944.
85 TNA FO 371/43692. Summary of Reports, 12 September 1944. See also report to Anthony Eden from Leeper, 4 September 1944.
86 TNA FO 371/43692. Warner to Leeper, 12 September 1944.

87 TNA WO 170/4410. War Diary, HQ 2nd Independent Parachute Brigade, entries October 1944. See also: Report "Activities of 2 Indep[endent] Para Bde in Greece from October 44 to Jan 45," n.d., 1.
88 Leeper, *When Greek Meets Greek*, 77–8.
89 C. Goulter, "The Greek Civil War: A National Army's Counter-Insurgency Triumph," *Journal of Military History*, no. 78 (July 2014), 1017–55.
90 Ministry of Defence, Army Historical Branch, War Office, "Operations of British Troops in the Insurrection in Greece," 52. See also: Appendices A20 and C; AHB RAF, RAF Narrative, *RAF in Maritime War*, vol. 7, part 2, Mediterranean, 830–46, 863–8.
91 TNA PREM 4/19/8. TUC Report, February 1945, 9–10.
92 E. Smith, *Victory of a Sort: the British in Greece, 1941–46* (London: Robert Hale 1988), 220.
93 War Office, "Operations of British Troops in the Insurrection in Greece," Appendix A20; Appendix C. Although precise figures for ELAS losses are not known, estimates done by the British HQ suggest that the insurgents lost ten people for every one British Commonwealth casualty. During the Second Round, one source suggests that 212 British personnel were killed. Another postwar calculation suggests that 237 personnel were killed. It is reasonable to propose that between December 1944 and January 1945, ELAS lost 2,500 to 3,000 out of a maximum force of 35,000.

13

Gender and Community during War
The Amorous Relationships of Western POWs and German Women in Nazi Germany

Raffael Scheck

While the prevailing orthodoxy of the "People's War" discourse advances the centrality of hatred, animosity, and violence to characterize relationships between representatives of combatant nations, recent scholarship seeks to emphasize more nuanced perspectives. This chapter presents an account of amorous encounters between Allied prisoners of war (POWs) and German women, which challenges much of that narrowly drawn consensus. By presenting love, rather than hatred, as a driver of behaviour, the chapter advances perspectives that enrich the thematic pursuits of this volume. The dynamics that emerge from detailed analysis of individual relationships challenge the friend-foe dichotomy so prevalent in wartime propaganda, revealing individual behaviour at stark odds with official desires. These relationships often created tensions within wartime society by challenging dating patterns and by disrupting families and communities. In this regard, the subversive side to amorous relationships between German women and Western Allied POWs should be interpreted as surpassing the norms between combatants and, instead, representing a broader societal renegotiation of conventional European gender roles, owing to the contrasting statuses of free German women and incarcerated Allied POWs. The man in the relationship was a community outsider and occupied a lower legal and often, in Nazi eyes, a lower racial rank than the woman. However, individual interaction stood in marked contrast to official diktats because both had something to offer to each other, and both often ran great risks for love, companionship, or support.

This chapter focuses, by necessity, on POWs drawn from among the armed forces of the Western Allies. Although a few German women became involved with Polish and Soviet prisoners, Nazi racism and the refusal to recognize international law with respect to Polish and Soviet POWs placed these relationships in a different category: the POWs were usually hanged, and the women received very long penitentiary sentences or were sent to concentration camps.[1] In dealing with western prisoners, the Nazi authorities by and large respected the 1929 Geneva Convention on Prisoners of War, which stipulated that accused prisoners had the right to a military trial with oversight by the protecting power. It is, predominantly, these records that shed light on this widely unknown aspect of wartime accord.

OFFICIAL ANXIETY OVER AMOROUS RELATIONSHIPS BETWEEN WESTERN POWS AND GERMAN WOMEN

The German High Command prohibited amicable relations between POWs and civilians, especially German women, because it argued that during the First World War, friendly relations with POWs had undermined German morale and the will to pursue the war to the end. German women who were unfaithful to their soldier husbands or boyfriends, and especially those women who consorted with POWs, were accused of "sexual treason."[2] The relations of POWs and German women thus became a facet of the stab-in-the-back myth, which sought to "explain" the German defeat in 1918 as a consequence of moral collapse on the Home Front. The Nazi regime added a racial hygienic argument to this notion by stressing that the love relations of foreign POWs with German women threatened "the purity of the German blood" and led to racial decay and the dissolution of the German family.[3] In Nazi parlance, the term "enemy" therefore assumed an additional meaning, including also the "racial" enemy at home. Getting intimately involved with an enemy POW meant betraying one's people and race.[4] Nazi officials never tired of reminding the German public that the POW remained an enemy keen to exploit the generosity of friendly civilians to pursue espionage, sabotage, and escape.[5]

Both world wars triggered anxiety about the role of women in the absence of many men in the corresponding age group, and both wars opened new sexual opportunities – consensual, transactional, and violent – due to increased mobility and disruption. Many wartime societies were particularly concerned about the faithfulness of the wives of soldiers, fearing for the soldiers' morale.[6] Most army commands in both world wars therefore restricted the relationships between POWs and civilians. The 1929 Geneva Convention on Prisoners of War stipulated that POWs had to follow the rules and regulations in force in the army of the detaining power and provided rules for disciplinary punishments (up to four weeks) and for judicial procedures against POWs (Articles 45 to 67). Although there was usually no equivalent to the ban on friendly relations with civilians for soldiers of the detaining power's army, it was legal to give certain orders to POWs and to punish them if they disobeyed them, as long as the POWs were treated with respect and in a humane fashion (Article 2).[7]

Nazi Germany had ratified the Geneva Convention and agreed to abide by it for western prisoners of war. Unlike the western countries, however, the German High Command severely punished all POWs' close contacts with civilians. Whereas the United States and Britain treated such incidents as a disciplinary infraction leading to a punishment of up to four weeks of arrest, Germany treated them as military disobedience (s. 92 of the German military law code).[8] Disobedience in wartime was a severe crime that could lead to a prison or penitentiary sentence of several years, and in serious cases, to a death sentence.[9] A POW embracing a German woman was therefore treated like a German soldier who refused to obey an order to attack. As a consequence, punishments for POWs involved with women in Nazi Germany were much harsher than they were for German prisoners in Britain or the United States. The western POW in Nazi Germany would receive a sentence in military prison ranging from six months (for a kiss) to four years (for repeated sexual contact). As the number of cases increased rapidly, Hitler requested that military tribunals sentence prisoners who had sex with a woman married to a German soldier to a penitentiary, which meant forced labour under hard conditions.[10]

German civilians faced similar restrictions under wartime law. Amicable relations with POWs counted as violations of the infamous Decree for the Protection of the Will to Resist. An addendum to this decree stipulated that all relations with prisoners that "crudely violate the healthy feeling of the *Volk*," would lead to prison sentences and, in severe cases, to a penitentiary. Civilians who violated these decrees usually had to appear in front of a so-called special court, an institution that the Nazi state had created before the war to deal with political opposition. Special courts had a reputation for harsh sentences. They were meant to be, in the words of Roland Freisler, one of the most avid Nazi judges, "the court martials of the inner front."[11]

ASCERTAINING THE EXTENT AND CHARACTER OF AMOROUS RELATIONSHIPS BETWEEN WESTERN POWS AND GERMAN WOMEN

The harsh punishments did little to deter forbidden relationships, however, as POWs and German women mingled freely on farms, in small businesses, and in factories. The decentralized deployment of POWs, instituted first for the French and Belgian POWs and later also for some British prisoners, made economic sense but did not allow close guarding, especially in light of the *Wehrmacht's* increasing manpower shortages. In the countryside, the prisoner might live and work on the family farm, and "guarding" might consist of an elderly reserve soldier on a bicycle checking once a week to see whether the prisoner was still there. The prisoner, sometimes with a few comrades or forced labourers from eastern Europe, worked in the fields and barns, usually in the presence of female employees and the farmer's wife. Hiding places for illicit encounters were easy to find in a barn, a forest, or the fields. In the factories, prisoners worked in larger groups but socialized with German women on the same shop floor. The prisoners typically spent the night in a closed restaurant or school with one or two guards, but these locales were not secured well, and the guards also needed sleep. It was relatively easy for a prisoner to sneak out at night for a couple of hours. On Sundays, prisoners could go on outings freely, and they often met a girlfriend outdoors or in her abode.[12]

French prisoners were by far the largest group of western soldiers in German captivity; nearly 1.6 million of them came to Germany in the summer of 1940, and close to one million were still there in 1945. Records of over 17,000 military trials against French prisoners have survived, and three-quarters of them concern forbidden liaisons with German women.[13] The actual number of trials is certainly higher because records were lost, particularly during the last year of the war. One also has to assume the existence of a large number of love relationships that were never discovered, especially in remote villages. These relations were not only forbidden, they also involved intimate and often adulterous acts that both partners usually wanted to hide from the public.

The number of unreported cases was likely particularly high for French POWs because Vichy France was a friendly neutral and the stigma attached to relations with French prisoners decreased rapidly after the campaign of 1940.[14] The diplomatic representation of French POWs was first entrusted to the American government (until December 1940) but then transferred to the Vichy authorities for the rest of the war. The Vichy office responsible for the POWs, the Scapini Mission, did not discourage amorous relations but tried to convince the German High Command to drop the charges or at least reduce the punishments. Many French prisoners and their German lovers wanted to marry after the war, but Free French military regulations, popular sentiment in liberated France, and often also rejection of the German bride by the prisoner's family made it extremely difficult to realize these plans.[15]

Belgian prisoners experienced similar situations to the French. After most prisoners from Flanders had been dismissed in 1940 according to a Hitler order, French-speaking Walloons predominated, although a sizeable group of POWs with Flemish or mixed ancestry remained. Approximately 90,000 Belgian POWs were left in the spring of 1941. Initially, the United States served as the protecting power for Belgian POWs, but after the American entry into the war in December 1941, Nazi Germany refused to accept a new protecting power. Instead, a Belgian commission, the *Délégation du service de liaison avec les prisonniers* (DSLP) under the leadership of Count t'Serclaes addressed the needs and complaints of Belgian POWs, while refusing to take on a formal role as protecting power.[16]

The bulk of the Belgian trial records was destroyed by a fire in the Belgian military archives in Evere, outside of Brussels, but some documents remain in other collections in Brussels, the German Foreign Ministry, and the American National Archives. The proportion of Belgian POWs on trial for amorous relations seems to have been even higher than it was for the French: a prisoner representative from a big camp in East Prussia testified after the war that 6 per cent of his comrades had to stand trial for forbidden relations – a revelation that caused a scandal among Belgian veterans.[17] In 1945, some Belgian prisoners wanted to stay in Germany and marry their girlfriends, but the military police brought them home *manu militari*. A few Belgians did manage to marry their German girlfriends sooner or later after the war, however.[18]

Given that German hostilities with Britain continued, the nearly 165,000 prisoners from Britain and the Empire were guarded more strictly and had less contact with German civilians. Unlike the French and Belgians, British authorities strongly discouraged prisoners from dating enemy women. Scholars who have studied the behaviour of British POWs argue that relationships with German women were very rare because most prisoners lost their sexual desire in captivity, while those few who did feel adventurous tended to date non-German women.[19] This image requires some modifications, however. While British prisoners in the German-occupied parts of Poland did indeed try to befriend Polish women, they ran into trouble because of the ambiguities of citizenship, ethnicity, and national identity in these regions. Many local women had been accepted onto the German People's List (*Deutsche Volksliste*) and acquired German citizenship, which meant that POW relations with them were punishable. To avoid legal ambiguities, several military district commanders in these regions prohibited prisoner contact with *all* women, not only women with German citizenship. Still, there were a significant number of British liaisons with German women both in the German-Polish regions and also in Austria and the Sudetenland. The files preserved in the archives of Switzerland, the protecting power for the British after December 1941, show a dramatic increase in cases throughout 1944 and early 1945, although hundreds of cases did not come to trial because of the chaotic circumstances toward the end of the war.[20]

Only a few love-related trials against American prisoners occurred. Most Americans came to the Reich late in the war. Given that it took time to distribute them to the smaller work detachments, many Americans did not come into contact with German women until very late. Many American POWs, moreover, were aircrew, who tended to be guarded relatively strictly in *Luftwaffe* camps.[21]

For German women, the war brought increasing pressures as more and more men had to join the armed forces and as the casualty lists grew longer. After 1941, German society became increasingly lopsided; most younger women were German and most younger men were foreigners, either POWs or foreign labourers. The milkmaid on a farm or the female worker in a factory would normally have dated a German man working next to her, but this became increasingly difficult. Married German women faced a particular conundrum because of the prolonged absence of a husband serving in the armed forces. The time between home leaves could be over one year, and the leaves could exacerbate marital tensions. Enforced absence, along with divergence in direct experience of front-line combat conditions could alienate couples and lead to estrangement.[22] Women also heard rumours that German soldiers were unfaithful abroad. The prisoner often seemed to be more understanding and helpful than the husband. Quite a few relations between married women and prisoners became intimate after a husband's home leave had led to marital strife.[23]

In the later years of the war, fatalism and desperation spread, particularly among urban German women. The insecurity of life under the bombs encouraged living in the moment. Moreover, as the German defeat loomed ever larger, the future became a source of insecurity and anxiety. With extremely long and tedious workdays, shortages, and bombings, German urban women became desperate for love, affection, and tenderness. The same may also be said, with some limits, for POWs working in urban centres. Although they might take satisfaction from the prospect of an impending Allied victory leading to their liberation, their immediate future also seemed insecure and threatening.

While the prisoner had little contact with his home, he was not completely isolated from the dynamics of his home community. Many married western prisoners heard from family or neighbours that their wife had become close to another man – in the case of Frenchmen or Belgians, this man might even be a German soldier. The problem for the prisoner was that he was forced into a new world with only tenuous connections to his pre-war life and did not know when his new existence would end. Some prisoners, especially on farms, integrated themselves so well into the local community that they began to fully identify with it. The exceptional situation created by the war became an alternative normality.

GENDER ROLES AND EXPERIENCE WITHIN AMOROUS RELATIONSHIPS BETWEEN WESTERN POWS AND GERMAN WOMEN

The French historian Patrice Arnaud has suggested that the relations between POWs and German women represented a reversal of gender roles, and Cornelie Usborne, in a recent article based on the study of files from women tried by the special court in Munich, has bolstered this argument. Usborne even suggests that some women frivolously engaged in affairs with POWs, taking advantage of the power that the Nazi regime conferred on them in relations with people supposed to be racial inferiors.[24] Nazi authorities, especially SS chief Heinrich Himmler, worried greatly about the apparent decline of morals among women in German wartime society. The high number of these illicit relationships helped to conjure up anxiety about a profound crisis of gender norms, maybe even a sexual revolution.[25]

The 2,000 court martial proceedings examined against French, Belgian, and British POWs and nearly 500 trials against women by the special courts in Kiel, Nürnberg, Vienna, Potsdam, Oldenburg, Bremen, Hannover, Darmstadt, Frankfurt, and Katowice, do not confirm a clear gender reversal, but they indicate that the gender dynamics were both more complicated and more flexible than conventional norms. The prisoner and the woman both had something to offer, including material goods and services (which often started the relationship). The prisoner received quality goods in his aid parcels that were rare in wartime Germany, such as chocolate, real coffee, perfumed soap, and good cigarettes. The woman might offer the prisoner additional food, especially home baked goods, which were much appreciated but pointed to older gender roles. The woman and the prisoner could offer each other some services, too, but most of them were also grounded in traditional gender roles. Women might be mending a prisoner's clothes or washing his laundry. The prisoner might be splitting wood or repairing doors and windows for the woman, replacing the proverbial but absent *Mann im Haus* (man in the house).

Although the prisoner seemed to stand on a lower rank than the German woman, it is important to keep in mind that he had rights. Unlike a forced labourer from Eastern Europe, a western POW could lodge a complaint against his employer and request a transfer to a different workplace.[26] On farms, this could be a serious threat given the labour shortage in Nazi Germany. According to Maria S., who was sentenced to two years of penal servitude by the special court in Nürnberg in June 1942, the French POW on her farm pressed her into sexual intercourse in the cow barn because he said he would work better if they had sex.[27] Other women argued that they had tolerated the sexual advances of the prisoner because they had been afraid to lose a good worker.[28] The special courts usually disregarded these defences, which occurred during trial and therefore have to be considered with caution, but they do reflect the power a POW had during a time of acute labour shortages.

Figure 13.1 This photo represents the predominant image of POWs in an all-male environment. While this was the reality for officers and members of special forces (such as airmen in this case), the vast majority of western prisoners were in close daily contact with civilians, including women. © Imperial War Museum, IWM HU20951.

It is notable that women often played an active role in initiating the forbidden relationship and openly admitted their attraction to a prisoner, even expressing a right to sexual satisfaction. According to French POW Marcel R., a German soldier's wife one day seduced him by giving him wine to drink and saying: "[Y]our wife is in France, my husband in Russia, and we are having no fun."[29] A woman on trial in Nürnberg stated: "I engaged in sexual intercourse with the Frenchman P. because I am very hot-blooded and because I have not received sexual satisfaction for 16 months."[30] The farmwoman Elisabeth A., from a village near Darmstadt, explained to the police that her husband, who had been drafted into the Wehrmacht, could not satisfy her sexually and that she had taken up an intimate relationship with two French prisoners because she had a very lively sex drive (interestingly, the husband confirmed all this information in a letter to the court).[31] A butcher's wife, Else B., in Frankfurt am Main, grew close to the French POW Émile Le P. who was assigned to the butcher shop as a helper. They had sex in the marital bed until her husband surprised them one day. In front of the special court in Frankfurt on 18 February 1944, she defended her right to sexual satisfaction, explaining, however, that the prisoner had always experienced premature ejaculation and that she had remained unsatisfied.[32] In a hamlet near Regensburg, French POWs and local women worked together in the fields. One day, Magdalene S. told the French POW André C. that he should let his comrade Georges ("Schorsch") M. know that he could have sex with her if he brought her some chocolate. The comment unleashed a series of flirtatious comments, and soon four French POWs were having sexual relations with the German farm maids, who boasted to each other about their sexual exploits and compared the "qualities" of their French lovers.[33] Of course, one has to treat statements reported by the police or court officials with caution, but most of these statements were confirmed by witnesses, including the prisoner or the husband.

Many group relationships seem to have been motivated by a mutual desire for fun and erotic adventure in the grim circumstances of the war. In Tilsit (East Prussia), for example, two young German women, both married, walked to the Belgian POW residence in town in March 1942 and asked José M., who happened to stand outside, whether he knew the handsome prisoner who worked at a local hair salon. M. realized immediately that they meant his comrade Jean ("Jonny") D., but as a joke, he said that he himself was that handsome prisoner. M. and the women agreed to meet at night in the city park, and he promised to bring a second prisoner. He more than kept his word and brought along three of his comrades for nightly unions with the two women over the next few months, including the real "Jonny" D., whose reputed good looks had inspired the women. The couples met many times in the city park and later in the apartment of one of the women. The relations were discovered for unknown reasons in July, and the special court in Königsberg sentenced the women to three and five years of penal servitude (the woman who had offered her apartment was punished more harshly). The court martial in Königsberg sentenced M. and another POW to four and a half years and two others, who had been less involved, to two and a half years in prison.[34]

A similar case occurred with three British POWs and three German women in a brewery in Danzig-Langfuhr. They flirted during work and talked about meeting at night in the apartment of one of the women if the prisoners could find a way to leave their sleeping quarters. Aided by a picklock and some agility, the prisoners managed to get outside. The women waited for them with a suitcase containing civilian clothes (belonging to the husband of one of them), so that the

POWs could shed their uniforms and walk to the apartment unrecognized. The three couples managed to have three nightly unions in March 1944 until they were caught. It is not clear who took the first step in this case, but the women were equal partners in deciding for the unions and in facilitating the nightly escapes.[35]

Some women on trial openly protested against the prohibition. In front of the special court of Nürnberg, for example, a woman pointed out that her soldier husband had not been home for a year and defiantly exclaimed to the judge: "[J]ust let our husbands come back to us!" The judge, greatly annoyed, sentenced her to fourteen months in the penitentiary, a harsh sentence given that sexual intercourse had not been proven in this case.[36] A woman on trial in Kiel justified her own relationship with a French POW by pointing out that in her village all the young men were either forced labourers or POWs.[37]

In many cases, the desire for emotional warmth and comfort motivated the forbidden relations. The prisoner or the woman could be the provider of comfort, or it could be a mutual relationship. Gustave E., a thirty-year-old French POW, was a textile worker from Dunkirk who was married with five young children. In February 1941, he was assigned to a farm east of Vienna. The farmwoman, sixty-one-year-old Barbara W., felt pity for the prisoner, who missed his family. One day, she proposed that he sleep in her bed with her, and they had sex five or six times. The court martial in Linz sentenced him to only eight months in prison on 9 September 1941. His concern for his family and the fact that the age of the woman "had ruled out any danger for the German blood" served as mitigating circumstances.[38]

In a Nürnberg brewery, a thirty-year-old French POW, Henri A., a teacher from Algeria, noticed that a worker, Emma E. (twenty-eight), a divorced woman with two children, was always sad. The prisoner tried to cheer her up and occasionally helped her during work. One day, he said to her with compassion in broken German: "E. *kaputt*. Too much work." They hugged and kissed each other. On 27 May 1941, the guard followed the prisoner and caught them. The woman offered the guard money, so that he would not denounce them, but he refused. The court martial sentenced the prisoner to six months in prison. The special court sentenced Frau E. to fifteen months in prison on 4 August 1941.[39]

Many other relationships involved deep love and a commitment to marry after the war. The love and commitment were mutual, and these relations did not normally involve a role reversal. Car mechanic Ernest

A., for example, thought that he had found the love of his life in Germany. A. was a widower and had one child. Born in Birmingham in 1899, he had emigrated to Canada. He was captured in May 1940 and placed in a small forestry work detachment housed in an isolated farmhouse near Elbing (West Prussia). A married German woman, Frau K., regularly took walks through the forest with her six-year-old son. In June 1942, she and A. began talking to each other. He gave her chocolate, soap, honey, and a sweater, and she brought him baked goods and paper for letters. An intense love relationship developed. He wrote her extremely tender letters in which he mentioned his intention to take her to Canada after the war and to marry her. He pointed out that he had a lucrative business and would take good care of her. On four or five occasions, they had sex in the bush. The relationship went on for many months until it was discovered, for unknown reasons. In front of the court martial, A. repeated his sincere desire to marry Frau K. after the war. The justification of the judgment and the report of A.'s attorney reveal that the judges were touched by the genuine love he professed for a German woman and that they found it hard to punish him with the required severity. They sentenced him to three years in prison, the bare minimum for a very involved relationship that had not been facilitated by working together, and that, as the court suggested, had probably ruined Frau K.'s marriage.[40]

Gender reversal did happen occasionally if the prisoner had escaped and gone into hiding in the apartment of a woman. In these cases, the woman was the provider and usually the prisoner's only contact with the outside world. This happened, for example, in the case of French POW Marcel H., who was performing construction work near the train station of Jena (Thuringia) in 1941. During work, he befriended Anna S., a widow with two children, who drove a delivery truck and often passed by the train station. He gave her chocolate and received bread in exchange. After several nightly meetings under rail tunnels and in her truck, he decided to escape on 28 September 1941, and he went to Frau S.'s apartment. She hid him for three weeks, until he was discovered. The special court in Weimar sentenced her to three and a half years of penal servitude, and the court martial in Kassel sentenced him to three years of prison on 22 January 1942. Her punishment was higher because she had assisted him in his escape, while escape could not motivate a judicial punishment against a POW.[41] On the surface, this relationship looks like a clear case of gender reversal. She drove him around in her truck, and, after his escape, she provided for him entirely while he watched her children. But we do not know whether they shed previous gender roles during sex, which assigned the active role to the man and put a premium on *his* satisfaction rather than hers. The trial documents are silent on this question because the two defendants immediately admitted sexual relations and the judges therefore did not probe into details. Like many of these couples, Marcel H. and Anna S. talked of getting married after the war. We cannot know for sure, but it seems rather unlikely that the role reversal would have continued under "normal" circumstances.

One factor that prisoners and women had in common was that they both faced severe punishment. The prisoner, however, could expect that his punishment would not carry a social stigma after the war. Sentences for having committed "disobedience" might even be regarded as a form of heroism. The worst long-term legal consequence a married POW might have to expect would be a divorce suit from his wife if she found out the real reason for his conviction (the families usually learned only that the POWs had been sentenced for "disobedience"). For the women, the social stigma of having gone to prison or, worse, the penitentiary, was likely harder to bear. A penitentiary sentence, the default for women in relations where consensual sex had been proven, also meant a loss of civic rights.[42]

While the court martial took place under international observation and with a defence attorney paid by the protecting power, many women could not afford an attorney and were regularly shamed in court. Some women had to submit to humiliating examinations to determine whether they were still virgins or whether their bodies displayed signs of "feeble-mindedness" and "degeneracy," which would lead to compulsory sterilization. The names of the convicted women appeared in shaming newspaper articles and public posters. Not surprisingly, a number of women committed suicide during pre-trial custody. Among the worst consequences for a woman could be pregnancy, which very often led to the discovery of the forbidden relationship. Some women had to give birth in the harsh and cold setting of a penitentiary; others were allowed to go home for a short time, but the child would be taken away from them and placed with relatives or in an orphanage.

When it came to intimacy, women on trial often stated that the man had taken the first step and that they had resisted to some degree. Some women claimed to have been raped, at least the first time the sexual encounter occurred. The special courts in most cases dismissed these arguments by pointing out that the woman did not call for help even though this would have been possible and by highlighting that she repeated the sexual contact after the first occurrence, even though she could have reported the alleged rape or at least kept more distance from the prisoner. In some cases, the fact that the woman had followed the prisoner to a hiding place or that sexual intercourse had occurred in a position that required significant cooperation from the woman, for example while standing, also indicated to the judges that the sexual advances of the prisoner were not unwelcome.

It is difficult in each individual case to evaluate the claims and counterclaims based mostly on documents produced in the context of a trial, where the stakes were high. But it does seem that in certain environments, women could have a hard time resisting the advances of a prisoner. This applies in particular to farms, where a maid, for example, would often work alone with the prisoner in the fields or in the barn. Some teasing, roughhousing, kissing, and touching could occur, and if a prisoner wanted to go farther, it could be difficult for a woman to say no, given that she had already compromised (and inculpated) herself to some degree through the more harmless forms of contact. There were some clear-cut cases of sexual assault, but the prisoners found guilty were sentenced under the German law code (*Reichsstrafgesetzbuch*, s.176) in addition to s.92 of the military law code (disobedience). These cases were very rare, however, even though one must keep in mind that the bar for proving sexual coercion was high. Arnaud reaches the same conclusion based on a sample of cases involving French POWs and forced labourers, although he points out that the fantasy of rape often dominated the post-war accounts, providing the defeated and disarmed soldier with a "redemptive" victory over the enemy.[43]

Clearly, the lack of close male supervision provided many opportunities for German women to engage in amorous relations. This is true for relationships in general, not only with prisoners of war. Correspondingly, the POWs' transfer to a different environment also loosened restraint and created opportunities. But a reversal of gender roles rarely happened, and if it did, it was temporary and situational. Every couple negotiated gender roles in their own ways, depending on the context, and therefore a comprehensive characterization seems elusive. But generally, one can say that the love relations between western POWs and German women showed a more egalitarian gender dynamic than was normal in peacetime, in Germany and elsewhere.

COMMUNITY REACTION TOWARD AMOROUS RELATIONSHIPS BETWEEN WESTERN POWS AND GERMAN WOMEN

Women and POWs who were involved with each other habitually negated the dichotomy between enemies. The numerous relations that involved emotional comfort or even marriage plans reveal a recognition that the "enemy other" was human and well-intended. This was the case with French, Belgian, and also with British POWs. Although it seems that casual affairs represented a larger share of British POWs' forbidden relations, this may be explainable by the fact that they tended to be more rigorously guarded than the French and Belgians and therefore often did not have the daily closeness and intimacy that triggered the desire for, and commitment to, a long-term relationship. But how did German communities react to the widespread relationships between POWs and women? The expectation of the Nazi regime was that citizens witnessing such a "traitorous" relationship would immediately denounce it. After all, the law applying to the women invoked the "healthy feeling of the *Volk*."

Admittedly, denunciations were common. As other researchers have shown, however, the motivations were predominantly private. Neighbours might complain about suspicious noise in the apartment across the hallway rented by two unmarried women and trigger the discovery of a forbidden group relationship. Whether they were primarily outraged by the noise or by the fact that the women were consorting with POWs (if they were aware of this fact at all) is usually unclear. Some denunciations resulted from intensely private motives. For example, a mother-in-law who had never really liked her daughter-in-law might notice something between her and a prisoner and alert the police. Many husbands finding out about their wife's relationship denounced her in a fit of rage. In both cases, the denouncer would likely also have reported a German man if she or he could have brought him in front of a court.[44] Many other denunciations resulted from outrage over public impropriety. Given that many forbidden encounters took place in forests or fields, an accidental witness, often a child, discovered them and alerted the police. But it is hard to determine whether this witness objected more to the relationship itself or to the indecent behaviour in a public space. Some denunciations also came from eastern forced labourers jealous of the relative privileges of a western prisoner, although the police and the courts often gave little weight to denunciations and testimonies coming from those labourers.[45]

Yet, in many cases, German witnesses, and also many guards, hesitated to denounce an illicit relationship. Many employers and guards warned the couple but did not report them, as would have been their duty. Some guards and employers were openly complicit and protected the couple. French POW Jacques K., for example, had a relationship with a woman married to a Luftwaffe officer in Greifswald. K. worked as a translator, and the guard always accompanied him on his missions. They became closer, and the guard began delivering letters between the lovers. One day, he and K. met the woman and a friend in the street, and they all went into a wine shop and drank wine together. The relationship was only discovered when the woman's husband came home on an unannounced leave. The guard, who had acted as an accomplice, received a court martial himself.[46]

Rural communities often cast a veil of silence and hidden solidarity over the affairs. Farmers had to weigh the loss of two valuable workers against the risk of being punished for not intervening. Very often, a couple received multiple warnings before being denounced. Once an affair became part of the village rumour mill, however, it was dangerous for the employer to ignore it. For example, a farmer, Alois K., and his wife, employed a married farm maid Anna K. on their farm in Furth im Wald (Bavaria). K. had three children aged three to twelve. Neighbours noticed that she often looked out of the window when the prisoners returned from work and marched through town. A neighbour once warned her against getting closer to a POW. The farmers themselves noticed that Anna K. was on cordial terms with French POW Marie Arthur W., who was assigned to the farm, and they warned her, too. Anna K. ignored the many warnings and started an intimate relationship with W. in February 1941. In July 1941, the farming couple again confronted her, probably after having witnessed something (they were tight-lipped in court because they did not want to disclose the full extent of their knowledge). Anna K. admitted the affair but implored the farmers not to denounce her. Yet, Alois K. pointed out that he would be prosecuted and punished if he failed to report her. The special court sentenced her to three years of penal servitude on 28 August 1941; W. received three and a half years in prison. The farming couple was obviously reluctant to denounce Anna K. It was only the finding of new evidence and the fact that the forbidden relationship had become part of the village rumour mill that convinced them a denunciation could not be postponed.[47]

Factory managers also had an interest in protecting their workforce from arrest. One example illustrates the messy context of denunciations and community reactions. In the honey cake factory "König" in Brandenburg in 1941, 50 German women were working alongside French POWs. The management soon noticed that much flirting took place during work. They therefore invited a local party official, who gave a speech to the women reinforcing Nazi propaganda about POWs remaining enemies. The management also separated prisoners and women who were suspiciously close by assigning them to different shifts. Yet, one day a woman worker, a party member, denounced a fellow worker, Leni S., who had allegedly exposed her underwear to the French POWs. This rumour turned out to be unfounded, but when the police searched Leni S., they found love letters from a French POW, revealing an intimate relationship with marriage plans. The woman who had denounced her claimed to speak for the majority of "truly German women," and the police and the judge felt vindicated because the "healthy feeling of the *Volk*" seemed to have worked properly in this case. Yet, they were disappointed to find out that it was the denouncing woman, not Leni S., who became ostracized after the discovery. The judge also severely criticized the factory management for having chosen a soft approach to the forbidden relations.[48]

A few women were publicly shamed after being caught with a French prisoner, but in many cases, they had already been on the margins of local society, often with a reputation for adultery or promiscuity. Here, too, it is hard to evaluate whether it was more the infidelity and promiscuity that prompted outrage, or the fact that the woman had been involved with a foreign POW, although this might have added piquancy to any scandal. It is, however, significant to note that Hitler forbade officials to initiate these shaming procedures because public opinion surveys revealed that they often evoked as much compassion as condemnation and provoked critical comments about double standards, given that German soldiers could freely socialize with western women.[49]

While the discovery of a forbidden relationship often revealed a complex web of solidarity as well as ostracism motivated by a mix of motives, the arrest and conviction of thousands of women involved with POWs had a disruptive impact on German wartime society. Women who had been convicted of having sex with a prisoner were sent to a penitentiary for one to six years, usually far from home. For milder offences, a woman still received twelve to eighteen months in prison. In either case, children were left unattended, older parents had to cope without help, and the shop or farm collapsed. The women's court files therefore often contain thick folders with clemency pleas from relatives. Even many husbands begged the court to release their wife, arguing that they had been forgiven and that the thought of their wife's incarceration was terrible for their fighting morale. Farmers' wives and female farm helpers appeared to be irreplaceable. Even local leaders of the Nazi farmers' league endorsed the clemency pleas and often wrote their own, arguing that the production quotas required all hands on deck. While most women did receive leave from the penitentiary to give birth to the prisoner's child or to help out during the harvest, the authorities always added the leave time to the sentence.

The convicted prisoners disappeared from the community in which they had lived temporarily. Initially, convicted POWs went to Wehrmacht prisons in their region, but in early 1942 the German authorities earmarked the fortress at Graudenz in West Prussia as the default prison for the POWs. Graudenz had a system of branch camps in West Prussia and in the industrial belt of eastern Upper Silesia. French and Belgian POWs sent to the Graudenz complex were treated very harshly in the beginning: violent guards, hard physical labour under partly unhealthful conditions, dark and damp rooms, and, above all, insufficient nutrition. The British and American POWs in Graudenz were generally treated a little better. The Scapini Mission pressed the German authorities to allow camp inspections and deliver aid parcels to the convicted POWs, and conditions started to improve in early 1943, although sporadic abuses occurred right up to the end, including a few killings of prisoners.[50] Thousands of POWs involved with women married to German soldiers entered the penitentiaries from 1943, where they usually occupied separate wings. POW agencies such as the Scapini Mission also insisted on inspections of the penitentiaries and urged the German High Command to concentrate all POWs in one location (the penitentiary Brandenburg-Görden was chosen for French POWs), but the chaos of the last months of the war hampered these efforts.

THE AFTERMATH OF THE INTERNATIONAL WARTIME RELATIONSHIPS

After the war, the relationships between prisoners and German women were largely ignored. The former prisoners declared that they had been punished because of an unruly or rebellious act. This was not strictly untrue, since the relationships had violated orders, but the ex-prisoners typically obscured that their "unruly" acts had consisted of kissing, embracing, or loving a German woman. The women sentenced for forbidden relations either fled in the chaos of the last weeks or were dismissed after the end of the war. Most applied for their convictions to be deleted from the penal registry, usually with success given that convictions based on the prohibition counted as Nazi oppression and were revoked in 1945. Some of the children grew up in foster care, but many women kept the former prisoner's child. While some husbands filed for divorce, many reconciled with their wives, and some accepted the foreign child.

Quite a few women settled down in new communities, although the stigma attached to infidelity and a birth out of wedlock was often difficult to erase. A few women applied for restitution payments as victims of Nazism in the 1950s, pointing out that the penitentiary had damaged their health, but the Federal Republic of Germany rejected their claims on the grounds that they had not been persecuted for what they were but for what they had done and that they had freely engaged in a forbidden relationship. A woman sent to the Ravensbrück concentration camp after a love relationship with a Polish POW (he was hanged, and their child, to whom she gave birth after her arrest, was taken from her and killed) even battled the authorities throughout the 1950s and 1960s without receiving compensation.[51]

The disruptions to communities and gender roles ultimately promoted calls for a return to normalcy. Sarah Fishman has shown in the case of French POW marriages that divorces did briefly increase after the war but that this may be explained by the difficulties of many women to obtain a divorce during their husband's captivity. But the increase in divorces was temporary and remained below wartime expectations.[52] Hester Vaizey has shown a similar trend toward normalcy in her study of German marriages in the war and post-war period.[53] Through their extreme disruptions, the war years created new opportunities for love and erotic adventure and an alternative reality in which women and prisoners of war were able to approach each other on relatively equal terms. But the trials and fearful punishments tore apart even those who wanted to make the alternative reality more permanent by getting married. For many of the prisoners and their German lovers, the war years became a bracket in their biography that was difficult to integrate but easy to forget, at least for the prisoners.

CONCLUSION

This chapter explores the role of love in determining relations between individuals on opposing sides of the Second World War. In this respect, it diverges from much scholarship, including the other chapters in theme 4 that prioritize adversarial behaviours. German officialdom strove strongly to prohibit amorous relationships between German women and Allied POWs. Ostensibly, such attitudes seem to conform to the wartime norm, and were to be expected on the part of combatants and civilians. However, the extent of official anxiety attests strongly to the following three findings: first, relationships between German women and western POWs were relatively common, numbering, at the very least, in the tens of thousands. Such relative ubiquity reflects an important sub-strand of behavioural divergence from nationally mandated policy. Second, within the confines of these relationships, the difference in liberty and status often challenged conventional European gender norms, undermining the notion of male figures as providers, initiators, or controlling figures within both societal and wartime contexts. Rather, relationships often unfolded on more equitable lines, with both parties benefiting from mutual intimacy and support. Finally, the degree of compassion from the community, evidenced through active complicity, passive condonement, or through Hitler's reluctance to allow local officials to chastise "wayward" women lest they secure societal sympathy, serves to show that the narrowly constructed parameters of the "People's War" narrative do not always apply.

NOTES

1 Ulrich Herbert, *Hitler's Foreign Workers: Enforced Foreign Labor in Germany under the Third Reich*, trans. William Templer (Cambridge and New York: Cambridge University Press, 1997), 75–7, 269.
2 Lisa M. Todd, *Sexual Treason in Germany during the First World War*, Genders and Sexualities in History (Cham: Palgrave MacMillan, 2017); George S. Vascik and Mark R. Sadler, eds., *The Stab-in-the-Back Myth and the Fall of the Weimar Republic: A History in Documents and Visual Sources* (London: Bloomsbury, 2016).

3 This formulation comes from many court-martial sentences passed in 1941 and early 1942: Raffael Scheck, "Collaboration of the Heart: The Forbidden Love Affairs of French Prisoners of War and German Women in Nazi Germany," *The Journal of Modern History* 90, no. 2 (2018): 355.
4 Silke Schneider, *Verbotener Umgang. Ausländer und Deutsche im Nationalsozialismus. Diskurse um Sexualität, Moral, Wissen und Strafe* (Baden-Baden: Nomos, 2010), 191.
5 For a sample, see Niedersächsisches Staatsarchiv Oldenburg, Best. 135 B, especially the brochure "Kriegsgefangene" edited by the OKW (High Command) in 1939 and sent to the government of Oldenburg on 13 November 1939, and the pamphlet "Feind bleibt Feind."
6 Dagmar Herzog, "Introduction: War and Sexuality in Europe's Twentieth Century," in *Brutality and Desire: War and Sexuality in Europe's Twentieth Century*, ed. Dagmar Herzog (New York: Palgrave Macmillan, 2009), 11–12; Birthe Kundrus, *Kriegerfrauen. Familienpolitik und Geschlechterverhältnisse im Ersten und Zweiten Weltkrieg*, Hamburger Beiträge zur Sozial- und Zeitgeschichte (Hamburg: Christians, 1995); Birthe Kundrus, "Forbidden Company: Romantic Relationships between Germans and Foreigners, 1939 to 1945," *Journal of the History of Sexuality* 11, nos. 1/2 (2002); Matthias Reiss, *Controlling Sex in Captivity: POWs and Sexual Desire in the United States During the Second World War* (London: Bloomsbury, 2018), 2–6.
7 For all references to the Geneva Convention Relative to the Treatment of Prisoners of War (1929), see Jonathan Vance, ed. *Encyclopedia of Prisoners of War and Internment* (Santa Barbara: ABC-CLIO, 2000), 508–27.
8 Thomas Werther, "Kriegsgefangene vor dem Marburger Militärgericht," in *Militärjustiz im Nationalsozialismus. Das Marburger Militärgericht*, ed. Michael Eberlein (Marburg: Geschichtswerkstatt Marburg, 1994).
9 Penitentiary was a significantly harsher form of detention than prison. It involved forced labour and the loss of civil rights as well as a series of tight restrictions on privileges, such as visits from relatives and correspondence.
10 Reiss, *Controlling Sex in Captivity*, 2; Scheck, "Collaboration of the Heart"; Bob Moore, "Illicit Encounters: Female Civilian Fraternization with Axis Prisoners of War in Second World War Britain," *Journal of Contemporary History* 48, no. 4 (2013).
11 Werther, "Kriegsgefangene"; Freia Anders, *Strafjustiz im Sudetengau 1938–1945*, Veröffentlichungen des Collegium Carolinum (Munich: Oldenbourg, 2008); Peter Lutz Kalmbach, "Das System der

NS-Sondergerichtsbarkeiten," *Kritische Justiz* 50, no. 2 (2017); Karl-Heinz Keldungs, *Das Duisburger Sondergericht 1942–1945*, Forum juristische Zeitgeschichte (Baden-Baden: Nomos-Verlagsgesellschaft, 1998); Gerd Weckbecker, *Zwischen Freispruch und Todesstrafe. Die Rechtsprechung der nationalsozialistischen Sondergerichte Frankfurt/Main und Bromberg* (Baden-Baden: Nomos Verlagsgesellschaft, 1998); Hans Wüllenweber, *Sondergerichte im Dritten Reich. Vergessene Verbrechen der Justiz* (Frankfurt: Luchterhand, 1990).

12 Scheck, "Collaboration of the Heart," 359–60.
13 The most complete collection is in the Archives nationales, Pierrefitte-sur-Seine (AN), série F9.
14 A report of the SS Security Service concluded on 15 November and 13 December 1943 that the French POWs were particularly well liked by German farmers: Heinz Boberach, ed., *Meldungen aus dem Reich 1938–1945: Die geheimen Lageberichte des Sicherheitsdienstes der SS*, vol. 15 (Herrsching: Pawlak, 1984), 6017 and 6141.
15 Jean-Paul Picaper, *Le Crime d'aimer. Les enfants du STO* (Paris: Éditions des syrtes, 2005); Fabrice Virgili, *La France "virile." Des femmes tondues à la Libération* (Paris: Éditions Payot & Rivage, 2004); Fabrice Virgili, *Naître ennemi. Les enfants des couples franco-allemands nés pendant la Seconde Guerre mondiale* (Paris: Editions Payot, 2009); Scheck, "Collaboration of the Heart."
16 There is little work on Belgian POWs in Nazi Germany. For a fine summary, see the series of articles by E. Gillet, "Histoire des sous-officiers et soldats belges prisonniers de guerre, 1940–1945," *Belgisch tijdschrift voor militaire geschiedenis/Revue belge d'histoire militaire* 27, no. 3 (1987).
17 Georges Smets to Mr Georges Paulus, 11 January 1976, in Musée Royal de l'armée, Brussels, Fonds Hautecler, Farde 34.
18 Lt-col Lescrauwaet to Baron de Guben, 21 September 1945, in Archives du Ministère des Affaires étrangères, Bruxelles, Film 408: Dossier général 1942–48. Gillet, "Histoire des sous-officiers et soldats belges prisonniers de guerre, 1940–1945," 362. See also the notes in Musée Royal de l'Armée et d'Histoire Militaire, Evere, Fonds Gillet, box 1, no. 4 affaires juridiques, 301.
19 Simon Paul MacKenzie, *The Colditz Myth: British and Commonwealth Prisoners of War in Nazi Germany* (Oxford and New York: Oxford University Press, 2004), 213–15; Vasilis Vourkoutiotis, *Prisoners of War and the German High Command: The British and American Experience* (New York: Palgrave, 2003), 93; Midge Gillies, *The Barbed-Wire*

University: The Real Lives of Allied Prisoners of War in the Second World War (London: Aurum Press, 2011), 48–9.

20 Schweizerisches Bundesarchiv Bern (CH-BAR), Vertretung Berlin, Dossier Schutzmachtangelegenheiten, vols. 72–88. According to my counting, these files, which are incomplete because of war damages, refer to 452 cases, with 348 coming to trial (32 acquittals). An additional 104 cases were waiting to go to trial at the end of the war.

21 Arieh J. Kochavi, *Confronting Captivity: Britain and the United States and Their POWs in Nazi Germany* (Chapel Hill and London: University of North Carolina Press, 2005).

22 Matthew Stibbe, *Women in the Third Reich* (London: Arnold, 2003), 158; Kundrus, *Kriegerfrauen. Familienpolitik und Geschlechterverhältnisse im Ersten und Zweiten Weltkrieg*, 369–73; Elizabeth D. Heineman, *What Difference Does a Husband Make? Women and Marital Status in Nazi and Postwar Germany* (Berkeley and Los Angeles: University of California Press, 1999), 44 and 54–6; Michael Löffelsender, *Strafjustiz an der Heimatfront. Die strafrechtliche Verfolgung von Frauen und Jugendlichen im Oberlandesgerichtsbezirk Köln 1939–1945*, Beiträge zur Rechtsgeschichte des 20. Jahrhunderts (Tübingen: Mohr Siebeck, 2012), 54–5, 57–8.

23 A typical example is the case of Ida M., Landesarchiv Schleswig-Holstein (LASH), Schleswig, Abt. 358 Staatsanwaltschaft beim Sondergericht Altona/Kiel, vols. 2406–7.

24 Patrice Arnaud, "Die deutsch-französischen Liebesbeziehungen der französischen Zwangsarbeiter und beurlaubten Kriegsgefangenen im, 'Dritten Reich': vom Mythos des verführerischen Franzosen zur Umkehrung der Geschlechterrolle," in *Nationalsozialismus und Geschlecht. Zur Politisierung und Ästhetisierung von Körper, "Rasse" und Sexualität im "Dritten Reich" und nach 1945*, ed. Elke Frietsch and Christina Herkommer (Bielefeld: transcript Verlag, 2009); Cornelie Usborne, "Female Sexual Desire and Male Honor: German Women's Illicit Love Affairs with Prisoners of War during the Second World War," *Journal of the History of Sexuality* 26, no. 3 (2017): 486–7.

25 Schneider, *Verbotener Umgang*, 219.

26 Mark Spoerer, "Die soziale Differenzierung der ausländischen Zivilarbeiter, Kriegsgefangenen und Häftlinge im Deutschen Reich," in *Das Deutsche Reich und der Zweite Weltkrieg*, ed. Jörg Echternkamp (Munich: Deutsche Verlags-Anstalt, 2005).

27 Bayerisches Staatsarchiv (BStA) Nürnberg, Akten der Staatsanwaltschaft beim Sondergericht, vol. 1528.

28 This transpired for example in the case of Roger T.: Feldurteil, Baden-Baden, 20 September 1941, in Politisches Archiv des Auswärtigen Amtes (PAAA), R 40883.
29 Feldurteil, Graudenz, 1 April 1944, in AN, F9, 3644. See also Usborne, "Female Sexual Desire and Male Honor," 477–8, 486.
30 "Ich habe mich deshalb mit dem Franzosen P. auf einen Geschlechtsverkehr eingelassen, weil ich sehr vollblütig bin und bereits seit 16 Monaten keine geschlechtliche Befriedigung mehr fand." BStA Nürnberg, Sondergericht, vol. 2046.
31 Judgment, Sondergericht Darmstadt, 23 May 1944, in Hessisches Staatsarchiv Darmstadt (HStAD), Fonds G 24, Nr. 955/2: "Bekanntgabe von Urteilen wegen Umgangs mit Kriegsgefangenen an die Gauleitungen."
32 Case file Else B., Hessisches Hauptstaatsarchiv Wiesbaden, Abt. 461 Nr. 9869.
33 BStA Nürnberg, Sondergericht, vols. 1455 and 1716.
34 Feldurteil, Gericht der Kommandantur der Befestigungen Ostpreußen, Königsberg, 14 September 1942, in CEGESOMA, Brussels, AA 244.
35 Feldurteil, Danzig, 10 August 1944, in CH-BAR, Vertretung Berlin, Schutzmachtangelegenheiten, 78a.
36 Case of Käthe P., BStA Nürnberg, Sondergericht, vol. 1278.
37 LASH, Abt. 358, vol. 6111.
38 Feldurteil, Linz, 9 September 1941, in PAAA, R 40884.
39 Feldurteil, Nürnberg, 6 January 1942, in PAAA, R 40905, and BStA Nürnberg, Sondergericht, vol. 1196.
40 Feldurteil, Danzig, 11 May 1943, and Dr. Marx to Schweizerische Gesandtschaft, 11 May 1943, both in CH-BAR, Vertretung Berlin, Schutzmachtangelegenheiten, 86b.
41 Feldurteil, Kassel, 22 January 1942, in PAAA, R 40909.
42 Nikolaus Wachsmann, *Hitler's Prisons: Legal Terror in Nazi Germany* (New Haven and London: Yale University Press, 2004), 2.
43 Arnaud, "Die deutsch-französischen Liebesbeziehungen," 187–8. Arnaud mentions that former prisoners and forced labourers described the sexual encounters in quite aggressive form, similar to imagined rapes. This helped restore their self-esteem and to justify them in French postwar society, in which the former prisoners were often seen as losers and even collaborators.
44 Although Nazi authorities generally agreed on the desirability of harder sanctions against relations with soldier's wives, this remained difficult to implement. German men engaging in a relationship with a soldier's wife could only be sued for offending the husband, and the punishments were light.

45 Hinrich Rüping, "Denunziation und Strafjustiz im Führerstaat," in *Denunziation. Historische, juristische und psychologische Aspekte*, ed. Günter Jerouschek, Inge Marßolek, and Hedwig Röckelein, *Forum Psychohistorie* (Tübingen: Edition discord, 1997), 129; Scheck, "Collaboration of the Heart," 36. For an example, see the case of Gilbert M., Feldurteil, Linz, 28 November 1941, in PAAA, R 40904.
46 Feldurteil, Stettin, 17 October 1941, in PAAA, R 40894.
47 BStA Nürnberg, Sondergericht, vol. 1206, and Feldurteil, Nürnberg, 20 November 1941, in PAAA, R 40887.
48 Brandenburgisches Landeshauptarchiv Potsdam, Staatsanwaltschaft 12C Berlin II, vol. 6845. There were many other cases of multiple relationships in factories.
49 See, for example: *Feldurteil* against Armand Le G., Frankfurt, 24 October 1941, in PAAA, R 40890, and the case of Louise B., in Hessisches Hauptstaatsarchiv Wiesbaden, Abt. 461 Nr. 8285. See also Fabrice Virgili, *Shorn Women: Gender and Punishment in Liberation France*, trans. John Flower (Oxford and New York: Berg, 2002), 261–2 and 269–76; Kundrus, *Kriegerfrauen*, 383.
50 AN, F9, 2721.
51 See the case of Sabine B., Hessisches Hauptstaatsarchiv Wiesbaden, Abt. 518 Nr. 4061.
52 Sarah Fishman, *We Will Wait: Wives of French Prisoners of War, 1940–1945* (New Haven and London: Yale University Press, 1991).
53 Hester Vaizey, *Surviving Hitler's War: Family Life in Germany 1939–1948* (New York: Palgrave Macmillan, 2010).

THEME FIVE

The History and Memory of "People's Wars"

14

Framing Myths of the Second World War through Ministry of Information Propaganda Posters

Katherine Howells

Myths dominate British cultural memory of the Second World War, and they are formed and communicated through the circulation and consumption of media. Three core myths – the "People's War," the "Blitz Spirit," and the "Dunkirk Spirit" – are especially influential in British media and prevalent in the national cultural memory of the Second World War. Their establishment and perpetuation rests both on how they are encoded into media and how that media is received by audiences. These audiences act to reconcile the media they consume with their own existing unique set of memories and accept, adapt, or reject the mythic narratives they interpret from the media. These productive relationships between media, myth, and memory are fundamental to any understanding of how myths about the past develop and persist in culture, becoming touchstones for numerous aspects of contemporary society, from business to politics.

Because the Second World War occupies such an influential place in British cultural memory, it provides an instructive example of how myths interact with media and memory. This chapter investigates relationships between memory and myth and a case study of Second World War media in the form of famous wartime propaganda posters produced by the Ministry of Information (MoI), drawing important conclusions about how these relationships function. It also explores how cultural memory and historical myths can be effectively investigated using social research methods, methods that so far have been largely overlooked for these areas of study. By doing so, it demonstrates that these posters operate as part of a cultural circuit, with individuals interpreting them, imbuing them with meaning, and using them to perpetuate or contest mythic narratives and define identities. This productive collaborative relationship between media and people can best be explored by employing social research methods that focus on the response of the individual.

Memory is not a direct reflection of the past, but it is constructed in the present, as many authors have argued, including Maurice Halbwachs, Lucy Noakes, Juliette Pattinson, and Ann Rigney.[1] Its construction thus relies on a collection of influences, which are unique to each individual, but which often include cultural media that in many cases perpetuate mythic narratives. The concept of "cultural memory," as defined by Noakes, Pattinson, and Rigney, takes these cultural influences into account. Cultural memory of the Second World War has been heavily influenced by strong mythic narratives that tie into concepts of British identity and so has become a powerful tool for those wishing to influence the British people. Politicians have leveraged the Second World War myths to justify certain actions and promote the idea of British exceptionalism.[2] This demonstrates that memory of the Second World War is not a passive remnant of past events, but an active force in modern society. Studying how it operates is therefore vital to understanding its power. This study is important because it contributes to our understanding of these areas and does so by using innovative social research methods that focus on the interactions between media and individual people.

The MoI was established in 1939 at the outbreak of war to inform and influence the British public and improve morale, as well as produce propaganda materials for the populations of allied and enemy countries. The Ministry produced a vast quantity of material to support Home Front objectives, including posters, pamphlets, film, radio, and exhibitions.[3] The seeds of myths were planted in these propaganda materials, influencing the development of cultural memory in the 1940s and beyond, as they are still being reproduced and influence cultural memory today. This process was also buttressed to some extent by the actions of American journalists, as discussed in Sean Dettman's chapter.

This chapter focuses on case studies of famous propaganda posters produced by the MoI. It questions why some posters are well known today and others are not, and how the popularity of an image continues to influence memory and perpetuate myths of the conflict. The reasons for this are complex and depend on how the posters have been used in the decades since their creation. Some posters have been reproduced in books, magazines, and marketing material and displayed in schools, on television, and in exhibitions. They have been used as designs for products and are also reproduced in multiple versions on the internet. Some posters have been reused relatively consistently over the years since the Second World War; the reuse of others, *Keep Calm and Carry On* in particular, has only intensified in the first two decades of the twenty-first century. The reuse of these images in recent years clearly links closely to increasing enthusiasm for nostalgia both on the part of consumers and marketing professionals, and the ongoing concept of the "People's War."

To better explore the relationships between media, cultural memory, and myth, this chapter focuses on a small set of MoI propaganda posters that are well known today: *Dig for Victory* (figure 14.1), *Go Through Your Wardrobe* (figure 14.2), *Keep Calm and Carry On* (figure 14.3) and *Women of Britain Come into the Factories* (figure 14.4). The arguments made in this chapter derive from the results of survey and interview research conducted with members of the British public. The research reveals that while propaganda posters do communicate cultural myths of the Second World War, individuals' reception of these myths is complex. Viewing visual media helps individuals to formulate their own personal cultural memory of the Second World War and situate it within a national shared memory.

Social research methods such as surveys and interviews make it possible to examine directly the self-reported thought processes, thoughts, and feelings that take place when an individual person looks at an image. Using these methods to investigate cultural memory and the development of historical myths is an original approach, since most studies in this area focus on interrogating the media itself rather than individuals' reception of media. It is important to employ these methods to avoid making uninformed assumptions about the collective reception of media. The main objective of this research was to identify how people use MoI images to develop their cultural memory of the Second World War and acknowledge, reinforce, and subvert the dominant myths of the war experience.[4] The survey, circulated online and in print in the spring of 2017, presented five MoI posters alongside open questions asking participants whether they recognized the image, what thoughts came to mind when they looked at it, and how far they considered it to be well known or memorable.[5] In total, 301 surveys were completed.[6] Following analysis of the survey data, 16 volunteers were recruited from those who completed a survey to take part in a one-to-one follow-up interview.[7] Each interviewee was shown 10 posters[8] and asked in-depth questions about their memories of the image, the thoughts that came to mind when viewing it, and any concepts and emotions associated with it. While interview data was collected relating to 10 images, this chapter focuses in depth on four, the responses to which exhibit the most interesting aspects of cultural memory.[9]

UNDERSTANDING CULTURAL MEMORY AND MYTH

Cultural memory is an important concept for fully understanding the phenomena observed in the survey and interview responses, because it is a broad definition of memory that takes into account the effect of media, the memory of events not experienced by the individual, and the role of identity. Cultural memory is a term developed out of other similar definitions of memory: collective memory, popular memory, public memory, mediated memory, postmemory etc.; which also attempt to come to terms with influences beyond individual psychological memory. The first of these concepts is "collective memory," proposed by Maurice Halbwachs in 1925, which conceives of remembering as a process fundamentally structured by the social group.[10]

Many newer memory concepts have been developed from or in reaction to Halbwachs's concept. Jan Assmann refers to cultural memory as one of two sub-concepts of collective memory, the other being communicative memory (social), which are entirely distinct from individual memory.[11] To Assmann, cultural memory is a form of "stable and situation-transcendent" semantic memory that is stored in symbols, objects, and institutions.[12] Lucy Noakes and Juliette Pattinson present a less rigid definition of cultural memory in their book *British Cultural Memory and the Second World War*. They argue that cultural memory is the product of the amalgamation of different kinds of memory (including Assmann's individual, communicative, and cultural memory), which interact freely and influence one another in a "cultural circuit."[13] Ann Rigney presents a concept of cultural memory with a similar focus and argues that this memory is communicated through cultural artefacts and media and is "collectively constructed and reconstructed in the present."[14] The concept of cultural memory considered in this chapter is influenced by the ideas of Rigney, Noakes, and Pattinson; it is constituted from multiple memories, some communicated through objects and media.

By recognizing the importance of the communication of memory between people through objects and media, it is accepted that cultural memory can be transferred across generations to those without any direct personal memory of an event. The factor that underpins the significance of cultural memory is not its relation to direct experience but its relevance to identity. This is supported by Assmann, who argues that "cultural memory reaches back into the past only as far as the past can be reclaimed as 'ours'."[15] A similar argument is made by Barry Schwartz, who suggests that "we cannot, in truth, be oriented by a past in which we fail to see ourselves."[16] Cultural memory plays a key role in the development of personal and collective identities and is itself shaped by these identities. The strong link between cultural memory and identity informs discussion of the results of the research presented in this chapter.

One important concept for discussion of cultural memory is myth. Myths are narratives or perceptions of the past that influence cultural memory, are transmitted and perpetuated through the exchange of cultural artefacts and media, and often help to unite people who believe in them around a collective identity. Myths of the Second World War, and in particular those that relate to the British experience of the war, have been explored in some depth by historians and can be closely associated with the development of British national identity. "The Blitz Spirit" refers to a mythic narrative about the character of British people, exhibited by their behaviour during the Blitz. It refers to characteristics of community spirit, endurance, and positivity in the face of aerial bombing. Lucy Noakes and Juliette Pattinson describe how it has become a "rhetorical device, shorthand for wartime unity and stoicism."[17] It has been appropriated to refer to the pinnacle of the British character as being one of solidarity and stoicism in the face of adversity.

The "Dunkirk Spirit" is another mythic narrative that shares characteristics with the "Blitz Spirit." It refers to the spirit of courage and determination shown by British soldiers and the British volunteers who rescued them from the beaches of Dunkirk in 1940. By extension, the myth of the "Dunkirk Spirit" is applied to Britain in general, as a nation that possesses the spirit to fight on against all odds. Mark Connelly has argued that the underlying myth of the British character and experience, "standing alone, fighting weird, wonderful and incomprehensible foreigners of all sorts against great odds," had existed for many years before the Second World War, and Dunkirk was just the latest historical event to be imbued with these national concepts.[18] Both of these myths rest upon the concept of high morale, incorporating the concept of stoicism and solidarity, as well as positivity, courage, and strength. The two myths are appropriated for modern purposes, again to show British national identity in a positive light, and to present modern hardships in light of the Second World War experience.[19]

The myth of the "People's War" conceptualizes the Second World War in Britain as a war that involved everybody, including ordinary people on the Home Front, working together to achieve victory. It encourages an egalitarian view of wartime Britain as an era of camaraderie and solidarity, which heralded a democratic revolution welcoming greater social equality and political participation. The myth was popularized even during the war, notably by Winston Churchill, to secure civilian cooperation.[20] Geoff Eley highlights its association with ideas of common sacrifice, egalitarianism, and the victory of democracy over fascism that framed the "People's War" as a "narrative of popular democratic accomplishment."[21] Some of the historical assumptions at the root of the myth have been debunked, most notably by Angus Calder in 1969,[22] and others have commented on the absence of some groups, such as women, children, and ethnic minorities, from commemorations of the Second World War and discussion of the "People's War" as a concept. Lucy Noakes, for example, highlights how the sacrifice of women and children has often been ignored in official commemorations.[23] Sonya O. Rose has discussed how portrayals of British national identity during the Second World War underplayed the effect of class and gender difference to promote unity.[24] Despite its complexity, the myth still persists in the popular imagination.[25] The phrase is commonly used today as a shorthand for the role of ordinary people during the Second World War.

Individuals shape their cultural memory by drawing on a variety of different media,[26] and media often communicate those myths of the Second World War outlined above. The consequence of this is that these myths can occupy powerful roles in the cultural memory of many people. The importance of media in the development of cultural memory is highlighted by Mark Connelly, who argues that the state of public memory of the Second World War, and thus the mythic narratives that exist within it, can be ascertained by looking at the "sheer homogeneity of its popular culture artefacts."[27] He also suggests that this public memory is strongly influenced by the myths outlined above, including those relating to the Blitz and Dunkirk, which actively help to unite people around a collective sense of identity.[28] People shape their cultural memory by drawing on media and myths of the Second World War, which in turn assist them in defining their identity as part of a group.

These historians have described how media may communicate myths of the Second World War, increasing the influence of myths in people's cultural memory and affecting their sense of identity. However, this chapter differs from previous research in that it focuses on assessing individuals' perception of a small set of cultural artefacts, rather than surveying a larger cultural landscape and assuming a certain kind of collective perception. This ensures that conclusions are drawn from direct evidence of perception, taking into account the breadth of individual experience, and thus avoids making uninformed assumptions about perception based only on the existence of certain cultural artefacts.

THE INFLUENCE OF MYTH IN CULTURAL MEMORY OF THE SECOND WORLD WAR

While other authors have previously established that myths can be dominant forces in the development of cultural memory, the results of this research reveal the level of influence of myths in the memory of individuals and show how these individuals use images to help them make sense of those myths. The dominance of the national myths of the "Dunkirk Spirit," the "Blitz Spirit," and the "People's War" is demonstrated by the fact that they draw on a shared vocabulary relating to these myths to make sense of the MoI images they are looking at. Participants often interpret the images with reference to the concepts of solidarity and stoicism, which are integral to the three mythic narratives referred to above. Participants also spontaneously refer directly to the myths themselves when discussing the images, indicating the role of the mythic phrases as "rhetorical devices" and "shorthand" in a shared vocabulary.[29]

Figure 14.1 "Dig for Victory," 1941. © Imperial War Museum, IWM PST 0059.

In 1939, in reaction to Germany's blockade on British shipping, the MoI devised a campaign to encourage domestic food production and self-sufficiency.[30] The slogan "Dig for Victory" was created for the campaign and used in a variety of propaganda material, in print, on film and on the radio. One of the most famous posters for this campaign, produced in 1941, depicted a photograph of a boot pushing down a spade set into a red background with the "Dig for Victory" slogan in white lettering (figure 14.1).[31]

The dominance of the "Blitz Spirit" and "People's War" myths in the minds of participants is demonstrated through their frequent references to the concept of solidarity when discussing *Dig for Victory*. The concept of solidarity is a fundamental part of these myths, because it frames a story of British people supporting one another and working together for the common good. In explaining their interpretation of the *Dig for Victory* image, participants[32] refer to members of the wartime generation working hard in a community effort to achieve victory, promoting the idea that British people all "mucked in" together in the fight against Nazism.[33] Participants say that the image "taps into,"[34] "evokes,"[35] and "typifies"[36] the feelings of solidarity associated with the "Blitz Spirit" and "People's War" myths. One participant describes the poster as evoking an "idea of country coming together in a common purpose,"[37] while another explains that "we were all in it together" and "everyone had a role to play in the war effort,"[38] referring to an idea of camaraderie and collective cooperation that underlies the mythic narratives of the "Blitz Spirit" and "People's War."

In the case of *Dig for Victory*, the poster itself is so simple, with only the phrase "Dig for Victory," the background colour and the photograph of the boot and spade potentially signifying meaning, that it is clear that these interpretations of the image draw on a wide range of other memories and knowledge possessed by the participants. The myths of the "Blitz Spirit" and "People's War" are included within the participants' memory and knowledge, so that they are able to draw on elements of the myths to form their interpretation of the images.

In reaction to textile shortages, the MoI and the Board of Trade created a campaign called "Make-do and Mend" to ease the introduction of clothes rationing in 1941. Donia Nachshen, who designed a variety of MoI images, produced one poster with the slogan "Go Through Your Wardrobe" to encourage women to be more economical with their clothing (figure 14.2).

Figure 14.2 "Go Through Your Wardrobe," 1942. © Imperial War Museum, IWM PST 4773.

Go Through Your Wardrobe was also interpreted in a similar way to *Dig for Victory*. Survey participants refer to ideas of ordinary people "doing their bit,"[39] "doing what they can," and "working together for the common good,"[40] linking closely to concepts of solidarity and hard work in the pursuit of victory and the myth of the "People's War" and the "Blitz Spirit." Again, these concepts are already part of the cultural memory of participants and the poster encourages them to be drawn out, strengthening the myths in the process. Responses to these two posters support understandings of cultural memory, put forward by Noakes, Pattinson, and Rigney, suggesting that people draw on multiple cultural artefacts and media, which often communicate mythic narratives, to form their own cultural memory.[41] They also demonstrate that an encounter between an individual and an MoI poster is a constructive interaction that builds upon their cultural memory while at the same time perpetuating an already understood myth.

The first three posters the MoI produced were described as the "red posters" and included the now-ubiquitous image *Keep Calm and Carry On*. The other two designs were similar but instead displayed the slogans "Your courage, your cheerfulness, your resolution will bring us victory" and "Freedom is in Peril. Defend it with all your Might." A survey was conducted on the reception of these two posters in 1939, which suggested that they were generally disliked by the British people, some of whom interpreted the slogans as condescending and paternalistic.[42] The results of this survey led to the decision not to display *Keep Calm and Carry On*,[43] and many of the remaining copies were pulped.[44]

Participants' responses to *Keep Calm and Carry On* present the clearest examples of how they interpreted stoicism, a fundamental concept to the myths of the "Blitz Spirit" and the "Dunkirk Spirit." These myths are linked closely to perceptions of the British national character exhibiting stoicism and determination in the face of danger and hardship. One survey participant writes of "calmness and stoicism and courage in hard times"[45] and another reports that "my thoughts are of stoicism, that is what "we Brits" did and it just served as a reminder to carry on as normal. Something that I felt the people were proud to do."[46] This is the main way that *Keep Calm and Carry On* is interpreted by participants. References to the Blitz are most commonly made in direct response to *Keep Calm and Carry On*, one participant stating that "it seems to sum up the British wartime spirit of trying to ignore the Blitz and continue with normal life."[47] This

Figure 14.3 "Keep Calm and Carry On," 1939. The National Archives, EXT 1/116 (3).

indicates a close association between this image and the myth of the "Blitz Spirit." Like the *Make-do and Mend* example mentioned previously, the idea of "carrying on" and not complaining despite great suffering and danger is seen by participants as an admirable national trait embodied by *Keep Calm and Carry On,* just as it is embodied by the "Blitz Spirit" and the "Dunkirk Spirit." The poster is imbued with meaning derived from existing cultural memory and at the same time contributes to this cultural memory, increasing the influence of the mythic narratives mentioned.

The clearest evidence for the power of Second World War myths in the cultural memory of individuals is their spontaneous direct references to the myths in their responses to the images. In response to *Dig for Victory,* one participant explains, "I believe this image is widely known because it encapsulates the Blitz Spirit which has been romanticised by popular culture."[48] Another describes *Go Through Your Wardrobe* as having "Very 'spirit of the blitz' connotations."[49] In referring directly to the "Blitz Spirit," they indicate how the myth phrases function as elements of a shared vocabulary of British cultural memory. Participants did not feel the need to explain the meaning of the phrase or their particular use of it, but rather used it as a meaningful symbol, assuming the reader shared that level of understanding. The role of myths as linguistic elements of a shared vocabulary is supported by Noakes and Pattinson in their description of the "Blitz Spirit" myth.[50]

BELIEF AND DISBELIEF IN SECOND WORLD WAR MYTHS

When viewing MoI images, many participants take the opportunity to express their active agreement with the Second World War myths expressed above. Not only are these myths dominant aspects of cultural memory that are seized upon as convenient communicators of meaning, but they are often believed by participants. In response to *Dig for Victory*, one participant states that "we were all in it together and everyone had a role to play in the war effort,"[51] indicating total agreement with that perception of the nature of the British Home Front. Another states that the poster reminds him "of the community spirit that seemed to pervade everything during the war,"[52] giving the impression that he may have experienced this community spirit during the war, despite the fact that he was born in 1943. The participant's statement demonstrates his certainty that the myths of the Second World War were true. This shows how cultural memory is influenced far more by media than by direct experience and indicates how the poster can help to reinforce an existing cultural memory and even give credibility to a myth.

In the example below, by viewing *Dig for Victory* the interview participant's mind is drawn toward ideas associated with the "Blitz Spirit" and "People's War" myths, ideas of "working together" with a "sense of community." She demonstrates her agreement with the interpretation of the Second World War home front encompassed by these myths, suggesting that people were united in opposition to an external threat; the fight against the Nazis provided "something to get behind":

> It makes you feel a little bit, you know, that whole thing about the sense of community, everybody, you know, that that represents, that idea of World War Two, so you know that is that, everybody was working together and you know actually after the blackout a lot of awful things happened, but that that represents I suppose we're all at war, but it represents, you know compared with what we're all like at the moment, where everybody's tense and angry with each other, that feels a little bit more like we were all a bit more, you know, there was something to get behind, that sort of thing. So maybe it feels a little bit of a simpler time, even though there was a massive struggle for survival going on. If that's not too controversial.[53]

Most significantly, this example demonstrates the importance of nostalgia to the myth, as the participant compares her positive perception of the Second World War experience to "what we're all like at the moment," concluding that the war period was a "simpler time." This demonstrates the power of the myth in the cultural memory of individuals, and at the same time shows how the development of nostalgia can be a reaction to interpretations of present circumstances.[54] Belief in the myth is strengthened by comparison to the modern experiences of the participant.

The quotation also demonstrates a degree of complexity to the interpretation of the myth. The participant supports the mythical interpretation, but also expresses some ambivalence, questioning the interpretation even as she makes it, by saying "you know actually after the blackout a lot of awful things happened." This demonstrates the importance of not assuming that mythic narratives are always accepted unquestioningly by people. Mythic narratives present in media do not necessarily reflect the cultural memory of individuals, which is often more nuanced and reflective. This observation supports the idea that it is vital to analyze the perception of these cultural artefacts and the responses of real people to understand cultural memory. The importance of studying perception has been noted by Jean R. Freedman, who argues that "popular ideas are often assumed to be equivalent to the representations created by popular culture, governmental directives, and wartime propaganda," when, in reality, interpretation is often mixed and must be analyzed in detail.[55]

While participants usually recognize the existence of the dominant myths of the "Blitz Spirit," the "Dunkirk Spirit," and the "People's

War," they sometimes disagree with these interpretations. There is a distinct element of scepticism running through the survey and interview responses as people communicate their opinions in reaction to what they perceive to be the dominant narrative. This again highlights the need to study personal responses to cultural artefacts directly instead of assuming that dominant myths are accepted and agreed upon.

Dig for Victory is, in general, interpreted in a way that corresponds with the narratives of the "Blitz Spirit" and the "People's War." However, some participants express discomfort with this interpretation. When viewing *Dig for Victory,* one participant discusses the concept of solidarity, stating that the poster encourages people to "pull together," and they recognize that this concept successfully encourages feelings of patriotism, but they make clear that rationally they find this interpretation of the image "an uncomfortable thing."[56]

Participants in the survey demonstrate their cynicism about the dominant Second World War myths they interpret from *Dig for Victory* and *Keep Calm and Carry On.* They describe the myths as "romanticised" and "sentimentalised," juxtapose them with serious contemporary societal problems and question their veracity. One participant expresses "irritation," "boredom," and "frustration" at the images and criticizes the sentimental obsession with the "Dunkirk Spirit" myth "at a time when we are experiencing a real international crisis around refugees and Brexit and so much more."[57] One participant argues that the images encapsulate "the Blitz Spirit which has been romanticized by popular culture,"[58] another complains that the British "sentimentalise" the "Dunkirk Spirit" instead of dealing with a "real international crisis."[59] One participant indirectly refers to the 2008 financial crisis as a cause of the popularity of these images and myths, suggesting that the images capture a sense of the "'Blitz spirit' that appealed to national sensibilities following 2008."[60] Another participant questions the existence of a "Blitz Spirit" during the war, referring to it as "so-called" and asking "was there really one?"[61]

These examples demonstrate the subtle responses people have to images, which require in-depth interviewing to be fully revealed. People interpret historical images through the lenses of contemporary concerns, their own personal beliefs, and the memories and historical knowledge that make up their complex cultural memory. They may interpret an image in light of a dominant myth and even refer to the myth to communicate their interpretation, but this does not necessarily mean that they believe the myth. Myths can be a part of cultural memory even when they are questioned and treated with scepticism. This may relate to Svetlana Boym's concept of "reflective nostalgia" a kind of nostalgia in which a person dwells on the mixed feelings they experience when considering the past, cultural memory, and myth.[62] People can experience nostalgia about a mythic past, while at the same time questioning it and expressing discomfort with the emotions it generates. This demonstrates how complex and highly personal the interaction between posters and the cultural memory of individuals is.

DEFINING IDENTITIES THROUGH IMAGE AND MYTH

Participants actively use the MoI images to define their own personal identities, whether related to nation, gender, or class, by interpreting the images in light of the concepts fundamental to national myths of the Second World War.

National Identity

The examples above have already indicated how participants define the British people as possessing the idealized characteristics of solidarity and stoicism implied by the myths of the Second World War. They also identify themselves as belonging to this group. Many responses to the images include first person pronouns and specifically references to "me," "myself," "our," and "ourselves" to demonstrate the participant's identification with the concepts being discussed. In the example below, an interview participant talks about the stoicism of the British people, interpreted from *Keep Calm and Carry On* and associated with the "Blitz Spirit" myth. In the course of her response, she moves from talking about the British people as "they" to referring to "we," "ourselves," and "us," defining herself as part of the British community:

> The idea of "carry on" to me really suggests that that's the Blitz Spirit. It's that people in Britain whatever happens, they just carry on. It's the kind of stiff upper lip as well. It's like even if the bombs are falling, even if everything is a disaster, you just keep calm and carry on. That's what you do if you're British.[63]

Survey participants use similar language in response to *Keep Calm and Carry On* to define national identity. One describes how "it has totally embedded into our collective psyche. I think British people would see this as actually summing up what we think we are good at – facing challenges and being brave when needed,"[64] while another argues that "now it is seen as 'Britishness' in a phrase. We are all proud of it and want to say 'this is us'."[65]

Another example from the interviews demonstrates the complexity of defining national identity when viewing and responding to *Dig for Victory*. The participant discusses the concept of solidarity in the face of hardship, a positive trait they associate with British national identity, and feels a sense of patriotism. At the same time, however, this feeling causes them discomfort due to nationalistic connotations, and they feel it is important to clarify their sense of national identity.

It makes me feel like, yeah, yeah, yeah, pull together – and that's slightly uncomfortable, in the sense of – in terms of nationalism, yeah, yeah, pull together, we will defeat enemies – that is slightly uncomfortable, now– it makes me feel like patriotic and that has a double edged sword, now, that's a very, that's an uncomfortable thing I think currently and I wouldn't have felt that years ago – but at the same time it's like this is part of my history, I'm English, I'm British, English, and this is part of my heritage.[66]

The participant expresses doubt as they attempt to identify themselves as English, and then British and then English again. They define their national identity both in accordance with the interpreted national myth but at the same time with ambivalence about it. This again demonstrates the importance of studying responses to cultural artefacts directly, to avoid making assumptions about the cultural memory and identity that those artefacts "reflect." It also supports the argument that, when people encounter media, they reflect upon their existing cultural memory and reassess their identity in a productive personal interaction.

Gender and Class

One feature of the myth of the "People's War" has been that the Second World War in Britain was total war, involving everybody, including men and women and the working, middle, and upper classes.[67] This emphasis placed on inclusivity in the myth masks real gender, class, and racial divisions, which have been remarked upon by historians.[68] This therefore raises interesting questions about how people reconcile the myth with their own gender and class identities. As people consider the complex "People's War" myth in the context of their own cultural memory and identity, they are inevitably encouraged to consider which people are included in the "People's War." When viewing the MoI images, participants spontaneously comment on gender and class issues.

The recruitment of men and women for war-related occupations was always a key objective for the British government and thus the MoI. In December 1941, the *National Service Act* was passed into law, requiring unmarried women under the age of thirty to join the armed services or enter war production.[69] This led the MoI to expand its female-focused propaganda material to support recruitment efforts and produce posters that depicted women in stronger, more traditionally masculine roles. One of these was *Women of Britain Come into the Factories* (figure 14.4), designed by *Daily Mirror* cartoonist Philip Zec in 1941,[70] which presented a positive image of a woman working in a factory.

One idea that links closely with the myth of the "People's War" is the idea of women's empowerment. Participants refer to this idea when they view certain images depicting women, explaining that they believe the Second World War was a time of great progress for the role of women in society. When participants in the interviews look at the poster *Women of Britain Come into the Factories*, they interpret it as an empowering image, symbolizing the achievements of women in the period. This is particularly noticeable for female participants, who sometimes explain that they personally identify with the woman in the image. One interview participant responds by saying "it feels like a real image and it feels like a very powerful gesture that this woman was making and I feel like I really identify with the woman because she just seems a really strong woman."[71] Another participant uses the term "us" to define her shared identity with strong empowered women:

> Women – sort of like empowerment and a sense of their liberation and I know that's not what that is meant to symbolise, I know she's looking more towards the men who are going to war, but that kind of image, it kind of signifies like a sort of sense of us finally, as women, moving forward a bit, breaking the traditional roles and breaking some boundaries.[72]

Figure 14.4 "Women of Britain Come into the Factories," 1941.
© Imperial War Museum, IWM PST 3645.

In another example, a participant comments on the image as not being "pretty" or "feminine" and describing the female figure as "prole," "solid," and "useful." She also states that "that's what draws me in and endears this image to me."[73] This demonstrates the participant's identification with working-class and progressive gender identity and shows how an interaction with the poster enables this identification to be realized and communicated.

Unlike *Women of Britain*, which corresponds to participants' already-formed narrative of Second World War empowerment, *Go Through Your Wardrobe* undermines this narrative by casting the woman in a traditional role. Many participants refer to the image as "sexist" and question the role of the woman presented.[74] One participant states "again – sexist. No man in the picture, yet there is a pair of men's trousers ready for the woman to fix,"[75] while another questions "why is it her responsibility to look after his clothes?"[76] The image is received negatively because it presents a different vision of the role of women during the war that does not correspond to the positive vision of female empowerment that exists in many people's cultural memory. This demonstrates how participants draw on a variety of different kinds of memory to form their cultural memory, as indicated by Noakes, Pattinson, and Rigney,[77] and suggests that when these memories and interpretations are in conflict, a sense of cognitive dissonance can arise. Trying to reconstruct their cultural memory and identity from different conflicting influences can cause confusion and dissatisfaction, and this is an important facet of an individual's personal interaction with media.

Class is another issue on which participants comment in response to the MoI posters. Again, some of the images fit closely into participants' vision of a "People's War," which emphasizes egalitarianism and the role of the working class.[78] Some participants interpret a class message from *Dig for Victory*, suggesting that it is a working-class image and associating it with socialism and the Labour movement. One interview participant interprets this from the red colour in the image, suggesting that "I suppose red is striking, it's [sic] – tends to be an aggressive colour, it's a Labour colour, maybe there's a Labour sort of message in that. It's not aimed I suppose at the gentry."[79] Another makes the same interpretation of the image of the boot, stating that it represents "the working class."[80] In talking about members of their own family in relation to *Dig for Victory*, participants position them as members of a group of "ordinary people" who participated in the "People's War" and toward whom *Dig for Victory* is aimed. In doing this, they attempt to specify their own class identities in connection with the "People's War" myth.

Other MoI images provoke reactions from participants again because they subvert the expected narrative of "ordinary people" participating in the "People's War" in an atmosphere of equality. *Go Through Your Wardrobe* sometimes provokes comment on the issue of class, due to the perceived quality and fashion of the clothes depicted. One participant compares the "beautiful wardrobe," which she believes to be the clothes of somebody "quite well to do," with her mother's clothes, which she believes were not as high-quality, stating "I doubt if my mother's wardrobe had anything looking like that in it."[81]

In making this comparison, the participant defines her own class identity in contrast to her perception of an upper-class target audience. Other participants comment on the fact that working-class people were already making do and mending out of necessity and did not need to be directed by the government to do so. One participant is irritated by the class implications, stating that they find it "patronising" because "most working class people had to do this anyway."[82] These examples demonstrate the capacity of cultural artefacts and the myths they carry to divide people as well as unite them. An interaction with an MoI poster enables an individual to draw on various influences in their life to construct their cultural memory and sense of identity both in accordance with, or in reaction to, the meaning they interpret from that poster. This experience is highly personal and can elicit positive or negative emotional reactions, but at the same time it is constructive because it further develops the individual's cultural memory.

CONCLUSION

MoI posters have a continuing role in popular British cultural memory of the war that has been underappreciated to date. For some people, the posters have been imbued with memories of all kinds, from personal and family memories to wider cultural and historical knowledge. The posters therefore function as media that influence the construction of cultural memory. In doing so, they communicate and perpetuate myths of the Second World War.

Survey and interview participants associate the MoI images with concepts of stoicism and solidarity, necessary elements of the "People's War," "Dunkirk Spirit," and "Blitz Spirit" myths. In many cases, participants' responses are both informed by and reinforce these myths. They draw upon the myths, which have long been part of their cultural memory, to communicate to the reader or listener exactly what they mean in a more efficient way. This indicates that the phrases of this myth have entered the language of British people and function as elements of a shared national and cultural vocabulary. They use these phrases to symbolize complex combinations of ideas including stoicism, solidarity, determination, and hard work, because they believe that the person receiving their response will share their understanding of the meaning of the phrases.

The relationship between myth and cultural memory is not one of automatic acceptance. Participants may draw on and refer to the myths as facets of their cultural memory, but they do not always agree with the ideas they suggest. Ideas and identities can be framed and communicated not only in accord with associated concepts and myths, but also in reaction to them. Participants also use the MoI materials to frame their own personal identity. By interpreting British national character or gender or class roles from the image, the participants are then able to situate their own identity in accordance with or in contrast to those roles. They sometimes demonstrate complex nuanced understandings of identities, showing agreement, scepticism, and ambivalence simultaneously and define their own identities in response to the national, class, and gender roles framed by the MoI images.

Images can have long-term and complex effects on the way people think about the past. An image such as a propaganda poster acts as one of many different influences on the mind of a person when they consider their own sense of nation, history, and self. As a person encounters and interprets an image, they are also able to make sense of their own conception of history through the cultural frame of that image. This research demonstrates the importance of closely studying individuals' reception of such media, through social research methods, to uncover the complexities of how cultural memory is constructed.

NOTES

1 Maurice Halbwachs, *On Collective Memory* (Chicago: University of Chicago Press, 1992), 43; Lucy Noakes and Juliette Pattinson, *British Cultural Memory and the Second World War*, (London: Bloomsbury,

2014), 5; Ann Rigney, "Plenitude, Scarcity and the Circulation of Cultural Memory," *Journal of European Studies* 35, no. 1 (March 2005): 13–14.

2 Mark Connelly, *We Can Take It! Britain and the Memory of the Second World War*, (Abingdon: Routledge, 2014), 271–94.

3 Ian McLaine, *Ministry of Morale: Home Front Morale and the Ministry of Information in World War II* (London and Boston: Allen & Unwin, 1979); Michael Balfour, *Propaganda in War, 1939–1945: Organisations, Policies, and Publics, in Britain and Germany* (Abingdon: Routledge & Kegan Paul, 1979); James Chapman, *The British at War: Cinema, State, and Propaganda, 1939–1945* (London: I.B. Tauris, 1998); Henry Irving, "Towards 'A New Kind of Book': Publishing and the Ministry of Information, 1939–46," *Publishing History: The Social, Economic and Literary History of Book, Newspaper, and Magazine Publishing* 75, no. 1 (2016): 53–76; David Welch, *Persuading the People: British Propaganda in World War II* (London: British Library, 2016).

4 The research detailed in this chapter formed part of a larger research project titled "A Publishing and Communications History of the Ministry of Information, 1939–45," which was a collaboration between the Institute of English Studies and the Department of Digital Humanities at King's College London, funded by the Arts and Humanities Research Council. For more information, visit the project website at http://www.moidigital.ac.uk.

5 Limiting the number of posters to five ensured the survey would take no more than ten minutes to complete. Demographic questions on the age, gender, place of birth, and education of each participant were included. The survey was circulated online using the *SurveyMonkey* platform and it was also printed and distributed from physical information stands erected in public places in four locations, in Ealing, Kew, Nottingham, and Croydon; these stands were run for seven days combined.

6 Ninety-two completed surveys were collected from the information stands and 209 from the online platform. Ethical approval for the survey was received from the King's College London A&H Research Ethics Panel (LRS-16/17-4214).

7 Interviews were conducted with nine women and seven men who came from a broad spread of age groups and were born between 1925 and 2001. The interviews were audio-recorded with the permission of the participants and lasted between forty-three and ninety-three minutes. Interviewees were encouraged to be as open and expansive as possible during the interview and allow thoughts to develop and be communicated naturally and spontaneously.

8 The ten images presented in the interviews included the same five images presented in the survey along with five others in order to broaden the range.
9 Ethical approval for the interviews was received from the King's College London A&H Research Ethics Panel (LRS-16/17-4718).
10 Halbwachs, *On Collective Memory*.
11 Jan Assmann, "Communicative and Cultural Memory," *in A Companion to Cultural Memory Studies: An International and Interdisciplinary Handbook*, ed. Astrid Erll and Ansgar Nünning (Berlin/Boston: De Gruyter, 2008), 109, http://ebookcentral.proquest.com/lib/kcl/detail.action?docID=364668.
12 Assmann, "Communicative and Cultural Memory," 111.
13 Noakes and Pattinson, *British Cultural Memory and the Second World War*, 5.
14 Rigney, "Plenitude, Scarcity and the Circulation of Cultural Memory," 13–14.
15 Assmann, "Communicative and Cultural Memory," 113.
16 Barry Schwartz, "Frame Images: Towards a Semiotics of Collective Memory," *Semiotica*, 121, nos. 1–2 (2009): 2, https://doi.org/10.1515/semi.1998.121.1-2.1.
17 Noakes and Pattinson, *British Cultural Memory and the Second World War*, 17.
18 Connelly, *We Can Take It!*, 56–60.
19 Noakes and Pattinson, *British Cultural Memory and the Second World War*, 10–11.
20 Angus Calder, *The People's War*, (London: Jonathan Cape, 1969), 17.
21 Geoff Eley, "Finding the People's War: Film, British Collective Memory, and World War II," *The American Historical Review* 106, no. 3 (1 June 2001), 821.
22 Calder, *The People's War*.
23 Lucy Noakes, *War and the British: Gender and National Identity, 1939–91* (London; New York: I.B. Tauris, 1997), 2–3.
24 Sonya O. Rose, *Which People's War?: National Identity and Citizenship in Wartime Britain 1939–1945* (Oxford: OUP, 2003), 6–7.
25 Geoff Eley, "Foreword" in Noakes and Pattinson, xiv; Noakes, *War and the British*, 3.
26 Noakes and Pattinson, *British Cultural Memory and the Second World War*; Rigney, "Plenitude, Scarcity and the Circulation of Cultural Memory."
27 Connelly, *We Can Take It!*, 3.

28 Ibid., 2–4.
29 Noakes and Pattinson, *British Cultural Memory and the Second World War*, 17.
30 Richard Slocombe, *British Posters of the Second World War* (London: Imperial War Museum, 2010), 35.
31 Slocombe, *British Posters of the Second World War*, 34.
32 All quotations are reproduced with the participant's unique identification number, their gender, year of birth, and place of birth.
33 Eley, "Finding the People's War," 821; Calder, *The People's War*.
34 6229266833, Female, 1989, East of England.
35 TNA448, Male, 1970, London.
36 6208614763, Female, 1996, South East.
37 TNA448, Male, 1970, London.
38 6208614763, Female, 1996, South East.
39 6208599442, Female, 1965, North West.
40 6165997579, Female, 1965, North East.
41 Noakes and Pattinson, *British Cultural Memory and the Second World War*, 5; Rigney, "Plenitude, Scarcity and the Circulation of Cultural Memory," 13–14.
42 Mass Observation, "Government Posters in War-Time: Report from Mass-Observation," 18 October 1939, TC BOX 1, The Kee.
43 Bex Lewis, *Keep Calm and Carry On: The Truth Behind the Poster* (London: Imperial War Museums, 2017).
44 Lewis, *Keep Calm and Carry On*, 58.
45 CC2749, Male, 1930, London.
46 6143275846, Female, 1946, London.
47 6186933511, Male, 1974, North West.
48 6141648519, Male, 1990, West Midlands.
49 6173155957, Female, 1996, London.
50 Noakes and Pattinson, *British Cultural Memory and the Second World War*, 17.
51 6208614763, Female, 1996, South East.
52 6150025179, Male, 1943, London.
53 6165997579, Female, 1965, North East.
54 Boym, *The Future of Nostalgia*, xvi; Niemeyer, *Media and Nostalgia*.
55 Jean R. Freedman, *Whistling in the Dark: Memory and Culture in Wartime London* (Lexington: University Press of Kentucky, 2015), 177–9.
56 Female, b.1969, speaking about Dig for Victory.
57 6140780367, Female, 1971, North West.
58 6141648519, Male, 1990, West Midlands, "Dig for Victory."

59 6140780367, Female, 1971, North West, "Keep Calm and Carry On."
60 6210396462, Female, 1997, South East, "Keep Calm and Carry On."
61 6135515088, Male, 1947, South East, "Keep Calm and Carry On."
62 Boym, *The Future of Nostalgia*, xviii.
63 6139902292, Female, 1987, South West.
64 6210515801, Female, 1954, London.
65 CC27411, Female, 1953, Yorkshire and the Humber.
66 6143866229, Female, 1969, East Midlands.
67 Calder, *The People's War*, 17.
68 Noakes, *War and the British*, Rose, *Which People's War?*
69 Slocombe, *British Posters of the Second World War*, 13.
70 Ibid., 16.
71 6139902292, Female, 1987, South West.
72 6165982650, Female, 1992, East of England.
73 LM1451, Female, 1949, Wales.
74 "I mean probably I have to sort of touch on the sort of mild sexism [laughter] it's obviously a woman who's gonna be sort of referring to the make do and the mends and of course she's the one, I think she's standing in a very feminine pose." 6165982650, Female, 1992, East of England; 6229266833, Female, 1989, East of England; 6166008009, Male, 1998, East of England.
75 6229266833, Female, 1989, East of England.
76 6166008009, Male, 1998, East of England.
77 Noakes and Pattinson; Rigney, "Plenitude, Scarcity and the Circulation of Cultural Memory."
78 Calder, *The People's War*, 17; Eley, "Finding the People's War", 821.
79 LM1451, Female, 1949, Wales.
80 6165997579, Female, 1965, North East.
81 LM1451, Female, 1949, Wales.
82 6179435145, Male, 1986, International.

15

Beyond a "People's War"

The Polish Past and the Second World War in Contemporary Perspective

Jadwiga Biskupska

Historians of the Second World War both profit from and are uneasy about the popularity of their subject, balancing what publics desire while questioning what has conventionally been accepted about the war. New models and approaches add much but still stumble over the awkward exceptionality of the Polish case. This "Polish problem," demonstrated in the continuing political turmoil over the wartime past in Poland, reveals how much both traditional and revised narratives of the war have taken for granted and how much they still have to encompass to claim a global purview. The reason for this "Polish problem" of the Second World War in the present lies firmly in the past: the Polish experiences of the war were fractious and disorienting, changing such basic factors as who counted as Polish and where (or if) the Polish state was between 1939 and 1945. Recent developments in Second World War historiography that question geographical conventions and reconsider the conflict as a series of "People's Wars" provide a way forward. This chapter argues that re-examining Polish wartime experience clearly explains why fractiousness continues into the present, characterizing both the historical narrative and in many cases public policy. To do so, the chapter starts by tracing the contours of Polish wartime exceptionality and then reveals how that has resurfaced in various historical-political controversies after the end of the communist period and the re-emergence of a free press and scholarly community in Poland.

PEOPLE'S WARS IN THE EAST

The war outside of western Europe and the United States does not lend itself to the narrative clarity that western-focused recounting provides; it is impossible to call the conflict a "good war" outside of that privileged space. It certainly did not end in 1945, festering across contested territories after the declarations of V-E and V-J Days and fanning out into revolution, occupation, forced migration, and decolonization conflicts.[1] Considerations of the war "elsewhere" undermine comfortable narratives and complicate politics outside of narrow national spheres. Eastern Europe, in particular, has the potential to explode conventional western wisdom. The region's wartime volatility was grounded in the vulnerability of the Versailles order, which Nazi Germany and the Soviet Union allied to destroy – and which they succeeded in doing both during the war and thereafter, despite the breakup of their 1939 alliance. Then, with the advance of the Red Army westward in 1944, this territory was occupied and influenced by the Soviets, isolating it from western historical memory for more than a generation.

Multiple nations and empires have claimed portions of eastern Europe; though Czechs, Ukrainians, south Slavs, and Baltic peoples all shared a "bad" Second World War, the conflict began in, and over, Poland, and it is the Polish case that provides the focus here. During the war, Poles – or simply people living in the territory of what had been the Second Polish Republic – fought and died not alongside or under or united with their government, but effectively in the absence of one. That made for a different sort of war and a very different memory of it. With the revolutions of 1989 and then the collapse of the Soviet Union, the East-West divide across Europe receded, joining the two parts of the continent. With them into the project of European integration, these "new" Europeans brought raw and uncomfortable understandings of the Second World War, some of which were mutually incompatible and none of which reconciled neatly with already established western narratives. It was not simply that these narratives were incompatible: they spoke to the zero-sum game of the years after 1941 when the participation of the Soviet Union in a "Grand Alliance" with western Europeans and the United States meant that victory for *either* the Axis Powers *or* the Grand Alliance meant continued occupation for east-central Europe rather than peace or victory.

Eastern Europe, despite its radically different experiences of the war, may provide fertile ground for interpretations pioneered further west, especially the "bottom-up" approach of considering the Second World War as a series of dynamic "People's Wars" rather than the purview of governments and their armies. Considering whole societies and wider demographics in western states and their empires has expanded understanding into cavernous regions of family life, home fronts, local politics, and the thoughts of "ordinary" fighting men and women. Work on whole societies at war illuminates the conflict as a prolonged moment when "citizens and subjects ... joined together united" in a common project of defence – or offence – in which popular support was vital to maintaining war efforts, even if some participated more than others or for reasons that differed profoundly below the surface.[2] Nicholas Stargardt's *The German War*, for instance, considers the fraught and malleable relationship between the Nazi German state and the German people, why they supported fighting the war, and how they interpreted its burdens and setbacks as they lost it.[3] Work on Soviet society and the consensus that allowed for a "Great Patriotic War" and its final victory confirms this.[4] Such approaches place governmental ability to coerce and persuade heterogeneous populations to adopt war aims for themselves as the backbone of victory and they show us much that "top-down" or "army-out" approaches cannot see.

Again, though, the Polish case rankles, revealing the unfitness of even expanded models of the conflict: in the heart of eastern Europe there was no government–people relationship to be finessed or fumbled: strictly speaking, there was no government. Though multiple entities made some claim to govern Poland, none did in the sense in which the United States, the United Kingdom, or even the invaded Soviet Union was governed during its Great Patriotic War. The question of how Poland was governed must be answered in the plural and with caveats: this was one of the central contested territories of the war, changing hands from the initial Molotov-Ribbentrop Pact through the development of the Grand Alliance. The last national government of the Second Polish Republic evacuated Warsaw in the night of 4/5 September 1939 ahead of a genocidal German *Wehrmacht*, abandoning its citizenry and remnants of the Polish armies, and decamped to less-than-neutral Romania.[5] This meant that while political independence was often the object of deep longing during the horrific war years, Poles had very mixed feelings about the last pre-war government and the return of anything similar post-war.[6]

A handful of opposition politicians assembled an exile government following the provisions of the constitution of the Second Polish Republic in the west, first in Angers and then in London in 1940. Though many Poles looked to this institution as the conduit of Western Allied material support, it was distant and fragile – and weakened as the Soviet Union rose in importance within the Grand Alliance and sidelined it. The impotence of the government in exile was revealed during the disastrous Warsaw Uprising in 1944 when it was unable to secure substantial aid for Polish insurgents from any of its supposed allies. A cluster of elites also assembled a "secret state" in Warsaw as the civilian counterpart to various emerging paramilitaries, a kind of Polish "underground state" with aspirations for post-war political power through cooperation with the London exiles.[7] Nazi Germany's General Government administration ruled rump Poland (including Warsaw) under Hans Frank on behalf of the Third Reich until Frank's ignominious flight ahead of the Red Army. Frank's General Government created massive Jewish ghettoes and then housed the Operation Reinhard death camps, turning Polish territory into a centre of Holocaust murder.[8] Other German and Soviet occupation structures ruled pieces of the Second Polish Republic (planning "de-Polonization" and long-term "incorporations"), though both the Soviet occupiers of the eastern Polish borderlands and the German occupiers of western Poland were unseated during the war. Finally, a Soviet-backed Lublin Committee ushered in the Moscow-friendly government of the Polish People's Republic (PRL) in 1944–45 amid a cloud of controversy.

The coalition of powers that won the war was distinctly different from Nazi Germany's original enemies. The Poles were an awkward holdover from the initial alliance, made most troublesome by the essential participation of the Soviet Union in the victorious coalition – despite its 1939 invasion of Poland. Polish troops, indeed, were fighting within the Red Army and several other Allied armed forces, primarily with British units, as the war ended. When these men received word in summer 1945 that the Lublin Committee had been recognized by the Grand Alliance, there was "bitter resentment" and mutiny among them. Their commanders tried to keep the information quiet because "they could not guarantee that there would be no incidents" if Polish troops concluded that their country had been occupied by the Soviet Union with the Allies' acquiescence.[9] Unfortunately for the Poles at home and scattered abroad, none of these myriad wartime occupations, evacuated governments, or post-war administrations functioned as a Polish government in a conventional sense; only a few of them even aspired to be.

Competing bids for control of Polish territory led inevitably to competing war narratives. At the end of the twentieth century, some of these bids lost and those that have survived have stifled their competitors. In Poland, part of post-war political power has been the ability to rewrite this recent past. There are therefore multiple Polish stories to tell, some of which are out of vogue. A snapshot of the Polish wartime experience *na kraj* – at home – emphasizing Warsaw, the country's largest city, will demonstrate that even this "centre" of Polish experience is difficult to capture in a single narrative.

POLISH RESISTANCE AND THE HOME FRONT QUESTION

Each eastern European interwar state project had its strengths and weaknesses, but their unmaking after 1938 meant that eastern European peoples were directly subjected to the might of professional armies and the genocidal police forces that accompanied them, unlike populations to their west.[10] Nazi Germany in particular conducted "a war against civilians."[11] Vulnerable states shattered under the threat and then the reality of war, contentious interwar minority and class politics exploded into conflicts of their own,[12] and non-combatants enjoyed none of the protections of a "home front" existence: they hosted the war and its atrocities and the follow-on revolutions it inspired. Polish military casualties were just short of a quarter million men in total, with 16,000 dead and 32,000 wounded during the 1939 invasion and the rest lost in other Allied military efforts. These losses were dwarfed by the number of Polish civilian losses.[13] Indeed, in spite of the small size of the Polish state, it sustained one of the highest percentages of population fatalities of any belligerent. Their homeland was literally a front, and the one on which Poles took the most casualties.[14]

Though the Polish experience has been peripheral to western understanding, it was central to the war's unfolding. This centrality denied its citizenry – even civilians, itself a blurry category – the privilege of front and home front separation. The bifurcation of experience and protection of non-combatants that Americans and Britons (and Germans for much of the conflict) took for granted was crucially denied to Poles and other eastern Europeans: they hosted the war as the French hosted the Great War. They also therefore hosted many of its atrocities, and became victims, bystanders, and willing and unwilling collaborators in a number of occupier genocides, most importantly the Holocaust.[15] This victim-bystander-collaborator division is vital. Such categories raise moral questions about non-Jewish Polish behaviour that are less often asked about western European civilians. They also make it possible to marginalize Poles and re-conceptualize Polish agency in wartime histories: some of the most provocative questions interrogate how non-Jewish Poles observed, reacted to, and participated in the persecution of those they often came to view as "other," especially Polish Jews.[16] Further, German and Soviet occupations with differing policies held Polish territory, and therefore Poles "at home" differed in their conceptions of wartime enemies and post-war hopes. A Varsovian intellectual feared different things than a civil servant in Lwów (now Ukrainian L'viv), a peasant boy from Poznania, or a Polish-Jewish woman in Kraków. Poland's Jewish community tended to see the Soviets positively, since they were not habitually murdering Jews like Nazi Germany and occasionally protected them; Poles who saw the Soviets and Germans as equal enemies considered this a betrayal. The Red Army "liberation" of Poland was regarded with mixed emotions by non-Jewish Poles but Polish Jews who survived the Holocaust saw it as salvation.[17]

Radical experiential differences may be the most important aspect of the Polish war but they should not obscure the substantive attempts to maintain civil society: to keep occupied Poles fighting together as a "front" in step with the Grand Alliance. Metaphors of fighting, struggle, and national defence dominated underground publishing. Maintaining a sense of national community was one of the central day-to-day projects of underground organizations, ahead of long-term goals of military uprising or the reconstituting of an independent state. The *Information Bulletin* (*Biuletyn Informacyjny*), which appeared regularly in Warsaw from May 1940 and achieved the largest circulation of any underground periodical in Axis-occupied Europe, issued multiple rallying cries to Varsovians about politically correct behaviour in the face of occupation persecution.[18] The conglomerate Home Army (*Armia Krajowa*), formalized in February 1942, eventually claimed the loyalty of most Poles (though not fascists nor communists, who refused to join) including the editor of the *Bulletin*, Aleksander Kamiński, who simultaneously held the position of chief of the Bureau of Information and Propaganda (BIP) within it. Still, becoming an insurgent outright was atypical. Kamiński saw this disconnect between "ordinary" Polish life and radical resistance early. He bridged the gap by encouraging accessible forms of patriotism. His call for "petty sabotage" (*mały sabotaż*) in the *Bulletin* in fall 1940 attempted to unite Poles and connect them to a wider *patria* despite occupation divisions:

> There are certain forms of sabotage that are not just acceptable at the present moment, they are required. Each of us – men, women, children, members of organizations and people still unaffiliated – each of us must take part in the action of "petty" sabotage. This sabotage, which does not put anyone at risk, can still make everyday life exceptionally difficult for the occupant … What is important is that this sabotage is implemented every day and everywhere.[19]

This was a bold move to democratize resistance and channel anti-German sentiment into specific behaviour, reminding Poles that they, too, were a front against the Axis. Kamiński suggested six everyday ways to make life difficult for the occupiers and express patriotism without great risk, including dragging one's feet at work and responding "I don't understand" whenever queried by Germans.[20] The goal was to build opposition consensus among the masses, inconvenience the occupiers, and give those leading resistance organizations (conspiracies, as Poles called them) a sense of whom to trust and recruit. Instances of petty sabotage – defaced placards, patriotic graffiti on buildings – appear frequently in Polish memoirs, indicating that Kamiński's suggestions were widely embraced, infusing daily life with a sense of common struggle. Conveniently, these behaviours could also be self-serving, but this did not necessarily undermine the shared patriotism of those who witnessed such activity: Kamiński planted in the minds of sympathetic Poles the idea that they were part of an invisible community, ready to rise up at the right moment.

This community maintenance under duress was much more successful as an ethno-national project than it was across ethnic and religious lines. Community bonds between ethnic Poles and minorities of various sorts – Jews, Ukrainians, Germans – frayed and split. Religious faith tied the majority Roman Catholics together but divided them from non-Catholics whose faiths were often associated with foreignness.[21] In fact, one of the revolutions of the war was the homogenization of Polishness it provoked. Wartime events, from the murder of the Jewish population, to the Nazi empowerment of the German "Volksdeutsch" minority and then their expulsion from the new Polish state territories after 1945, to the seizure of the eastern borderlands and removal of their Ukrainian and Belorussian populations into the Soviet Union made Poland more Polish in an ethno-national sense. This meant that war narratives with protagonists who became "normal" Poles after 1945 dominated and those that centred on national or religious minorities were de-emphasized or re-categorized into other fields, such as German or Holocaust history.

BACKWARDNESS OR SEPARATENESS: MANAGING A COMPLEX PAST

This fractured wartime experience led to immensely difficult historicizing and commemoration. The absence of clear continuity in governance, diverse and conflicting individual experiences, scattered military forces fighting abroad and resisting at home, and the Grand Alliance shifts that left Poles in a very different situation vis-à-vis their allies in 1945 than they had been in 1939 were unique to Poland. Historical controversies have nevertheless been portrayed as a problem of contemporary eastern European "backwardness" compared with the enlightened west when they are in fact a product of wartime fracture and trauma. In Poland, the uncomfortableness of the "where" and "who" of this history (or these histories) in light of western models is an ongoing problem with little chance of speedy resolution.

Categories and ideas developed further west fit uneasily onto Polish experience; even distinctions like those between "war" and "Holocaust" or between "resistance" and "collaboration" are simultaneously distinct and muddled. American anthropologist Erica Tucker, who interviewed Polish survivors of the occupation of Warsaw in the 1990s as eastern and western Europe reunited, ran into a terminology problem, realizing that "for my [American] friend[s] resistance to the Nazis meant to help Jews." For her Polish interviewees, however, "resistance" meant nothing of the sort: "[T]he main goal of those involved in the Polish resistance was not to save Polish Jews but to prevent the disintegration of Polish society as a whole and ultimately to liberate Poland from Nazi control. Ironically, aiding Jews, which many Americans see as the epitome of Nazi resistance, is something that few ... described as opposition."[22] For non-Jewish Poles, including those in Warsaw, the heartland of resistance, the fate of the country's Jewish population was sometimes tangential to the goal of recreating an independent Polish state: war and occupation meant different things than they did to the western Allies. Resistance and opposition, thus, also did. This was true in the 1990s; it has stayed true.

This divorce from western models is grounded in Second World War experiences and their repression during the Soviet-dominated Polish People's Republic (though one might be forgiven for thinking that the Polish experience of state vulnerability has deeper roots). The Poles lacked the opportunities for open debate and publication available to West Germans, whose *Historikerstreit* during the 1980s exposed academic politics and eventually provoked a larger public conversation about the Holocaust, Nazi crimes, and the responsibility of "ordinary Germans" for the war and its genocides. One of the major points of contention in those debates was whether Nazi Germany and its behaviour during the Second World War was unique or whether it was best understood in comparison with fascist and totalitarian regimes elsewhere. In general, those on the left thought Nazi Germany and the Holocaust were unique and those on the right preferred comparative approaches.[23] East Germans had a different relationship with the Second World War and Nazism, and their reintegration with West Germany in October 1990 began uneasy German-German conversations that prefaced in microcosm the reintegration of eastern with western Europeans.[24] Though they are not very far in the past, these German debates appear distant and the Polish – and Hungarian, Ukrainian, Russian, and Czech – historical controversies that have flared up with increasing frequency in the twenty-first century seem aberrant, a testament to the abnormality and backwardness of eastern Europe. Those looking for overarching explanations point to lingering controversies about the Second World War and the past in general as signs of dangerous political trends, of the rise of a "new right" or "new fascism." Of course, the debates have their politics; all historical debates do. But they run much deeper and are less new than such current diagnoses suggest; if they are symptoms of a disease, it is one of the twentieth and not the twenty-first century.

Outsiders who focus on the "now" of public conversations in eastern Europe misunderstand them. They are not merely about the present but fundamentally about the past. Occupied Poland itself looked to its own recent past as a model for wartime behaviour, and Polish wrestling with that past has unfolded since before the dawn of the Third Republic, the first non-communist Polish state after the Second

World War.[25] The right to rethink their own past and revise and reject "traditional historical master narratives" was key to the work of dissidents in communist Poland, and they had comrades across the region engaged in the same project.[26] With political independence, historical debates returned in full force. Rafał Stobiecki, writing in 2008, considered that Poles were then in the midst of at least their "third great debate" post-independence: the first was the lustration controversy over the legacy of the communist state and how to punish or integrate those who served it.[27] The second, primarily Polish but with international reverberations, followed the publication of Jan Tomasz Gross's book *Neighbors* at the turn of the millennium. *Neighbors* was a microhistory of a Polish village occupied by the Soviet Union in 1939 and then Nazi Germany in summer 1941 in which the Polish villagers burned their Jewish neighbours to death in a barn one day as the Eastern Front unfolded around them, events that Gross asserted were initiated by Poles, not Germans. More important, although the events were widely remembered after the war, they were not condemned or even much discussed.[28]

Neighbors confronted the Polish Third Republic with the accusation (levelled by a Pole publishing bilingually from the United States) that Poles shared blame for Holocaust violence and were not merely co-victims of Nazi and Soviet atrocities alongside the Jewish people but agents of persecution themselves. However many waves of debate follow 1989, post-*Neighbors*, the question of Polish complicity is always present. The Holocaust, the occupation, and the war are inseparably intertwined even if one story that considers them all thoroughly is still impossible to assemble. This expansion of the franchise of culpability and muddying of the wartime narrative parallels debates in other nations at other moments: the German Historikerstreit and the American reconsiderations of the Second World War from a "good war" to a war that was much better for some than others.[29]

In the Polish case, however, the stakes are especially high and seem to grow higher with time. Polish debates about the past turn both on interpretations of events and on who counts as Polish and are therefore the proper subject of Polish history: Polish Catholics (almost always); Polish Jews (sometimes but not always); national minorities living within the borders of a Polish state, such as Germans, Ukrainians, or Belarussians (it depends); Poles living abroad either in exile or by choice (it depends): the ethnic segregation arising from wartime occupations has outlived them. The vulnerability of Polish statehood is the source of the difficulty. Multiple Polands with varying borders and political systems have graced the map of Europe since the Renaissance – or vanished from it. Multiple occupations and the absence of a recognized government at home during the Second World War confound the creation of any unified top-down history and explain the prevalence of military narratives as there was (eventually) a dominant army "at home" in Poland – the Home Army – the actions of which can form the skeleton of a unified story of "the" Polish experience.[30] Indeed, telling Polish wartime history through the lens of Polish soldiers and their contributions to the Allied war effort has attempted to square this circle: it is the story of an army that was actually many armies fighting not on behalf of but *in the hope of* a state.[31] The *who* and *where* of Polish history have thus themselves been contested in a way unimaginable to societies with more peaceful pasts and more durable borders and bureaucracies.

MUSEUMS AND LAWS AND OTHER FIGHTS

Simmering conflicts bubble to the surface when grand new narratives of the twentieth century emerge. Books and films have occasionally had this power but it has been museums that have provoked the greatest upset in Poland.[32] Museums, after all, aspire to educate a country's population (including its children) and foreign visitors. Two museums threatened expansive narratives of the war and occupation: POLIN, the Museum of the History of the Polish Jews, unveiled in 2013–14 in Warsaw; and the Museum of the Second World War in Gdańsk. Moreover, their multilingual exhibits had the potential to promote these narratives to a global audience.[33] The Gdańsk museum was caught between rival historical interpretations as it opened in 2016. The main exhibition attempted a single, global story of the long Second World War from the rise of totalitarianism to the early Cold War, stressing thematic comparisons and assembled by a team of historians and curators under an international board of advisors. This was intellectually (and physically) hard to construct as a single exhibit and the result was a series of interconnected galleries, some of which were thematic and others of which focused on a particular moment and place.

The Gdańsk exhibitions lavished attention on civilians and took as their subject the lives of ordinary people in the extraordinary experience of the war, highlighting atrocities and experiments conducted upon them by warring regimes. This contrasts with the more traditional "trophy" style museum with tanks and artillery pieces and pennants fluttering – like the spectacular National Museum of the History of Ukraine in the Second World War in Kyiv or the Museum of the Great Patriotic War in Moscow. Kamiński would be proud of the depiction of such people – his petty saboteurs – as historical actors. Poles, Jewish and non-Jewish, were featured but did not dominate the presentation. Rather, according to its original director, Paweł Machcewicz, the exhibit was an attempt "to insert the experiences of Poland and east-central Europe into Europe's and the world's historical memory."[34] The exhibition depicted much human suffering, but it offered no redemptive victory like the projects in the former Soviet Union, the collections in the Imperial War Museum in London, or those in the National WWII Museum in New Orleans, Louisiana. The project constructed a global "People's War" perspective, pulling together the most provocative reimagining of the war's meaning and placing it on display in northern Poland.

Shortly before the official unveiling of the Gdańsk museum, the Polish government intervened from Warsaw to make changes to the exhibit. The opening was stalled, a merger proposed with a smaller museum, and finally the original director dismissed and a more politically friendly replacement found. The problem, from the perspective of the ruling Law and Justice (Prawo i Sprawiedliwość) party and its supporters, was the global context. In Poland, which had such a brutal war and occupation, the government considered it inappropriate that this experience be robbed of its particularity and subsumed in a global presentation. It thus wanted to re-nationalize the museum as a specifically Polish institution. The global purview struck the museum's critics as implicitly pacifist and an argument against the unique suffering of the Polish nation. This was the Historikerstreit in reverse: the traditionalists argued for Poland's unique wartime position (crucially, victimhood rather than perpetration); those further to the left were more eager for comparison. Historians both in Poland and abroad remarked on the decision, some with vehement protest at the audacity of the last-minute power play and others in support of the government intervention and its priorities.[35] The Gdańsk museum opened quietly, its main exhibit unaltered from the original conception, but with an uncertain future. This controversy played itself out over months in several languages, airing the dirty laundry of nascent Polish government policy internationally to curious spectators unsure why a museum might be so spectacularly controversial.

The museum debate was not the last attempt of the Law and Justice government, in power from 2015, to put forward its own historical policy emphasizing the particularity of Polish experience. In January 2018, a revision to the *Act of the Institute of National Remembrance* (*Ustawa o Instytucie Pamięci Narodowej*) passed in the Polish parliament, the 55th article of which stipulated steep fines and up to three years' imprisonment for those who "accuse ... the Polish state or people of involvement or responsibility for the Nazi occupation during World War II."[36] This was an addition of punitive powers to the original act, which had created educational initiatives, an archive, and a publishing centre focusing on recent Polish history. The severity of the new punishment was remarkable by the standards of international law. Though the Institute of National Remembrance was created in 1998 and has since been amended and updated, the new article was partially prompted by a simmering political controversy: the tendency of foreign politicians and dignitaries to use the phrase "Polish death camps" to refer to the Nazi German camps erected across occupied Europe, especially Auschwitz-Birkenau. The phrase highlighted global ignorance about war and occupation in eastern Europe. Those who objected saw it not as an innocent geographical shorthand but as part of a shifting of blame for Nazi German atrocities onto eastern Europeans. Here again a category from the West found itself ill-suited for eastern Europe. Article 55 criminalized "Polish death camps" gaffes, but also had implications for those interested in studying the Holocaust and wartime behaviour more broadly. It was a swipe at the still-muddled history and historiography of the war designed to "solve" the problem of that complexity by legislative means.

Historians, whose ability to research and publish in Poland was placed in question by Article 55, despite a provision protecting intellectual freedom for "scientific" work, reacted strongly. A number of high-profile figures spoke against the change, calling it a form of mandated Holocaust denial, and some Polish politicians leapt in to defend it. The ensuing debate about these and other regulations involved prominent Poles, Americans, and Israelis and drew further attention to the region's unquiet wartime past and its enduring political ramifications. Jan Tomasz Gross, interviewed for *The Atlantic*, called the laws "terrible" and warned that they imperilled Holocaust survivors giving testimony and discussing their experiences.[37] The debate became a bone of contention between the Polish and Israeli governments. Israeli

Prime Minister Benjamin Netanyahu, no stranger to controversy himself, accused the Polish government and its representatives of "Holocaust denial" and "whitewashing Polish history."[38] Historians ranging across the political spectrum from right to left questioned the government's actions and demanded clarification about its implications for their work.

Attempting to get ahead of the controversy, Law and Justice Prime Minister Mateusz Morawiecki defended the act's updates inside and outside Poland. He explained the stakes of the recent Polish past to bewildered Americans for *Foreign Policy*:

> My government's recently adopted bill dealing with the falsification of Polish history ... has a very simple aim: to protect the truth about World War II and about those who were truly responsible for it. It penalizes public accusations against Poland, contrary to all facts, of responsibility or complicity in Nazi German crimes. Attributing complicity in the Holocaust to Poland blurs the responsibility of Nazi Germany ... Instead, when the Holocaust started, Poland's government in exile endeavoured to make the world hear about the tragedy of the Polish Jews and to convince the Allies to undertake appropriate action. The Polish Underground State not only created an organized platform to help Jews called the Polish Council to Aid Jews, known by its code name Zegota, but also punished by death those who helped Germans in murdering Jews.[39]

This summary of the Polish past oversimplified matters, as politicians are wont to do. The prime minister's defence of his government's historical policy intertwined a number of wartime actors and institutions, some of which we have already established as distinct: the Polish government in exile, the Polish underground state, the Polish Council to Aid Jews (Żegota), and the diverse Polish-Jewish community.[40] Each of these groups and its behaviours has been subject to robust historical examination in Poland (and occasionally outside it); few historians would so blithely intertwine them as Morawiecki did. The brief explanation implicitly conflated institutions that sometimes quarrelled and blurred individual Polish agency, subsuming everything under a narrative of Polish wartime unity: one (exiled) government; one (underground) state; one definition of who was Polish; one posture toward the Holocaust.

The reality of the war was more complex, and even linked organizations like the government in exile in London and the underground "secret state" diverged sharply over key matters – especially the developing Holocaust and appropriate responses to it.[41] Żegota was not an initiative of the Polish underground state but of individuals, especially the conservative Catholic author and activist, Zofia Kossak, who brought in colleagues to sustain it and sought the financial support of the London Poles; she later left the group, frustrated at the inclusion of Polish Jews among its expanded leadership. These qualifications might appear trifling, but they are not: organizational initiative and the control of networks are vital to understanding the power and durability of underground movements in wartime. Did the London Poles take the initiative in broadcasting information about the Holocaust in Poland, or were they prompted to do so by the work of actors "from home" like Jan Kozielewski Karski, who brought some of the first reports about the murder of Jews to London and then the United States, receiving a chilly reception?[42] Did any of these institutions clarify differences between the fate of Polish Jews and non-Jewish Poles for international audiences? Should they have? That the specificity of Polish-Jewish victimhood was downplayed or misunderstood by the London Poles and other institutions abroad, including the Catholic Church, remains a subject of serious contention.[43] The role of Karski is demonstrative because he remained in long-term post-war exile in the United States and published extensively on the war and the Holocaust. His reporting suggested that it was the initiative of Warsaw's Jews – not the London Poles or the Polish underground leadership – that demanded "appropriate action" by the Allies in the face of the Holocaust.[44] Karski's politics and behaviour were exceptional during the occupation, which does not make them less important but may make him inappropriate as a standard-bearer for the Polish experience.

Some of these matters are hairsplitting; others are of staggering importance. All of these topics and the articulation of these groups' visions and behaviours have been subject to reasonable debate: that is the point of historical scholarship on wartime Poland and on the global war. Indeed, some scholars would agree broadly with Morawiecki's presentation of the period; others would dismiss it. The story is not closed nor is it univocal, and the 2018 law operated as if it were. Those who supported the law's passage preferred the narrative of the Polish past that Morawiecki had sketched and were interested in quieting those who would complicate it – and especially those who would air those complications abroad.

CONCLUSION:
AN UNQUIET WARTIME HISTORY

The Law and Justice government is not the first Polish government to attempt to channel and control what is known and believed about the Polish past; it will not be the last. Other governments across the globe, not just in eastern Europe, have toyed with restrictive historical policies, educational curricula, and nationalist commemoration. In an age of global news media, however, what might once have been an internal Polish debate over a book or a museum or a law instantaneously became international. This awkwardly parallels the war that began in Poland in 1939: it might have started as a local one, but it became an international one, bigger than those who first fought to determine its outcome – a phenomenon affecting them but beyond their control. Western Europe and the United States, unlike eastern Europe, East Asia, and a number of places in the Global South, did not host the major atrocities of the Second World War. Eastern Europe did. In particular, Poland did. It also did so in a space divided by multiple occupation boundaries and segregation policies designed to undermine community and prevent opposition which some Poles – like Kamiński with his petty-sabotage manifesto – fought fiercely.

The political circumstances of the later twentieth century left huge portions of that wartime past unprocessed – or at least not fully publicly examined. It also left those in western Europe and the United States blithely ignorant of many of the events there, an ignorance that has persisted into the present, to westerners' detriment. Historical controversies are always historiographical controversies since some of the stakes of study depend on the freedom to examine such questions and write about them at all – a freedom that could not be and cannot be taken for granted in the eastern European and post-Soviet space in the way it has further west, where debates are hardly settled or narratives unchallenged. Continued debate is, after all, the best testimony to the war's transformative importance.

In eastern Europe, the historiography of the Second World War and Holocaust is deeply unquiet foremost because those experiences were contested and various during the events themselves. The mere passage of time will not put back together what war tore apart; neither will the imposition of external categories and assumptions, though some might suggest ways forward. The goal of those of good will (in Poland and outside it) should not be to uphold clear narratives and conventional wisdom about the past that necessitate marginalizing eastern European complexity. The war, after all, began in this space, and understandings that exclude or simplify it are in fact misunderstandings. An embrace of the fractiousness and disquietude of the eastern European experience rather than an attempt to "solve" it is necessary for a truly global picture of the war to emerge; it is not enough to fit eastern European experience into western narratives. Rather, such narratives must be formed anew to allow for eastern European – and Asian and African – realities, past and present.

Poles had the peculiar experience of fighting both world wars – so essential to the historical consciousness and global position of other states – as peoples detached from any single sovereign state. If Poles fought "People's Wars," they fought them by default rather than by choice. If those who experienced the war years disagreed about what they meant and how they should be understood and who should be included in their pantheon of heroes and martyrs (to say nothing of their villains), then their descendants will also do so and the voices of those who died without issue or are now outside that national community will grow faint. And if Polish governments have attempted to wrangle these sloppy pasts into a neat story that serves their agendas, this should never surprise us and it is useless to mark it as aberrant or backward: it is different than western trends because the war was different there and its legacy must therefore also be. However, there should be some comfort in the assurance that such simplification initiatives have and will likely fail in controlling the past. After all, no Polish government led or directed the actual war that Poles – all of them, in all the definitions of them – experienced, so no subsequent such institution is likely to control its legacy. For historians of the whole global war, this is both a warning and an opportunity

NOTES

1 Robert Gerwarth's *Vanquished* shows that a "world" war exacerbated regional conflicts and civil wars, making 1918 a closing date for few (Gerwarth, *Vanquished: Why the First World War Failed to End* [New York: Farrar, Straus and Giroux, 2016]); Jochen Böhler's *Civil War in Central Europe, 1918–1921: The Reconstruction of Poland* (New York: Oxford University Press, 2018) details the Polish case. For the Second

World War, Anita Prażmowska's *Civil War in Poland 1942–1948* (London: Palgrave Macmillan, 2004) considers 1944–45 an inappropriate end date.

2   Jonathan Fennell, *Fighting the People's War: The British and Commonwealth Armies and the Second World War* (New York: Cambridge University Press, 2019), 4.

3   Consider especially his discussion about Holocaust guilt and the perception of Western Allied bombing as retribution for it (Nicholas Stargardt, *The German War: A Nation under Arms, 1939–1945: Citizens and Soldiers* [New York: Basic Books, 2015], 366–79).

4   On the mobilization of non-traditional groups defending the Soviet Union, see: Svetlana Alexievich's *Unwomanly Face of War: An Oral History of Women in World War II* (New York: Random House, 2018); Roberto J. Carmack's *Kazakhstan in World War II: Mobilization and Ethnicity in the Soviet Empire* (Lawrence: University Press of Kansas, 2019); Julie K. deGraffenried's *Sacrificing Childhood: Children and the Soviet State* (Lawrence: University Press of Kansas, 2014).

5   Julian Kulski, *Z minionych lat życia, 1892–1945* (Warszawa: Państwowy Instytut Wydawniczy, 1982), 229; Władysław Bartoszewski, *1859 dni Warszawy* (Kraków: Wydawnictwo Znak, 1974), 26–7.

6   Notably, some of those eager for a new Polish government were Catholic conservatives on the right like Jerzy Braun and Zofia Kossak who wanted a larger role for the Catholic Church in post-war Poland (BN Mf. 43293, Prawda, "Deklaracja Frontu Odrodzenia Polski" Kwiecień 1942 r., 2–3; AAN 2-1440– 0 sygn. 344/1, Unia [Organizacja podziemna z siedzibą w Warszawie], "Unionizm: podstawowe zasady doktryny," [1942–1943]).

7   Stefan Korboński told the story of this group – of which he was a leader – in *Fighting Warsaw*. It was democratic but small and its reach beyond Warsaw uneven (Stefan Korbonski, *Fighting Warsaw: The Story of the Polish Underground State, 1939–1945*, repr. ed. Scholar Select [London: George Allen & Unwin, 1956]).

8   See: Martyn Housden's *Hans Frank: Lebensraum and the Holocaust* (New York: Palgrave Macmillan, 2003); Christopher Browning's *The Origins of the Final Solution: The Evolution of Nazi Jewish Policy* (Lincoln: University of Nebraska Press, 2004); Yitzhak Arad's *The Operation Reinhard Death Camps: Belzec, Sobibor, Treblinka* (Bloomington: Indiana University Press, 2018); Joshua D. Zimmerman's collection, *Contested Memories: Poles and Jews during the Holocaust and Its Aftermath* (New Brunswick: Rutgers University Press, 2003).

9   Gen. Władysław Anders was the commander quoted in the British report (TNA WO 106/3973, Attitude of Polish Allied Forces to the Formation

of the Lublin Government, telegram 23 June 1945–24 June 1945, [1]; telegram 30 June 1945–1 July 1945, 2).

10 Poland saw military invasions from east and west and two genocidal police forced targeting Polish citizens. For police atrocities against civilians in 1939–40, see: Maria Wardzyńska's *Był rok 1939: Operacja niemieckiej policji bezpieczeństwa w Polsce: Intelligenzaktion* (Warszawa: IPN, 2009); Alexander B. Rossino's *Blitzkrieg, Ideology, and Atrocity* (Lawrence: University Press of Kansas, 2003); Anna M. Cienciala, *Katyń: A Crime without Punishment* (New Haven: Yale University Press, 2008).

11 Mark Mazower, *Hitler's Empire: How the Nazis Ruled Europe* (New York: Penguin Books, 2008), 4.

12 This was not just true of Poland. For the influence of the radical right in Austria before the *Anschluss*, see Janek Wasserman's *Black Vienna: The Radical Right in the Red City, 1918–1938* (Ithaca: Cornell University Press, 2014). For the collapse of Czechoslovakia and the rise of a clerical fascist Slovak state, see James Mace Ward's *Priest, Politician, Collaborator: Jozef Tiso and the Making of Fascist Slovakia* (Ithaca: Cornell University Press, 2013).

13 Steven Zaloga and Victor Madej, *The Polish Campaign 1939* (New York: Hippocrene Books, 1985), 156.

14 Polish casualty numbers "at home" are the hardest to count, but they are higher than military losses by many times. Victor Davis Hanson's global treatment of the war lists Poland's "over 16 percent" fatalities of 5.6 to 5.8 million as the highest of any participant (Victor Davis Hanson, *The Second World Wars: How the First Global Conflict was Fought and Won* (New York: Basic Books, 2017), 489); the best Polish numbers are found in Wojciech Materski's and Tomasz Szarota's, *Polska 1939–1945: Straty osobowe i ofiary represji pod dwiema okupacjami* (Warszawa: IPN, 2009), 9.

15 A subject of enormous controversy. For collaboration, see: Barbara Engelking, "*Szanowny panie gistapo:*" *Donosy do władz niemieckich w Warszawie i okolicach w latach 1940–1941* (Warszawa: Wyd. IFIS PAN, 2003), and Jan Grabowski's *Hunt for the Jews: Betrayal and Murder in German-Occupied Poland* (Bloomington: Indiana University Press, 2013) and his *Na posterunku: Udział polskiej policji granatowej i kryminalnej w zagładzie Żydów* (Wołowiec: Wydawnictwo Czarne, 2020).

16 The matter of collaboration versus aid is fraught. On aid, see Nechama Tec, *When Light Pierced the Darkness: Christian Rescue of Jews in Nazi-Occupied Poland* (New York: Oxford University Press, 1987).
17 The most famous of many Polish Jews saved by the arrival of the Red Army was pianist Władysław Szpilman (see Szpilman's *The Pianist* (London: Picador Books, 2000) or Roman Polanski's 2003 Focus Features film of the same name).
18 It appeared weekly from 31 May 1940, but there were occasional issues from November 1939 (BN Mf. 45815, *Biuletyn Informacyjny*, 31 May 1940 r.).
19 BN Mf. 45815, *Biuletyn Informacyjny*, 1 listopada 1940 r., 1.
20 The six precepts were: 1. To work [for Germans] as slowly as possible, 2. To make "mistakes" in all work done for Germans, 3. To give Germans wrong answers and bad information when asked (driving directions, etc.), 4. To answer "I don't understand" to German questions [even for Poles who were multilingual], 5. To be inefficient and disrespectful in the implementation of German commands, 6. To make anonymous denunciations of Volksdeutsch to the Gestapo (BN Mf. 45815, *Biuletyn Informacyjny*, 1 listopada 1940 r., 1).
21 The Germans followed a *divide et impera* policy in the General Government and the territories annexed to the Third Reich; even administrative reporting broke down by ethnicity and the "Jewish residential district" was always discussed separately from Polish, German, and Ukrainian communities. (See discussion of reporting from Warsaw to the head of the General Government in Kraków in *Raporty Ludwiga Fischera: Gubernatora Dystryktu Warszawskiego, 1939–1944* (Warszawa: Książka i Wiedza, 1987) 134–6). For the long association between Polishness and Catholicism, see: Brian Porter-Szücs's "Polak Katolik" in *Faith and Fatherland: Catholicism, Modernity, and Poland* (New York: Oxford University Press, 2011), 328–59.
22 Erica L. Tucker, *Remembering Occupied Warsaw: Polish Narratives of World War II* (DeKalb: Northern Illinois University Press, 2011), 139.
23 Ernst Nolte was the central traditionalist, arguing against Nazi uniqueness – and the idea that Germans therefore had unique guilt. His first study of Nazi Germany was the comparative *Three Faces of Fascism* (London, Weidenfeld and Nicolson 1965), published in German in 1963.
24 Jeffrey Herf, *Divided Memory: The Nazi Past in the Two Germanys* (Cambridge, MA: Harvard University Press, 1999).
25 Jan Tomasz Gross's *Polish Society under German Occupation* begins with this point on the backward focus of Poles during the war: "A reader of the

underground Polish press during World War II found it largely devoted to Polish history" (Gross, *Polish Society under German Occupation: The Generalgouvernement, 1939–1944* [Princeton: Princeton University Press, 1979]).

26 Michal Kopeček considered the historical rethinking of Poles, Czechs, and Hungarians in the 1970s and 1980s – Adam Michnik among the Poles – key to dissidence, Kopeček, "Human Rights Facing a National Past. Dissident 'Civic Patriotism' and the Return of History in East Central Europe, 1968–1989," *Geschichte und Gesellschaft* 38, no. 4, Neue Menschenrechtsgeschichte (2012), 577.

27 Rafał Stobiecki, "Historians Facing Politics of History: The Case of Poland," in *Past in the Making*, ed. Michal Kopecek (Budapest: Central European University Press, 2008), 179–180.

28 *Neighbors: The Destruction of the Jewish Community in Jedwabne, Poland* (New York: Penguin Books, 2002); for some indication of the breadth of the controversy in English, see: Antony Polonsky's and Joanna B. Michlic's *The Neighbors Respond: The Controversy over the Jedwabne Massacre in Poland* (Princeton: Princeton University Press, 2003). For an oral history of the Jedwabne controversy stretching before the publication of Neighbors, see: Anna Bikont, *The Crime and the Silence: Confronting the Massacre of Jews in Wartime Jedwabne* (New York: Farrar, Straus and Giroux, 2015).

29 Shifting American mentality can be seen between Studs Terkel's *The Good War: An Oral History of World War Two* (New York: Pantheon Books, 1984) and John Bodnar's *The Good War in American Memory* (Baltimore: Johns Hopkins University Press, 2011) a generation later. On the development of myth and popular memory regarding Britain's war, see for example the chapter by Katherine Howells in this volume.

30 The Home Army had complex origins in 1939 and many competitors; Feliks Gross called it a "jungle." (Feliks Gross, "Some Sociological Considerations on Underground Movements," in *The Polish Review* 2, nos. 2/3 (1957), 33–4, 44.

31 This parallels histories of Poland under partition written in the west which privilege diplomatic history as it offers the possibility of a single narrative. See Piotr S. Wandycz, *The Lands of Partitioned Poland, 1795–1918* (Seattle: University of Washington Press, 1975). For the Second World War, Halik Kochanski's study calls itself a story of "Poland and the Poles in the Second World War" (Kochanski, *The Eagle Unbowed* (Cambridge, MA: Harvard University Press, 2014).

32 Film may be one of the more provocative battlegrounds for the eastern European past with its profound narrative appeal and resistance to

censorship. Bracketing film about the war in eastern Europe made elsewhere, Agnieszka Holland's 2011 *W ciemności* (*In Darkness*), Paweł Pawlikowski's 2013 *Ida*, Wojciech Smarzowskis's 2016 *Wołyń* (*Hatred*) and Konrad Lecki's 2017 *Wyklęty* (*Cursed*) have all claimed audiences inside and outside of Poland and offer cinematic comments that defy easy categorization on the perpetrators of war and genocide and their wider societal effects.

33 The 2004 museum of the Warsaw Uprising (Muzeum Powstania Warszawskiego) might also have, but its multilingual exhibit on Polish resistance in 1944 has been less controversial in Poland and less known outside it.

34 Rafał Wnuk, inter alia, *Museum of the Second World War: Catalogue of the Permanent Exhibition* (Gdańsk: Muzeum II Wojny Światowej, 2016), 8.

35 In support of the government intervention, see Sławomir Cenckiewicz, "Historical Truth Told Differently" in *Do Rzeczy*, 20 September 2016, https://polska.pl/social-issues/social/historical-truth-told-differently. In support of the museum's original vision, see: Michał Wachnicki, "Prof. Andrzej Nowak i Timothy Snyder bronią Muzeum II Wojny Światowej: 'Wystawa ta oddaje prawdę historyczną,'" *Gazeta Wyborcza*, 13 August 2016; and Anna Muller, "Objects Have the Power to Tell History," *Krytyka Polityczna*, 4 November 2016.

36 Act with all current articles, "Ustawa o Instytucie Pamięci Narodowej – Komisji Ścigania Zbrodni przeciwko Narodowi Polskiemu," *Lex Lege*, https://www.lexlege.pl/ustawa-o-instytucie-pamieci-narodowej-komisji-scigania-zbrodni-przeciwko-narodowi-polskiemu. For United States coverage, see: Tara John, "Poland Just Passed a Holocaust Bill That Is Causing Outrage. Here's What You Need to Know," TIME, 1 February 2018, http://time.com/5128341/poland-holocaust-law.

37 Rachel Donadio, "The Dark Consequences of Poland's New Holocaust Law," *The Atlantic*, 8 February 2018, https://www.theatlantic.com/international/archive/2018/02/poland-holocaust-law/552842.

38 "Poland Holocaust Law: Talks in Jerusalem Aim to Ease Row," BBC, 2 March 2018, https://www.bbc.com/news/world-middle-east-43251964.

39 Mateusz Morawiecki, "Poland's Misunderstood Holocaust Law," *Foreign Policy*, 19 March 2018, http://foreignpolicy.com/2018/03/19/polands-misunderstood-holocaust-law.

40 The official history of the Home Army, published in London after the war, asserted that "Polish society felt the tragedy of the Jewish population very deeply. Thanks to Polish help many Jews were saved from certain death, and many Poles paid for this help with their lives." Komisja Historyczna

Polskiego Sztabu Głównego w Londynie, *Polskie Siły Zbrojne w Drugiej Wojnie Światowej*, vol. 3, *Armia Krajowa* (London: Instytut Historyczny im. Gen. Sikorskiego, 1950), 47. Such a summary has been unpacked in the decades since, especially with regard to Polish societal attitudes and rescue; Morawiecki revived it unqualified.

41 Joshua Zimmerman has documented tensions between the London exiles and the underground. These were complicated by the fact that the Home Army differed in its behaviour across occupied Poland with regard to treatment of Polish Jews and the perception of Jewish "threat." Zimmerman, *The Polish Underground and the Jews, 1939–1945* (New York: Cambridge University Press, 2015), 177, 249–56, 360.

42 Jan Karski, *The Great Powers and Poland, 1919–1945: From Versailles to Yalta* (New York: Rowman & Littlefield, 2014), 357 and 365–6; Rafael Medoff, "The Man Who Told FDR About the Holocaust," *The Algemeiner*, 17 July 2013, https://www.algemeiner.com/2013/07/17/the-man-who-told-fdr-about-the-holocaust.

43 "Vatican Broadcasts on Persecutions in German-Occupied Poland" in *The Persecution of the Catholic Church in German-Occupied Poland: Reports Presented by H.E. Cardinal Hlond, Primate of Poland, to Pope Pius XII, Vatican Broadcasts and Other Reliable Evidence* (London: Burns Oates, 1941), 115–23.

44 Jan Karski, *Story of a Secret State: My Report to the World* (Washington, DC: Georgetown University Press, 2013), 302.

Contributors

MARK BAKER is a lecturer in Chinese history at the University of Lincoln. He was a career development fellow in modern global history at Balliol College, Oxford. He gained his PhD from Yale University in 2017 for the thesis titled "Making Cities, Making Countryside: Zhengzhou, Kaifeng, and the Henan Hinterland, 1905–1960." He also holds a BA (Hons) and MPHIL from Oxford University.

JADWIGA BISKUPSKA is assistant professor of history at Sam Houston State University in Huntsville, Texas, where she teaches the history of the Second World War and the Holocaust. She received her PhD in Central European History at Yale University in 2013 and has held fellowships at the Woodrow Wilson Center and United States Holocaust Memorial Museum. Her first book, *Survivors: Warsaw under Nazi Occupation*, appears with Cambridge University Press in 2022.

ANDREW N. BUCHANAN is senior lecturer in the Department of History at the University of Vermont. He completed his PhD at Rutgers University in 2011 and his first book, *American Grand Strategy in the Mediterranean during World War II*, was published by Cambridge University Press in 2014. His latest book, published by Wiley in 2019, is *World War II in Global Perspective, 1931–1953: A Short History*. Buchanan is currently working on a book for Bloomsbury Press on the transition from the Second World War to the post-war world. It is provisionally titled "Ending the Long War: Revolution, Decolonization and the Rise of the United States."

NICOLÒ DA LIO earned his PhD at the Università degli Studi del Piemonte Orientale. His research interests are war and societies studies, Italian social and political history, and the cultural history of the Armed Forces. His publications include *La guerra non è né bella né comoda. Il Gruppo di combattimento "Cremona" nella guerra di Liberazione. 1943–1946* (Ravenna: Istituto Storico della Resistenza e dell'Età Contemporanea in Ravenna e Provincia, 2012) and "The Italian Regio Esercito Co-Belligerent Soldiering, 1943–1945: A Grassroots Perspective" in *Italy and the Second World War: Alternative Perspectives*, ed. Emanuele Sica and Richard Carrier (Brill: Leiden, 2018).

RICHARD V. DAMMS is associate professor of history and head of the Division of Arts and Sciences at the Mississippi State University Meridian campus. He holds a PhD in history from The Ohio State University. His research focus is on the intersection of science and national security. His most recent book is *Scientists and Statesmen: Eisenhower's Science Advisers and National Security Policy* (Republic of Letters, 2015). His latest essay, "Eisenhower's Farewell Address in history and memory," was published in *Constructing Presidential Legacy: How We Remember the American President*, ed. Michael Patrick Cullinane and Sylvia Ellis, in 2018.

FABIO DE NINNO is assistant professor of contemporary history at the University of Siena and is secretary of the editorial staff for the journal *Italian Contemporanea*. He is the author of various books, articles, and chapters published in international journals such as *War in History*, *The Journal of Military History*, and *The Journal of Modern Italy Studies*. His latest books are *Piero Pieri, Il pensiero e lo storico militare* (2019) and *Fascisti sul mare: La Marina e gli ammiragli di Mussolini* (Laterza, 2017).

SEAN DETTMAN lectures in the Department of Social Sciences at University College Jersey and is the director of the Jersey International Centre of Advanced Studies. He is in the final stages of publishing his PhD thesis, titled *America and Blitz: The Aerial Bombardment on London and other UK Cities 1940–41 and its Impact on US policy of Aid to Britain*. Sean received fellowships from the George C. Marshall foundation in Lexington Virginia, and the Hoover Institute on War, Revolution and Peace, Stanford University, to help research this project.

JONATHAN FENNELL is reader in modern history at the Defence Studies Department at King's College London. He completed a doctorate in modern history at Oxford in 2008. He is a director of the Sir Michael Howard Centre for the History of War and president and co-founder of the Second World War Research Group. Jonathan is the author of two books, *Fighting the People's War: The British and Commonwealth Armies and the Second World War* (Cambridge University Press, 2019) and *Combat and Morale in the North African Campaign: The Eighth Army and the Path to El Alamein* (Cambridge University Press, 2011).

EDWARD J.K. GITRE is assistant professor of history at Virginia Tech specializing in the history of the interdisciplinary social and behavioural sciences and war and society. He holds a PhD in history from Rutgers University and two Masters degrees, including one from the University of Manchester. He has held fellowships at the Center for Cultural Analysis and the Institute for Advanced Studies in Culture. His research has appeared in the *Journal of the History of the Behavioral Sciences* and *History of the Human Sciences* journal and has been supported by the American Philosophical Society, Rockefeller Archive Center, and National Endowment for the Humanities.

CHRISTINA GOULTER is senior lecturer at King's College London, and teaches at the UK Defence Academy. She was formerly associate professor of strategy at the US Naval War College, and is currently co-director of the Sir Michael Howard Centre for the History of War and head of the King's Air Power Studies Research Group. Her publications include *A Forgotten Offensive: Royal Air Force Coastal Command's Anti-Shipping Campaign, 1940-1945*, and other works on intelligence, the Special Operations Executive in the Second World War, and counter-insurgency warfare. She is co-author of a RAND study, *Precision and Purpose: Airpower in the Libyan Civil War* (2015), and other edited volumes on the Libyan air campaign of 2011. Her next book deals with British intervention in the second round of the Greek Civil War, with a particular focus on urban counterinsurgency.

RICHARD HAMMOND is a senior lecturer in the History and Politics Division at Brunel University, London. He holds a PhD from the University of Exeter (2012), which has been adapted into a book, *Strangling the Axis: The Fight for Control of the Mediterranean during the Second World War* (Cambridge University Press, 2020). Elsewhere, he has published articles in the *International History Review*, *War in History*, *Journal of Military History*, and the *Journal of Strategic Studies*. Two of these articles have won prestigious awards. He is also a vice-president of the Second World War Research Group.

KATHERINE HOWELLS is a visual collections researcher at the National Archives, specializing in art, design, and photographic records. She holds a PhD in digital humanities from King's College London. Her doctoral research focused on Ministry of Information propaganda images and British cultural memory of the Second World War. She also holds an MA from the same institution and a BA (Hons) in history from the University of Warwick.

KEVIN NOLES is a doctoral candidate in history at New College, University of Oxford. He also holds an MST with distinction from the same institution. His doctoral research focuses on the experiences of Indian prisoners of war of the Japanese during the Second World War.

JACOPO PILI obtained his PhD at the University of Leeds in January 2020, with a thesis on the image of Great Britain in Fascist Italy. He has published on the subjects of the Italian *Regia Aeronautica* involvement in the Spanish Civil War, on the Italian military attachés in Western Europe during the fascist era, as well as on fascist espionage in Yugoslavia in the interwar period. His first monograph, "Anglophobia in Fascist Italy," is a forthcoming publication with Manchester University Press.

RAFFAEL SCHECK is professor of modern European history at Colby College in Waterville (Maine). He is the author of six books and more than thirty articles and chapters on German history from 1871 to 1945, including *Hitler's African Victims: The German Army Massacres of Black French Soldiers in 1940*, *French Colonial Soldiers in German Captivity during World War II*, and *Love Between Enemies: Western Prisoners of War and German Women in World War II*, all with Cambridge University Press. He is currently writing a book for Hoffmann & Campe on the western campaign of May to June 1940 in light of the experience of the First World War.

BEN H. SHEPHERD is reader in history at Glasgow Caledonian University, and focuses on German and Austrian history, 1914–45. His key publications include *Hitler's Soldiers: The German Army in the Third Reich, 1933–1945* (London and New Haven, CT: Yale University Press, 2016); *Terror in the Balkans: German Armies and Partisan Warfare* (Cambridge, MA: Harvard University Press, 2012); and *War in the Wild East: The German Army and Soviet Partisans* (Cambridge, MA: Harvard University Press, 2004).

EMANUELE SICA completed his PhD at the University of Waterloo on the Italian military occupation of southeastern France in the Second World War, 1940–43, with a particular emphasis on the occupation policy of the Italian army and its effects on the relationship between the Italian soldiers and the local population. This has since been published as *Mussolini's Army in the French Riviera: The Italian Occupation of France* (Chicago: University of Illinois Press, 2016). He is also the editor, along with Richard Carrier, of *Italy and the Second World War: Alternative Perspectives* (Brill, 2018) and has written on Italian military history in English, Italian, and French.

ALEXANDER WILSON is lecturer at the Defence Studies Department, King's College London. He completed a PhD at the same institution in 2018. He is a regional director of the Second World War Research Group with responsibility for Europe, the Middle East, and North Africa, and a councillor of the Army Records Society. His research focuses on the Indian Army in the Second World War and it has taken him to battlefields from Italy to Myanmar and archives in the UK, India, and Nepal.

Index

Page numbers in italics refer to figures.

Abbas, Ferhat, *Manifesto*, 26
Aboriginal peoples, in British-Imperial forces, 21
Abyssinia, 23, 238
Act of the Institute of National Remembrance (Poland), 365
Africa: anti-colonial sentiment, 22; French mobilization of, 24–5; Greek government in Cairo, 280–5, 288, 290, 291; Italian colonial occupation, 238, 239; Italian mobilization of, 23–4; Italian propaganda and, 78–9
African Americans, in US military, 34–6, 121, 128
agency: in anti-partisan brutality, 221–2; in Italian occupation policies, 242–4; in Polish wartime histories, 358
Algeria, 25, 26, 310
Ali, Subedar Barkat, 266
Allied Control Commission (ACC), 137, 141–2, 146
Allied Military Government of Occupied Territories (AMGOT), 146

Allied occupation and Italian health care, 144–7, 148, 149–50, 153
Ambrosio, General Vittorio, 234, 235
American Civil Rights movement, 35
amorous relationships, Nazi Germany: aftermath, 317–18; community response to, 314–17; extent and character of, 303–6; gender roles and experience, 306–13, *308*, 319, 323n43; official anxiety over, 301–3; People's War narrative and, 300, 319. *See also* anti-partisan warfare, German; Germany
Anders, General Władysław, 27
Anglophobia, 71
anti-Bolshevism, 212, 213, 215
anti-British propaganda. *See* propaganda, Italian
Anti-Fascist Air Force Organization (AOA), 286
Anti-Fascist Military Organization (ASO), 286
Anti-Fascist Navy Organization (AON), 286
anti-partisan warfare, German: background, 207–9; geography

or national setting, 209–11; heritage and ideology, 211–13; immediate conditions, 219–20; individual experience and agency, 221–2; organizational culture, 214–19, 223. *See also* amorous relationships, Nazi Germany; Germany; occupation policies, Italian
Antonescu, Ion, 32
Appelius, Mario, 76
Arbe (Rab) concentration camp, 236
Armed Forces Radio Service, 126
Armellini, General Quirino, 239, 243
Armistice of Cassibile (1943), 143
Arnaud, Patrice, 306, 313
Asia-Pacific War, 99, 100, 102–3
askaris (Eritrean soldier serving in Italian colonial army), 23
Assmann, Jan, 330, 331
atomic energy, 173–5, 177
Atomic Energy Act (1946), 175
Atomic Energy Commission (AEC), 175, 177
Auchinleck, Claude, 22
Auftragstaktik (mission tactics), 214–19, 223
Australia, 21, 124, 256, 268
Austria, 216, 221, 305
Averoff (Greek flagship), 287
Azad Hind newspaper, 268
Azeris, as non-German volunteers, 34

Bader, General Paul, 237
Badoglio, Pietro, 59, 238
Balkan region: anti-partisan measures, Serbia, 211, 213, 216, 219, 221; anti-partisan measures, Yugoslavia, 210, 216, 218; Bulgarian occupation of Greece, 278, 289, 290; Italian occupation policies in, 234–7; Macedonian resistance organizations, 279; Romanians under German command, 30, 32
Banat region, 234
Bao Wenyue, 105
Barbarossa Decree (1941), 214–15, 217
Barzini, Luigi, 74, 77
Bastianini, Giuseppe, 241, 243
Bataan Death March (1942), 36
BBC (British Broadcasting Corporation), 189
Begin, Menachem, 27
Belarus, 210
Belgium: German anti-partisan brutality, 211; on the Ostfront, 31; POW-civilian relations, 304–5, 314; Royal Air Force and, 27
Belich, James, 36
Ben Bella, Ahmed, 26
Berling, Zygmunt, 28
Beveridge Report (1942), 153
Bhandari, Subedar, 262–3
Bhonsle, Major, 267, 268
Biroli, General Alessandro Pirzio, 239, 242
blanchiment (whitening), 26
Blitz bombing campaign: American journalism and, 189–93; in British cultural memory, 327, 331, 333–9, 334, 336, 338, 341; Edward Murrow's *This is London*, 185, 187–8. *See also* journalism
Boehme, General Franz, 216
Bologna, Italy, 138
Bose, Subhas Chandra, 251, 268
Bosnia, 211, 235, 237
Bowen, Harold G., 171
Bowles, Edward L., 171
Bowman, Isaiah, 164–5

Boyle, John Hunter, 97
Brandenburg-Görden penitentiary, 317
Brar, Captain, 267
Brazil, 36
Brereton, Lewis, 124
Brignoli, Pietro, *Santa Messa per i miei fucilati*, 236
Britain Can Take It! (1940), 194
British exceptionalism, 328
British New Deal, 196–7
British Raj, 21–2, 258–9
British Special Operations Executive (SOE), 279, 281–4, 291, 293
Brogi, Dino, 80–1
brutality versus restraint. *See* anti-partisan warfare, German; occupation policies, Italian
Bulgaria, 278, 289, 290
Bureau of Information and Propaganda (BIP), 358
Burgess, Ernest, 121
Burgwyn, James, 230
Burma, 20–1, 22
Bush, Vannevar: atomic energy and, 173–4, 175; national defence and, 172; vision for post-war science, 162–3, 168–9, 177; wartime mobilization of science, 165–8
Byelorussia, 30

Cairo, Egypt, 280–5, 288, 290, 291
Calamandrei, Pietro, 73
Calder, Angus, 186, 187, 191, 332
Calder, Ritchie, 190
Cameroon, 25
Campbell, W.W., 165
Canada, 21
Caporilli, Pietro, 75
Capra, Frank, 126

Carnegie Corporation, 116, 118, 122
Carnegie Institution of Washington, 166
Carr, E.H., 190
Caserta, Italy, 290
Caucasians, as non-German volunteers, 34
Chad, 25
Chand, Major Prakash, 267
Chang, Lily, 98
Chase, Stuart, 116
Chatterjee, Lieutenant Colonel, 262
children: exclusion from People's War narrative, 332; German anti-partisan measures, 218; illicit amorous relationships and, 312, 318; Italian health care and, 137, 148, 151
China: conscription to Imperial Japanese Army, 19; national narratives, 5–6; perceptions of by American soldiers, 123. *See also* mobilization in China
Chowdry, Lieutenant, 264
Churchill, Winston: British intervention in Greece, 287, 292; in Italian propaganda, 82; People's War narrative popularized by, 332; support of Greek monarchy, 283–4
Ciancarini, Ovidio, 61
Citino, Robert, 30
civilian deaths, Polish, 357. *See also* anti-partisan warfare, German; health care, Italian
civilian evacuations, 140–1, 148–9
Civil Rights movement, 35
class, in People's War imagery, 332, 346–7
COGEFAG (General Commissariat for War Production), 48, 49–50, 55

Index

Cole, George Douglas Howard, 199–200
collaboration politics, China, 90–1, 95–102, 105–6
collective memory, 330. *See also* cultural memory
colonial experience, and Italian occupation policies, 238–42
colonial rule (British), and wartime mobilization, 22
Columbia University, 164, 167, 176
Combined Services Detailed Interrogation Centre (India) (CSDIC(I)): INA dissolution, 267, 268; INA historiography, 252; INA recruitment, 257–8; interpreting texts from, 253–4, 264. *See also* prisoners of war (POWs), Indian
Commando Order (1942), 216, 217
communicative memory, 330
communism: within exiled Greek forces, 286; French resistance, 26; German anti-partisan warfare and, 211, 212, 216; Greek Communist Party (KKE), 276–7, 278–9, 285, 289, 291–3; Greek resistance and, 281; Italian occupation policies and, 235, 236; occupation-collaboration ideology and, 95–6, 101, 102; post-communist Poland, 353, 360–8. *See also* occupation and resistance in Greece
Communist Military Organization Middle East (KSOMA), 286
Communist Party of Yugoslavia (KPJ), 235
Compton, Arthur Holly, 164
Compton, Karl T., 164–5, 166, 168, 171

Conant, James B., 166, 167, 175
concentration camps, 236, 256, 263–4, 266, 356
Confucianism, 95–8
Connelly, Mark, 332, 333
Constantine I, king of the Hellenes, 277
Il Corriere della Sera newspaper, 73, 79, 82
Cossacks, 8, 29, 33, 34. *See also* Ukraine
Cottrell, Leonard S., Jr, 122
counterinsurgency, Balkan region, 234–7. *See also* anti-partisan warfare, German; occupation policies, Italian
Crasta, John Baptist, 254
cultural memory: characterized, 330–1; and myth, 328, 331–3, 347–8; of the Second World War, influence of myth on, 333–9, 334, 336, 338
Cunningham, Admiral Sir John, 287
Cyrenaica, 77, 78
Czechoslovakia, 27

Dallolio, General Alfredo, 46–7, 48, 49, 52
Dalmatia, 234, 243
Dalmazzo, Renzo, 239
Damms, Richard V., chapter by, 162–84
Darwin, John, 6
Davis, Elmer, 195
Debre Libanos massacre, 238
Decree for the Protection of the Will to Resist, 302
De Felice, Renzo, 71–2, 74, 82
Defenders of Northern Greece (YVE), 279
Delaney, Douglas E., 6

Delegation du service de liaison avec les prisonniers (DSLP), 304
Demertzis, Konstantinos, 278
democracy: attempts to mobilize in Britain, 198–9; Black soldiers' perspectives, 128; British post-war social revolution, 187–8, 193–7, 199–201; fascist depictions of British military, 82–3; public opinion and, 115; US media and "People's War effect," 189–93. *See also* ideology; propaganda, Italian
Democratic Republic of the Congo, 25
Denmark, 31
Dig for Victory poster (MoI), 329, *334, 335,* 338–9, 341, 343, 346–7
disease: deaths in the First World War, 135–7; malaria, 145, 146, 256; tuberculosis, 140–1, 142–3, 148–51, *150*; venereal, 147. *See also* health care, Italian
Division Azul (Blue Division), 31–2
Dollard, John, 122
Douds, G.J., 252, 253, 257, 268
Duara, Prasenjit, 98, 102
DuBridge, Lee A., 167, 174
"Dunkirk Spirit," 327, 331–2, 333–8, *334, 336, 338,* 341
dysentery, 256

Éboué, Félix, 25
Eden, Anthony, 283
EDES (National Democratic Greek League), 276, 279, 282–5, 291
Edgerton, David, 6
Egypt, 24, 280–5, 288, 290, 291
Ehrenburg, Ilya, 28–9
Eisenhower, Dwight D., 122, 171

EKKA (National and Social Liberation), 279–80
ELAS (Greek Popular Liberation Army), 276, 278, 279, 281–5, 289, 291–3
Electronics Research Lab (Stanford University), 172
Eley, Geoff, 332
ENDIMEA (National agency for the distribution of allied medicines), 147
Eritrea, 23–4, 238
ethno-cultural identity, 258–62, 269
eugenics, 116, 137
European Theatre of Operations (ETO), 113–14, 122, 123–4, 125

Fascist regime: Franco-Italian relations and, 231–2; Italian health care and, 137, 138, 141–2, 152–3; Italian military justice, 54–5, 56–61, *57, 59, 60*; Italian occupation policies, 238–44; Italian society and, 47–8, 61–2. *See also* mobilization, Italian; occupation policies, Italian; propaganda, Italian
Favagrossa, General Carlo, 49
Fay, Peter, 252, 253, 257
Fennell, Jonathan, 6, 189
Fermi, Enrico, 176
Field, Geoffrey, 186, 196
Finland, 30, 31, 123
First World War: and anti-partisan brutality, First World War, 216, 221, 222; deaths from disease, 135–7; enlistment statistics for the Second World War versus, 120–1; Greek national schism and, 277–8; Italian war mobilization and,

45, 46–7; National Socialist ideology and, 212; restraint versus radicalized behaviour, 214
Fishman, Sarah, 318
Florence, Italy, 145, 150
Foreman, Paul, 176
The Forgotten Army (Fay), 252
Forrestal, James V., 172
France: German anti-partisan brutality, 211; ideology and youth, 101; Italian occupation policies, 231–4, 241–2; mobilization of colonial person-power, 24–6; POW–civilian relations, 303–4, 308–9, 314; Royal Air Force and, 27
Franco, Francisco, 31
Frank, Hans, 356
fraternization. *See* amorous relationships, Nazi Germany
Freedman, Jean R., 340
Free French forces, 24–6, 304
Freisler, Roland, 303
Freri, General Orlando, 74, 75, 78
Fujiwara, Major Iwaichi, 254, 255, 267

Gabon, 25
Galeazzi, Ernesto, 47
Gambara, Gastone, 239
Gandhi, Mahatma, 256, 257, 258, 265, 266, 268
Gaulle, Charles de, 24–5
Gdańsk museum exhibition, 363–4
Geldern-Crispendorff, Colonel Joachim von, 222
gender: illicit amorous relationships and, 306–13, *308*, 319, 323n43; in occupied China, 97, 99; in People's War messaging, 332, 343–6, *345*. *See also* women

General Commissariat for War Production. *See* COGEFAG
Geneva Convention on Prisoners of War, 301, 302
Genoa, Italy, 138, 141, 150
geography, German anti-partisan brutality and, 209–11
George II, king of Greece, 283, 285, 286, 288, 289
Georgians, as non-German volunteers, 34
Gerarchia (Italian fascist magazine), 73, 74, 78, 80
German Army: 201st Security Division (Germany), 220; 221st Security Division (Germany), 218, 219–20, 221–2; 342nd Infantry Division (Germany), 218–19, 221; 718th Infantry Division (German), 218; Security Battalion 242 (Germany), 219
Germany: colonial experience and wartime brutality, 238; community response to illicit relationships, 314–17; counterinsurgency in Balkan region, 237; discourse around wartime behaviour, 361; mobilizing non-German forces, 30–4; national narratives, 6; non-Russian populations and, 29; occupation of Greece, 278, 280–1, 285, 290–1; occupation of Italy, 139–47; occupation of Poland, 356, 358–60. *See also* amorous relationships, Nazi Germany; anti-partisan warfare, German
Geyer, Michael, 3
Ghosh, Kalyan, 252
Gilani, Lieutenant Colonel, 267
Gill, Naranjan, 254
Giraud, Henri, 25

Gobetti, Eric, 239
Go Through Your Wardrobe poster (MOI), 329, 335–7, *336, 339, 346, 347*
Governorate of Dalmatia, 234
Graudenz prison complex, 317
Graziani, Marshal Rodolfo, 77, 238, 239–40, 241
Grazioli, Emilio, 243–4
Great Britain: attempts to mobilize US in, 198–9; intervention in Greece, 277, 281, 282–4, 287, 290–3; Italian ideology around, 82–3; in Italian propaganda, 71–9, 80–2, 85n29; mobilization of imperial forces, 20–2; myths and cultural memory, 327, 328, 331–2, 333–5, *334, 336, 338,* 341; national narratives, 6; post-war social revolution, 186–8, 193–7, 199–201; POW-civilian relations, 302, 305, 309–10, 314; recruitment of Indian POWs, 254–5; surrender of Singapore and, 258–9; US Army morale research and, 122–4, *123*; US media and "People's War effect," 189–93. *See also* military formations: British Commonwealth; propaganda, British
Greece. *See* occupation and resistance in Greece
Greek Communist Party (KKE), 276–7, 278–9, 285, 289, 291–3
Gross, Jan Tomasz, 362, 365
Grossunternehmen (large-scale operations), 209–11
Guidelines for the Conduct of the Troops in Russia (1941), 214–15
Guo Zhongtian, 93, 98
Guttman, Louis, 119

Halbwachs, Maurice, 328, 330
Harling Mission, 293
Hauteclocque, Philippe de, 25
health care, Italian: disparities in data, 151–2, *152*; gaps in research, 135–6; military operations and, 143–7; post-war reform, 153–4; spread and mortality of disease, 148–51, *150*; systemic weaknesses, 136–43, *141*. *See also* Italy; mobilization, Italian; occupation policies, Italian; propaganda, Italian
Henan Province, China, 90, 94, 95, 100, 103, 105
Hilfswillige "Hiwis" (willing helpers), 30, 33, 34
Himmler, Heinrich, 307
Hinghofer, General Walter, 221
Hitler, Adolf: approving Cossacks for front lines, 33; National Socialist ideology, 213; POW-civilian relations policy, 316; on Romanian forces, 32
Holocaust, 356, 358, 360, 361, 362, 365–7
Horne, John, 7
Hovland, Carl, 122
Hull, Isabel, 238
Hungary, 30, 32

identity: cultural memory and, 331; ethno-cultural, 258–62, 269; gender and class in image and myth, 332, 343–7, *345*; national identity through image and myth, 342–3
ideology: attempts to mobilize US ideology, 198–9; British post-war social revolution, 186–8, 193–7, 199–201; collaboration politics, China, 90–1, 95–102, 105–6;

fascist depictions of British military, 82–3; German anti-partisan brutality, 211–13; Italian occupation policies, 238–42; Nazi race-based, 210–11; US media and "People's War effect," 189–93. *See also* democracy; mobilization in China; propaganda, British; propaganda, Italian
illicit relationships. *See* amorous relationships, Nazi Germany
Imperial Japanese Army (IJA): conscription of non-Japanese soldiers, 19–20; INA dissolution and, 267, 268; Indian POWs and, 251, 260; occupation of Singapore, 255–7, 266. *See also* Japan; prisoners of war (POWs), Indian
Independent State of Croatia (NDH), 210–11, 216, 218, 234–5
India: mobilization of British-imperial forces and, 21–2; propaganda, 252, 255–6, 262–6, 268, 269. *See also* prisoners of war (POWs), Indian
Indian commissioned officers (ICOS), 255, 257–8, 259, 263, 265–6
Indian Independence League (IIL), 255, 257, 265, 267
Indian independence movement, 22
Indian National Army (INA): dissolution, 267–8; establishment, 251, 256, 261–2; existing scholarship on, 252–3; recruitment to, 255–6, 262–6. *See also* prisoners of war (POWs), Indian
Indigenous peoples, in British-imperial forces, 21

industry: inefficiencies in, Italy, 51–5; Italian military justice and, 56–61, 57, 59, 60. *See also* labour
Ingersoll, Ralph, 193, 195–6
institutional culture, and Italian occupation policies, 242–4. *See also* organizational culture and German anti-partisan warfare
insurgency, Balkan region, 234–7. *See also* anti-partisan warfare, German; occupation policies, Italian
Ireland, 27
Italian Americans, serving in US military, 35
Italian Armistice Commission with France (CIAF), 242
Italian Governorate of Montenegro, 234, 235, 239
Italian National Bureau of Statistics (ISTAT), 149
Italian Red Cross, 137
Italian Social Republic (*Repubblica Sociale Italiana* [RSI]), 140, 142
Italy: departure from the Axis, 211; German Soviet invasion and, 32; imperial mobilization, 22–4, 23; national narratives, 6; occupation of Greece, 278; perceptions of by American soldiers, 123. *See also* health care, Italian; mobilization, Italian; occupation policies, Italian; propaganda, Italian

Jackson, Ashley, 6, 257
Japan: American perceptions of, 123; conscription of non-Japanese soldiers, 19–20; INA dissolution and, 267, 268; Indian POWs and, 251, 260; national

Index

narratives, 6; occupation of Singapore, 255–7, 266. *See also* Imperial Japanese Army (IJA); prisoners of war (POWs), Indian
Japanese Americans, serving in US military, 35
Japanese-occupied China. *See* mobilization in China
jawans (junior soldiers), 254, 255, 262, 265–6, 269
Jewett, Frank B., 165, 166, 168
Jews: German anti-partisan brutality, 210–11, 216; German anti-partisan ideology, 212, 213; mobilization of, Italy, 51, 65n37; Polish resistance and, 360; Polish wartime histories and, 358, 362, 365–7
Jim Crow policies, 128
Johnson, Edwin C., 174
Johnson, Louis A., 173
Joint Army and Navy Committee on Welfare and Recreation (JANC), 117
journalism: British social revolution and, 187–8, 193–7, 199–201; mobilizing US efforts in Britain, 198–9; Edward Murrow's *This is London*, 185, 187–8; "People's War effect" and, 189–93. *See also* media

Kaifeng, China. *See* mobilization in China
Kamiński, Aleksander, 358–9, 368
Karski, Jan Kozielewski, 367
Kassala, 76
Keep Calm and Carry On poster (MoI), 329, 337–8, 338, 341, 342–3
Keppel, Frederick, 116
Khan, Shah Nawaz, 254
Khan, Yasmin, 6

Kiani, Major Mohammed Z., 254, 260, 262
Kilgore, Harley M., 168, 169, 177
Killian, James, 175–6
King's Commissioned Indian Officer (KCIO), 255
Kita Seiichi, 100
KKE (Greek Communist Party), 276–7, 278–9, 285, 289, 291–3
Klopsteg, Paul, 176
Kluge, Field Marshal Günther von, 32
Knox, MacGregor, 77
Korea, 19–20, 36, 37
Korean War, 163, 176, 177
Kossak, Zofia, 367
Kufra (Libya), 25

Laboratory for Nuclear Science and Engineering (MIT), 171
labour: assembling of, Italy, 46–51; illicit amorous relations and, 303, 307, 314, 316–17; inefficient use of, Italy, 51–5, 62. *See also* industry
Laski, Harold, 196–7
Latvia, 29
Law and Justice government (Poland), 364–6, 368
Lawrence, Ernest O., 174, 176
Lebanon Charter, 289
Lebra, Joyce, 252
Leclerc de Hauteclocque, Philippe, 25
Leeper, Reginald, 284, 288, 291
Legnani, Massimo, 46
Levenson, Joseph, 98
Li, Lincoln, 95
Life magazine, 118
Li Qiuju, 95
Li Shiwei, 98
List, Field Marshal Wilhelm, 213, 217

Ljubljana Province, Italian occupation, 234, 235, 243
Löhr, General Alexander, 217
London Can Take It! (1940), 194
Libya, 23–4, 25, 77, 78, 238

MacArthur, Douglas, 124
Macedonia, 279
Machcewicz, Paweł, 364
McMahon, Brien, 175
Maghreb, 25–6
Magnuson, Warren G., 169
malaria, 145, 146, 256
Malaya, 20–1, 22
Man, Captain Dilsukh, 267
Manchuria, 19
Manhattan Project, 163, 167, 168, 176
Manifesto (Abbas), 26
Manifesto della razza [Manifesto of Race] (1938), 240
Maori people, in British-imperial forces, 21
marginalized histories, 12–13, 19–20, 359–60
Marinos, Lieutenant Themis, 282
Marshall, George C., 115, 118, 121, 124, 127
Marston, Daniel, 252, 253, 257
martial race theory, 21, 23, 29, 36, 254
Massachusetts Institute of Technology (MIT), 164, 165–6, 167, 171, 174
May, Andrew J., 174
Mazzolini, Serafino, 242
media: British social revolution and, 187–8, 193–7, 199–201; mobilizing US efforts in Britain, 198–9; "People's War effect" and, 189–93; relationship to myth and memory, 327–8, 339. *See also* propaganda, British

memory. *See* cultural memory
Metaxas, Ioannis, 278
Mexican Americans, serving in US military, 35
Milan, Italy, 138, 141, 142, 143, 148
military justice: Italian society and, 47–8, 61–2; mobilized workers and, 54–5, 56–61, 57, 59, 60
military formations
– British Commonwealth: 2nd Independent Parachute Brigade (United Kingdom), 291; Fourteenth Army (British Commonwealth), 20–1; 23rd Armoured Brigade Group (United Kingdom), 291
– French: 7th Algerian Tirailleurs, 26; Armée B, 25–6; Armée d'Afrique, 25; French Expeditionary Corps (CEPI), 25. *See also* Free French forces
– German. *See* German Army; Waffen-SS
– Greek: 3rd Brigade (Greece), 288
– Indian (colonial): 1/14th Punjab Battalion, 255; 2/10th Baluch Regiment, 265; 5/11th Sikh Regiment, 262. *See also* British Raj
– Italian: Second Army (Italy), 234, 235, 236; Fourth Army (Italy), 232, 239, 241, 242; Tenth Army (Italy), 77; Fourteenth Army (Italian), 235
– New Zealand: 28th Maori Battalion, 21
– Polish: First Polish Army, 27–8; Anders Army, 27, 28; Armia Krejowa (Home Army), 28; Berling Army, 28
– Red Army (USSR): 16th Latvian Rifle Division, 29

– United States: 2nd Armored Division (United States), 25; Fifth Army (United States), 25, 36; 9th Infantry Division (United States), 113; 65th Infantry Regiment (United States), 35; 442nd Regimental Combat Team (United States), 35
– Yugoslav: Chetnik Detachments of the Yugoslav Army, 235, 237; Garibaldi Division (partisan unit), 237
military technology. *See* scientific research
Milizia Volontaria Anti Comunista (MVAC), 237
Ministero della Cultura Popolare (Ministry of Popular Culture), 78, 80, 81
Ministry of Information (MoI): establishment of, 328; propaganda and cultural memory, 333–9, 334, 336, 338. *See also* propaganda, British
Ministry of the Interior (MOI), 137, 138, 141, 142
mobilization: of African forces, 25; broader implications, 36–7; of imperial armies, 20–6; of minorities in US military, 34–6; non-national soldiers in national armies, 27–34. *See also* journalism; mobilization, Italian; mobilization in China; morale research, United States
mobilization in China: background, 90–2, 92; disengagement and detachment, 105–6; militarization and, 102–5; youth and collaboration politics, 95–102; youth and occupation-collaboration state, 93–5. *See also* China

mobilization, Italian: inefficiencies in, 51–5, 62; phases of, 45–6; Verona military court, 56–61, 57, 59, 60; workforce assembly, 46–51. *See also* health care, Italian; Italy; occupation policies, Italian; propaganda, Italian
mobilization, United States: of African forces, 25; journalistic attempts at, 198–9; of minorities, 34–6. *See also* morale research, United States
Montenegro, 234, 235, 239
morale research, United States: implementation, 118–24, 123; implications and limitations, 126–8; morale research program creation, 115–18; responses to, 113–14, 125; success of, 125–6. *See also* scientific research; United States
Morawiecki, Mateusz, 366, 367
Morse, Philip M., 172–3
Mouvements unis de Resistance (MUR), 233
Murata Seiji, 99, 100–1
Murrow, Edward: on the Blitz, 190–3; journalistic legacy, 199–201; mobilizing US efforts in Britain, 198–9; on post-war social revolution, 194, 195, 196, 197; *This is London*, 185, 187–8
Museum of the Second World War, 363–4
Muslims, 26
Mussolini, Benito: foreign policy toward Britain, 73, 75, 77, 83; Italian health care, 138; Italian military justice, 61; Italian occupations in Africa, 238; Italians as "mobilized army," 47, 51
Myers, Brigadier Eddie, 282, 283–4

myth: belief and disbelief in, 339–42; in cultural memory, 328, 330–3, 347–8; cultural memory of the Second World War and, 333–9, 334, 336, 338; media and, 327–8; national identity through, 342–3
The Myth of the Blitz (Calder), 187

Nachshen, Donia, 335
Naples, Italy, 139, 143, 144, 149, 150
National Academy of Sciences (NAS), 163, 173
National Bands Agreement (1943), 282–3
National Defense Research Committee (NDRC), 166, 167
national identity: "People's War" concept and, 5–6, 7, 186; through image and myth, 342–3
nationalism: collaboration ideology, China, 95–102; in India, 251, 255–6, 261–6, 268; national identity, 342–3; Polish historical policies, 365–8. *See also* mobilization in China; propaganda, British; propaganda, Italian
National Liberation Front (EAM), 278, 282–4, 288, 289, 292
National Liberation Front (FLN), 26
National Research Council (NRC), 164, 165
national schism (Greece), 277–9
National Science Foundation (NSF), 169, 171, 177
National Science Foundation Act (1950), 169–70
national security: atomic energy, 173–5; scientific research and, 170–3, 175–7

National Security Act (1947), 172
National Service Act (1941), 344
National Socialist ideology, 208, 210–11, 212, 213
National War Organization, 47–8
nation-states: imperial armies and, 20–6; national narratives, 5–6, 7; non-national soldiers in national armies, 27–34
Native Americans, in US military, 35–6
Nedić, General Milan, 234
Nee Soon POW camp, 256, 260
Neighbors (Gross), 362
Nertherlands, 22, 31, 38n18
Netanyahu, Benjamin, 366
New Deal, 196–7
New Deal for science, 164–5. *See also* scientific research
New Guinea, 124
New Mediterranean Order, 240
New World thinking, 193
The New York Times, 118
New Zealand, 21
Nimbu (prison camp staff), 263–4
Noakes, Lucy, 328, 330, 331, 332, 337
North Africa: French mobilization of colonial forces, 25; Italian mobilization of colonial person-power, 23–4; Italian propaganda and, 78–9; mobilization of British-imperial forces, 22
Norway, 31
nostalgia, 329, 339–40, 342

occupation and resistance in Greece: civil war overview, 276–7; early resistance, 279–85; Greek mutinies, 285–9; national schism, 277–9; re-entry into Greece, 290–3, 292

occupation-collaboration politics: ideology and, 95–102; Kaifeng youth and, 93–5. *See also* mobilization in China
occupation policies, Italian: agency and institutional culture, 242–4; in Balkan region, 234–7; colonial experience and fascist ideology, 238–42; divergent approaches, 230–1; in France, 231–4, 241–2. *See also* anti-partisan warfare, German; health care, Italian; Italy; mobilization, Italian; propaganda, Italian
O'Connor, Lieutenant-General Richard, 77
Office of Naval Research (ONR), 170, 171
Office of Scientific Research and Development (OSRD), 163, 166, 167, 172, 177
Operation Animals, 282
Operation Barbarossa, 30
Operation Husky, 282
Operation Reinhard, 356
Operation Schwartz, 236–7
Operation Trio, 236–7
Operation Weiss, 236–7
Oppenheimer, J. Robert, 163, 174
organizational culture and German anti-partisan warfare, 214–19. *See also* institutional culture and Italian occupation policies
Osborn, Frederick: morale research implementation, 118–19, 121–4, 126–7; morale research program, 114, 116–18

Pacific War, 99, 100, 102–3
Paget, General, 286
Palestine, 27
Pan-Hellenic Resistance Organization (PAO), 279
Papandreou, George, 288–9, 290, 291
Pariani, Alberto, 72–3
Patterson, Robert, 170
Pattinson, Juliette, 328, 330, 331, 337
Pavelić, Ante, 235
Pavese, Roberto, 75
Pavolini, Alessandro, 79
PEAN (Pan Hellenic Union of Fighting Youths), 280
Pearl Harbor, attack on, 113, 119
Pei Yuanyou, 106
People's War: amorous relationships and, 300, 319; in British cultural memory, 327, 328, 331–2, 333–5, 334, 336, 338, 341; class and, 332, 346–7; concept of, 4–7, 5; gender and, 332, 343–6, 345; individual agency, 208, 221–2; marginalized histories, 12–13, 19–20; mobilizing US public opinion, 198–9; national narratives, 5–6, 7, 186; nation-states and imperial armies, 20–6; non-national soldiers in national armies, 27–34; Polish wartime exceptionality, 354–7; post-war social revolution and, 186–8, 193–7, 199–201; racial and ethnic minorities in US military, 34–6; US media and "People's War effect," 189–93. *See also* amorous relationships, Nazi Germany; anti-partisan warfare, German; health care, Italian; journalism; mobilization; mobilization, Italian; mobilization in China; morale research, United States; occupation and resistance in Greece; occupation policies,

Italian; Poland; prisoners of war (POWs), Indian; propaganda, British; propaganda, Italian; scientific research
The People's War (Calder), 186
Persico, Joseph, 200
Pétain, Maréchal Philippe, 232
Petragni, Giovanni, 140
Petrella, Luigi, 71, 80
Pettinato, Concetto, 81
Philippines, 36
Piazzoni, Sandro, 239
Piovene, Guido, 73
Pipitone, Cristiana, 239
Plaka Agreement (1944), 284–5
Planning Survey I (ETO), 113–14, 122, 123–4, 125
PM (American publication), 193
Poland: backwardness or separateness, 360–3; Gdańsk museum debate, 363–4; historical policies, 365–8; the "Polish problem," 353; Polish wartime exceptionality, 354–7, 362–3; POW-civilian relations in, 301; recruitment in national armies, 27–8; resistance and the home front question, 357–61; Royal Air Force and, 27
POLIN Museum of the History of Polish Jews, 363
Polish Army, 27–8
Polish People's Republic (PRL), 356
Polish Third Republic, 362
Political Committee of National Liberation (PEEA), 285, 287
Pozzi, Laura, 98
Prezzolini, Giovanni, 73
Priestley, J.B., 190, 192
prisoners of war (POWs), Indian: divided loyalties, 258–62; existing scholarship on, 252–3; INA dissolution, 267–8; INA establishment, 251, 256, 261–2; INA recruitment, 259, 262–6, 269; interpreting CSDIC(I) texts, 253–4; quantifying participation, 257–8; in Singapore, 254–7
prisoners of war (POWs), Western Allied. *See* amorous relationships, Nazi Germany
propaganda, British: background, 328–30, 349n5, 349n7; belief and disbelief in, 339–42; class and, 332, 346–7; cultural memory and myth, 328, 330–3, 347–8; gender and, 332, 343–6, 345; media and people, 327–8, 339; myth in cultural memory of the Second World War, 333–9, 334, 336, 338; national identity through, 342–3. *See also* Great Britain
propaganda, Indian, 252, 255–6, 262–6, 268, 269
propaganda, Italian: final phase of, 80–2; Great Britain as enemy, 72–5, 85n29; ideology and, 82–3; periodization of, 76–9; traditional interpretations, 71–2. *See also* health care, Italian; Italy; mobilization, Italian; occupation policies, Italian
Psarros, Dimitris, 279–80
Puerto Rican National Guard, 35
Pyle, Ernie, 193–4

Quit India campaign, 256, 257, 258, 265, 269

Rab concentration camp, 236
Rabi, Isidor I., 176–7
race: Black enlistee expectations, 121; divided loyalties among Indian POWs, 259; INA recruitment and, 258; Italian

occupation policies and, 239, 240–1; Jim Crow policies, 128; martial race theory, 21, 23, 29, 36, 254; minorities in US military, 34–6; National Socialist ideology, 210–11, 213; Nazi policy on POW-civilian relations, 301
Radiation Laboratory (Rad Lab, MIT), 167–8, 174
radicalization, in German anti-partisan warfare, 214–19
Raghavan, Srinath, 252, 253, 257
Rai, Rajesh, 253, 268
Ramperti, Marco, 74
rape, 312–13, 323n43
Red Army (USSR), 28–30, 33, 210, 216, 354, 356, 358
reflective nostalgia, 342
refugee health conditions, Italy, 140–1, 148–9
Regia Aeronautica (Italian Royal Air Force), 73, 76
Regia Marina (Italian Royal Navy), 73, 77
research. *See* morale research, United States; scientific research
Research Laboratory for Electronics (MIT), 171
resistance: insurgency in Balkan region, 234–7; Polish, 357–61. *See also* anti-partisan warfare, German; occupation and resistance in Greece
Reynolds, Quentin, 194
Rigney, Ann, 328, 330–1, 337
Roatta, General Mario, 235, 236, 243
Robertson, Ben, 193
Robotti, General Mario, 235, 243–4
Rochat, Giorgio, 239, 242
Rochester University, 167

Rodogno, David, 239
Romania, 30, 32
The Roman Peace in Libya (Graziani), 239–40, 241
romantic relationships. *See* amorous relationships, Nazi Germany
Rome, Italy, 149
Roosevelt, Franklin D.: "arsenal of democracy" speech (1940), 199; on Blitz bombings, 196–7; on democracy and public opinion, 115; government-science relations, 164, 165, 166; relationship with Frederick Osborn, 117
Roper, Elmo, 115
Rose, Sonya, 6, 186, 192, 332
Royal Air Force, ethnic diversity within, 27
Russia: German anti-partisan measures, 210, 212–13; non-Russian forces, 29; Soviet patriotism and homogeneity, 28–9. *See also* Soviet Union
Russian Liberation Army (RLA), 33
ruthlessness. *See* anti-partisan warfare, German

Sala, Teodoro, 240
Sardana, Major, 263, 264
Sareen, Tilak, 254
Schwartz, Barry, 331
Science Advisory Board (SAB), 165, 166
scientific research: atomic energy, 173–5, 177; Bush, Vannevar, and, 162–3, 165–9, 172, 173–4, 175, 177; government-science partnerships, attempts at, 163–5; national security and, 170–3, 175–7; visions for post-war

science, 168–70; war as catalyst for, 177. *See also* morale research, United States; United States
Scobie, Lieutenant-General Ronald, 290, 291
scorched earth measures, 211
Second Polish Republic, 354, 355–6
Second World War: gaps in historiography, 3–4; marginalized histories, 12–13, 19–20; national narratives, 5–6, 7, 186; People's War concept, 4–7, 5. *See also* People's War
Selvi, Giovanni, 74–5
Senegalese Tirailleurs, 25
Serbia: German anti-partisan measures, 211, 213, 216, 219, 221; Italian occupation, 234
Service de travail obligatoire (STO), 233
Servizio Sanitario Nazionale (National Health Service), 154
Sevareid, Eric, 194–5
sexual treason, 301. *See also* amorous relationships, Nazi Germany
Sheppard, Rufus, 281
Sherry, Michael, 175
Siantos, Giorgis, 289
Sidi Barrani, 76
Sikorski-Maisky Agreement, 27
Singapore: Indian prisoners of war in, 254–7; surrender of, 258–9. *See also* prisoners of war (POWs), Indian
Singh, Captain Mohan: INA dissolution, 267; interviewed by Hugh Toye, 252; loyalties among Indian POWs, 259, 260; memoir of, 254; as POW, 255–6; volunteer recruitment, 261–3, 269

Singh, Gajendra, 253
Singh, Gurbakhsh, 254
Singh, Lieutenant Colonel Gurbakhsh, 261
Singh, Pritam, 255
Sino-Japanese war (1937–45), 90–1
Slim, William Joseph Slim, Viscount, 20–1
Slovenia, 211, 234, 235
smallpox, 145
Social Science Research Council, 118
Somaliland, 24, 76
Somervell, Brehon B., 124
Soviet Union: German anti-partisan measures in, 210–11; German invasion of, 30–1, 212–13, 215; national narratives, 5; occupation of Poland, 354, 356, 358; POW-civilian relations, 301; Red Army, 28–30, 33, 210, 216, 354, 356, 358
Spain, 31
"Spanish flu," First World War, 137
Special Service Branch (US Army), 121–2, 124
Stahel, David, 30
La Stampa newspaper, 73, 77, 78, 80, 81
Stanford University, 172
Stargardt, Nicholas, 355
statistical research. *See* morale research, United States
Stewart, Andrew, 6
Stimson, Henry, 116, 117, 118
Stobiecki, Rafał, 362
Stoler, Ann, 101
Stouffer, Samuel, 118–19, 121
Sundaram, Chandar, 252
Sun Jingqing, 104
Sun Yat-sen, 96
surveys. *See* morale research, United States

Tachibana Shiraki, 100
"taking it" construct, 193–7
Taiwan, 19–20
Taylor, Jeremy, 97
technology. *See* scientific research
Tei, Gaetano, 47
Testa, Temistocle, 241
Thimayya, Captain, 265
Thimayya, K.S., 265
This is London (Murrow), 185, 187–8
Thompson, E. P., 36
Thrace, Greece, 279
Tilsit (East Prussia), 309
Tito, Josef Broz, 235
Todman, Daniel, 6, 187
Tooze, Adam, 3
Toye, Hugh, 252, 253, 264, 265
Truman, Harry S., 169–70, 174–5
Tsouderos, Emmanuel, 278, 286, 287
tuberculosis: deaths in the First World War, 136; Italian health care and, 140–1, 142–3, 148–51, 150
Tucker, Erica, 360
Tunisia, 25
Turin, Italy, 141, 144, 148, 150–1
Turkmens, as non-German volunteers, 34

Ukraine, 30, 210, 214. *See also* Cossacks
Ulio, James, 115–16, 118
United Kingdom, People's War narrative in, 6. *See also* Great Britain
United Nations Relief and Rehabilitation Administration (UNRRA), 147
United States: armed forces and scientific research, 170–3; British social revolution and, 187–8, 193–7, 199–201; journalistic attempts to mobilize, 198–9; mobilization of African forces, 25; mobilization of minorities, 34–6; national narratives, 5; "People's War effect" and US media, 189–93; POW-civilian relations, 302, 305; Royal Air Force and, 27. *See also* journalism; morale research, United States; scientific research
United States Armed Forces, and scientific research, 170–3
United States Army Morale Branch. *See* morale research, United States
University of California, Berkeley, 167, 176
University of Chicago, 167, 176
Urey, Harold, 176
Usborne, Cornelie, 306–7
Ustasha regime, 211, 216, 234–5, 237

vaccination campaigns, 146
Vaizey, Hester, 318
Valori, Aldo, 77
Velouchiotis, Aris, 289
Ven, Hans Van de, 90
venereal disease, 147
Venizelos, Eleftherios, 277–8
Venizelos, Sophocles, 287
Vercellino, General Mario, 232
Verona Military Court, 46, 56–61, 57, 59, 60
viceroy's commissioned officers (VCOS), 253, 255, 257, 259, 263, 265–6
Vichy Regime, 24–5, 231–4, 304
Vlasov, General Andrey, 33
Volga Tatars, as non-German volunteers, 34

Waffen-SS, 31; 5th SS Panzer
  Division Wiking, 31; 11th SS
  Panzergrenadier Division
  Nordland, 31; Jagdkommandos
  (hunter units), 219
Wallace, Henry A., 164
Wallace, Major David, 291
Wang Fanyi, 97
Wang Jingwei, 100
War Aims (Cole), 199–200
war crimes, 208, 239. *See also*
  anti-partisan warfare, German;
  occupation policies, Italian
War of Resistance (1937–45), 9,
  90–1
Warsaw Uprising (1944), 356
Waterman, Alan T., 171
Weapons Systems Evaluation
  Group (WSEG), 172, 173
Webster, Wendy, 6
Wehrmacht. *See* anti-partisan war-
  fare, German; German Army;
  Germany; Waffen-SS
West Africa, 24–6, 27–8
Why We Fight films (1942–45), 126
Wiemann, Colonel Hans, 221–2
Wilson, General Sir Henry
  Maitland, 284, 285, 290
women: anxiety around women's
  roles, 302; deaths from
  tuberculosis, 148, 151;
  gender roles in amorous
  relationships, 306–13, *308*, 319,
  323n43; German anti-partisan
  measures, 218; in Indian
  propaganda, 263; maternal
  health care, Italy, 137, 142;
mobilization of, Italy, 51–2, 61,
  66n47; in occupied China, 97,
  99; in People's War messaging,
  332, 344–6, *345*; pressures on,
  305–6; venereal disease, 147.
  See also amorous relationships,
  Nazi Germany
*Women of Britain Come into the
  Factories* poster (MoI), 329,
  344–6, *345*
Woodhouse, Colonel Monty,
  282, 284
workers. *See* labour

Xie Xiaopeng, 90
Xie Ziling, 99
Xing Hansan, 93, 94, 98, 99
Xinminhui (Renovate the People
  Association), 94, 95–6, 100, 101,
  102, 104, 105

Yang Fuli, 97
Yang Jingwen, 98
Yi Shuqing, 102–3
Young, Donald, 122
youth. *See* children; mobilization
  in China
Yugoslavia: German anti-partisan
  measures, 210, 216, 218; Italian
  occupation policies in, 234–7;
  National Socialist ideology, 213

Zec, Philip, 344
Żegota Council to Aid Jews,
  366, 367
Zervas, Napoleon, 279
Zhang Zhengfang, 96, 99